The 2001/2002 ASTD Distance Learning Yearbook

Also available from McGraw-Hill

The 2001 ASTD Training and Performance Yearbook, edited by John A. Woods and James W. Cortada

The Quality Yearbook, 2001 Edition, edited by James W. Cortada and John A. Woods

The Supply Chain Yearbook, 2001 Edition, edited by John A. Woods and Edward J. Marien

The 2001/2002 ASTD Distance Learning Yearbook

Karen Mantyla
John A. Woods

McGraw-Hill

New York   Chicago   San Francisco   Lisbon   Madrid
Mexico City   Milan   New Delhi   San Juan
Seoul   Singapore   Sydney   Toronto

McGraw-Hill

*A Division of The **McGraw·Hill** Companies*

1 2 3 4 5 6 7 8 9 0 DOC/DOC 0 9 8 7 6 5 4 3 2 1

ISBN: 0-07-137792-1

The sponsoring editor for this book is Richard Narramore. Maureen Harper was the manufacturing supervisor. Tama Harris was the editing supervisor. Design and production services were provided by CWL Publishing Enterprises, Madison, WI, www.cwlpub.com.

Printed and bound by R.R. Donnelley Company.

All McGraw-Hill books are available at special quantity discounts to use as premiums and sales promotion, or for use in corporate training programs. For more information, please write to the Director of Special Sales, Professional Publishing, McGraw-Hill, Two Penn Plaza, New York, NY 10121. Or contact your local bookstore.

To my family, especially my mother and father who have provided role model examples for my life. My father always told me that I could do anything in the world, and my mother cheered me on as I followed my heart's dream. And of course, my son Michael, who can do anything in the world, and I cheer him on as I watch his dreams become reality.

To my wonderful distance learning clients in the U.S. and in Saudi Arabia, for providing the opportunities to help support their success.

—Karen Mantyla

For my wife Nancy, who works as hard on these books as I do.

—John Woods

Contents

Contents

Foreword

The e-learning revolution is changing the field of learning and performance. We're experiencing the same upheaval as other industries reshaping themselves around the Internet.

- Rapid growth and change: John Chambers' now famous quote: "E-learning is the next killer ap for the Internet. It will make e-mail look like a rounding error."
- Decline of the classroom: Gartner predicts that the traditional classroom model will represent less than 30 percent of all formal corporate learning programs by 2003.
- Growth of soft-skills learning online: IT training has dominated e-learning since its emergence, but that picture is about to shift dramatically. Analysts at IDC tell us that business and soft skill content for e-learning programs is experiencing a 123% compound growth rate and should surpass IT training by 2003.
- New strategic role for e-learning: As a component of enterprise-wide change, and as a tool for educating customers to be more comfortable with e-commerce.

Because the e-learning revolution is seeping through the business world, we are seeing the very fundamentals of the profession being reinvented from instructional design, to evaluation, to product pricing, to who owns learning in the organization.

We know there are challenges for the profession in making a bold change in direction from traditional classroom instruction to distance learning and e-learning. Technology puts the learner in charge. Online authoring tools enable almost anyone to create and publish learning programs. Learning portals dazzle and confuse learners with choices. Technology itself has a tendency to take center stage. Our familiar yardsticks, hours and money invested in training, don't work in our favor when we are asked to deliver better performance for less money via technology. No one said a change this sweeping would be easy, but there is no doubt it is exhilarating.

The 2001/2002 ASTD Distance Learning Yearbook, compiled by capable editors Karen Mantyla and John Woods, is designed to help you understand the problems, approaches, successes, failures, and distance learning "lessons learned" from training professionals and from leading experts in the field of technology. If you can take one idea from this book and turn it into a profitable, productive learning experience for the learners in your organization, then your investment will be returned many times over. ASTD is pleased to sponsor this Yearbook knowing that the information provided will be used as an authoritative resource in guiding you on your e-learning journey.

Tina Sung
President
American Society for Training & Development
Alexandria, Virginia

Acknowledgments

The specialists who surround the world of distance learning are currently a small cadre. We are fortunate to have the shared expertise of many distance learning specialists in the articles that follow and original writings from recognized experts in the field. We also want to thank the different publishers who have extended their permission to reprint the many articles in this book. In addition, special thanks to:

Richard Narramore at McGraw-Hill for providing the opportunity to work collaboratively with John Woods.

Karen White, Manager, Reference Services at ASTD headquarters in Alexandria, VA, for her rapid-speed response in providing a wealth of article references for review.

Dr. Christine Olgren at the University of Wisconsin-Madison for creating an up-to-date glossary for 2001.

Dr. Matthew Champagne, IOTA Solutions, and Dr. Robert Wisher, U.S. Army Research Institute, for writing original and timely evaluation materials for this book.

—Karen Mantyla

This book would not have happened without the help of Robert Magnan and Nancy Woods of CWL Publishing Enterprises, and I want to express my appreciation for their help at every stage of development.

—John Woods

Introduction

E-learning, distance learning, collaborative learning, digital learning, mobile learning ... anyone dizzy yet? Even though we are right in the beginning of the 21st century, the new changes in learning technologies and software applications are multiplying faster than nearly any of us could have imagined. The future appears to offer more than we can justifiably imagine today. Along with those changes, and always the stimulus of all of it—learning.

Too often we are enthralled with the gizmos and bells and whistles of technology-assisted learning. As well, we succumb to the excitement and promises of the sizzle without ensuring that the learning is at dead center surrounded by the right selection of technologies, careful instructional design, and well-prepared trainers to enhance and support the learning experience. Somehow, learning is not always what drives decision making.

Are we focusing too much on the technology and not enough on the learning? It's a good enough question to ask. We need to stop and think about that before we make strategic decisions backed by an infusion of money and human resources. We want to get it right the first time.

As organizations around the world embrace and fine-tune the use of learning technologies to meet both internal and external customer needs, many aspects of the distance learning equation come into play. It is the goal of *The 2001/2002 ASTD Distance Learning Yearbook* to look at those key aspects that will have a great impact on your success.

The articles included here are from experts in the field and come from real-world experiences. This book contains information, tips, ideas, and resources to help you succeed. Even though our learning world is continuously changing, this book will give you a firm foundation for your successful distance learning initiatives and what naturally follows, positive results.

This book is designed to be a comprehensive and current anthology covering the field of distance and e-learning. It consists of 11 parts, 10 of which include articles, with Part Eleven being a guide to distance learning resources. Let's briefly review what's in Parts One to Ten.

- **Part One. The State of Distance Learning**, in which we include an eclectic group of articles that overview trends and statistics and rationales for implementing distance learning in organizations of all types.
- **Part Two. Technology Overview: E-Learning Leads the Way**, which we have divided into three parts: E-Learning/Web/Computer-Based Training, Blending Traditional Classroom Training and E-Learning Technologies, and Video/Teleconferencing and Synchronous Techniques.
- **Part Three. State of the Art: Corporate Distance Learning**, in which we include articles describing how distance learning is being implemented in business.
- **Part Four. State of the Art: Distance Learning in Government**. Here, you'll find material documenting how different government agencies are using distance learning in their training programs, including the military.
- **Part Five. State of the Art: Distance Learning in Higher Education**, where we look at topics like virtual universities and how distance learning is affecting higher education and the students being served.
- **Part Six. Instructional Design for Distance Learning**, in which you'll find articles that explain how to effectively design courses that will be delivered using computers and other technology.
- **Part Seven. Teaching Strategies for Distance Learning**, which includes several how-to pieces for developing sound techniques for teaching at a distance.
- **Part Eight. Evaluating Program Success** includes articles that explain how to measure the success of your program and figure out how to improve it.
- **Part Nine. Distance Learning Case Studies**, in which you'll find case studies of DL implementation in companies like IBM and others.
- **Part Ten. Benchmarks for Successful Distance Learning Programs,** where we look at studies that document best practices in several companies.

Distance learning and the other related technology-driven approaches to training are rapidly being adopted by organizations in every sector of our society. As someone working in this field, thank you for purchasing and using this book. We hope it meets your needs and expectations.

Part One

The State of Distance Learning

———————————————

I n the field of training and employee performance improvement, things are changing. Technology is the primary cause and it has facilitated the rapid expansion of
distance learning as a viable and more economic method for delivering training
and instruction in organizations and educational institutions. This fact is the rai-
son d'être of this book. And it is our purpose in Part One to document some of the
trends and statistics to help you better understand what's going on today.

We've included a variety of articles from authoritative sources. The book starts
with a detailed piece by Clark Aldrich of the Gartner Group. This article started as a
presentation that he has given to various groups and deals with trends in the strategic
implementation of e-learning. In it, the author carefully explains each of his conclusions. If you want a good sense of where e-learning is going, read this article.

Next we include ASTD research director Mark E. Van Buren's description of findings from the 2001 ASTD state of the e-learning study and report based on surveys of
365 organizations. What are others doing and investing in? Get the answers to these
questions and more in this article. See why the previous documented trends are moving in an opposite direction and how you can learn from this information.

Here's a brief rundown on the other pieces included in this part to help you better understand the state of distance learning:

- "Trend Watch: E-Learning Goes Soft" by Tom Barron looks at how e-learning is
  expanding from its IT training focus to skills across the organization.

- "The Evolution of Learning Devices" by Chris Dede documents how learning
  technology has evolved and is evolving. The article includes some interesting
  case studies.

- In "21st Century Teaching and Learning Patterns: What Will We See?" by Judith
  V. Boettcher, the author lays out seven predictions for changes in learning, driv-
  en by technology and customer demand.

- "E-Learning: Economic Drivers" by Brandon Hall is a short piece that makes the economic case for technology-driven training. The lower costs of distance and e-learning are frequent themes in the articles in this book.

- "Distance Learning Trends in Higher Education" by Eduardo Rivera and George Kostopoulos documents how distance learning is changing and will change higher education, another focus of this book (see Part Five for more on this subject).

- In "Episodic Learning: Experiences with Distributed Education" by Molly D. Campbell we learn about on-demand training in educational institutions and on the job.

- Distance learning has brought about new markets for technology and the content it can deliver. The final article in Part One, "Marketing Distance Learning" by Edward L. Davis III, examines this new market and some of the hardware, software, and content companies that seek to serve it.

We've chosen an eclectic group of articles here, but we wanted to give you a broad sense of the state of distance education. We think when you've finished going through these pieces, you will see that this really is not a trend anymore, but a done deal that will only grow as time goes by.

Strategic E-Learning: Trends and Observations
Clark Aldrich

This piece by Gartner Group consultant Clark Aldrich looks at a variety of trends in distance and e-learning. It is an eclectic piece but gives you a very good overview of the field and things to think about in understanding the directions e-learning is going to train employees, customers, and more. There are four parts to this report: (1) Where are we today? (2) New uses, (3) New models, and (4) New types of vendors. Some sections include what the author calls "action items," which suggest what you can do to take advantage of this information.

Report Conclusions

- E-learning spending will double in enterprises through 2001.
- E-learning will become higher-profile, supporting both enterprise transformations and CRM.
- The form of e-learning will evolve toward blends including performance support, immersive simulations, and convergence with knowledge management.
- The market is rapidly changing. Select vendors today that can generate near-term ROI. Don't limit your flexibility with long-term contracts.
- The traditional training group will have to improve their relationship with the business units. Those that do not will continue to be marginalized in many organizations as many business groups work directly with specialized vendors.

E-learning is the leveraging and automation of key pieces of the educating process. It has found some conventional sweet spots, including off-the-shelf IT professional training, virtual classrooms for salespeople, and enterprise-wide learning management systems. And in all of these cases the use of e-learning is growing between 50% and 100% a year.

But the leading users of e-learning are doing so much more than that. Strategically deployed, e-learning can enable the alignment of entire organizations around new strategies, acquisitions, competencies, and products every six months, even every three months, instead of every five to ten years. As well, teaching customers alongside employees brings the market advantage of intimacy.

Advanced uses of e-learning will both necessitate and fund advanced models of e-learning. Classroom replication will still play a role, but increasingly alongside immersive simulations, performance support systems, even assisted collaboration.

To meet these needs, the vendors as well will have to evolve, playing well as best of breeds today, but preparing to be providers of either end-to-end infrastructures or high-end strategic content around 2002. Many leaders today won't make the transition to the new models as upstarts build their entire architecture around them.

E-learning is a young discipline, but evolving fast. Its roots are in the focused, humble training world, rather than the boil-the-ocean challenge of intellectual brother knowledge management. Yet the focused processes, multiplied, refined, measured, and projected, can have a staggering impact on workgroups, extended enterprises, industries, even cultures.

This presentation will explore the emergence of the e-learning marketplace and how e-learning will enable the agile workplace.

Action Item: Build a pool of discretionary funds to begin experimenting.

Where Are We Today?

Approaches to E-Learning

Figure 1 shows 14 approaches to e-learning, each with different risks and rewards. Companies with no threshold for failure will want to invest only in technologies by the *plateau of productivity* with understood methodologies and proven results. Highly competitive organizations will look at the *technology trigger* area as well. Some examples:

- **Training for High-Turnover Positions**. For jobs with turnover over 60% a year, especially in lower-paying positions such as bank teller and retail outlet cashier, creating two or three hours of high-quality new employee programs, often still CD-ROM-delivered, improves service and retention while freeing up managers.
- **Learning Management Systems (LMSs)**. Although expensive and difficult to choose and customize, LMSs are nonetheless reducing training costs through automation, self-service, and the enabling of e-learning, while increasing the surgical use of all formal learning events.

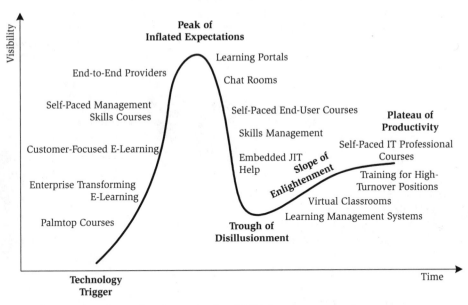

Figure 1. Corporate e-learning hype cycle, 2000 (Source: Gartner)

- **Skills Management**. Skills management will be the common feature of a future generation of business success stories. Yet today it is expensive and has a high failure rate, in part because it often gets bogged down tracking irrelevant skills, and in part because the goals are often contradictory (such as employee satisfaction and rigorous accuracy).
- **Self-Paced End-User Courses**. People already uncomfortable on computers —who become unable to do their jobs because of a new application and actively resent the time needed to learn the application—make teaching via computer an option that is still too painful for most enterprises.
- **Learning Portals**. Although proliferating wildly, portals eventually will bump into issues involving fulfillment, overcharging, security, competition, and a lack of profitability.
- **End-to-End Providers**. Currently, any vendor that claims to have true end-to-end capability has either a cripplingly limited vision or an overly empowered marketing department. Not until the end of 2001 will enterprises consistently choose comprehensive players over best of breeds.

Action Item: Identify e-learning with the most aggressive risk profile tolerable to your organization.

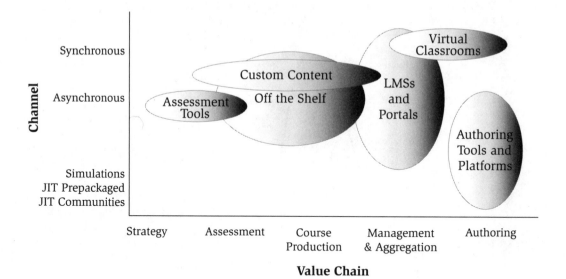

Figure 2. Six types of traditional e-learning vendors (Source: Gartner)

E-Learning Vendors

In today's market, there are six categories of e-learning vendors:

- Learning Management Systems, to deliver the right content to the right student at the right time in the right format,
- Virtual Classroom Tools, to provide an infrastructure for same-time, different-location courses, as well as an authoring tool for capturing and integrating experts' voices, slides, and gestures,
- Off the Shelf Content, including business and IT skills courses, allowing companies to give up customization for lower price and/or higher production values,
- Self-Paced Authoring Tools, which allow enterprises to build their own course creation capability,
- Custom Content creation capability, to outsource the course creation process, and
- Assessments, which are pre-built systems to evaluate skill levels of large audiences.

Still an Early Market

Keeping IT professionals' hard skills current using off-the-shelf e-learning is so compelling that a strong argument has to be made for why enterprises should not use self-paced IT professional courses. The content is up to date and increasingly well-pre-

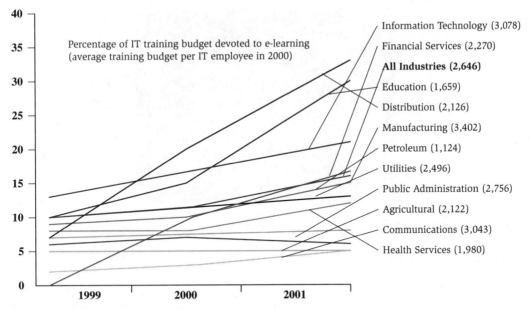

Figure 3. Still an early market (Source: Gartner)

sented, and the competition is fierce. It is also the most mature part of the e-learning market, estimated to show usage trends about two years earlier than other parts.

Having said that, it's worth noting that this type of hard IT skills (product and technology) will make up less than 30% of skill portfolio by 2005, as business skills fill the gap.

Gartner surveyed our client base in the *2000 IT Spending & Staffing Survey*. The results show a steady increase in the percentage of the budget for IT professional training dedicated to e-learning versus traditional classroom.

The e-learning market is still in its early, high-growth stages. Even the most mature component, IT professional training, is showing no sign of leveling off.

Constraints to E-Learning Market Size

There are some significant barriers to an e-learning explosion.

- **Cultural issues**: Employees have spent years learning the non-intuitive skills of how to take a classroom course. Some people realize they have to ask a lot of questions to focus themselves in classes. Others like to read ahead in the written material provided. E-learners will need to invest as well in understanding how to best absorb content delivered via computers. Issues for employees to resolve include: should they take notes or not, where to take the courses, how to keep from being interrupted, and even how to break up a long course.

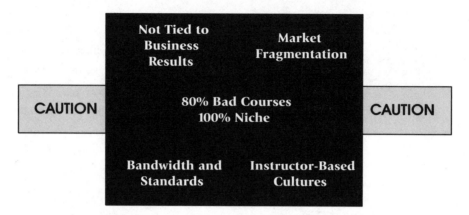

Figure 4. Barriers constraining e-learning market size

- **The market remains fragmented**, paralyzing many decision makers with overwhelming choices.
- **Pushed instead of pulled**: Traditional training is pushed (e.g., "the class begins at 10 a.m."). Often when courses can be taken at any time, they are never taken at all. There are also *technical issues*: To take an e-learning course, employees may have to find the site, find the course they want (from hundreds of entries), download and install any plug-ins, fill in any registration material, download the content in some cases, find some headphones and the jack on the computer. Expect attempts by e-learning providers to gain representation on users' desktops.
- **Bad courses**: Most courses do not meet the needs to the users. The percentage of good courses won't necessary improve, but expect better navigation and rating tools.
- **Standards** are still immature and do not aid in content reuse or integration yet. Further, most training management systems, authoring tools, and industry standards are built around a slide show/quiz metaphor. Innovative content producers have difficulty tying into this restrictive environment.
- **Bandwidth**: Through 2004, more than 50% of consumers will still access the Internet at low bit rates. Corporations have always been good at training people within driving distance of their headquarters. It is the ubiquity, the commonality of experience, that is essential to a successful e-learning rollout.
- **Too theoretical**: Many courses need a hands-on application. This includes the learning of both technical and management content.

New Uses
The Need

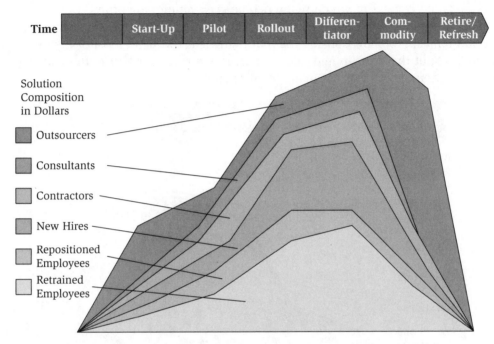

Figure 5. A traditional view of training ... a back-end support tool (Source: Gartner)

New projects often require skills that do not exist within a business unit, creating a gap that needs to be filled across the project's life. To produce the right portfolio of skills over the life of the project, managers have to juggle between:

- outsourcers,
- consultants,
- contractors,
- new hires,
- repositioned employees, and
- retrained employees.

Some organizations have outsourced everything, a strategy that gave them the immediate ability to compete, but ultimately was too expensive and rigid. Other companies have tried to develop the capacity from within, only to find that it took too long and the window of opportunity passed.

Many leading organizations have taken a hybrid path. They have begun with bringing in outside experts in different capacities and jump-started the process. While the project was being designed, they also began a parallel track of building an internal capacity, through training and hiring and shadowing. At some inflection point, the responsibility could be shifted from external to internal.

This is the context in which many people see training: important, to be sure; but a small, supporting role in a larger drama; a convenient, slow, cost-effective solution to a non-critical problem. Considering that many leaders spend most of their energies worrying about the start-up and pilot stages, it is no wonder that traditional training has never been on the radar of many in command.

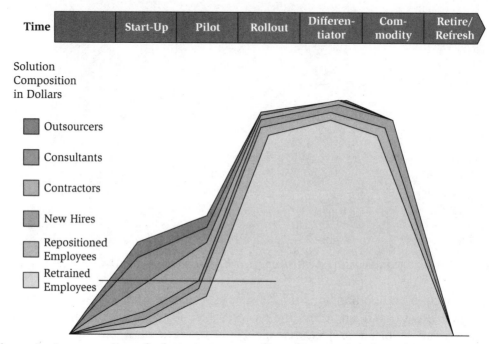

Figure 6. A newer view of e-learning ... to align the organization

A New View of E-Learning

Increasingly, projects require (re)training an entire enterprise. Examples include taking advantage of a recent merger, shifting to new business models, or building a new competency. When a project scales to this level, the traditional competency sourcing options of outsourcers, consultants, contractors, new hires, repositioned employees, and retrained employees dwindle considerably.

Getting the work done externally is much less of an option. A handful of new hires and consultants can bring some understanding of both the change process and the "to be" state. But because every job is affected by this new view, every work process and internal dialogue needs to incorporate aligned words and perspectives. This need for ubiquity requires a combination of perspectives that is simply not available outside.

Repositioning employees can be a small part of the solution. But where the skills do exist internally, they are in short supply by a factor of over a thousand.

The only comprehensive solution is retraining most, if not all, of the enterprise. In these scenarios, not only is training important, but e-learning is critical. This leveraging of the learning process provides speed, consistency, and cost-effectiveness, all necessary elements for success.

Examples of Enterprise Alignment

Xerox, 1984
- Threatened with high-quality Japanese copiers
- Required broad cultural change
- Spent over four years training 100K employees
- Successfully grew business against intense competition, won National Quality Award

KPMG Consulting, 1999
- Needed to change its revenue mix to include e-business
- Required broad cultural change
- Spent 12 weeks training 8K employees, ramped up to over 22K employees
- Would have taken 7 years to do it internally, 3 years to do it through outsourcing
- Since then increased e-business revenue 50%
- Now is offering service to its customers

Using massive learning programs as a way of changing cultures is not new.

Xerox, when faced with dozens of Japanese competitors in its core business of photocopiers, embarked on an enterprise-wide quality program. It involved training over one hundred thousand employees, four years, and many tens of millions of dollars. They were so successful that they were able to reverse the tide against the competitors.

Through e-learning, however, changing cultures becomes both faster and more measurable. KPMG had to change its revenue mix to include e-commerce and e-business. They looked into classroom training, but it would have taken seven years through using their own facilities, and still three years if they outsourced the project. Instead, they developed a hybrid course that involved Web-based, CD-ROM-based, and classroom-based training, and were able to train the first eight thousand employees in just 12 weeks. Soon, over 22 thousand employees had gone through the program. As of today, they have booked a billion in new e-commerce business attributable to the program.

Using e-learning to facilitate the transformation of a culture and enterprise is a new and therefore somewhat risky activity. Some best practices are emerging.

Enterprise-Aligning E-Learning Must Be ...

- Driven from the board room
- Broadcast, not rolled out—first student to last—in less than four weeks
- Around acquisitions, new enterprise strategies
- Designed to address new skills, business strategy, organizational culture, and operational infrastructure
- 8 to 24 hours of instruction
- Evolved in real time
- Mandatory

Enterprise-transforming e-learning (ETeL) needs to be driven from the board room and require a larger commitment for development time, mapping out the goals, and senior communication, than a reorganization.

The program has to address at least three components: *Business Strategy*, including Markets, Services, and Competencies, *Organizational Culture*, including Values and Leadership Style, and *Operational Infrastructure*, including Organizational Structure, Business Process, and Technology.

To evolve the program in real time, ETeL needs to be online-deployed for versioning control, use real-time tracking tools to monitor where the courses are doing well and where they are confusing, and include a live help desk. They must be like a CNN 24-hour coverage of a breaking story.

Over 90% of these programs will be developed with consultants, system integrators, or vendors, with little or no participation beyond back-end support from the traditional training organization.

Strategic E-Learning Portfolio

Every major new product introduction should be treated as an enterprise transformation.

One of the most common organizational transformations will be the release of new products—because when a product is announced, customers won't buy it, sales people can't sell it, sales channels can't push it, and service and financing can't support it, until they "get it."

To make the challenge more biting, we are seeing situations where new offerings are coming out well before the various parties have understood the last generation. Speeding up the "time to get it" is a necessary competency.

This will have all of the characteristics of enterprise-aligning e-learning, including being ASPed and carefully managed, but also extend to the supply chain, sales channels, and, of course, customers.

In both *Enterprise Aligning* and *Support of a New Offering*, the content then has to be distilled into a lasting infrastructure. Content and lessons learned from the *alignment* work must be embedded in *new employee orientation tools*, or their work will be

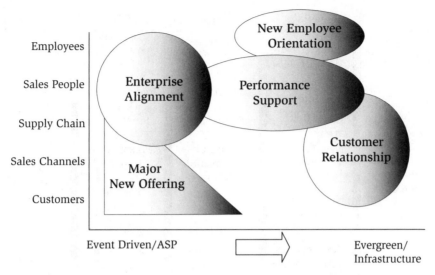

Figure 7. A portfolio of strategic e-learning

eroded quickly by time, and also *performance support tools*. Likewise, the information from *new rollouts* must be embedded in sites for both *customers* and *sales channels*.

Having said that, the handoff between the *event* and the *infrastructure* is more than just repurposing.

- From a technology perspective, many organizations will want to maintain their strategic e-learning infrastructure themselves, holding it behind the firewall, not ASPed.
- Vendors will have to sell and support it more as a software licensing arrangement than the more expensive consulting model.
- From an organizational perspective, the control will move from the CEO to IT or other staff function.

Given the gyrations necessary, what will be more difficult, having one vendor try to do it all or successfully handing off the content and responsibility?

Customer Education

Rolling out changes to an enterprise's customers is the *sine qua non* of any transformation. Six e-learning models are emerging to support it:

- **Changed/New Market Focus:** When brand name companies switch or add a market focus, preparing a high-value, free course establishes their credentials in their new area of focus (e.g. Charles Schwab).
- **New Interface (Consumer)**: New features on a camera don't entice people whose VCR is still blinking 12:00. Giving potential customers a walkthrough of an unfamiliar interface, and even teaching them how to navigate it before they

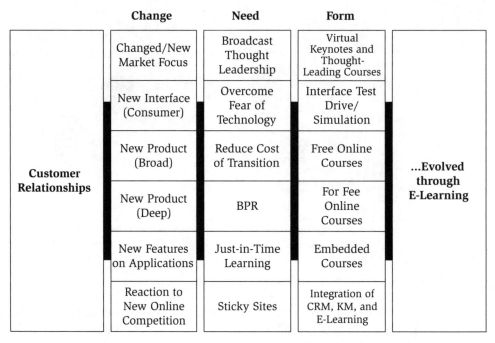

	Change	Need	Form	
Customer Relationships	Changed/New Market Focus	Broadcast Thought Leadership	Virtual Keynotes and Thought-Leading Courses	**...Evolved through E-Learning**
	New Interface (Consumer)	Overcome Fear of Technology	Interface Test Drive/ Simulation	
	New Product (Broad)	Reduce Cost of Transition	Free Online Courses	
	New Product (Deep)	BPR	For Fee Online Courses	
	New Features on Applications	Just-in-Time Learning	Embedded Courses	
	Reaction to New Online Competition	Sticky Sites	Integration of CRM, KM, and E-Learning	

Figure 8. Educate your customers or someone else will

buy, will encourage them to buy (e.g., Palm OS).

- **New Product (Broad)**: Increasingly vendors will have to bear the brunt of transitioning the user base. This will be accomplished primarily through free self-paced courses (e.g., Dell).
- **New Product (Deep)**: When broad courses still leave holes, high-value-add additional e-learning courses can be sold profitably. This will be accomplished primarily through synchronous (same-time, different-location) courses (e.g., SAP).
- **New Features on Applications**: Providing proactive help in bite-size chunks is evolving from annoying to essential (e.g., Microsoft).
- **Reaction to New Online Competition**: Free courses can make sites and relationships more valuable and provide reams of data on customer interests and issues (e.g., Barnes and Noble).

Key Issue: How can e-learning be exploited for customers, suppliers, and trading partners?

Palm Computing made the decision to recognize not traditional characters in the handwriting recognition software, but a stylized version called "Graffiti." This increased the long-term user satisfaction with the product significantly, but added a barrier to adoption for new users. As many as 30% of high potential customers put off the purchase for fear that learning how to use their Palm Pilot would be too difficult.

To address these pre-purchase concerns, Palm developed a mini-tutorial, written internally in C++, available on their web site. The program had three explicit goals: it was primarily developed to illustrate how easy it is to use Grafitti for text entry. Secondarily, it was developed to show how quickly Grafitti could be learned. And finally, it was one part of an overall program to show the three ways one could enter data into their Palm handheld.

Palm used the number of hits as a metric for the success of this page, and it became one of their top 10 most requested pages.

Action Item: Identify where complexity might be a product or service barrier, and create tutorials.

What we are seeing now in leading vendors is a glimpse of how many e-businesses will look in 2003. Asynchronous content will be given away. It will be aligned with the marketing department and be treated and funded as advertising. New e-learning campaigns will be launched. New courses for employees, customers, and channel partners will be introduced with new products and offerings. It will also be a source of information about customer and channel partner attitudes and questions.

In contrast, synchronous classes (same time, different location) will be sold. These will be high-quality courses with very good instructors that will maintain their premium prices over time.

As the market evolves, expect to see pure plays will continue, such as Interwise, NotHarvard, LearningBrands, eHelp, and Spire, as well as CRM vendors, advertising agencies, and e-business infrastructure providers.

Over 90% of these programs will be developed with consultants, system integrators, or vendors, with little or no participation beyond back-end support from the traditional training organization. Further, it will off-load about 30% of an average training group's current responsibilities.

New Models

The form of e-learning will evolve away from classroom replication to include performance support, immersive simulations, and converging with knowledge management.

More sophisticated uses of e-learning, such as enterprise transforming and customer-focused, will require more sophisticated models of e-learning.

The first generation of e-learning was based on the "tell and test" classroom model. It was often delivered just in case, days or weeks before the skills were needed, and with more information than any individual student needed; it was also delivered with the goal of convergence, producing a nearly identical experience for all participants as they step through the application. It is no surprise that this model is

	Convergent (Discrete-Path)	Divergent (Infinite-Path)
Just in Time	**Performance Support/ Embedded Help** • ERP Support • Microsoft Office Assistant • Palm Apps • KnowledgeShop	**Knowledge Management** • Traditional KM Vendors • Pensare • LMS Vendors • gForce • Mindlever
Just in Case	**Classroom Replication** • Certification Training • New Employee Training • Virtual Classroom Sessions	**Immersive Simulations** • Military • Computer Games • Ninth House • Cognitive Arts • Imparta • OCI

Figure 9. New e-learning models beyond classroom replication (Source: Gartner)

referred to as "sheep dipping."

At least three new models are emerging.

- One model is *performance support*, with the goal of transmitting small pre-packaged moments of understanding at the point of need.
- The second model is *simulations*. People crave new experiences. Shortcutting the experiential learning process through immersive, frustrating, fun simulations will be the dominant form of prepackaged management training for the Nintendo generation.
- The third model borrows from *knowledge management*. As the speed of business continues to accelerate, knowledge workers don't need old theory, they need new ideas.

Course Creation Problem

The biggest skeleton in most training groups' closet is the process used to create a course. A sponsoring organization finds some subject matter experts (SMEs). These people are SMEs because they had some experiences out in the marketplace that were viewed as successful. The sponsoring organization then produces a learning program, usually using the rule of:

- 20 hours of development time for every finished hour for classroom,
- 40 hours of development time for every finished hour of self-paced e-learning,

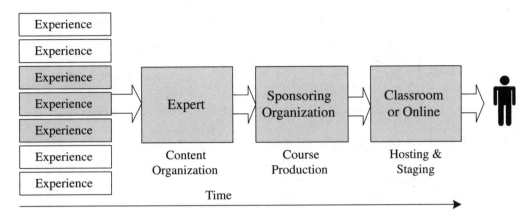

Figure 10. The traditional training model doesn't support the agile enterprise

- 7 hours of development time for every finished hour of virtual classroom/live e-learning.

Students then take the course, learn, and then put this new knowledge to use. But the average time between original experience in the field and the time it again reaches the field is, for non-technical training, *two years and three months*. Sales courses teach techniques that are older than most products. Management courses tend to lag even more significantly. Worse, the process filters out some of the great ideas that were simply never identified.

Today, while some courses teach bad habits, almost all courses teach old habits. As the speed of business continues to accelerate, custom course content, like fruit, airplane seats, and consulting hours, becomes a highly perishable good, either used or lost. Merging with KM will not be easy. But with the advent of learning chunk tools, the last technology and process excuses have been eliminated. It will be increasingly hard for either group to fulfill their missions without the other.

Just-in-Time E-Learning

The next vendor battleground in e-learning will be for control over the smallest piece of content. These small pieces of content that capture individual moments of understanding are becoming the currency of e-learning. *And the technology around chunks will finally enable the convergence with knowledge management, the effective use of just-in-time learning, and will challenge to the position of many current best-of-breed vendors.* For an enterprise to get value from knowledge chunks, however, they have to piece together several different components, today (sigh) sold by different vendors. Components include:

- **Centralized Authoring Tools**, for course developers, to create chunks. Examples of such tools include Macromedia Authorware and Coursebuilder,

---

The Emerging Just-in-Time E-Learning Ecosystem

- *Centralized Authoring Tools*, for dedicated experts to create small chunks;
- *Decentralized Authoring Tools*, for everyone, including very busy subject matter experts (SMEs), to create small chunks, ideally as a by-product of their work;
- *Authoring Platforms*, for organizing, storing, and real-time assembling of small chunks;
- *Search Engines,* for organizing and finding the right content;
- *Deployment Systems*, quasi knowledge management behind the firewall, which also contain limited authoring capabilities;
- *Sales Outlets*, places that sell premium chunks.

Digital Lava, ToolBook II, and HTML templates.

- **Decentralized Authoring Tools**, for everyone, including very busy subject matter experts, to create content, ideally as a by-product of their work. Examples include Centra, Interwise, Microsoft Office tools, text, and media files.
- **Authoring Platforms/Content Management**, software systems for organizing, storing, and real-time assembling of small chunks and the heart of the movement. Vendors include Knowledge Mechanics, MindLever, Peer3, even WBTSystems.
- **Search Engines**, for organizing and finding the right content. Early examples include Verity, Autonomy, even Yahoo and Google.
- **Deployment Systems**, knowledge management hybrids, behind the firewall, often capable of predicting when users need help and pushing the chunks out to them, and which also contain limited authoring capabilities. Examples include gForce, MindLever, Athenaeum, Communispace, Worklinks, Ventix, Microsoft Office Assistant (a.k.a. That Damn Paperclip), and Arista.
- **Compatible Off-the-Shelf Content**, into which custom chunks can be inserted. Vendors include SmartForce and NetG. Not surprisingly, both are traditional library vendors that always thought of themselves as just-in-time content providers (they never minded high dropout rates of their courses—students were picking up what they needed and moving on), in contrast to the more classroomesque models favored by DigitalThink. These components will interoperate through a pidgin of Web (including XML and HTML) and emerging e-learning standards; In fact, expect any real progress on broader Web-based training standards to be made primarily by the abovementioned chunk vendors. Because their success depends on it, they will be the most pure advocates and have the most practical knowledge.

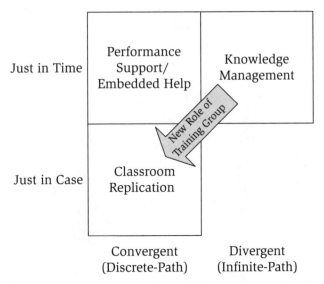

Figure 11. New e-learning models beyond classroom replication

New E-Learning Models

Observation: The form of e-learning will evolve away from classroom replication to include performance support, immersive simulations, and converging with knowledge management.

More sophisticated uses of e-learning, such as enterprise transforming and customer focused, will require more sophisticated models of e-learning.

This new world will require a modified role of the training department. Their mission increasingly will be to:

- wade into the cacaphony (read "that mess") of knowledge management content,
- identify the valuable threads (using both their own savvy and the reactions of others), and
- weave these pieces into coherent, more linear modules, often interspersed with off-the-shelf content.

Let's say, for example, that GE's top Java programmer did a learning lunch on external Web page requirements using live e-learning technology. Imagine she spoke for about 40 minutes, with 15 minutes of question-and-answer. The obligation of the training group would be to tear apart the record of the presentation, edit out the best moments, clean up the sounds of people eating and rustling plates, and then intersperse these new chunks in the appropriate prepackaged GE courses. This brings in customization and good stories, and can make heroes of the right people.

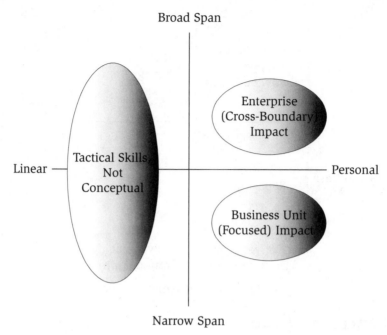

Figure 12. The most important aspects of advanced learning programs—personal and broad

Advanced Training: Personal and Broad

Training has traditionally been a narrow-reaching activity. Classrooms touch only dozens of students at a time. Different instructors teach the same material differently, and even the same instructor will evolve his or her material during the three-week span of a traditional national tour. The also explains why the industry has been as fragmented, supporting not only so many mom-and-pop organizations, but also sometimes shops of just pop.

E-learning has introduced broad, measurable, formal learning programs. But while the concept of "broadness" tends to favor technology, by itself scalability does not make a program broad. "Broadness" also describes content. A course on double-entry accounting could be available to all employees, but would be used only by less than 1%. As well as e-learning has done in the first part of broadness, it has failed in the second part. Therefore most e-learning today feels like special-interest cable channels: wonderful if you care about the plight of African baobab trees or the Battle of the Bulge, but not for bringing a group together.

Broadness is critical because there is a network effect with training. Just as having two fax machines in the world is more than twice as good as having one fax machine, so having multiple people sharing similar experiences is logarithmically more effective than fewer. Programs that are not broad can only have a limited effect on the enterprise as a whole and therefore the bottom line.

Finally, from a supplier perspective, broadness leverages the intellectual property necessary to create a program, and therefore justifies larger budgets and more TLC per project.

The other critical criterion for a program is the ability to make it personal. We have all been in programs that weren't this way. So many training programs are "sheep dipping." The expectation of the course is that all students will leave the program with the exact same body of knowledge. Tests are given. Evaluations of content learned are used. Students are expected to memorize 70%, 80%, even 90% of the available material. And to be fair, linear programs work well to teach tactical skills, like those taught in IT certification courses.

Nonstandard Approaches

But when most people think back to their most profound learning moments, it was personal. Perhaps it was a story they heard while they were an apprentice. Or a technique they uncovered while role-playing with a colleague. Or an insight into a work

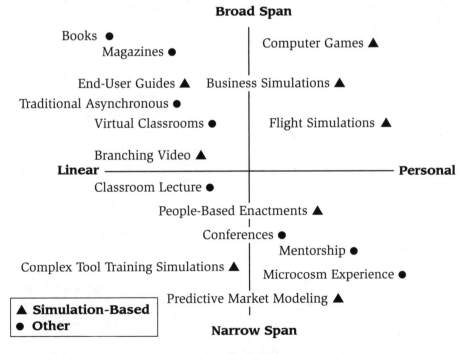

Figure 13. Personal and broad require nonstandard approaches

process they learned while in a pilot or skunk works. Making an experience personal, an order of magnitude above "customization," requires the ability of the program to provide such a rich experience that the students intuitively pick and choose the 5% to 10% of skills and information they need, instead of having to learn it all.

Ironically, any good college course is personal, but all tests to determine your grade are linear. Personal experiences tend to be learner-out, not instructor-in. They are self-driven, relying on discovery and invention, not memorization. They teach at the intuitive, not just intellectual, level. Critically, people can share personal experiences, even if what they walk away with is unique.

Linear experiences can only teach tactical skills (although often disguised as business skills). Programs aimed at the personal level but that are not scalable can affect individuals, workgroups, maybe divisions, but not organizations. It is the ability to impact an organization across boundaries, meshing personal experiences with broad reach, that is required for learning programs to impact the bottom level. The models for these programs will have to be brought in from outside the training world. Templates include next-generation knowledge management programs, movies, television shows, commercials, or my current area of focus, computer games.

Simulations and Just-in-Time Content

The third model is *infinite path simulations*.

As evidenced by the popularity of video games, high-adventure team-building courses, and high-tech simulation theme parks, people crave new experiences—virtual and real. To paraphrase Winston Churchill, they want to learn, not be taught. In the military, role-based and organization unit simulations have demonstrated very high value: by learning the lessons critical to survival in combat, individuals and units own the lessons.

Cognitive Arts and Ninth House Network have laid some ground here, but have relied too much on pre-canned streaming video and not enough on dynamically generated computer animation. Like it or not, computer games are to the e-learning industry what racing cars are to the automobile industry. Two remarkable e-learning programs are role models: one, built by Imparta for McKinsey, shows that streaming video can be taken to an incredible degree of sophistication, and the other, built by OC Inc. for the military, represents the most successful use of computer-generated animation for e-learning.

During late 2001 and early 2002, a slew of off-the-shelf business simulation will be available. But they may disappear by 2003. Building a good simulation is a high-stakes gamble for the vendor; and because of the number of options that will be available, choosing a good simulation will not be easy for the enterprise.

Further, there are still some political difficulties that need to be overcome. The good simulations will be CD-ROM-delivered for a while, although some synchronization will happen over the Web. The computers will also need drivers such as DirectX

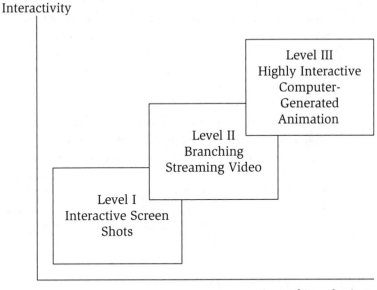

Figure 14. Simulations: evolving just-in-time content (Source: Gartner)

and more horsepower than the traditional corporate standard. (Employees' home machines will be up to the task.)

Building Business Simulations. Here are seven rules for building effective business simulations.

1. **Real, identifiable situations**. Although some early simulation providers use metaphorical settings, the scenarios must feel authentic and directly relevant to the employees' task at hand. "Realism is only a technique," Shakespeare scholars may say, but in this case, it is the technique of choice.

2. **Real time**. The pressure of immediate decisions breaks through the attempts of most students to "psych out" a course. This is also valuable as these tools are used for evaluations. As with life, time moves ahead, and doing nothing has to be an option (and sometimes even the right one).

3. **Infinite pathing within a finite world.** The user must have the feeling of unrestricted options, albeit within the relatively small simulated world, much like an ant's sense of freedom on a basketball. Every wall hit by the user breaks the mood. Simulations should be an analog, not discrete, experience. This strongly favors computer animation over video. Further, video cannot be updated over time, while computer animation cannot.

4. **Built-in coaching and reflection**. Learning requires some mulling. In some cases, these tools will even act as a stand-alone performance support tool that

the students can access well after the simulation is over.

5. **The learning takes place from, not between, interactions**. So many early, misguided models revolved around an "entertaining" setting framing drier content, such as a loud game-show veneer on multiple-choice questions. The lessons have to come instead from the way the environment responds to the student, including the "physics" of the business model, and the domain knowledge of autonomous characters. Only this will drive the learning at the multi-processing intuition level over the linear logical level.

6. **Replayability taking on different approaches**. Just as a pilot in a flight simulator can try conservative and aggressive strategies, so too in business simulator must users be able to try out different personalities and approaches.

7. **Core engine with easily customizable scripts**. When businesses spend large sums on simulations, they should expect to customize the experience to their unique culture, as least as much as people buying new cars can customize style and options.

New Types of Vendors

In today's market, there are six different categories of e-learning vendors. Most of us would like all six categories to be handled by the same vendor. But today there are two legitimate, show-stopping concerns with the offerings of the current players.

First, by far most vendors have offerings in only one or two of these areas. The top-tier players proudly describe themselves as being best of breed. When others distract with talk about being end-to-end, they really mean that they offer a handful of different services in one category, often including hosting/ASP services, while desperately hoping you will not think about the other five.

Second, the few vendors that actually are end-to-end—IBM, Calian, NIIT, and Mentergy—tend to sell services that are a far cry from best of breed, with clumsy integration between the various newly acquired pieces. These are offerings similar to the first generation of so-called multi-function devices that combined faxes, printers, scanners, and copiers via brute force rather than actual design. Most of these companies' wins will still be by category for the near future.

Part of the reason is that when enterprises are picking out vendors, they often already have some of the e-learning mosaic and are looking to fill in a few more pieces. Or they want to pilot some aspect of e-learning, perhaps off-the-shelf courses for their IT professionals or virtual classrooms for their sales people (two choices for safe e-learning bets). In either case, the last thing they want is end-to-end.

For these common buying decisions, as well as most others, a much more critical characteristic, even over any specific feature, should be the vendor's custom integration with both your preferred vendors and best of breeds in the other categories. They must commit to seamless compatibility for the life of the product (about two years).

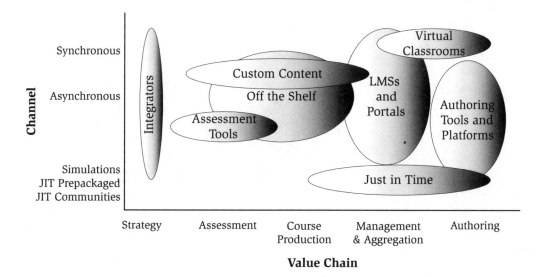

Figure 15. Six (or eight) types of e-learning vendors through 2002 (Source: Gartner)

The partnership criterion correlates with, as well as causes, the best vendors. Because partnerships take work on both sides, vendors make them only with the most relevant companies, as determined by both their research and their customers. For example, it has gotten to a point where the easiest way to create a short list of learning management vendors is to look at publicly identified partners of Centra.

Observation: Because of the speed of evolution, do not make a contract longer than two years.

Integrated Offerings

Integrated offerings from large organizations will begin to be more compelling than best of breed for many organizations beginning around the beginning of 2002, because of their ability to provide strategy and full implementation services, knowledge management capabilities, and dramatically better content.

Single vendors will provide most e-learning needs (although they will subcontract out parts), through proprietary content and tools. Best-of-breed vendors that had excelled previously will have to find partners quickly or be left out, perhaps banding together to form a new enterprise themselves. Web store fronts such as Thinq and vertical vendors such as medschool.com will continue to carve out a profitable niche.

Technology infrastructure companies focusing on e-learning will reach their apex of influence during this stage. This is the chance for organizations such as IBM, Microsoft, Knowledge Universe, and perhaps Mentergy and NIIT to dominate the task of making enterprise employees smarter. Meanwhile, because formal learning pro-

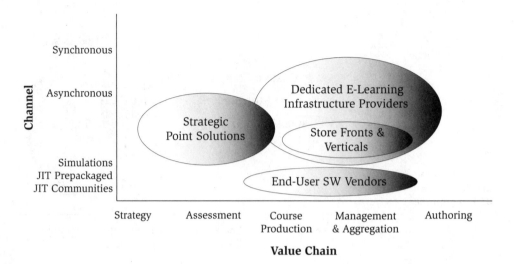

Figure 16. E-learning vendors 2002-2003: end-to-end/strategic (Source: Gartner)

grams will be a standard part of any large organizational transformation efforts, all the Big Five consulting companies, as well as hundreds of other smaller players, will develop focused competencies.

Amid the focus on technology, however, a few brilliant directors—the Steven Spielbergs of this new medium—will leave the fold and usher in a new era.

Foundational Platforms

With the recent spate of alliances and acquisitions, foundational platforms might be taking form.

The stated attraction of learning platforms in the short term will be greater quality (no one thinks today's HTML-based content is cutting it), ease of deployment, and improved tracking over comparable stand-alone pieces. Over the next 18 months, they will set the standards that other vendors have to use and build on (similar to B2B e-business platforms Commerce One, SAP, Ariba, I2, IBM, Oracle) for next-generation e-learning products.

The immediate challenge for all of these vendors is how quickly they optimize content around their platform.

If they do it too fast, they cut off too many platforms for their content and content for their platforms. Imagine all of the VHS-Beta issues, but with six standards instead of two. Ironically, this would limit the amount a company could invest in an individual course, defeating the value of proprietary platforms in the first place.

If they add proprietary capabilities too slowly, there is no added value with the platform. They will still be training systems at their core, built around only minimally

---

> ## Contenders for E-Learning Foundational Platforms
> - DigitalThink, since their acquisition of Arista
> - SmartForce and Docent
> - Thinq, with their acquisition of TrainingSoft
> - Saba
> - ElementK and Isopia (perhaps)

---

enhanced classroom replication material (read that "tell-and-test slide shows"), with very little just-in-time, virtual classroom, simulation, and knowledge management capabilities.

Strategic E-Learning: Epilogue

The new uses of e-learning ping such CEO hot spots as:

- Through educating *customer*s, building brand loyalty, increasing e-business acceptance, and generating incremental revenue; and

- Through educating *employee*s, significantly changing entire cultures in weeks instead of months and years, perhaps towards realizing new visions, or after a merger or acquisition, or even in support of new bet-the-farm offerings.

This should be a boon for the training people. After all, they have been the enterprise omsbudmen for formal learning for decades. In fact, one should expect the person responsible for learning programs to be invited to the same meetings and retreats as the top operations officers, or at least the CIO.

That is not happening. The situation has strong parallels to the Information Technology departments five years ago. When you look at IT-centric innovations such as supply chain management, Intranets, ERP implementation, sales force automation, and data warehousing (just to name a few), virtually none were introduced or effectively championed by the IT department. Instead, they were pushed by the product vendors, systems integrators, and the consulting community. IT's involvement, if any, became maintenance.

History is repeating itself. Top officers are paying attention to strategic learning initiatives—but not to training departments.

Just as with the businesses they support, training groups need to treat e-learning models as both threat and opportunity. It will require strong planning and execution to make the transition to a highly strategic organization, but it is so much more fun leading the parade than sweeping up after it.

Implementers of formal learning programs should consider 10 steps to stay relevant.

1. Outsource the non-strategic programs like end-user training. No one cares.

2. Build a pool of discretionary funds of at least 20% of your total budget. You need some risk room for investments.

3. Know the business's two-year plan as well as they do. Constantly evaluate how learning programs can help achieve their goals.

4. Look into Learning Management Systems. Remember it's a great Web front-end to order books still shipped from a warehouse that makes Amazon.com an e-business.

5. Make your workforce e-learning-compatible. For most employees, this means starting with business skills courses. Carefully manage that first use, providing as much help as the student needs.

6. Support the new strategic initiatives and associated e-learning as they emerge. Don't take on the role of professional curmudgeon. The IT approach of pointing out flaws in the business's strategy didn't work, and they were labeled as a speed bump. Proactively find and suggest partners, and earn your way on the evaluating team.

7. Work harder at competitive analysis. Go to their Web sites and interview their students. The companies that are really using e-learning as a strategic differentiator aren't sharing much beyond marketing at conferences and user-groups. That would defeat the whole purpose.

8. Develop a custom e-learning capability—only licensing generic courses will trap you in the maintenance space.

9. Eliminate teach-speak. Say things like "design methodology" and "Level 2 evaluation" only when no business people are around.

10. Consider merging with the knowledge management group, if you have one. They have the budget and the alignment, if not the successes. Get the combined vision and organization in place immediately, and then work on processes and technology.

Conclusions

- E-learning spending will double in enterprises through 2001.
- E-learning will become higher-profile, supporting both enterprise transformations and CRM.
- The form of e-learning will evolve toward blends including performance support, immersive simulations, and convergence with knowledge management
- The market is rapidly changing. Select vendors today that can generate near-term ROI. Don't limit your flexibility with long-term contracts.
- The traditional training group will have to improve their relationship with the business units. Those that do not will continue to be marginalized in many organizations as many business groups work directly with specialized vendors.

Recommendations

For Implementers of Learning Programs

- Outsource the non-strategic programs like end-user training.
- Build a pool of discretionary funds.
- Know the business's two-year plan as well as they do.
- Look into Learning Management Systems.
- Make your workforce e-learning compatible.
- Support the new initiatives e-learning as they emerge.
- Develop a custom e-learning capability.
- Eliminate teach-speak. Talk in business terms.
- Consider merging with the knowledge management group.

For Vendors

- Earn "best of breed" today from your customers, but plan to migrate.
- Build partnerships with other Bests of Breeds.
- Don't be trapped by classroom replication. Prepare for next generation of content (Simulations, Performance Support, Knowledge Management).
- Content providers: build an IT soft skills curriculum.
- Don't use your VC presentation as your perspective client presentation.

Clark Aldrich is currently researching how full-featured simulations can be designed for the e-learning marketplace. Through a privately funded pilot project, working with subject matter experts from universities including Harvard and game manufacturers, he is resolving the outstanding issues around content and process.

In 2001, he has been identified as one of Training's New Guard by the American Society for Training and Development. In 2000, he was chosen as one of three e-learning gurus by Fortune *magazine, and was named one of* Training *magazine's 16 visionaries of the industry. He was the research director at Gartner Group responsible for launching and building their e-learning practice, where he developed strategies with Global 1000 organizations, vendors, and venture capitalists.*

Previously, Mr. Aldrich was a member of Gartner's Best Practices service, doing case study work with both organizational learning issues and the demonopolization of internal IT groups.

E-Learning Proving a Tough Nut to Crack

Mark E. Van Buren

This is a report on the state of the industry in 2001 dealing with e-learning. It includes two useful charts showing the movement toward the adoption of e-learning over classroom learning and the use of different learning technologies.

In 2000, ASTD held the fourth round of its Benchmarking Service, an annual process that collects information from all types of organizations on the nature of their employer-provided training expenditures, practices, and outcomes. Over 950 organizations, more than a third of which were located outside the United States, participated in the service. The Benchmarking Service provides some of the most systematic evidence that exists on trends in the use of learning technologies.

Of the participants in the 2000 Benchmarking Service from the United States, 365 organizations provided enough valid and comparable information on their 1999 training investments and practices to be included in detailed analyses of trends in learning technologies. The average Benchmarking Service respondent employed over 2,679 employees in 1999 with an annual payroll of about $98 million. Nearly 40 percent had fewer than 500 employees and just under 63 percent were for-profit companies.

In this summary, we contrast trends in the Benchmarking Service with two comparison groups. One group consists of firms in the ASTD Benchmarking Forum, an elite consortium of world class companies that engage in a reciprocal and open annual benchmarking process. The typical Benchmarking Forum firm was much larger than the average Benchmarking Service firm in 1999, serving over 55,000 employees with an annual payroll in excess of $2.8 billion.

The second comparison groups is a set of firms we have labeled "Training Investment Leaders." These are firms whose data indicate that they have made a dedicated commitment to developing the knowledge, skills, and abilities of their employees. To identify the Training Investment Leaders, we ranked firms in the Benchmarking Service and the Benchmarking Forum according to five measures:

- Percent of employees eligible for training that received training in 1999
- Total training hours per employee eligible for training in 1999
- Percent of training time in 1999 delivered through learning technologies
- Total training expenditures in 1999 per employee eligible for training
- Total training expenditures as a percent of payroll in 1999

To qualify as a Training Investment Leader, a firm had to score in the top 10 percent of an index that combined all five measures. These cutting-edge firms employed 16,000 employees on average in 1999 at an annual payroll of $962 million. Over 36 percent of these organizations had fewer than 500 employees and 62 percent were for-profit companies.

For several years now, the *ASTD State of the Industry Report* has found that organizations have projected they will be delivering less and less of their training in the classroom with corresponding increases in technology-delivered training or "e-learning" (see Table 1). The growth of e-learning and the decline of instructor-led, classroom training has been widely heralded for several years. In fact, projections made by 1998 participants in the Benchmarking Service indicated that, on average, 23 percent of all training time would be delivered via e-learning in 2000. These projections were made after the same firms reported an average of 9.1 percent of e-learning in 1997.

The projections made, as well as the actual training delivered, by participants in the Benchmarking Service since then, however, belie this trend. E-learning projections made for 3 years out by the 1999 and 2000 participants have actually fallen to 19.8 percent for 2001, and finally to 18.2 percent for 2002. These figures suggest that, while firms still remain hopeful about the future of e-learning, they have been growing increasingly less optimistic.

The decline in optimism may be a product of the difficulties firms have been experiencing in adopting e-learning in the late 1990s. In fact, the actual amount of e-learning that Benchmarking Service firms have provided reached its highest level of 9.1 percent in 1997. In 1998, the average amount of e-learning in Benchmarking Service companies fell to 8.5 percent. The same figure for 1999 (8.4 percent) gave no indication that the projected growth in e-learning had begun to materialize.

At the same time, the average firm in ASTD's Benchmarking Service increased the percent of its training delivered in the classroom from 77.6 percent in 1997 to 79.9 percent in 1999. Likewise the projection for classroom training for three years out from the same periods rose steadily from 61 percent to 67.5 percent.

	Classroom, 1999	Classroom, + 3 Years	Learning Technologies, 1999	Learning Technologies, + 3 Years
Benchmarking Service				
1999	79.9	67.5	8.4	18.2
1998	78.4	64.5	8.5	19.8
1997	77.6	61.0	9.1	23.0
Training Investment Leaders				
1999	77.0	66.0	14.9	24.4
1998	70.3	56.9	18.3	30.3
Benchmarking Forum				
1999	79.1	62.2	13.8	27.4
1998	78.7	61.5	12.3	25.2
Number of Employees				
1-499	81.0	70.0	8.0	18.1
500-1999	80.3	67.9	8.2	16.9
2000 +	78.3	63.3	11.1	21.6
Industry				
AMC	81.6	69.0	4.3	16.3
Technology	77.8	63.2	10.3	20.4
Non-durables	77.4	64.1	9.5	18.7
Durables	83.5	71.9	6.0	13.0
TPU	71.6	62.7	13.8	21.0
Trade	64.5	55.5	6.0	16.1
FIRE	87.4	70.6	6.7	20.5
Services	81.2	70.0	10.9	20.9
Health Care	77.2	63.3	10.3	21.1
Government	79.8	72.1	6.7	10.9

Table 1. Delivery via classroom and learning technologies (% of training time spent)

The continued growth of classroom training supports conjectures we raised in our previous report that perhaps organizations are finding e-learning difficult to do well. To understand this trend more fully, we contacted some of the companies that participated in the Benchmarking Service in both 1999 and 2000 whose numbers showed the same pattern.

Several respondents told us they were facing declining enrollments in e-learning courses as a result of negative experiences learners had had with e-learning previously. A study recently conducted by ASTD and the MASIE Center, in fact, found that learners who reported negative previous experiences with e-learning were significantly less likely to take future e-learning courses offered to them. This finding emphasizes the importance to getting e-learning right the first time. We fear that this is one obstacle to e-learning that will be particularly difficult to overcome.

In other companies, the growth of classroom training was attributed to a rise in training using some form of technology, but which occurred in a classroom or learning center setting. Given a choice between e-learning and classroom training, these firms reported these as instances of the latter. This form of training, which is clearly neither e-learning nor classroom training, is one of a number of emerging forms of training which combine more than one form of learning. Such "blended learning," not e-learning, we believe, is the more likely successor to traditional classroom, instructor-led training.

Finally, we found evidence that perhaps e-learning is not doomed for the history pages, but only taking a breather. Some firms shared with us that, in 1999, they held the amount of e-learning steady while making significant new investments in e-learning systems and courses. These firms told us that their e-learning levels had since grown in 2000. However, it is increasingly clear that firms wanting to providing large amounts of e-learning to their employees must overcome significant up-front development and implementation costs to reach their ambitions.

The e-learning picture for the Training Investment Leaders is much the same. Although selected partly for their e-learning levels, this year's group of leading firms reported significantly less e-learning in 1999 than last year's group (18.3 percent and 14.9 percent, respectively). Likewise their e-learning projections for three years out fell sharply from 30.0 percent to 24.4 percent.

By contrast, members of the Benchmarking Forum exhibited the opposite trend. The percent of training time delivered via e-learning grew from 12.3 percent in 1998 to 13.8 percent in 1999, just short of the level of the average Training Investment Leader. In fact, their three-year e-learning projection (27.4 percent) was several percentage points higher than that of the leaders.

The results from the Benchmarking Forum lend support to the notion that, thus far, the growth of e-learning is occurring primarily among large companies. The e-learning figures for Benchmarking Forum companies, most of which are very large, mirror the averages among the largest Benchmarking Service firms. The latter reported 11.1 percent e-learning in 1999 and projected 21.6 percent e-learning in 2002. Similarly, classroom training among large organizations was projected to drop to 63 percent of all training by 2002. We suspect that the foremost advantages of the present forms of e-learning accrue mostly to large firms. With many employees, they can reap savings in distribution costs and travel expenses due to economies of scale.

When examined by industry, ASTD's data show that those sectors reporting the highest levels of e-learning technologies included transportation and public utilities (13 percent of training time), services (10.9 percent), and technology (10.3 percent). Bringing up the rear was the agriculture, mining, and construction sector (4.3 percent of training time). The health care sector experienced a notable increase in e-learning, from 5.0 percent in 1998 to 10.3 percent the next year.

In addition to measuring the extent to which organizations are using learning technologies, ASTD's Benchmarking Service data reveal what types of technologies are being used. For clarity's sake, we have split learning technologies into two categories. The first includes technologies, such as text-only computer-based training and multimedia, that relate to the format in which training is *presented* or "presentation methods." The second category includes technologies that are used to *distribute* training or "distribution methods." Examples are cable TV, CD-ROMs, and company intranets.

As shown in Table 2 (on next page), the most popular technology among the presentation methods remained multimedia—used by 64.9 percent of Benchmarking Service organizations in 1999. This was closely followed by text-only computer-based training (CBT) applications (64.4 percent). Training Investment Leaders also reported these two categories as their top presentation technologies, although the percentage of these organizations using both technologies was remarkably higher (80 percent each).

Among distribution methods, the most frequently mentioned technology among all Benchmarking Service participants remained CD-ROMs, which were used by 61.5 percent of organizations. Coming in next were e-mail (46.5 percent), local area networks (40.9 percent), and intranets (39.8 percent). The greatest growth in distribution methods between 1998 and 1999 occurred in the percentage of companies using the Internet and intranets for training (15.5 and 7.5 percentage points, respectively).

The averages for the Training Investment Leaders were notably different from those of the larger group. Although CD-ROMs also held the top position (84 percent), intranets were the second most popular distribution method, used by a full 60 percent. E-mail, by contrast, ranked 7th in use, while simulators were being used by a healthy percentage of companies (43.5%). The shares of Benchmarking Forum companies using most presentation and distribution methods were higher yet, with 87.5 percent using CD-ROMs and 65 percent using intranets.

Projections for 2001 suggest that the spread of these technologies across organizations is likely to continue. By then, significant majorities of all three groups expect to be using multimedia. Anywhere between 23 and 26 percent of courses are projected to have a multimedia presentation. Among distribution methods, for the first time, more companies in all three groups expect intranets to be the most widely used technology.

Mark E. Van Buren is director of research for the American Society for Training & Development. Contact him at mvanburen@astd.org.

Percentage of Organizations (Courses) Using:	Benchmarking Service, 1999	Benchmarking Service, 2002	Training Investment Leaders, 1999	Training Investment Leaders, 2002	Benchmarking Forum, 1999	Benchmarking Forum, 2002
Presentation Methods						
CBT	64.4 (9.7)	79.3 (16.4)	80.0 (6.2)	83.3 (6.9)	83.3 (10.0)	81.0 (9.2)
Multimedia	64.9 (16.2)	91.0 (26.1)	80.0 (14.5)	92.0 (24.0)	95.2 (14.3)	100.0 (23.1)
Interactive TV	19.7 (1.0)	37.0 (3.0)	36.0 (2.0)	43.5 (2.4)	45.2 (2.4)	61.9 (4.4)
Teleconferencing	35.9 (2.1)	63.0 (6.6)	44.0 (2.0)	65.2 (4.4)	66.7 (3.0)	81.0 (7.4)
Groupware	33.1 (3.8)	60.7 (9.0)	40.0 (.86)	70.8 (6.0)	47.6 (7.0)	85.7 (10.9)
Virtual Reality	2.1 (0.7)	21.8 (3.2)	11.5 (3.5)	20.8 (4.0)	14.3 (1.1)	33.3 (2.5)
EPSS	15.7 (1.3)	44.8 (6.1)	40.0 (2.1)	66.7 (8.0)	50.0 (2.9)	76.2 (7.7)
Distribution Methods						
Cable TV	10.2 (0.7)	19.4 (1.2)	4.2 (0.6)	13.0 (0.9)	26.2 (0.8)	28.5 (1.0)
CD-ROM	61.5 (5.8)	82.7 (14.8)	84.0 (4.7)	83.3 (6.2)	95.2 (6.0)	95.2 (8.5)
E-Mail	46.5 (5.2)	62.1 (8.5)	32.0 (1.0)	39.1 (61.7)	50.0 (6.1)	52.4 (7.5)
Extranet	17.3 (2.1)	32.8 (4.9)	24.0 (0.7)	36.4 (2.4)	42.9 (1.8)	66.7 (9.2)
Internet	38.0 (3.0)	70.5 (10.8)	36.0 (1.4)	63.6 (7.9)	45.2 (1.9)	81.0 (7.7)
Intranet	39.8 (5.0)	83.3 (16.8)	60.0 (8.8)	91.7 (19.0)	71.4 (10.3)	100.0 (24.9)
LAN	40.9 (6.2)	62.0 (12.2)	45.8 (13.9)	45.5 (2.5)	57.1 (5.4)	52.4 (4.0)
Satellite TV	18.8 (0.8)	28.2 (1.9)	39.1 (1.2)	52.4 (2.3)	64.3 (2.1)	76.2 (4.5)
Simulator	19.7 (2.2)	29.8 (4.0)	43.5 (3.5)	42.9 (4.5)	61.9 (3.8)	69.0 (6.3)
Voicemail	11.0 (3.0)	18.4 (3.7)	8.7 (0.3)	9.5 (0.1)	16.7 (0.1)	26.2 (0.3)
Wide Area Networks	14.7 (1.3)	30.2 (4.5)	16.7 (1.9)	27.3 (2.8)	40.5 (4.2)	47.6 (3.9)

Table 2. Use of learning technologies

Trend Watch:
E-Learning Goes Soft

Tom Barron

E-learning adopters and providers are expanding their focus from the IT topics that helped establish the medium to broader business skills needed to support organizational change.

Until e-learning changed the economics of training delivery, training on so-called soft-skills topics was often the first to be lost in the annual budget scrutiny of an organization's cost centers. But the new knowledge economy ethos and the growing adoption of technology for delivering and managing learning have altered the equation. Though only one-third the size (in terms of content volume) of IT-related e-learning, the market for soft-skills e-learning is in the midst of an expansion consultants say is certain to dwarf that field in a matter of two years or less.

In many ways, the success of IT e-learning has paved the way for this broader adoption of technology for nontechnical skills. Having proved its worth to many CEOs in "upskilling" technical staff quickly, more executives are approving wider rollouts of the learning medium to nontechnical staff. And as technical staff increasingly find themselves in roles that call for business knowledge, they, too, become targets for soft-skills training.

What is soft-skills e-learning? Given its breadth, it's tempting to define it by what it is not: training on technical topics that enable straightforward testing, measurement, and certification. Instead, soft skills encompass a broad sweep of topic areas outside the IT domain, including management education, sales training, compliance-related topics such as sexual harassment training, other employee skills such as project management and customer service, even training to orient new employees to a company's mission. It's a far more amorphous entity than the IT arena, one reason the soft-skills market is notoriously difficult to characterize and measure.

Analysts are all but unanimous in forecasting that e-learning's biggest impact will come from the development and adoption of this nontechnical content, including areas that thus far have remained largely rooted in instructor-led delivery. They point to factors ranging from the growth of learning management software, increasing availability of high-speed connections to the Internet, satisfaction with early e-learning implementations often centered on IT skills, and the growing stocks of content in soft-skills topics offered by content vendors, vendor alliances, and end-to-end providers. Growing acceptance of the hosted or ASP delivery model, which allows vendors to provide content and learning management as a subscription-based package, is also fueling use of soft-skills content.

"We expect non-IT corporate e-learning spending, much of which will be focused on soft skills, to grow explosively as content providers take advantage of technology and increased bandwidth to deliver their offerings via the Internet," wrote analyst Michael Moe and colleagues at Merrill Lynch in a report on the e-learning market last year. Several subsequent investment bank studies have echoed that prediction, and Internet market research firm IDC last spring backed it with some jaw-dropping numbers. A survey by the firm of corporate buyers in five vertical markets forecast a compounded annual growth rate (CAGR) of between 18 and 19 percent for adoption of business-skills training content from 1999 to 2004. Growth for the entire soft-skills market during that timeframe was forecast as a whopping 123 percent CAGR; a more recent analysis trimmed that figure slightly to 106 percent.

And, a Drake Beam Morris survey of training professionals who attended ASTD's annual conference last spring found that 70 percent plan to use e-learning for soft-skills training in the next 12 months.

Recent events, including mounting evidence that overall economic growth is slowing, together with a wholesale retreat of technology stocks—those of newly public e-learning firms among them—are clouding the rosy forecasts of early 2000. "I do think growth will be bumpy, and there's likely to be a glut of overlapping content followed by a shakeout on the vendor side," cautions analyst Trace Urdan of H.R. Hambrecht + Company.

Still, anecdotal evidence from industry consultants suggests a continued robust expansion. E-learning technology consultant Brandon Hall points to the sheer breadth of topics in the arena he prefers to term "business skills," together with growing interest by vendors—including IT e-learning veterans—as factors. "I estimate [that in] 18 to 24 months the volume of business-skills training will overtake IT," Hall states.

Perhaps the most convincing evidence is the fact that e-learning content providers that made their name in the IT sector, including SmartForce, NETg, and DigitalThink, have begun pursuing the soft-skills market. NETg and SmartForce introduced e-business curricula aimed at managers recently, while several of DigitalThink's recent contracts involve custom development of business-skills content.

Business Drivers

Judging from the activities of major soft-skills content providers, the market is expanding with gusto in certain areas, less so in others. At the market's top end—in terms of the target audience—is a flourishing of Web-based content for management education through a spate of partnerships between e-learning content and platform developers and postsecondary education providers. Most visible in that niche is Pensare, which in recent months announced alliances with the business schools affiliated with Duke University, the University of Pennsylvania, and UCLA. The company, which provides a content-platform combination, also launched an e-commerce education program in conjunction with three professors from Stanford, one of several such e-learning offerings for e-business training to be unveiled in recent months.

Pensare and such competitors as Corpedia, Harvard Business School, Quisic, and UNext.com are seeking to entice with business-skills education in a format convenient to time-challenged executives. Harvard, for instance, recently announced it was spinning off an executive education e-learning division as a separate, nonprofit organization, HBS Interactive. Some corporate buyers are providing those offerings as part of their compensation packages or as retention incentives. The strategy some analysts observe among e-learning providers is to appeal to the top echelon first, then broaden offerings to the larger employee base after a client relationship has been established.

Large corporations looking to improve their agility or reinvent themselves see the same need for business-skills training for their rank and file. The notion that employers need to help foster a well-rounded education for employees—particularly technical staff—in order to achieve business goals is helping push interest in business skills and other soft-skills topics, say e-learning company executives.

"We think the outlook is expansive because everyone needs to learn these skills," says Lee Ritze, senior director of marketing for SkillSoft, considered the largest producer of off-the-shelf soft-skills content. "We're seeing a number of new workforce competencies being defined in the past few years, and the notion of lifelong learning is reaching deeper into organizations." Ritze is a cofounder of the publicly held, Nashua, New Hampshire-based firm, which counts 350 titles in areas ranging from customer service and leadership to finance and business strategy and claims one million user seats among its largely *Fortune* 500 clientele.

Ritze points to several areas of interest for companies migrating to e-learning. E-business training is one; customer service, where attrition rates are high and there's a need to develop skills quickly, is another. "We have some telco customers who have been able to cut their 13- or 14-week training program for customer service reps down to four or five weeks through use of e-learning," with a compelling return-on-investment, he says. Project management is another topic that has seen surging interest, he adds.

The trend toward less hierarchical, more team-driven organizational structures among companies, led by nimble Internet companies and emulated by brick-and-mortar counterparts, is another driver, says Ritze. "We're seeing more companies interested in leadership and management training for nonmanagement employees in these work environments. When companies flatten out organizationally, it serves them well to provide employees with these types of skills."

Ninth House Network, a developer of soft-skills content and pioneer in the use of streaming-video methods to deliver it, reports a similar escalation in demand that senior vice president of market development Tom Fischmann attributes to "the pain businesses are experiencing" in shifting to the Internet economy.

"Organizations are trying to scale themselves very rapidly, or consolidate after a series of mergers and acquisitions, or trying to remake themselves from the bottom up into an e-business," says Fischmann, a cofounder of the San Francisco-based company. Those changes "don't call for technical skills so much as the need for people to be able to communicate effectively," he says. Many of the company's newer offerings, including a series of Web-based videos that portray a 100-year-old company as it works to get into the e-business game, focus on building basic communication and management skills, he says. "Demand is being driven by the need to solve business problems, and the people in charge of business lines are turning to e-learning for help."

Ken Dickens, vice president of marketing for e-learning giant SmartForce, says demand for soft-skills topics is growing steadily among users of its combined content and learning management system. "Virtually all of our customers are asking for solutions in areas such as sexual harassment, diversity, and other areas," he says. The company's interest in expanding its soft-skills offerings is evident in two recent alliances, one announced last spring with business simulation developer Strategic Management Group (SMG) and an October agreement with classroom-based soft-skills provider Provant.

Technology Drivers

A clear catalyst in the growth of soft-skills e-learning is technology advancements that improve the ability to deliver and manage it. When learning technologies began migrating from the lush environs of CD-ROM-based multimedia to the bandwidth-spare world of WBT, many eulogized the loss of video and other interactive features considered vital to teaching behavioral skills. It's one reason—surging demand for IT skills is another—why soft-skills content has lagged behind IT content in the e-learning era, some say.

Bandwidth-heavy graphics, animations, and streaming video, increasingly accessible as a result of the growth of broadband connectivity, are often cited as keys in helping to turn the tide. Web-based video using one or more competing browser-based players or Java-based applets is becoming a component of more soft-skills offerings.

"The technologies are catching up to where it now makes sense to develop Web-based soft-skills training," says Anthony Karrer, a developer of custom e-learning with Technical Empowerment who also teaches Web development at Loyola Marymount University. Karrer's firm recently developed a Web-based course on interviewing skills for LMU students that relies on video and a simulation approach to illustrate how best to handle interview questions; the e-learning course can be viewed at www.careers.lmu.edu.

"The technology is available now to do the modeling of behavior that is important in training on behavioral skills," says Karrer.

Other analysts point to the growing sophistication of off-the-shelf courseware, more of which are employing simulation methodologies. "The best ones are not necessarily the most media rich, but excellent business-skills simulations do require rich, complex scenarios, and are as a result difficult and expensive to develop," notes Brandon Hall.

Among developers pursuing simulation are SkillSoft, which recently rolled out a new product line called SkillSims that uses a browser-based Java player to deliver images, audio, and rapid-fire interactivity to simulate scenarios for business-skills training. Its first SkillSim simulations target customer service representatives and provide an environment for practicing skills taught in its existing courseware library. "We went the extra mile and designed this without the need for a plug-in," says SkillSoft's Ritze. "Our plan is to build one or more for every popular course we have."

SmartForce is also developing soft-skills simulation courseware through its partnership with SMG. And a plethora of smaller firms, including Cognitive Arts, led by learning and simulation expert Roger Schank, are seeking to carve stakes in what's anticipated to be a booming market for business-skill simulation.

Another driver cited by consultants is the growth of learning management systems that provide a framework for organizations to manage their e-learning and instructor-led training. Once in place, those systems simplify the delivery and management of learning, making courseware more accessible. But at least one observer says indecision by buyers in the crowded field of LMS products and services is acting as a damper rather than driver of soft-skills content adoption.

Yet another catalyst is the evolving discipline of competency or skills management, in which various employment positions are analyzed from a skills and knowledge perspective and tied to appropriate learning. The field traces its roots to the IT sector, where such mapping is comparatively straightforward, but it has evolved to encompass a growing number of nontechnical positions and competencies. Hank Riehl, founder of SkillView Technologies, one such provider of a skills-management system, says the methodology provides a context for employers to match e-learning content with training needs.

"The principle has been accepted most readily in IT organizations, where constantly changing skill sets have made it very valuable," says Riehl. But as more technical staff have soaked up IT training without business-skills training, the need to map their positions to appropriate soft-skills courseware has grown. "Technical people in the trenches are not particularly fond of soft skills—we frequently hear they have a beef over what they're being trained on," he says. Skills management helps pinpoint training relevant to certain positions without bogging learners down with unnecessary courses. "Some of these folks are in positions that require dealing with customers, and that calls for skills many of them don't have but need."

Brandon Hall says skills management "will be essential for organizations needing to link their business skills e-learning programs to real competency-performance improvement needs."

One other phenomenon said to be helping propel soft-skills content is the growth of so-called blended approaches to delivering behavior-related learning, which combines e-learning with instructor-led training, in either a real or a virtual classroom. Blended learning answers the shortcomings of e-learning in illustrating subtle differences in social behaviors and in teaching social skills such as teamwork and acceptance of diversity. Consultants were first to stress the value of blended learning, but e-learning providers have since chimed in. SmartForce's alliance with ILT provider Provant is evidence of growing recognition by content vendors that buyers are intrigued by the combination approach. The best examples of blended approaches are still in the custom e-learning domain, says Hall, but he predicts that off-the-shelf content vendors will move quickly to embrace the blended model.

What's in a Name?

The downside to prospects for achieving the stellar growth forecast for the soft-skills market includes an overall economic slowdown that could affect corporate purchasing of technologies during the new year. The resilience of the e-learning field as a whole would be tested by a recession, analysts agree, since it has been incubated thus far in the longest economic expansion since World War II.

There's also plenty of room to improve content quality by making soft-skills e-learning more interactive, engaging, and sound from an instructional design standpoint. "Engaging the learners and holding their attention is much more challenging in soft skills than in IT training," says Hambrecht's Trace Urdan. "The quality of the content has to be very strong to survive."

Other complications include the increased difficulty in "cookie cutting" soft-skills content for overseas markets, where different cultural norms make it much harder to adapt content for those audiences. "It's a challenge for any company developing business and soft-skills content," acknowledges Ritze of SkillSoft. As a result, soft-skills content providers won't enjoy the same multiplier effect that IT providers have as international markets adopt e-learning.

Ironically, another barrier to faster growth is a lingering distaste for the term *soft skills*. Analysts say the term hearkens back to training's legacy as a cost center unallied with business objectives and hampers interest from executive buyers—especially those outside traditional training functions. "*Soft skills* seems to have a rather negative connotation," says Brandon Hall, whose research is abandoning the term and dividing the areas it comprises into business skills and people skills.

Another analyst speculates on whether dislike for the term will goad firms with *soft* in their titles to seek new names. Says Urdan: "It's enough of an issue that it wouldn't surprise me to see companies getting away from the term completely."

The extent to which e-learning in general, and soft-skills content in particular, is used by companies to support their transition to e-business will prove pivotal to achieving the swift growth consultants forecast for the content sector.

Tom Barron (tbarron@astd.org) is editor for Learning Circuits.

The Evolution of Learning Devices: Smart Objects, Information Infrastructures, and Shared Synthetic Environments

Chris Dede

What's going on in distance and e-learning these days? This article provides an overview of the different directions this new technology-driven approach is taking. Besides explaining the different technologies, the article includes examples of these approaches and how they're working.

Over the course of the Industrial Revolution, motors shrank in size and cost, disappearing inside household appliances and workplace tools to create new kinds of machines. Through a similar process, we are now embedding computers and telecommunications into our everyday context, making possible three innovative types of learning devices. *Smart objects*, with embedded microprocessors and wireless networking, explain their own functioning and help us create "articulate" educational environments that communicate with their inhabitants. *Information infrastructures* provide remote access to experts, interlinked archival resources, virtual communities, and "distributed" investigations involving many participants in different locations. *Shared synthetic environments*, by

Reprinted from the U.S. Department of Education's series of white papers, "The Future of Networking Technologies for Learning," www.ed.gov/Technology/Futures/index.html.

immersing us in illusion, help us develop a better understanding and appreciation of reality. The new messages emerging from these new media can dramatically improve instructional outcomes, but such an evolution of educational practice depends on careful design of the interface among the devices, learners, and teachers.

New Types of Learning Devices

High-performance computing and telecommunications are driving the rapid evolution of devices that facilitate learning. Imagine information technologies as forming something akin to a biological ecosystem, with each type of device a different species. First came the telegraph, then the telephone, then radio, television, videotape players, videodisc players.... Now this ecosystem is incredibly crowded; every few months a new species appears, such as the personal digital assistant. From their individual niches, a bewildering variety of species cooperate, compete, and become extinct, just as in nature's ecological systems.

The coming generation of computers and telecommunications is different from prior evolutions of information technology because it is dramatically reversing the century-old trend toward a crowded ecology of devices. Different species are fusing together; the radio, television, telephone, copier, fax, scanner, printer, and computer will eventually coexist in a single box. Soon, the ecology of information technologies will have only a few superspecies remaining that synthesize and extend the capabilities of all current devices.

One way of understanding this evolution is to classify these synthesis devices into three types—smart objects, information infrastructures, and shared synthetic environments—based on their relationship to our surroundings. *Smart objects* are artifacts in our immediate context that can explain themselves and, acting in concert, help us understand our surroundings. *Information infrastructures* are ways of extending our nervous systems so that we can communicate and learn across barriers of distance and time, exploring and contributing to remote archives and virtual think tanks. *Shared synthetic environments* are entire virtual contexts into which we immerse ourselves, much as Alice walked through the looking glass to become part of an artificial reality. Thinking about new educational media from this perspective highlights the crucial issue of how our relationship to these various devices shapes and makes possible different types of learning.

Smart Objects and Articulate Environments as Learning Devices

As microprocessors and wireless networking grow cheaper and more powerful, it is rapidly becoming more feasible to design embedded capabilities (including speech, imagery, and intelligence) into common objects, thereby enhancing their educational value. Smart objects used for learning might include, for example, intelligent manipulatives for young children. Imagine a child stacking blocks by size, from biggest to smallest, to form a tower. When he picks up a block whose size is out of sequence, the block could say, "Not me," while the correct block could light up and say, "My turn."

To illustrate some potential implications of smart objects, a vignette is presented below that depicts the daily routine of a university faculty member a decade from now. The ideas and situations in this vignette draw heavily from a scenario described by Weiser (1991). Brief descriptions in parentheses explain neologisms that may be confusing to readers. The purpose of this scenario is not to predict how university teaching will evolve, but to illustrate the types of smart devices that will permeate society in the future and the range of their instructional capabilities.

Vignette: Engineering Education via Intelligent Objects

Vesper is driving to work through heavy rush hour traffic. She is a faculty member in computational engineering at a university located far from her home in the suburbs. Despite the long drive, the position was irresistible because the campus serves as a test site for advanced networking technologies.

She glances in the "foreview" mirror to check the traffic. (Commuters' automobiles are hooked into a large network that uses data sent by cars and highway sensors to monitor and coordinate the flow of traffic. The foreview mirror presents a graphic display of what is happening up to five miles beyond her car along Vesper's planned route to work.) Noticing a traffic slowdown ahead, Vesper taps a button on the steering column to check for alternate routes that might be faster. A moment later, she cancels the request for rerouting as the foreview mirror reveals the green icon of a food shop on a side street near the next freeway exit. The foreview mirror helps her to find a parking space quickly, and she orders a cup of coffee while waiting for the traffic jam to clear.

While drinking her coffee, Vesper calls up some of her students' work on the screen and begins reviewing it. (This machine, about the size of a thick pad of paper, has the approximate processing power of today's supercomputers. It is linked via wireless networking to a large web of computers, including those at Vesper's campus.) The university's diagnostic expert system for debugging prototype designs can handle the routine misconceptions typical of most sophomore engineering students, but occasionally it is stumped by an unusual faulty procedure that some learner has misgeneralized. (A computer program trained to mimic human experts can handle many routine aspects of evaluating student performance, but complex assessments still require human involvement.)

Vesper has an uncanny ability to recognize exotic error patterns in student work, and she diagnoses three sets of student misgeneralizations before resuming her trip to school. Her new "bug collection" will be sent automatically to the national database on design misconceptions, where it will be entered into statistical records. Her notepad also forwards her diagnoses to the university's expert system on design, which incorporates the new bugs into its knowledge base and begins preparing tutorials to correct those particular errors. Later today, this instructional material will be forwarded to the appropriate learners' notepads to provide individualized remediation.

As Vesper walks into the engineering complex on campus, her personalized identity tab registers her presence on the university's net of security sensors. (Within a clip-on badge displaying Vesper's picture and name is embedded a small device that broadcasts information about her movements. This identity screening procedure is part of the university's security system. In this future world, these elaborate precautions unfortunately have become necessary.) A moment later, the machines in her office initiate a log-in cycle in preparation for her arrival. She realizes that she has left her car unlocked, but does not bother to retrace her steps; from her office, she can access the network to lock her car via a remote command.

As Vesper gets to her desk, the "telltale" by her door begins blinking, indicating that the department's espresso machine has finished brewing her cafe au lait. (A telltale is a remote signaling device that can be triggered to blink or emit a sound, advising people in its vicinity of some event happening elsewhere.) Vesper drinks a cup of cafe au lait every morning upon arriving. She heads down the hall to get the coffee; the espresso maker's brew will be much better than the vile stuff she had consumed at the food shop. On returning to her office, she instructs her desktop workstation to remind her not to stop there again. A copy of her evaluation is automatically forwarded to the food shop's manager and to the local consumer ratings magazine.

In the hour before class, as her sophomore students arrive, they wander around the halls visiting friends and faculty, gradually congregating in the engineering lab to work on projects for their exhibition portfolios. Vesper will join them in about half an hour to begin face-to-face instruction. She takes a break from viewing her videomail to fast-reverse through the electronic trails their movements have left on the security system. Valerie is still dallying too long before getting down to work; Vesper will have to speak with her. Richard has not arrived at the engineering complex, but no message has come in to indicate why he is later than usual. Vesper decides to wait another 15 minutes before taking action about his unexpected tardiness.

Her desktop workstation conducts a brief dialogue with the "intelligent" equipment in the lab, then reports its findings. (Just as with the identity badge and the telltale, classroom devices can have embedded microprocessors and wireless networking. This gives each set of objects limited abilities to sense what is happening and respond, guiding some forms of student learning.) Ronald is redoing activities he has already mastered rather than moving on to the new work she had assigned; Vesper notes that she needs to talk to him about this. Everyone else seems to be on task and involved enough to be occupied for another 15 minutes before she arrives at the classroom.

A small light on the edge of Vesper's glasses begins blinking. A phone call is coming in; it must be from someone not on the network. "Activate," says Vesper (the only word her glasses can recognize). A voice begins speaking, emanating from a small telephone receiver the size of a hearing aid located in her left ear. The voice is Richard's girlfriend, informing her that he is sick again. With a sigh, Vesper makes a note to prepare hardcopy homework that will be sent off by snailmail—what a hassle! (Many network users refer to traditional delivery services for paper copies as "snail-mail"; they prefer the rapid transmission of electronic mail via telecommunications.) She will be glad when the government finally recognizes that access to basic network services is a fundamental right of all citizens, even if that does mean subsidizing sub-scriptions for the poor. Her notepad automatically informs the attendance monitor in the registrar's office of the reasons for Richard's absence ....

As discussed earlier, the purpose of this vignette is not to suggest that Vesper's world is the most likely future, but instead to illustrate the types of intelligent devices that will permeate society in the future and the kinds of human capabilities that they can enable. Through the ubiquitous presence of smart objects, the everyday context itself can become an "articulate environment," able to communicate with its inhabi-tants. This situation is analogous to animistic cultures studied by anthropologists, in which people believe that objects have souls and personalities and thereby experience a very rich interaction with their surroundings.

Interface Issues for Smart Objects

The barriers to artifacts with embedded intelligence are more psychosocial than tech-nical and financial. For example, we do not want all the cereal boxes in the supermar-ket screaming, "Buy me or I'll die," on the day before they reach their expiration date.

Moreover, Vesper's environment may seem implausible—why would a person choose to live in such a machine-centered environment—but then, how would today's world of cellular phones, facsimiles, electronic mail, and answering machines have seemed two decades ago?

The vignette also deliberately incorporates a high level of surveillance; instruction is individualized by monitoring students' activities and by intrusively intervening if these do not match some predetermined pattern. From my perspective as an educator, such a "Big Brother" world would be unattractive. But I deliberately incorporated some dystopian aspects into this vignette to underscore that the design of powerful tech-nologies must be considered carefully to avoid unfortunate side effects. Advances in information technology have already stripped away much of our privacy; for example, supermarkets track our purchases and sell lists of our preferences and buying patterns to telemarketers. Unless care is taken with how smart objects are implemented, we may all live in "glass houses."

Information Infrastructures as Learning Devices

The global marketplace and the communications and entertainment industries are driving the rapid evolution of regional, national, and global information infrastructures that enhance our abilities to access and interlink materials in remote archives. These powerful channels for transmitting data are ways of extending our nervous systems so that we can communicate and learn across barriers of distance and time, exploring and contributing to virtual think tanks (Dede 1994). As a result, the means for creating, delivering, and using information in business, government, and society are swiftly changing. To successfully prepare students as workers and citizens, educators must incorporate experiences into the curriculum that enable students to create and utilize new forms of expression and that can be activated just in time, at any place, and on demand (Dede and Lewis 1995).

The "information superhighway" metaphor, now widely used to convey the implications of high-performance computing and communications, is an inadequate analogy. It is the equivalent of someone in 1896 declaring that the airplane will be the canal system of the 20th century. Backward-looking metaphors focus on what we can automate—how we can use new channels to send conventional forms of content more efficiently—but miss the true innovation: redefining how we communicate and educate by using new types of messages and experiences to be more effective. Since emerging forms of representation, such as hypermedia and virtual reality, are in their early stages of development, we are just beginning to understand how they shape not only their messages, but also their users.

Many people are still reeling from the first impact of high-performance computing and communications: shifting from the challenge of not getting enough information to the challenge of surviving amid too much information. The core skill needed in today's workplace is not foraging for data, but filtering a plethora of incoming information. The emerging literacy we all must master requires immersing ourselves in a sea of information and harvesting patterns of knowledge, just as fish extract oxygen from water via their gills. In this environment, educators must understand how to structure learning experiences that make this kind of immersion possible. Preparing students for full participation in 21st-century society will require expanding the traditional definitions of literacy and rhetoric to encompass "immersionlike" experiences of interacting with information.

Two new forms of expression that take advantage of the unique power of information infrastructures are knowledge webs and virtual communities. Both illustrate how information infrastructures can have a major impact on conventional instruction by expanding learning resources beyond the individual teacher and classroom materials, to encompass rich, widely distributed sources of information, expertise, and fellowship.

Knowledge Webs

"Knowledge webs" give people distributed access to experts, archival resources, authentic environments, and shared investigations. We are accustomed to asking a well-informed person in our immediate vicinity for guidance, to consulting printed information or watching a news program, to visiting exhibits like zoos to learn about different types of environments, and to conducting informal experiments to understand how reality works. Often, these information-gathering and -creation activities are constrained by barriers of distance, restricted access, scheduling difficulties, and limited personal expertise in investigation methods.

Via information infrastructures, educators and students can join distributed conferences that provide an instant network of contacts with useful skills—a personal brain trust scattered geographically, but offering just-in-time answers to immediate questions. Eventually, these informal sources of expertise will utilize embedded "groupware" tools to enhance collaboration. On the Internet, online archival resources are linked increasingly into the World Wide Web, accessible through "webcrawler" programs such as Netscape. In time, guides based on artificial intelligence will help users navigate through huge amounts of stored information.

Another type of emerging electronic environment is the virtual exhibit that duplicates museums and other real-world settings. Virtual exhibits make possible a wide variety of experiences without the necessity of travel or scheduling. Distributed science projects enable students to conduct shared experiments dispersed across time and space; often each team member learns more than would be possible in isolation about the phenomenon being studied and about scientific investigation. Combined, all these capabilities to enhance information gathering and creation form knowledge webs.

Interface Issues for Knowledge Webs

Access to data does not automatically expand students' knowledge; the availability of information does not intrinsically create an internal framework of ideas that learners can use to interpret reality. While presentational approaches transmit material rapidly from source to student, often this content evaporates quickly from learners' minds. To be motivated to master concepts and skills, students need to see the connection of what they are learning to the rest of their lives and to the mental models they already use. Even when learners are drilled in a topic until facts are indefinitely retained—we all know that the sum of a triangle's internal angles is 180 degrees—this knowledge is often "inert"; most people don't know how to apply the abstract principles they memorized in school to solve real-world problems. To move students beyond assimilating inert facts and toward generating better mental models, teachers must structure learning experiences that highlight how new ideas can provide insights in intriguing, challenging situations.

The curriculum is already overcrowded with low-level information; teachers frantically race through required material, helping students memorize factual data to be regurgitated on mandated, standardized tests. Using information infrastructures as a fire hose to spray yet more information into educational settings would make this situation even worse. Without skilled facilitation, many learners who access current knowledge webs will flounder in a morass of unstructured data.

A vital, emerging form of literacy that educators ought to be communicating is how to transform archival information into personal knowledge. Moving students from access through assimilation to appropriation is no simple process, however. Teachers must provide unsophisticated learners with educational experiences that enable them to construct their own knowledge and make sense of massive, incomplete, and inconsistent information sources. In order to create a learner-centered environment in which students can take full advantage of information infrastructures, it is vital that educators augment the traditional curriculum with collaborative, learning-through-doing activities based on linked, online materials and orchestrated across classrooms, workplaces, homes, and community settings.

Virtual Communities

Virtual communities that provide support from people who share common joys and trials are a second means for enhancing student learning through information infrastructures. We are accustomed to face-to-face interaction as a way of getting to know people, sharing ideas and experiences, enjoying others' humor and fellowship, and finding solace. In a different manner, distributed learning via information infrastructures can satisfy these needs at any time, in any place. Some people—shy or reflective or seeking a little emotional distance—may even find asynchronous, low-bandwidth communication more "authentic" than face-to-face verbal exchange. They can take time before replying to compose a more elegant message or refine the emotional nuances they wish to convey. This alternative conception of authenticity may reflect a different kind of learning style than the visual, auditory, symbolic, and kinesthetic distinctions now used.

Virtual communities are an important component of new pedagogical strategies based on information infrastructures, one that can dramatically improve learning outcomes. Learning is social as well as intellectual. Individual, isolated attempts to make sense of complex data can easily fail unless the learner is encouraged by some larger group that is constructing shared knowledge. In addition, institutional evolution is a communal enterprise; educational innovators also need emotional and intellectual support from others who have similar challenges in their lives.

Moreover, formal education comprises only a small fraction of how students spend their time. No matter how effective the schooling, students are unlikely to make major gains in learning if the other parts of their lives are not educationally fulfilling. Virtual communities can help bring about close cooperation and shared responsibility for learning among all the educational agents of society—families, social service agencies, workplaces, mass media, schools, and higher education. For example, involving families more deeply in their children's education may be the single most powerful lever for improved learning outcomes. Virtual parent-teacher conferences and less formal social interchanges provide new opportunities for involving parents who will never come to a PTA meeting or a school-based event. In many regions across the United States, community networks are emerging that, among other missions, enhance education by enabling distributed discourse among all the stakeholders in quality schooling.

Peer tutoring is another educational use of virtual communities. This instructional approach aids all students involved, on both an intellectual and an emotional level, but is difficult to implement in traditional classroom settings. Outside of school, virtual interactions, enhanced by groupware tools, make it easy for students to relate to each other and also prepare them to use distributed problem-solving techniques in adult workplaces. Telementoring and teleapprenticeships between students and workplace experts are other ways of applying the capabilities of virtual communities to distributed learning.

Interface Issues for Virtual Communities

Creating a sense of communion among a distributed group linked by low-to-moderate bandwidth networking is a complex challenge. Some people favor technology-mediated communication as their most authentic way of sharing ideas and enjoying fellowship. Most people prefer face-to-face interaction, but find that the convenience of just-in-time, any-place access to others often outweighs the disadvantages of distributed sharing of ideas, experiences, and support. Groupware tools, a capable moderator, and shared interactivity and control are important for sustaining the vitality of virtual communities, as is occasional direct contact among participants.

To succeed in sustaining communion among people, distributed learning must balance virtual and direct interaction. A relationship based only on telephone conversation lacks the vibrancy that face-to-face interchange provides. Similarly, while digital video will broaden the bandwidth of virtual interactions via information infrastructures, teleconferencing will never completely substitute for direct personal contact. We can expect a variety of social inventions to emerge that provide the best of both worlds.

We are just beginning to understand how knowledge webs and virtual communities can reshape the content, process, and delivery of conventional distance education. Information infrastructures are the new type of learning device that is spurring this evolution, just as the steam engine was the driver for the Industrial Revolution.

Shared Synthetic Environments as Learning Devices

Shared synthetic environments, the third type of emerging learning device, are entire virtual contexts into which we immerse ourselves, just as Alice walked through the looking glass and became part of an artificial reality (Dede 1995). Communal virtual worlds that students can enter and explore have many educational uses. For example, single-user simulations allow an individual to interact with a model of reality, such as flying a virtual airplane. Distributed simulations extend this capability by enabling many people at different locations to inhabit and shape a common synthetic environment. As an illustration, the U.S. Department of Defense uses distributed simulation to create virtual battlefields on which trainees at remote sites develop collective military skills. The appearance and capabilities of graphically represented military equipment alter second by second as the virtual battle evolves ("dial-a-war").

Shared synthetic environments are a representational container that can accommodate a broad range of educational uses, such as virtual factories, hospitals, or cities. Moreover, this type of distributed learning strategy uses "edutainment" to build on the curiosity, fantasy, and motivation that the entertainment industry stimulates in youngsters. While home video game consoles are not now particularly powerful, in 8 to 10 years they will be quite sophisticated in graphics and distributed simulation capabilities, but still relatively inexpensive because so many are sold. Since video game consoles are widely found even in poor and rural households, they offer a promising installed base of learning technologies—if we develop educationally rich material that takes advantage of these systems.

Even without the added enhancement of visual imagery, the rise on the Internet of text-based shared synthetic environments (i.e., MUDs, MUSEs, MOOs) illustrates the fascination that people have with participatory virtual worlds. The continual evolution of distributed simulations based on participants' collaborative interactions keeps these shared virtual environments from becoming boring and stale. In contrast to standard adventure games, in which you wander through someone else's fantasy, the ability to personalize an environment and receive recognition from others for adding to the shared context is attractive to many people. Part of why we read fiction or watch dramatic productions is to escape the ordinary in a manner that increases our insights or refreshes us to plunge back into real-world challenges. Shared virtual experiences on the national information infrastructure can complement books, plays, television, movies, and concerts by taking us beyond the daily grind; the challenge, however, is to move past escapism into metaphorical comprehension and catharsis.

Sensory Immersion

Advances in high-performance computing and communications also provide the means for sensory immersion, whereby learners are involved in "artificial realities." Wearing computerized clothing and a head-mounted display, the participant feels as if he is "inside" an artificial reality, rather than just viewing a synthetic environment through a computer monitor's screen; virtual reality is analogous to diving rather than to looking through an aquarium window. Using sensory immersion to present abstract, symbolic data in tangible form is a powerful method of attaining insights into real world phenomena.

"Visualization," for example, is an emerging type of rhetoric that enhances learning by using the human visual system to find patterns in large amounts of information. People have very powerful capabilities to recognize patterns among images; much of our brain is "wetware" dedicated to this purpose. As a result, when tabular data of numerical variables—such as temperature, pressure, and velocity—are transfigured into graphical objects that shift their shape, texture, size, color, and motion to convey the changing values of each variable, learners also gain increased insights. For example, graphical data visualizations that model thunderstorm-related phenomena (downbursts, air flows, cloud movements) can help meteorologists and students understand the dynamics of these weather systems.

As information infrastructures increasingly enable people to access large databases across distances, visualization tools can expand human perceptions so that we recognize underlying relationships that would otherwise be swamped in a sea of numbers. One good way to enhance creativity is to make the familiar strange and the strange, familiar; adding sound and even tactile sensations to visual imagery can make abstract things tangible, and vice versa. Expanding human perceptions—for example, allowing a medical student to see the human body through X-ray vision like Superman's—is a powerful method for deepening learners' motivation and their intuitions about physical phenomena. My current research centers on assessing the potential value of sensory immersion and synthetic environments for learning material as disparate as electromagnetic fields and intercultural sensitivities (Salzman, Dede, and Loftin 1995).

Assessing the Impact of New Learning Devices on Conventional Instruction

The vignettes depicted above may seem financially implausible; where will schools and colleges find the resources to implement these sophisticated technologies? An analogy can be drawn to the early-1980s competition among cable TV vendors to receive exclusive franchises from communities. Those educators smart enough to participate in that bargaining process received substantial resources—buildings wired for free, dedicated channels, sophisticated production equipment—because the vendors knew public service applications would help determine who won. In the same manner, during today's much larger war in the information services industry, educators that have innovative alternatives to "talking heads" instruction can find vendors happy to share the costs in exchange for help with the regulators, legislators, and judges who are determining which coalitions will manage the nation's information infrastructures.

As with business, however, the evolution of technology creates new markets and expanded competitors for schools and colleges. As one illustration, prestigious universities may develop nationwide offerings of standard courses, such as Psych 101, taught by telegenic, internationally recognized authorities. Under this strategy, presentations with high production values would be coupled with frequent, interactive teleconferences, mentoring via electronic mail, and occasional face-to-face meetings of locally enrolled students led by a practitioner. This approach would not intrigue learners interested in a residential college experience, but could be very attractive to students at commuter campuses. With sufficient economies of scale, this delivery method would have lower costs than our present system of similar standard courses duplicated at every institution. While many faculty would disparage this type of instruction, state legislatures could easily see it as an attractive way to cut their expenditures for higher education—a method applicable to every course for which a substantial textbook market exists.

In this particular evolution of distance education, colleges and universities would be reshaped as profoundly as American business has been altered by the technologies that helped create the global marketplace. Given their responsibilities for socialization and custodial protection, public schools would be less affected by the erosion of geographic monopolies through distributed learning technologies. But the home schooling and educational voucher movements see emerging learning devices as an attractive alternative means of delivering instruction. If smart objects, information infrastructures, and shared synthetic environments are not incorporated into public school classrooms, teachers may find a decade from now that they have a smaller fraction of students enrolled and fewer taxpayers willing to provide funding.

Educators must help all students become adept at distanced interaction, for skills of gathering information from remote sources and of collaboration with dispersed team members are as central to the future American workplace as learning to perform structured tasks quickly was to the industrial revolution. Also, by increasing the diversity of human resources available to students, distributed learning can enhance equity and pluralism, while preparing young people to compete in the world marketplace. Virtual classrooms have a wider spectrum of peers with whom learners can collaborate than any local region can offer and a broader range of teachers and mentors than any single educational institution can afford.

In a few years, high-performance computing and communications will make knowledge utilities, virtual communities, shared synthetic environments, and sensory immersion as routine a part of everyday existence as the telephone, television, radio, and newspaper are today. This evolution of learning devices won't be a "silver bullet" that magically solves all problems of education, however. Thoughtful and caring participation is vital for making these new capabilities truly valuable.

How a medium shapes its users, as well as its message, is a central issue in understanding the personal impact of emerging learning devices. The telephone creates conversationalists. The book develops imaginers, who can conjure a rich mental image from sparse symbols on a printed page. Much of television programming induces passive observers; other shows, such as *Sesame Street* and public affairs programs, can spark viewers' enthusiasm and enrich their perspectives. Through the evolution of smart objects, information infrastructures, and shared synthetic environments, our society is encountering powerful new interactive media capable of great good or ill. Today's "couch potatoes," vicariously living in the fantasy world of television, could become tomorrow's "couch funguses," immersed as protagonists in 3-D soap operas while the real world deteriorates. The most significant influence on the evolution of education will not be the technical development of more powerful devices, but the professional development of wise designers, teachers, and learners.

References

Dede, C. and M. Lewis. 1995. *Assessment of emerging educational technologies that might assist and enhance school-to-work transitions.* Washington, DC: National Technical Information Service.

Dede, C. 1995. "The evolution of constructivist learning environments: Immersion in distributed, virtual worlds." *Educational Technology* 35(5) (September-October): 46-52.

Dede, C. 1994. *The technologies driving the national information infrastructure: Policy implications for distance education.* Los Alamitos, CA: Southwest Regional Educational Laboratory.

Laurel, B. 1991. *Computers as theater.* Menlo Park, CA: Addison-Wesley.

Rheingold, H. 1993. *The virtual community: Homesteading on the electronic frontier.* New York: Addison-Wesley.

Salzman, M., C. Dede, and B. Loftin. 1995. *Learner centered design of sensorily immersive microworlds using a virtual reality interface.* Proceedings of the Seventh International Conference on Artificial Intelligence and Education. Charlottesville, VA: Association for the Advancement of Computers in Education.

Sproull, S., and S. Kiesler. 1991. *Connections: New ways of working in the networked world.* Cambridge, MA: MIT Press.

Weiser, M. 1991. "The computer for the 21st century." *Scientific American* 265(3) (September): 94-104.

Chris Dede is Timothy E. Wirth Professor of Learning Technologies at the Graduate School of Education, Harvard University. Contact him at Chris_Dede@Harvard.edu.

21st Century Teaching and Learning Patterns: What Will We See?

Judith V. Boettcher

This article was written in mid-1999, but it is still a valuable preview of ways learning and training will change over the next few years. The author makes seven predictions about future trends that are food for thought in considering and planning your distance and e-learning efforts.

The time period for predictions is an important decision. If the time span is too short, the predictions can hardly qualify as they are in progress already. If the time span is too long, the predictions can get to be so outrageous that they might be easily discounted. A time span of seven years can be a good compromise—long enough so that we can be playfully optimistic and possibly totally impractical, yet short enough that planning is possible. And seven years is close enough that we ourselves will be impacted one way or another by what actually happens.

The Higher Education Enterprise and the Big Picture: Seven Predictions

William Gibson, a science fiction writer, says, "The Future is here; it is just not evenly distributed." This quote aptly describes both where the teaching and learning enterprise is today and how it will progress. We know that many groups within higher education are embracing new technologies while others hold back, some quite vigorously.

This perception of unevenness helps us to keep in mind that higher education will not change in a lockstep progression. The "uneven distribution" of the future will be emphasized as institutions that declare a new context for teaching and learning move forward with astonishing speed. A few institutions will constitute the leading edge, and others will be more conservative and shy away from the newer environments, tools, and processes.

With the help of a few data points, I can offer seven predictions of significant events and changes in teaching and learning that I think we will all see in the early part of the next century. These predictions both suggest and anticipate where higher education might be by the year 2007.

Prediction One: A "Career University" sector will be in place. This prediction highlights the explosive growth in the entire education market and the need to respond to the new requirements of the information age workforce. This workforce needs to constantly increase their knowledge base and upgrade their skills to support their multiple career changes.

A new career university sector will emerge, focusing on the non-traditional degree, certification, and career professional areas. The institutions in this new career university sector will design customized and flexible programs to meet the knowledge requirements, as well as the learning style needs, of career professionals. A closely related development will be a new set of national and global partnerships that extend institutions' specialties around the world.

The signs for these changes are already quite apparent. Over the last 10-15 years we have seen the development of Motorola University, National Technological University, Jones International, and the new set of virtual universities associated with existing institutions—including Penn State's World Campus, Western Governors University, and the Southern Regional Educational Board.

Another major shift will be manifested in the credibility of the for-profit companies. Jones International University just received accreditation from North Central in March of this year for their bachelor's and master's programs in business communications. The University of Phoenix is also well known for its wide range of accredited programs.

These new career university institutions will have expertise at teaching and reaching career professionals with flexible life-style and focused content-packaged programs, and the role of technology will be to support efforts to reach such learners. Tuition costs will not be kept low, however, as many companies that send their students to these programs will subsidize the time and the cost of these programs.

Whereas most major universities have branches of their expertise reaching out to career professionals, these branches will probably become institutions in their own right, with strong links to the originating institutions. The best institutions for working professionals will probably be focused institutions, extending the expertise of their current institutional image and supported by the research and knowledge creation of the research faculty. We can see the beginnings of this with programs like the Harvard, Wharton, and Penn State Executive programs; Duke University's Global MBA; and others.

Higher education institutions that wish to provide career professional programs will begin with a focus that extends their current strengths and images. If these programs are successful, they may spin off entire portions of the university into a non-profit foundation or a for-profit institution.

Prediction Two: Most higher education institutions, perhaps 60 percent, will have teaching and learning management software systems linked to their back office administrative systems. This prediction highlights the fact that our current teaching and learning support systems are still very traditional—unimpacted by most of the efficiencies that have transformed other service industries. This prediction is a prediction of dramatic change. Tools and systems for support of teaching and learning processes will become part of the critical mission infrastructure on higher education campuses, and they will be tightly integrated with current back office administrative systems. Today's Web course management tools will evolve into full-fledged systems for the management of teaching and learning, paving the way for the unbundling of the design, development, and delivery components of teaching. These software systems will bring the first major modernization of the work associated with the management and delivery of teaching and learning.

The administrative part of the higher education institutional infrastructure of the future is well under way. Many institutions recruit, admit, and screen students from afar. Students can register, pay bills, check on grades, and receive course and pro-grammatic consulting, all online. Comprehensive campus services available online will continue their rapid evolution. Lines on campus are being replaced by queues on the phone or on the Web. Library resources and other learning content resources are being accessed online from students' homes and from wherever students are. Student consulting and faculty office hours are being replaced by asynchronous e-mail, synchronous chat, telephone, and video conferencing.

The new systems will directly impact the teaching and learning processes. The current teaching and learning tools—Web course management tools, student tracking and collaboration tools—will be enhanced, reducing the amount of time and skill needed to teach and manage learning online. These tools already have templates for different types of courses, collaboration tools for supporting different types of faculty and student interaction, and assessment applications for testing, tracking, and managing student learning.

These systems will help faculty, but also change faculty control. These systems will reduce the amount of preparation time for faculty, as the systems will "hold" content in more organized, accessible ways. Courses will be packaged and "owned" more easily, and they will be delivered in different ways.

Prediction Three: New career universities will focus on certifications, modular degrees, and skill sets. This prediction highlights a shift of emphasis for many career professionals from a need for academic degrees to a focus on updating, certification, and skill sets. Web mastering, international communications, and the online MBA are all examples of these content areas. The degrees in such areas will be offered in flexible ways, including a modular degree approach, and be convenient, customized, and continuous.

Prediction Four: The link between courses and content for courses will be broken. This includes a number of related predictions, all having to do with the ability of the Web and the Internet to package and offer content resources in varying sizes and depths in unlimited combinations. The major prediction is that the course as a unit of design and development will be weakened. Rather than course databases, there will be discipline databases of knowledge clusters focused on developing competencies. These knowledge clusters will have a set of core concepts and principles linked to both knowledge and problems for applying these principles.

Publishers are quickly moving now to build large databases of content on the Web, suitable as "adoptable" content in conjunction with regular textbooks. These databases of content will become a larger percentage of a course. Rather than a faculty member "redeveloping" 40 to 60 percent of a course every semester, the faculty would only redevelop perhaps 30 to 40. The "adoptable" portion of a course will increase from an average of 30 to 60 percent, or more.

These databases of content could also become attractive portals for discipline knowledge. The trend for expert synchronous and asynchronous events is just getting under way. Each of the portals might become a Web channel for the learning and knowledge in those fields. These databases will be the same used by practicing professionals. As an example, we already have the Harvard Case Studies that are used by undergraduates, graduates, and learning professionals.

In some cases, publishers may spin off life-long learning businesses using their rich sources of content. Faculty now work for publishers as writers and editors; they may become faculty and discipline tutors. One company, CBT Systems, is doing something similar to this today. They offer self-paced high-end professional updating and certification tutorials and courses that come "packaged" with a mentor.

Prediction Five: Faculty work and roles will make a dramatic shift toward specialization. Higher education teaching and learning today is in many respects a cottage industry. We have one person, the faculty member, doing a whole course, from soup to nuts. From the design and development of the course through the delivery of the course, the one, the only faculty member, does it all. And this same process of creating and building the course is done every semester, because every time we teach a course it is somewhat different than the last time we offered it. This is the model of the master craftsman.

With the proliferation of the new technologies for teaching and learning, teaching is becoming a more "technology-intensive" part of the faculty member's responsibilities. The demands on the role of the faculty will be increasing until specialization must be acknowledged and supported. Not every faculty member will do everything. Some faculty will focus on design and development of programs. Others will focus on the delivery portion or managing a number of tutors who manage the actual interaction with the students.

Some faculty who delight in the combination of development and delivery may well become teaching and learning "personalities" who specialize in the development of resources to be used by many others. These faculty personalities may stay at universities, or they may become stars of the for-profit content publishers or for-profit institutions. Again, some faculty may keep doing what they are now doing for some time to come; but the up-and-coming new cadre of faculty will be expected to have a command of how to teach online.

The changing roles and responsibilities of the faculty also mean that we will have to develop new policies about who owns what in the area of courses. Do faculty own the courses? Do the institutions own the courses? The best policies will acknowledge that courses are probably best jointly owned in today's environment. Much work remains to be done here.

Prediction Six: Students will be savvy consumers of educational services. Over the coming years, students will become a formidable customer group. The expectations of students in the new career universities will be high. Students will expect efficient learning resources and access to quick and easy support for their learning needs. Courses—if there are courses—will need to be well designed, offering effective learning experiences with predictable outcomes in less time.

Many of these expectations will mirror the types of services that career professionals offer in their professions. They will be looking for similar types of services, customization, and responsiveness. New services that focus as guides and channels for career education programs will emerge. Students will pick up and piece together certifications, skill sets, and knowledge sets.

Universities will want to design programs that support the career learner in achieving more than one goal while attending educational programs. Programs that support multiple career goals, including networking with other professionals, will be attractive. These programs may also combine vacation and other types of enjoyable networking experiences.

The majority of learning has always occurred outside the classroom; this will increase. This means that students will be learning more online, and therefore more at home, at hotels, in transit (cars, planes, and so forth) and conference facilities. Learning is moving off campus: to the home, the workplace, the field, or wherever the learner is.

Prediction Seven: The tools for teaching and learning will become as portable and ubiquitous as paper and books are today. This highlights the need for constant monitoring and planning in the use of the technologies for teaching and learning. The decade of the '90s was the decade of the Web. The decade of the "aughts" will be the decade of mobile, portable, and wireless technologies that support teaching and learning anywhere and anytime.

The barriers for effective, one might say comfortable, virtual learning are coming down. Access to computing and to the Web will be virtually universal in another five years. But the basic economic model, that some will have more, will still be true. The good news is that basic computing power will be in the hands of all; the bad news is that it will be greater, more convenient, and more customizable for some than for others.

Further, I believe that the cost of access to content and information will grow to be an even more formidable challenge than issues of bandwidth and hardware. We will see a shift from the low cost of simple free Web access to the higher costs of accessing well-structured, easily researched content. The digital library of today is not free; the digital library of the future will probably not be free either. Just as we have subscriptions to many sources of content, e.g., magazines, cable, newspapers, we will have subscriptions to many varied databases of content.

We have already seen multiple generations of software agents come and go. Maybe by the year 2007 we will have become accustomed to personal robots—in the form of personal digital assistants—who can help us remember our preferences, who we interact with frequently. They could anticipate the articles that we want to read, help to formulate the questions we might have, and provide guides, hints, and insights. The new mapping systems becoming available in cars provide just one specific example of specific personal assistants. These mapping systems are our own personal navigators; in the future more sophisticated applications will certainly be by our sides and at our service.

Moving On

Many of the predictions stated above are extrapolations of current trends. But, we know that we will also be surprised by new developments. The Web surprised us all! And what marvelous, fearful, and satisfying patterns of teaching and learning are emerging from that surprise! What other marvels are out there? Let's keep our eyes open.

Judith V. Boettcher is Executive Director of the Corporation for Research and Educational Networking (CREN). She is also a Syllabus Scholar and contributes regularly to Syllabus *magazine.*

E-Learning: Economic Drivers

Brandon Hall

This brief description of the economic drivers of e-learning and distance learning is from a special report that appeared in Forbes *magazine. Other parts of this report appear elsewhere in this book.*

The Knowledge-Based Economy

Everywhere you look in financial reports, books on best business strategies and periodicals, you'll read comments about the New Economy. Before our very eyes, and within our lifetime, we have moved from the Industrial Age, to the Information Age, to the Knowledge Age. Information is everywhere, overwhelming in its mass and difficult to find when we need to use it. Yet, what we do with that information is valuable to the organizations we work for. Knowledge about our customers drives the products that we develop. Knowledge and experience often differentiate us from our competition, but only if our organizations can move quickly enough to take the advantage. "Business at Internet speed" is a phrase often used to describe today's work pace.

The cost of computing is dropping 25% per year, and the under-$1,000 PC market now represents one-half of all PCs sold. Ray Kurzweil, noted computer scientist, predicts that by 2019, a $1,000 computer (in 1999 dollars) will be able to perform 20 million billion calculations per second and will be equivalent in sophistication to the human brain. (After that it just keeps getting smarter.)

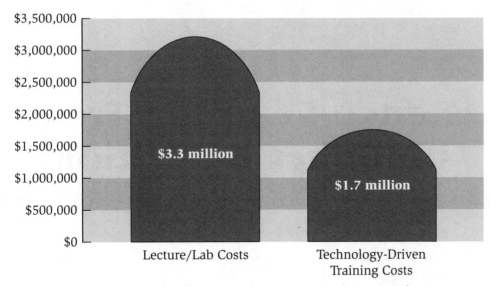

Comparison of total costs over 3 years at a sample company for
development and delivery of a course in lecture/lab format ($3,291,327)
vs. technology-driven format ($1,748,327)

Figure 1. Total training costs: lecture/lab training vs. technology-delivered training
Source: brandon-hall.com, Return on Investment and Multimedia Training, 1995

Shortage of Skilled Workers

Yet, in the midst of all this technology, information and potential access, the U.S. is facing a shortage of skilled workers. This is also a global problem. PricewaterhouseCoopers states that 70% of the world's 1,000 top-tier companies cite lack of trained employees as their number-one barrier to sustaining growth.

Department of Labor statistics show that occupations requiring a college degree are growing twice as quickly as others. By 2006 almost half of all U.S. workers will be employed in industries that produce or intensively use information technology products and services. In the U.S. alone, one out of every 10 computer-related positions, or approximately 350,000 jobs, are unfilled. Students graduating with computer science degrees are decreasing (Merrill Lynch, *The Book of Knowledge*, 1999).

See biography of Brandon Hall, information about brandon-hall.com, and contact information on page 439.

Distance Learning Trends in Higher Education

Eduardo Rivera and George Kostopoulos

This article examines the main trends of distance learning in higher education, and the challenges posed to traditional educational institutions. It also takes a look at the developing interdependence between distance learning and globalization.

Distance learning, a concept and phenomenon that slowly but steadily is revolutionizing education, continues to expand, penetrating practically every learning process. While it is still at its infancy, it represents a small, but not negligible, sector of higher education.

The future of distance learning is identified with that of the new media and of the information technologies, and its exponential growth is making it an issue that every educational institution has to deal with.

Despite its strategic importance, the overwhelming majority of academic institutions have no plans in place for the capturing this unprecedented opportunity to offer education to student constituencies that cannot access education in its traditional delivery mode.

Present State

In the year 2000, the administrations of practically all academic institutions are, to various extents, recognizing the need to take a position vis-à-vis distance learning. However, very few have actually incorporated cyberspace in the strategic planning. As a result, there is currently a disparity in higher education in this regard, with only about 200 institutions offering distance learning courses, while the remaining 2,000 are still contemplating the issue.[1] The reluctance in the introduction of cyber courses is attributed to the lack of standardization, the lack of incentives for faculty, and the failure of academic administrations to see the strategic benefits that await the successful cyber programs.

Some Background

Distance education is a general concept with numerous technological modes of implementation, such as correspondence, videotapes, television, and the Internet, with the large market being captured by the Internet. As a consequence of resulting cost reductions, distance education is extensively being used in the entrepreneurial world for all levels of training. In the general population, distance education is oriented more toward the adults and in higher education toward the graduate programs.

Many reasons can be cited for that, ranging from the fact that many adults are home- or work-bound, unable to attend traditional educational programs available next door, to the mere geographical distance that may separate them from the schools. It has to be recognized, however, that distance education is not for everyone, but only for those who have a certain level of Internet technology literacy and a strong desire for self-learning.

Some Trends

Cyber Institutions. Many new institutions specializing in distance education have emerged, and many more will continue to emerge. However, in the long run, only a few are going to survive, because of the increased competition.[2]

Academic Recognition. While only a few years ago, cyber courses enjoyed marginal recognition and cyber degrees even less, today, and even more in the future, they will be considered as being mainstream education.[3]

Hybrid Offerings. Traditional institutions of higher education are already feeling the pressure to provide cyber courses, as they are pressured to provide evening courses.[4]

Use of Multimedia. As for the delivery of the educational content, it will steadily improve in quantity and in quality, using streamed multimedia (text, images, sound, video, animation) and—most important—interactivity.[5]

Multilingual Offerings. Considering the significant investment that is required in a cyber course development, small incremental efforts will make the course multilingual.[6]

Teamworking. Another trend recognized in the current evolution of distance education is the incorporation of *cooperative learning*, through the use of groupware, that is, server and client software that facilitate text, voice, and video interaction.[7]

Conferencing. The use of video and voice simultaneously, under compression, offers an alternative to direct communication which is very appreciated for students who still want a personal touch. In business environments, distance conferencing is one of the hottest ways to save money and enlarges participation of workers in different courses and conferences.

Increased Bandwidth. Advanced technologies applied in modem design are steadily increasing the bit rates. Use of 1Mb/s ADSL (Asymmetric Digital Subscriber Line) modems, and especially wireless Internet access will enable crystal-clear audio and full-screen video.[8]

Course Authoring Tools. In this area we see a wide range of course administration templates available, but very little in course authoring tools. Unfortunately few places encourage students to use authoring as a learning tool.[9]

Custom Course Designs. With the increase in cyber instructors who are also Web designers, courses will remain unique in structure, reflecting the philosophy of their creator.[10]

Virtual Reality. The design of educational material using simulation and virtual reality, although very sophisticated and therefore still expensive, will change as a result of the emergence of more powerful and easier to use programming languages for the design of such material.[11]

Accreditation. Although there is an organization that is supposed to pass judgment on the credibility of distance learning programs, institutions of higher education still abide by the traditional regional and national accreditation bodies. We are currently observing an increase in regulations for distance education. This increase, while aiming at the prevention of low-quality courses that effectively are underselling academic credits, fears are that greater regulation may stifle innovation.[12]

Cost. As for the distance education cost, there is no obvious trend, with course charges widely varying from institution to institution.[13]

Class Size. It seems that the economies of scale concept does not apply here, because distance education demands individualized attention, which naturally limits class size. Many schools limit the size to about 18 students.[14]

High Technology. Advances in the communications and media technologies have a direct impact on distance learning. Most impact is expected from *wireless Internet access*, *streaming media technologies*, and *teleconferencing*.[15]

Competency Tests. The future of distance education belongs to the self-learners, because academic recognition will be eventually granted based on competency measures, like examinations or presentations.[16]

Certification. Recognizing that the academic world is lagging behind the real world, the various industries are offering specialized educational programs that lead to certificates. These programs, presently offered in in-class environments, will be made available over the Internet, for worldwide coverage and ease in updating.[17]

Cyber Libraries. Virtual libraries—exclusively electronically accessed libraries—will be the way of learning. Guidelines already are in place for such libraries. With time, most publications will have an electronic full version.[18]

Free Education. For those who are interested in the learning aspect of education, rather than in the social, the Internet already offers thousands of full courses and short specialized tutorials. Authors, as a global community service, are continuously posting their wisdom and knowledge, making it freely accessible. This trend will undoubtedly continue, eventually making the Internet humanity's knowledge depository.[19]

Enrollment. A recognized fact is that distance education student enrollment suffers from a high dropout rate. This is attributed to a variety of reasons, ranging from Internet illiteracy and lack of responsiveness to the absence of similar precedent experiences and poorly presented courses. As distance education matures, enrollment is expected to keep on increasing.[20]

Instructor Literacy. Currently, the academic world has two kinds of faculty: those who live inside the Web and those who look at it from the outside. This partitioning is mostly generation-related, but with time, practically all faculty will be integrated with the Web.[21]

Impact of Globalization

As with many of the new economic phenomena, globalization offers a big challenge for most countries and regions. It is aiming at the internationalization of economic affairs and the opening of markets to a global economy. Education, however, is something more than just another business.

Besides the fundamental education in which children learn values and culture, higher education is not only to prepare for professional life, but also the way in which the society regulates and creates its leaders and new executives. It is not evident that leaving it to the simple forces of the market will improve our education. We must ask about its pertinence and if institutions are preparing students in the way in which a local region needs. Institutions of higher education are also organizations that traditionally offer a service to society and preserve the local culture and humanities.

Challenges and Opportunities

As life-long learning becomes a reality, it seems that the only way to face this increasing demand for education and training is distance education. For many, the main challenge seems to be maintaining the quality of education—as if traditional education would always be of quality. Here, it seems to be necessary to innovate and to measure distance education with different parameters than those of traditional education, since quality is not a number of contact hours or just the GPA or the grade on a specific exam. Distance education offers an opportunity for education in geographically and educationally remote places, while adjusting the curricula to complement the existing offerings. This may seem to be a reasonable approach to the globalization of distance education.

Conclusion

Distance education has opened a new area of multidisciplinary research and innovation, as new technologies enter in the field. Distance education has enormous perspectives for application, due to the great demand for training, the need for continuous education, and the diversification of higher education. This is not the end of traditional education, since each form has its own merits and markets, especially at the pre-college level, but the beginning of an educational cooperation that will be created among institutions and countries in the formation of multinational educational consortia cooperating in distance education.

References

1. New Promise Distance Education, www.newpromise.com.
2. Jones International University, www.jonesinternational.edu.
3. Distance Education and Training Council, www.detc.org.
4. Mott Community College, www.mcc.edu.
5. Kostopoulos, George, "Global Delivery of Education via the Internet," *Journal of Internet Research*, Volume 8, Number 3, 1998, www.tamiu.edu/ ~ kostopoulos.
6. Gritsenko, V.I., and Anisimov, A.V., *Multilingual Environment in Cyberspace*, International Scientific and Training Center of Information Technologies and Systems, Kiev, Ukraine, www.unesco.org/webworld/infoethics_2/eng/papers /paper_9.htm.
7. PictureTel Internet Conferencing, www.picturetel.com.
8. InterWireless Services, www.interwireless.com.
9. WebCT Course Authoring Tool, www.webct.com.
10. WebBoard Course Design, www.webboard.com.
11. Virtual Reality in Education, www.ddce.cqu.edu.au/ddce/confsem/vr/present.html.
12. American Association of Colleges and Schools of Business, www.aacsb.edu.
13. New Promise Distance Education, www.newpromise.com.
14. United States Distance Learning Association, Archives, www.usdla.org/03_fact_ sheet.htm.
15. Real Networks Streaming Media, www.real.com.
16. Competency Tests, www.doe.k12.ga.us/sla/ret/crct.html.
17. Microsoft Certification Programs, www.microsoft.com/train_cert.
18. Electronic Library Services, www.elibrary.com.

19. Free Higher Education Campaign, www.interlog.com/~2mowchuk/fedcamp /fed01.html.

21. Berry, John, "Web Learning Starts to Pay Off," *InternetWeek*, November 15, 1999.

22. Smith, S.J., Tyler, M., and Benscoter, A. "Internet Supported Teaching: Advice from the Trenches," *Education at a Distance*, January 2000, Vol. 13, No. 1, www.usdla. org/ED_magazine/illuminactive/JAN_1999/Internet.htm.

Bibliography

1. Kostopoulos, George, "Instructor-Developed Online-Course Design," Eighth Annual International Conference on Distance Education, December 1-5, 1999, Guadalajara, Mexico. Co-authored with Ourida-Zoe Kostopoulos.

2. Kostopoulos, George, "Study of Issues Associated with Cyber Education," Eighth Annual World Business Congress, June 30-July 3, 1999, Monterrey, California, USA. Co-authored with Dr. Kamal Dean Parhizgar.

3. Kostopoulos, George, "Education for the Third Millennium," a Workshop conducted at the Annual International Conference of the Business and Economics International Society, July 17-21, 1998, Rome, Italy. Co-presented with Ourida-Zoe Kostopoulos.

4. Kostopoulos, George, "Global Delivery of Education via the Internet," *Journal of Internet Research*, Vol. 8, No. 3, 1998.

5. Kostopoulos, George, "Acceso Mundial a la Educación a través de la Red Internet." An invited address delivered in Spanish. Fourth International Congress on Educational Research, December 5-7, 1997, Victoria, Tamaulipas, Mexico.

Dr. Eduardo Rivera is associate professor and chairman of MIS of the MBA at the Graduate School of Management, St. Edward's University, Austin, Texas. He has extensive consulting experience in educational computing, curriculum development, databases, telecommunications and technology assessment in industrial or academic environments. He is the author of several books, among them Introduction to PC Computers *and* Computers in Education. *His Web site may be found at www.stedwards.edu/badm/mba/rivera. You may contact him at eduardor@admin.stedwards.edu*

Dr. George Kostopoulos is a member of the faculty at the College of Business Administration, Texas A&M University, Laredo. His areas of teaching and research are global delivery of education and cyber technologies. His Web site may be found at www.tamiu.edu/~ kostopoulos.

Episodic Learning: Experiences with Distributed Education

Molly D. Campbell

Episodic learning is a term that comes from being able to deliver training on demand and in "episodes." This article documents this trend and its implications in different venues.

At the beginning of the new millennium, a student sits in a classroom, taking a test that asks for the three factors leading up to the Civil War. The student, who stayed up late the night before doing his aviation "flight simulation" on the Internet, is not at all prepared for the test.

That same day, a manufacturer wonders how she will possibly be able to fulfill the latest contract for widgets. There just isn't enough people to hire, and the ones that are hired seem to lack the skills necessary to get the job done.

That night, a parent sighs after attending his daughter's high school "parents' night." It doesn't seem to him that life in the classroom is any different today than it was when he was in school. No wonder his daughter lacks real interest in academics.

These individuals have something in common: they are disenchanted with an educational system that is not reacting fast enough to the needs of today's students, the demands of the marketplace, and the evolution of technology as it impacts almost everything we do.

The problem stems from the way we look at education. Traditionally, the function of education has been to provide students with a "liberal arts" background in math, history, literature, language, and science in order to produce a "well-rounded" adult. This approach to education provided the foundation for commerce, government, and society as a whole: only well-rounded people could run businesses, make laws and set standards, educate others, and manage the republic.

The attitude toward education is changing. The old liberal arts approach is giving way to a new demand for knowledge and skills that have utility in the present time. Technology has changed our lives. It has changed the way we live, the way we think, and especially the way we work.

Just 20 years ago, a person working as a retail clerk had to be well rounded. He had to meet and greet customers. His job required counting inventory and stocking shelves. He had to know how to ring a cash register, make change, and keep track of regular and sale prices. If customers wanted merchandise to be sent, he had to know the procedures for shipping charges, packaging and sending items. He had to keep track of which styles were selling well and which ones were not, so that he could let the buyer know what to reorder.

In today's world, technology has changed the way retailers do business. One person no longer does a multitude of tasks: instead that clerk's job is "chunked" into many jobs, each one requiring specific technical skills. The customer calls a number or enters a Web site to place a catalog order. A worker at a PC receives the order. When inventory gets low, the computer signals a worker in the order center—miles away — to reorder the item. All orders are transmitted via computer to a warehouse at a third location, where workers pull the merchandise and pack items for shipping. If a customer has a complaint, a customer service representative handles the complaint at yet another computer terminal. What was done by one individual in the past is now chunked into a multitude of jobs, done by workers linked by technology.

Since jobs today are nothing like jobs 20 years ago, there is a requirement for a new type of learning. Today's students demand education that has utility in the present time. Jobs require technical skills. Since technology changes rapidly, what students want to learn changes rapidly as well. Instead of the academic degree that builds a curriculum over a period of semesters to a final body of knowledge, students want to learn concepts and skills that apply to what they need to know in order to do a job, get a promotion, or earn a credential. Employers demand constant upgrading of specific skills and are willing to provide training in those skills only.

The Relationship

At Miami-Jacobs, we believe that educators in this new world will have to respond to change and learn to see into the future. In the world of technology, training will be viewed as a means to an end rather than the end itself. Students will become consumers who buy "learning episodes" on an "as needed" basis.

For instance:

- A high school student interested in art may need to learn how to create an online portfolio to submit to a museum in France;
- A college graduate will need to learn how to do a PowerPoint presentation highlighting his skills to show to an employer;
- A manager feels that her employees should gain technical writing skills; and
- A company installs new software and wants to train employees to use it quickly.

The learning episode is the mandate; distributed education is the mode. At Miami-Jacobs, we believe that in a world of technology, students are becoming increasingly unwilling to travel to experience a learning episode when they can log on to a computer and link with experts from all over the globe. Traditional education is no longer cost-effective for students who desire a single learning episode. Many people have multiple jobs, which makes attending a specific class at a specific time impossible. Thus, distributed education makes sense as the transmission medium for episodic learning.

In order for a person to become a successful episodic learner online, certain skills are prerequisites:

- The ability to use self-assessment to determine learning objectives;
- The ability to work autonomously;
- The ability to manage time successfully;
- The ability to think logically and critically;
- The ability to organize information and ideas;
- The ability to write clearly and effectively;
- The ability to assimilate information independently of a teacher; and
- The ability to feel comfortable in the "cyber classroom."

With this end in mind, Miami-Jacobs has designed all of its distributed education courses to enable its graduates to become competent episodic learners. Coursework is designed so that students can improve the above skills while mastering content such as technical writing, customer service, project management, and portfolio development. All our students experience a distributed education course beginning with their first quarter at the college, and most students have at least one additional distance experience before they graduate.

Miami-Jacobs students who have successfully completed a distributed education experience:

- Love the convenience;
- Enjoy having control of their learning process; and
- Gain new skills in writing and thinking that they did not previously possess.

How Does Distributed Education Happen?

In many educational environments, much time and money is spent training instructors in the "nuts and bolts" of distributed education: teachers have to learn HTML, how to create Web sites, how to build threaded discussion areas, and how to design and manage the online classroom. This is costly to many institutions as well as intimidating to educators who are not technical by nature. It is time-consuming as well; bringing a staff of instructors up to speed in distributed education technology can take years. Even with distributed education software, training instructors can become an overwhelming task.

At Miami-Jacobs, it was decided early on that instructors should become proficient in designing the cyber experience as *content* experts rather than *context* experts. We looked for a company that could provide us with the technical expertise and support to build our cyber classrooms, administer them, and leave the education to the experts. We found the perfect partner in Embanet Corp.

At Miami-Jacobs, all online courses are designed by instructors and built by Embanet Corp. Instructors interact with Embanet staffers to create an environment in each cyber class for discussion, activities, team projects, and "lectures." Each student has a personal e-mail box for confidential communication with instructors. Online portfolios are created for each student to place examples of work that can be used as indicators of achievement and skill in a job interview. Students receive technical support 24 hours a day from the Embanet support team. By letting "distance architects" design our distance environment for us, Miami-Jacobs has been able to focus on what is most important: training students to be successful episodic learners.

Will episodic learning ever replace the traditional educational model? We don't think so. However, as students become more and more empowered to choose the educational experience they desire, the demand for cyber education will increase. We at Miami-Jacobs are training our students for the future now.

Molly D. Campbell is vice president for distance education and development at Miami-Jacobs College (Dayton, Ohio). She may be reached via e-mail at molly.campbell@ miamijacobs.edu.

Marketing Distance Learning

Edward L. Davis III

The advent of technology to facilitate distance education makes the "learning market" much more lucrative to companies that are in the position to develop content and use this technology to deliver it. This article looks at this new market for companies like IBM, Lucent, and many more and explores how they will promote and sell these services. It includes some hypothetical examples and provides some useful insights into this distance learning trend.

Many large companies and institutions are now preparing to enter the distance learning market. Some of them are publishers (e.g., Macmillan, Simon & Schuster, Pearson, Peterson's, McGraw-Hill, UOL), some are telecommunications companies (e.g., Lucent, GTE, Pac Bell, Bell South), some are computer companies (e.g., IBM, Sun Microsystems), some are learning conglomerates (CUC, NEC, Jostens Learning, Sylvan Learning Systems and Knowledge Universe), some are media conglomerates and cable companies, and many more are software companies, corporate training companies, colleges and universities.

As increasingly sophisticated software better enables the creation of a campus atmosphere with social interaction, collaborative learning, asynchronous conferencing, etc., the barrier to entry for anyone who offers learning materials becomes minimal. The entire market for learning is our largest, at close to $800 billion. Now that an inexpensive piece of software can eliminate the need to build or rent classrooms, many more enterprises will be formed to offer computer-mediated instruction.

Although the barrier to entry is low, the barrier to commercial success is high. A number of *Fortune* 500 companies, not to mention many smaller ones, have already failed miserably at distance learning ventures. The few companies that are achieving a measure of success have generally done so through a painful process of trial and error.

Preparing to enter the distance learning market begins with a game plan and the process of staffing up to achieve it. Although the strategy and business model are crucial, the ability to execute a plan will be the key. It will involve choosing people who know how to wisely use venture capital; but more important, it will necessitate managers who understand and maximize the use of human capital. Here's why.

First, let's choose a segment of the market to illustrate some fundamental issues and make my assertion real. I will use the continuing professional education market, as it is so enormous and up for grabs.

A company entering this marketplace may serve learners who are reached through corporations, labor unions, professional associations, direct marketing campaigns, targeted PR, or media advertising. It is likely, depending on the specific targeted market segment, that some combination of the above will be most effective. How does one arrive at the appropriate marketing recipe? First, by knowing what the consumer needs, and next, by knowing the entities that serve the consumer's professional needs and what they want.

Consumers of learning, especially for professional advancement, are notorious for seeking the advice and the endorsement of organizations and professional communities to which they belong. Furthermore, many of these organizations have already commandeered the role of promoting and/or sanctioning the professional progress of their constituents.

If you wanted to offer a series of professional certification courses to telecommunications workers, it would be useful, probably crucial, to know that they are served by a national union (the CWA) with over 600,000 members who belong to 1200 locals and are employees of 16 major corporations and a host of smaller ones. If 10% of this group are candidates for your courses, and you can get them to enroll, you have the basis for a lucrative and renewable business.

So, you develop a series of computer mediated "tele-courses" and you know your curriculum compares favorably to what's out there. You are the ABC Tele-training company. Students love your courses, finish them faster, and demonstrate a superior grasp of new technologies after completing them. You can prove that. Now what?

Let's start by going back to the consumer. It would be nice to develop courseware in conjunction with consumer. But wait, aren't the unions, professional journals, and employers consumers as well? They directly benefit from a better trained, professionally and economically advancing workforce. In developing courseware for this market wouldn't it be advantageous to seek the active participation of the national union, its locals, and the companies that employ its member?

Hypothetical Case in Point

CWA member goes to his manager at Nynex and says, "I want to sign up for a course series on digital switching." The manager asks, "How much does it cost?" "$700.00 for the whole series," says the employee. Manager: "I'd like you to wait two months until the Nynex-developed course comes out." Employee: "But this is a really good course offered by ABC Tele-training, and it's been approved by my union." Manager: "Nobody told me about it. If you want me to pay for it, wait two months. The Nynex course is going to be cheaper and it was developed with our own engineers. They even asked me a question or two. Besides, I'm not real big on those courses by computer."

Change the above scenario to a legal firm, a nurse's station in a hospital, a public school, or an accounting firm. Situations identical to the one described occur every day in multiple industries. How can you prevent them? To some the solution appears impossibly complex. The challenge has caused many a good marketer to withdraw from the training market, licking their wounds.

What did the marketer of this series of telecommunications courses need to know to avoid this imbroglio, and how can we extrapolate to apply these principles to any distance learning venture?

To understand the answer, one must first appreciate the simple fact that marketing in the world I've described is equivalent to sending a freshly minted Harvard MBA to Japan to start a business. Classical marketing methods can be useless without a full and sustained immersion in the business culture. Ask the long list of American companies that have unsuccessfully marketed products in Japan.

So first, the would-be marketer of tele-learning would need to know the cultures (and interaction of cultures) of all the constituents served by his or her product. Let's alter our troublesome Nynex scenario slightly. Suppose you (ABC Tele-training) had been the one to negotiate a contract directly with Nynex to develop a training program, in collaboration with Nynex engineers, technicians, and managers on new digital switching technologies. Nynex is paying you for the product, so they're obviously going to push it to their employees.

As I've already pointed out, these employees also belong to unions. Do you ignore the unions or just placate them? Obviously, neither. Unions may have less authority, but more influence over employees. Furthermore, the participation of a local union in creating a product for the advancement of its employees is an entrée into the national union as well as the back door of other companies that employ their members. A certificate of advancement issued by a union may be more valuable to the mobile employee than one issued by his/her employer.

The first order of business as a marketer of distance learning is to know the cultures of your target clients. They probably exist in several cultures whose business decisions are interlocking but not necessarily compatible. The skill of the marketer is to make them compatible, to make the agenda of one play into the agenda of another. The marketer of distance learning is skilled at making common cause between multiple and often countervailing cultures.

Inside a corporation or professional organization, how do you avoid getting caught between the line manager who has a need to get mobile technicians or salespeople trained quickly and the training manager who is convinced that the only way to do that is through line-of-site training? How do you talk to the principals of an association of engineering professionals who have already been convinced (but haven't signed on the bottom line yet) that live satellite delivery of instruction is the preferred form of distance learning when you are offering asynchronous delivery through PCs and modems?

Within every business culture is also a learning culture. It is comprised of tools and methods that training and IT managers prefer, and a set of logistics that do (or should) influence learning decisions. The logistics include the question "who gets paid for what?" One HRD department's bias is to develop training internally while another's is to purchase off-the-shelf products or outsource custom designed training.

Training managers are generally biased towards methods that preserve or expand their fragile power base within an organization. Methods of distributed learning are often perceived as threatening and vigorously opposed. Does this mean you go around the HRD department to seek a training contract—straight to a line manager who has the need?

A professional association may be motivated by the opportunity to sell professional improvement packages to their constituents with a commission paid to them. Within the same organization may be an influential who believes this is an unethical practice of influence peddling and that they (the association) should simply recommend a list of competing products and make money advertising them in their newsletter. How do you make the sale?

These and many others make up a set of questions and concerns that influence the decision-making process in marketing a professional training product. When you market soap, video games, books, or vitamin pills, you go directly to the consumer and the media that influence the consumer. In the learning industry, there are almost always intermediaries, organizations, and influencers that affect consumer decisions.

You can give away free soap, free books, and free vitamins all day long. It's not so easy to give away professional advancement. It requires the participation and approval of consumers, gatekeepers, and well-wishers to ensure widespread use. The marketing of learning must include consideration for the arbiters of knowledge. If knowledge is what you're selling, and it is, who is the buyer?

In high-technology marketing, you have the fundamental problem of "crossing the chasm" from early adoption by the technology elite to reaching a mass market. In marketing professional advancement, you have the reverse. Creating a product wanted and needed by your market is the easy part. Getting the knowledge elite to sanction and promote it is the challenge. It's the same chasm, but you start out on the other side.

Canon #1. Know the multiple (and sometimes countervailing) cultures and business organizations that influence your buyer's decision.

Selling knowledge to the professional world is best done in contracts. The contract may be with a corporation to train 4,000 employees on a new software application. It may be with a state bar association to provide 4 CEUs to legal clerks, or with the Interactive Services Association to provide an online seminar on developing EDI standards to its 18,000 members. The best consumers of professional development are not individuals, but organizations that can provide you recurring groups of individuals—organizations that frequently hire and promote new candidates for a course and/or organizations whose members need frequent "add-ons" to upgrade their skills.

Inevitably, when selling a training contract, you will come up against a training professional with an argument based on preferred methods, products, technologies, or delivery systems of training. If you are selling just-in-time, asynchronous, computer-mediated training based on a "cognitive" model of development, how do you respond to the following:

"We're about to sign a contract with Prosoft. They deliver live lectures so that you can interact with instructors in real time," or "How did you arrive at the behavioral objectives for this course?," or "We like your curriculum a lot, but we're used to dealing with the Forum Corporation, and are about to contract with them to produce a similar set of courses," or "How would you compare your course on HTML authoring to the one offered by XYZ company? Theirs is cheaper and it's used at Microsoft and yada, yada...." Of course, there are times when answering such questions amounts to beating a dead horse. But how do you learn *when* to answer as well as *how* to answer?

Canon #2. Know the tools and methods of the learning trade and how they're used by your competitors.

Many contract sales are won and lost on the ability to make pedagogical arguments. This requires some understanding of learning theory, instructional design, and the strengths and weakness of various delivery systems. This, of course, includes economic considerations. Above all, you must be able to effectively respond to real and perceived deficits to your instructional design and delivery system.

The prospect who believes that line-of-sight instruction (classroom, satellite, etc.) is vital to an effective training program will have certain prejudices and agendas. Without understanding the basis for such prejudices and agendas, it is difficult to either counter an argument or take it in another direction. If you make an economic argument (cost savings) over the top of an unanswered quality consideration, it is likely to go unheard and vice versa.

Purveyors of online learning are beginning to counter traditional objections with better product design, especially in the re-creation of missing elements from the traditional classroom (e.g., Q&A with instructors, live chat, asynchronous conferencing, online libraries, social interaction, collaborative learning processes, etc.). In the absence of these improvements one must be astute at making the strengths of a delivery system (or method) counter its deficits.

For example: Prospect says, "We know that non-verbal cues are a key to learning. What you pick up in the classroom is just not available in an emailed response to a lesson or instructor's questions." Salesperson says, "I absolutely agree with you, and that is, for some, a deficit of online instruction. However, have you considered how many of your employees are not only not picking up cues, but not even paying attention to what's being said in the classroom? What about all the people you bring into your training center the night before from the field? They're stressed from traveling. They may have partied a little the night before. And what about all your trainees who are taking this program after hours rather than leave their workplac? They're tired from a day's work and their attention span is diminished. If you added up all of those employees and put them in our program, they could work the various modules in when they had the time and the energy, and if they discovered they had 'spaced out' during the audio lecture, they can simply run it back 30 seconds and listen to it again."

One of the biggest mistakes that purveyors of online learning make in marketing or selling their products is the assumption that the features and advantages of their delivery system are obvious and obviously better. Many possible sales are lost because the biases of the prospect are not fleshed out and addressed in a manner that acknowledges yet effectively counters them. This kind of hubris stems from a lack of immersion in the thinking of others. Knowing your own product comes easy. Becoming intimately familiar with the assumptions and life experience that keeps others from seriously considering it comes only from the school of hard knocks.

The final arena that a marketing organization needs to know in depth is the medium in which online training exists. How do you tap usenet groups, online professional communities, subscriber lists, and potential allies in the online world to create prospects for your business? How do you build communities of existing and potential clients online? How do you set up effective online conferences and other events that use the word-of-mouth power of the online world to inform people about what you're up to?

The act of designing a compelling website, registering it with search engines, creating the root words, key words, and strings, setting up an auto-responder, etc., is only the preparation for using the vast power of the web to market learning.

Just for starters, anyone selling learning over the web should be an online publisher. Whether you publish curriculum or study aids or not, the circulation of free reports, executed properly, can generate tremendous interest and word-of-mouth.

As John Sculley (formerly of Apple) put it, the Web is a "you ask, you get medium." How do you build a "you ask, you get" website, and then most importantly, how do you get the right askers to come to it? How do you design a web-published newsletter that becomes a PR and marketing vehicle for your learning products?

If you have done the above effectively, you've covered a few of the fundamentals. The real work begins in seeking out web-based marketing partners. Most companies still think of the Web as a channel for advertising and distribution. The fact is, it offers many highly targeted venues for PR, advertising, and distribution.

One of the crucial marketing activities of professional development is effective follow-up. Every happy student and every happy client organization is a potential evangelist. If a client engages in measuring the results of your training, publish those results and post them on your website and theirs. If they don't measure, be sure to do it yourself so that you can make quantitative arguments to back up qualitative assertions.

What learning or knowledge organizations offer complementary products and services, and how can you partner with them to go after customers? How can their customers become yours and vice versa? For instance, if you provide training for accountants, would it be effective to link existing news services (directed to accountants) from your website?

How do you build or tap into web-based communities whose members would benefit from your services? The skills to address these questions effectively are vital to the purveyor of online learning. The message is the medium.

Canon #3. Know how to use the medium in which you operate (the Internet) as an effective means to disseminate and promote your services.

The business culture, the tools of the trade, and the Internet.... These are the professional currencies of an online learning venture. Many who set out to launch such a venture make the mistake of assuming the skill and assumptions they bring from another industry will translate. AT&T and IBM thought they could create a distance learning business as a vehicle to cross sell their products. Carnegie Mellon University thought it could create a standard for web-based curriculum development and instructional management. Publishers and software developers have made the mistake of assuming that the products they distribute in the physical world are promoted and sold by the same principles in the online world.

Due to the complicated dynamics of bringing a new, and sometimes threatening form of learning into an already complex marketing environment, staffing an online learning venture requires identifying the unique skill set necessary to execute a business plan with competence. The three canons set forth here are meant to establish the most basic requirements for the marketing and business development functions.

Edward L. "Ned" Davis III is president of learnNet (www.learnnet.com), an e-learning consulting firm. He is currently working on a new book, The Future of Learning. *You can e-mail him at ndavis@learnnet.com.*

Part Two

Technology Overview: E-Learning Leads the Way

P art Two provides a more detailed look at the specifics of technology and how it is influencing training. We've divided this part into three distinct sections that capture how organizations are implementing e-learning. This is the longest part of the book and provides an excellent perspective on the nature of distance and e-learning today. The three sections are:

- **E-Learning/Web/Computer-Based Training**, in which we include five articles dealing with the basics of technology-based training.

- **Blending Traditional Classroom Training and E-Learning Technologies**, that includes four articles that look at what many believe will be the major pattern for distance and e-learning programs. Blending is not a fad, but the way and wave of the future, where all organizations can take advantage of selecting different types of technologies and delivery options to maximize the learning event.

- **Video/Teleconferencing and Synchronous Technologies**, in which we look specifically at the distance learning technologies and how to effectively use them to deliver training.

The first of these sections includes five articles that explain the ins and outs of computer/web-based training in its most common forms. We start with Pam Pervenanze's "Developing a Strategy for Creating E-Learning Courses." This article reminds us of the importance of having a clear strategy for e-learning initiatives and what that involves. We also include the advocacy article, asking you to "Get on the E-Train" by Dylan Tweney, but it also reminds you to ask the right questions and look at whether it will work for you or not.

We've also selected pieces to help you figure out whether you're ready for e-learning, how e-learning is being used in Europe, and we conclude with Pat Galagan's (editor of *Training & Development*) piece she calls "The E-Learning Revolution." In it she talks about the future of training as well as the future of trainers. It's a good food for thought article to conclude this section.

The next section deals with blended learning, the combination of classroom and computer-based training. We've included four articles that look at the how and why of mixing the new with the old. We start with "Long Live C-Learning" by James N. Farrell, in which he describes the relative strengths of classroom and e-learning instruction and how to get the best of each. Then we have selected an article that documents how a healthcare facility has created a balance of classroom and e-learning to meet its training needs. This is followed by "Imagine That: Hybridizing Training" by Wendy Webb that looks at how US West has created its blended learning approach. It includes advice for anyone looking to do what they did. We conclude this part with a detailed case study of how a blended learning program was developed at the University of Wisconsin-Milwaukee.

The final section of this part of the book looks at synchronous e-learning programs. We've included three articles that explain the synchronous approach by Jennifer Hofmann, that include how to choose a synchronous approach, how to make it succeed, and a glossary of synchronous tool features. We conclude with Tom Barron's "Online Learning Goes Synchronous." In it the author, editor of *Learning Circuits*, explains how synchronous Web-based training works.

E-Learning/Web/ Computer-Based Training

Developing a Strategy for Creating E-Learning Courses

Pam Pervenanze

You don't undertake your e-learning initiative blindly. It must fit into the organization's strategy. This article addresses this issue and gives you several items to consider as you develop an effective e-learning strategy.

E-learning continues to grow at a tremendous rate. Brandon Hall, editor of *e-learning* magazine, predicts that by the year 2003, half of all training may be online. E-learning companies are springing up everywhere. It seems as though you can't pick up a business or training magazine without seeing articles about the benefits or the problems that are a result of e-learning. The field is growing at an amazing rate and its standards have yet to be developed or even agreed upon. So how in the world does a training department go about implementing an e-learning program in an organization? One way is to develop a strategy for creating e-learning courses that can serve as a guide or road map as you are working your way through the chaos.

To create your e-learning strategy, you need to:

- Link e-learning goals with business goals
- Ensure support from top management
- Work with your IT department to develop an understanding of your baseline technologies

- Work with your IT department to establish standards for working together
- Create a plan to help your training department handle the change
- Determine e-learning specifications
- Determine how you will measure the results
- Prepare a rollout plan

Link E-Learning Goals with Business Goals

Training efforts are frequently questioned—do they add value to the organization or are they simply a cost? These questions have resulted in a shift from training for training's sake to training for performance. Training professionals who want to be seen as providing value to an organization must create programs that are tied to business problems and opportunities, and these links must be understood and supported by management.

By linking the e-learning strategy to business strategy, you strengthen the training department's position in the organization and the perception of the value of the training that is provided. It is essential to link e-learning goals to business goals to ensure the ultimate success of the entire e-learning program.

In order to link the e-learning goals with business goals, you must first look at your business goals. It is probable that your organization is dealing with one or more of these pressures:

- Global employees
- Global competition
- Speed to market with new products
- An effort to implement cost savings
- The exponential rate of change in technology
- Demand for exemplary customer service
- Demand for high-quality goods and services

Many of the advantages of e-learning offer support in alleviating these pressures. For example, there can be significant cost savings when implementing an e-learning program, especially when travel of trainees is involved. IT departments have already made the leap to e-learning, with many departments relying on courses that are available over the Internet to keep their employees up-to-speed with the rapid pace of changing technology.

E-learning courses are available at any time, for employees working different shifts, or on other sides of the globe.

It is important to keep in mind that e-learning is not an absolute solution. E-learning should be integrated into ongoing training programs and should be viewed as a supplement to face-to-face instruction. This is called blended learning.

Ensure Support from Top Management

Without support from top management, an e-learning program will probably not survive.

E-learning programs require significant resources for development and support and the cooperation of several departments within the organization. If the support from top management isn't there, it needs to be developed. Aligning your e-learning strategy with business goals can be an important first step in gaining support from top management.

Do your homework to ensure that the development of the e-learning program isn't sabotaged. Prepare a project plan that includes a budget and a schedule, as well as any unusual resource needs and the assumptions that were used to develop the plan

Work with Your IT Department to Develop an Understanding of Your Baseline Technologies

There are two environments that you need to gather information about. One is the authoring environment, or the hardware and software that is required to create the e-learning course. Before selecting an authoring software, check with your IT department to make certain that it is consistent with company standards, such as programming language, and browsers and plug-ins that are supported. Other issues to consider include:

- Does the software accept the word processing and presentation software that your IT department supports?
- Does the software use a different graphics or database package than those that are currently supported in your organization?
- Will the purchase of this software require the upgrading of the computer systems that your training developers currently use?
- Will the purchase of this software require additional hardware, such as a zip drive or CD-ROM or a DVD drive?

The other environment is the delivery environment—the hardware and software that is needed to actually take an online course. Some of the issues to consider are:

- What are the minimum system requirements of the viewing equipment?
- What are the hardware and software platform requirements?
- What browsers will be used? Will there be multiple versions and which ones will be supported?
- Will any type of plug-ins be required and, if so, how will users obtain the plug-ins?

These are just some of the issues that you will need to make decisions about before you can move ahead with implementing an e-learning program.

Work with Your IT Department to Establish Standards for Working Together

It is critical to include your IT department early in the development of an e-learning strategy. Often IT is not included until the actual implementation and this can lead to the failure of the e-learning program. You will need to partner with IT because your e-learning initiative may require:

- Software installation
- Server space
- Customization
- Application development
- Maintenance
- Ongoing support
- Legacy system interface

The implementation of an e-learning program will require collaboration between the training department and the IT department. This collaboration will most likely be new to both departments, hence the need for establishing standards for working together. The standards should be established jointly, with both departments agreeing to expectations and roles.

Create a Plan to Help Your Training Department Handle the Change

When delivering e-learning courses, the locus of control shifts from the instructor to the learners. Training departments that are converting from instructor-led courses to interactive online courses will face the following issues:

- **Level of effort.** If the online course is truly a student-centered learning event, rather than a form of teaching media, it will take more time on the part of the trainer. There will be e-mail messages from students to answer on a regular basis and the course may need to be monitored in order to encourage all of the learners to participate.
- **Role shift.** The trainers will need to become comfortable making the shift from being the expert or the "sage on the stage" to facilitating the learning process or being the "guide on the side." Instead of relying on lectures, trainers will need to provide examples, demonstrations, and written materials.
- **New techniques and instruction methods.** A powerful instructional method is the asynchronous discussion. Asynchronous discussions between teachers and learners take place intermittently, not simultaneously, through links to HTML content or email, news, or discussion groups. Instructors need to provide insight, motivate learners, summarize discussions, keep the discussion on track, and coach learners.
- **Evaluation tools.** While many online courses include standard tests, these tests do not show if a participant has integrated the concepts and skills and is using this new knowledge on the job. If you require special projects to show this level of learning or enhanced performance, your trainers will need to provide facilitator support during the project, and assessment and feedback when the project is complete.

Determine E-Learning Specifications

If your organization does not currently maintain standards or guidelines for training materials and written documentation, this would be an excellent time to begin to establish those standards. Your guidelines should include:

- Style guidelines for headings, numbers, names, punctuation, and capitalization
- Corporate identity
- Graphics guidelines
- Screen designs
- Page layouts

In addition, you may want to consider these specifications for e-learning technologies in your organization:

- Quality or design requirements for new applications
- Maximum time that a web page takes to load
- Maximum graphic size per web page

Determine How You Will Measure the Results

Ask management what measurements they expect before you expend a lot of resources collecting evaluative data. Some management teams expect very little in terms of metrics. This may be especially true for management teams that value education and training, because they feel that what is important is providing training opportunities for employees and they are not as concerned about results. Be aware that this attitude can change with the addition of new members to the management team, changes in the financial position of the organization, or any number of other business factors, and be prepared to establish measurements very quickly.

If you decide to measure results, think about the current methods that you are using to measure training results. If you are currently using participant evaluations or standardized tests to measure training results, these methods are easily incorporated in e-learning programs. Some training departments measure the number of hours of training that each employee receives and report that metric to management. One of the problems with using such a metric is that when e-learning is introduced, the number of hours of training per employee is likely to go down. Unfortunately, that may lead some managers to believe that the training department can be streamlined, when in actuality trainers are spending more time per program than they did when the course was delivered using conventional methods.

Some companies, like Verizon, IBM, and Ernst & Young, are measuring performance, competencies, and intellectual capital. The tools that they are using include certification programs, portfolio assessments, and online job assessments by supervisors.

It is important to measure business results such as gains in productivity or the shortening of a learning curve. For example, perhaps after implementing an e-learning course, a production worker learns how to use a new piece of equipment in a week, compared to the month that it took using the previous method. The productivity gains that are a result should be measured and reported to management.

Prepare a Rollout Plan

Choose carefully the courses that you will convert from traditional delivery methods to online delivery. The first courses must be successful, or the entire program may suffer. When selecting a course, consider these issues:

- Is the subject matter objective, or does it require judgment or subjectivity? Objective subject matter is a better candidate for e-learning.
- Have training materials been developed? If so, are those materials already divided into sections or chunks of information? Does it incorporate multimedia? These types of programs don't take as long to convert to e-learning.
- How quickly does the subject matter change? There is an advantage to using e-learning when the subject matter changes often because updates are quicker to implement.
- What size is the intended audience? Small audiences generally are not cost-effective.
- Does the intended audience have the necessary technical skills? One of the major hurdles in implementing an e-learning program is getting learners accustomed to technology if they are not already technically adept.

Start with a small number of courses and create a plan for integrating e-learning into your current training programs.

Marketing your e-learning program should also be a part of your rollout plan. Marketing includes introducing the e-learning program, promoting it, and maintaining and increasing usage over time. Some ways to accomplish the marketing of your e-learning program include:

- Integrating e-learning programs into new employee orientation programs
- Incorporating e-learning programs into employee development plans and performance improvement initiatives.
- Educating managers and supervisors about the program and how they can incorporate it in employee development and performance improvement.
- Using e-mail to promote e-learning and its benefits by promoting specific courses and providing information about the benefits of e-learning programs.
- Providing for recognition of employees who take e-learning courses.
- Evaluating your e-learning programs so that you can improve the areas that are weak.

There are many issues to consider when you begin thinking about creating an e-learning strategy. This article should help you start creating a strategy that is customized for your organization's needs.

References

Carliner, S, "Build a Business Case for Online Learning Projects," *ASTD Learning Circuits*, February 2000.

Galagan, P.A., "Getting Started with E-Learning," *Training & Development*, May 2000, pp. 62-64.

Hartley, D., "All Aboard the E-Learning Train," *Training & Development*, July 2000, pp. 37-42.

Mayberry, E., "Laying the Foundation for Successful IT Partnering," *ASTD Learning Circuits*, January 2000.

Sevilla, C. and Wells, T., "Converting to Web-Based Training: Choices and Trade-offs," *ASTD Learning Circuits*, May 2000.

Pam Pervenanze, a former employee of Fredrickson Communications, has 11 years of experience in the training and development field. She will be completing a Master's of Education degree in the area of Human Resource Development from the University of Minnesota in May 2001. Pam is an active member of ASTD and serves on the Program Committee for the Southern Minnesota Chapter.

Want Smarter Employees? Get on the E-Train

Dylan Tweney

This article extols the virtues of distance and e-learning, including its economies. But it also suggests that e-learning is not the answer to all training problems and that a blended approach with classroom learning is more likely the choice for many in the long run.

Companies have been caught in a bind when it comes to training. Teaching new skills is critical to keeping employees motivated and productive. But classroom instruction is often expensive, slow, and ineffective. Besides, it takes people away from their jobs. Every minute your salespeople are sitting in a classroom listening to someone teach effective selling techniques is a minute they're not out there selling. How do you provide effective professional education without sticking people in mind-deadening classrooms for days at a time? E-training may be just the ticket.

E-training promises more effective teaching techniques by integrating audio, video, animation, text, and interactive material to help each student learn at his or her optimum pace. But the real argument for online training is that it can eliminate one of the biggest costs of real-world training: travel.

According to Brandon Hall of online-learning research firm Brandon-Hall.com, e-learning has produced training budget savings of 40 to 60 percent for large organizations such as Ernst & Young, IBM, the Internal Revenue Service, and Rockwell Collins. IBM, for instance, claims that its e-training initiative, Basic Blue, which teaches basic management skills to new managers, saved the company $200 million in 1999. Eliminating travel expenses formerly required to bring employees and instructors to a central classroom accounts for much of the savings. With an online course, employees can learn from any Internet-connected PC, right from their desks in the home office.

However, developing customized online courseware isn't cheap. Typically, e-learning service providers charge from $10,000 to $60,000 to develop one hour of online instruction, depending on the complexity of the topic and the media used (HTML pages are easier, and thus usually cheaper to develop; streaming-video presentations or Flash animations cost more). And the course content is just the beginning. A complete e-learning solution also includes the technology platform—computers, applications, and network connections—used to deliver the courses. Also known as a learning management system (LMS), this platform is either installed onsite or outsourced. Add to that the necessary investments in network bandwidth to deliver multimedia courses, and you're talking serious money. For the LMS infrastructure and a dozen or so online courses, the bill can easily top $500,000 in the first year.

The steep up-front costs mean that custom e-training is likely to be economical only for large organizations. "It's more expensive to create online content," says Hall. "But if you have a large audience, it pays for itself tremendously."

Attracted by such potentially huge savings, companies are pouring money into online training. International Data Corp. estimates that U.S. companies' 2000 bill for e-learning technologies, courses, and services will be $2.2 billion, and predicts that the expenditure will grow to $11.4 billion by 2003. By comparison, corporations spend $54 billion annually on all training (online and off), according to a *Training Magazine* study of 1,347 companies with 100 employees or more.

E-learning started life in IT departments more than a decade ago as relatively unglamorous computer-based training (CBT). CBT courses are usually delivered on CD-ROM, via stand-alone computers, and have traditionally been focused on providing technology skills—after all, it makes sense to train employees to use a database while they're sitting in front of computers. But the traditional CBT model doesn't work as well for teaching skills, like salesmanship, that require more interactive instruction.

Now e-training is expanding beyond CD-ROMs onto the Web, and it's encompassing all the capabilities of the new medium: streaming audio and video, interactive Flash animations, and, of course, plenty of PowerPoint slides. According to the *Training* study, 40 percent of all e-learning today is CD-ROM-based, but an increasing number of courses are delivered over company intranets (31 percent) and the public Internet (19 percent). About a third of online courses include interaction with other people (such as a remote instructor), but most still involve just the learner and a computer.

E-training is also rapidly growing beyond merely imparting computer skills to include a broad array of topics. The vast majority of all e-training in 1999 was IT-related, but that area will fall to less than half the market by 2003, according to IDC senior research analyst Cushing Anderson. "It's not just technology that you need to know, but technology combined with what business processes you need to change," he says. Accordingly, e-learning courses now encompass the full gamut of business issues, from accounting to employee wellness. "Every conceivable topic is available now as an online course," says research analyst Hall.

Eric Wortmann, director of product marketing for NEC America, uses e-learning services provided by Baltimore-based Caliber Learning Network to train his internal sales staff on the company's new telecommunications and networking products. Formerly, NEC America would send product managers, sales managers, and coaches on road trips to train remote sales staff. Besides racking up exorbitant travel expenses, this approach took key salespeople out of commission for weeks at a time. Now, Caliber produces training videos for the company, then delivers the videos through a webcast that salespeople can view live or access later at their convenience.

Reaction to the e-learning program has been tremendous, according to Wortmann. "When salespeople are fighting for their numbers for the year, spending a day and half in travel is a waste of their time and a waste of our money," he says. "To do this online is a real benefit for them and for us." Wortmann won't say exactly how much the company saved, but he says e-learning was a "no-brainer," given the reduction in travel expenses. According to a Caliber spokesperson, a typical one-day sales training class comparable to NEC's would cost about $150,000 to develop and deploy via Caliber—about half the cost of delivering the course in person at each of 40 different regional offices.

But saving money isn't the only reason to pursue e-training. Sometimes online training can help teach employees faster and more effectively than other methods. Consider Circuit City. The electronics retailing giant sells a lot of televisions and Walkmans, but its customer service is, well, terrible. High employee turnover and a rapidly changing high-tech inventory make it difficult to keep sales staff up to speed on the capabilities and limitations of the latest gadgets—thus the blank looks when you ask a Circuit City salesclerk about the advantages of one DVD player over another.

"It will always be a challenge to make sure the sales associates have the right information at the right time, and that they know what to do with it," acknowledges John McKeever, general manager of superstore training for Circuit City.

The old method of training new employees—piling them into a classroom for group training sessions—wasn't working, so Circuit City decided to try e-learning. Last May, Circuit City contracted with San Francisco-based e-learning outsourcer DigitalThink to develop a series of online courses for new employees. Circuit City's permanent training staff worked with DigitalThink designers to create 44 courses dealing with various aspects of sales, customer service, and operations. The system was deployed on Oct. 1, and within the first week, 19,000 sales associates were taking the online courses at Circuit City outlets.

DigitalThink provides the technology platform that delivers course content over the Internet to "training centers" (banks of Internet-connected computers) located in the employee areas of Circuit City stores. During orientation, each new salesperson is required to take a number of courses. The average course is 20 to 30 minutes long—

"Most people get pretty bored if it's any longer than that," says McKeever—and at the end of a course, employees get a printout detailing the in-store procedure or technical information, so they can immediately apply what they've just learned.

McKeever declines to say how much Circuit City spent on the program, but DigitalThink officials say a typical customer spends more than $600,000 for the company's full-blown e-learning solutions. Is it paying off? It's too soon to tell, says McKeever—but the results from the holiday season should be meaningful. The initial reaction from managers and employees alike has been overwhelmingly positive, he says. Managers appreciate not having to deal with outdated, bulky, printed training manuals. It's now possible to deliver individualized classes to employees one at a time, rather than relying on mass indoctrination. And, according to McKeever, the employees find the new courses engaging and entertaining.

Whatever route companies choose, e-learning isn't going to replace classroom instruction entirely. For one thing, bandwidth limitations still constrain multimedia over the Internet. Sure, it sounds like a great idea to have business guru Peter Drucker speaking to you via video or audio (as Corpedia courses offer). But when there are glitches in the audio stream and Drucker starts sounding like a stuttering Max Headroom, the technology's shortcomings become more apparent.

E-training also isn't a great way to impart cultural values or build teams, says research analyst Hall. If you have a unique corporate culture, such as Southwest Airlines's freewheeling good humor, it's hard to convey it to new employees through a 15-inch screen. Group training sessions work better in such cases, Hall says. Likewise, team-building coaches need not fear replacement by computer anytime soon. So far, e-learning technology just can't replicate the experience of falling backward off a chair into your co-workers' arms. (Darn.)

However, for teaching specific information or skills, e-training has a lot going for it. For instance, e-learning can be especially effective at helping employees prepare for IT certification programs. In a study commissioned by e-learning company KnowledgeNet, 94 percent of students passed an IT certification exam after taking a KnowledgeNet online course, compared with an industry-wide average of 74 percent. Hall says e-learning also effectively addresses topics such as sexual harassment education, safety training, and management training—all areas where a clear set of objectives can be identified.

When designing courses, interactivity is key. Having employees watch an on-screen talking head is no improvement over putting the same talking head at the front of a classroom. "Sitting and staring at the RealAudio Stream just isn't going to get it done," says Allen Gunn, chief technical officer and co-founder of e-learning service provider Pensare in Sunnyvale, Calif. "Feedback is important in any online context, but particularly in education. That feedback should drive my curiosity and my next set of inquiries."

Accordingly, Pensare (like many other e-learning companies) provides tools for online community interactions among students. Pensare's courseware also encourages students to share information and ideas off-line. For example, student profiles with phone numbers are attached to each course, so employees can easily contact one another for extended discussions.

Ultimately, experts such as Hall and IDC's Anderson recommend a "blended" approach combining online and in-person training. Circuit City's McKeever stresses that it's still important to include human interaction in corporate training, "E-learning is not the end-all solution," he says. But if it helps eliminate lost afternoons in windowless training rooms, e-learning is definitely a step in the right direction.

Dylan Tweney is an award-winning technology critic and currently a contributing writer for eCompany Now, *where his column, "The Defogger," appears online every Thursday at www.ecompany.com. You can e-mail him at dylan@tweney.com.*

Are You Ready for Web-Based Training?

Gary C. Powell

What's involved in preparing for Web-based training? That's the issue this article addresses, including looking at who, what, where, how, and when questions. It includes a useful table that summarizes the author's findings.

Web-based training (WBT) is here to stay. Many companies that previously viewed WBT as a fad are now quick to offer on-line training programs because of the supposed savings, flexibility, and interactivity these courses often provide. But is *your* organization ready for a web-based training delivery solution? Despite the excitement, possibilities and glamour associated with delivering courses over corporate Intranets and/or the Internet, jumping in headfirst without analyzing the who's, what's, where's, when's and why's could lead to disaster.

Given today's need for HR to justify training costs, provide evidence that training and development contributes to business success, link training intervention with the bottom line, and calculate the strategic value of training, why start down a path that could be doomed for failure? Too much is at risk to blindly launch a web-based training initiative, regardless of how new, in vogue, creative, flexible, cost-effective and exciting we hear it is.

Often, training departments are mandated to develop online learning initiatives (Driscoll, 1998). Such mandates are often instigated by a technological imperative—a pressing need to use Internet technology for the sake of technology. In some organizations, web-based training has been launched merely to justify the costs of the corporate intranet. Satisfying management's demand to develop or maintain an innovative or prestigious corporate image jumps some organizations onto the WBT bandwagon. While not the best reasons for ushering in a web-based training initiative, they can in fact lead to profit, cost savings, growth, marketability and prestige if they're done well.

For the fortunate, these courses help train, retrain and retain employees. Although these are wonderful benefits of successful web-based learning initiatives, they alone are not good reasons to enter the business of delivering WBT.

For whatever reason, the business of delivering WBT is steadily increasing. The popularity of WBT programs is growing at such an astronomical rate that about 500 products are now on the market for online learning (Torode, 1999). According to McGee (1999), "technology-based training, including Web-based solutions, will represent half of all training by the year 2002, up from 25% [in 1998]." Torode (1999) predicts that the next major shift in the training industry will be the hybrid approach: combining instructor-led training and technology-based training, which will include synchronous and asynchronous online training, CD-ROM's, and video and satellite broadcasts.

Training can be delivered using a multiplicity of media, such as the traditional classroom and computer-based training. Choosing Internet technologies to deliver training should occur only after careful consideration of a number of factors. These factors include what is taught, who is taught, where the teaching takes place, how the teaching is supported, and when the teaching takes place (see Table 1).

Who Is Taught

What is the culture of your organization? High-tech, fast-paced organizations—as opposed to "mom & pop shops"—will be more accepting of WBT. What is the value of "water cooler" dialog during training breaks? This refers to the informal interaction that employees, often from different offices, have as a result of coming together for training. This sharing is often one of the highlights for even attending a training session. If this kind of rapport is highly valued, you might run into an initial resistance to eliminating classroom-based for on-line training. Finally, consider how well your organization can accept the notion that training can actually occur at the desktop. Even though computer-based training (e.g., CD-ROM) has been around for awhile, not everyone is ready to accept non-instructor led training.

What is the size of your organization? If it's too small, it will be difficult to justify the investment. For populations greater than 200 students—especially when they are geographically dispersed—WBT becomes most cost effective compared to classroom training (if the course is presented several times). At that point, the cost of course development, delivery hardware, and production hardware/software is less than costs of trainee's salaries, material reproduction, travel, tuition, record keeping and administration.

Factors Affecting CBT Training				
What is taught	**Who is taught**	**Where the teaching takes place**	**How the teaching is supported**	**When the teaching takes place**
Domain of learning	Culture of the organization	Technical infrastructure	Administration	Just-in-time
Stability of content	Size of the organization		Technical support	Anytime
Importance of content consistency	Learner characteristics		Corporate support	Frequency
Content complexity	Number of learners		Union/labor support	
Media complexity	Geographic dispersion of learners		Instructor support	
Requirement for special equipment	Number of training sites		Developmental support	
Format of current materials	Consequence of time off the job			
Confidentiality	Preferences of learners			

Table 1. Factors to consider when deciding to adopt Web-based training

What are the characteristics of your learners? Learners that tend to succeed in on-line courses are self-disciplined, self-regulated, self-directed, independent and responsible. Likewise, learners should be focused, and not easily distracted. While WBT does offer the flexibility of learning anytime and anywhere (such as at home), the amount of potential distractions versus a traditional classroom are enormous. Bosses, co-workers, computer games, children, TV, pizza delivery guys...to name a few. Naturally, on-line learners need to be very comfortable with written communication, somewhat savvy with web technologies, and proficient with computers. Finally, another learner characteristic to consider is fear of job security. Some learners assume that since WBT involves a computer and Internet technologies, performance scores are automatically "zapped" to management and other HR decision-makers. Those who make such assumptions may be hesitant to use WBT.

What Is Taught

In what learning domain does the course content fall? As expected, psychomotor and hands-on topics are not well suited for WBT. While it is possible to teach foundations of forklift operations on-line, the actual operation of one is not possible. Also consider the stability of the course content, is it dynamic or static? For example, training topics that include laws, regulations, or sales figures would be dynamic, versus a training class on business-writing skills (static). Laws, regulations and sales figures are apt to change over time, whereas business-writing techniques would not. Software application training is also quite dynamic; each time a new software version is released, the training must be updated. Content that frequently changes is perfect for web-based delivery because it is relatively quick and easy to update. If content consistency is important, web-based delivery is ideal. Technology-based instructional systems do not have bad days or tire at the end of a long day. Technology-based instruction is delivered in a consistently reliable fashion that does not vary in quality from class to class, school to school or one company location to another. Web-based courses deliver the same information every time the course is used. (Note: this does not necessarily hold true for on-line classes that involve an instructor, such as a college course.)

How complex are your training courses in terms of content and media requirements? Topics that are highly complex (such as surgical procedures) can be better taught in more traditional settings. Topics that call for great amounts of media (such as video clips demonstrating how to properly extinguish a fire) will suffer from bandwidth constraints if delivered on-line. Consider special equipment requirements for students enrolled in the course. If special software or machinery is required, on-line learning may not be the best approach. Consider the format of current training materials. Naturally, those in a digital format will be more web-ready compared to those that are not.

Finally consider how confidential your training materials are. If they are highly confidential, resistance might come from those with a fear of hackers. While precautions can be implemented, some management staff may be nervous about putting confidential material on-line.

Where the Teaching Takes Place

What is the technical infrastructure of your organization? Consider the capacity and limitations of its network, Internet and Intranet connections (bandwidth). Consider the capacity and limitations of desktop computers and web servers. Naturally, if these systems are very limited (due to age, condition, etc.), a WBT initiative may not succeed. Consider whether or not your employees have permission to install extra software such as plug-ins on their desktop computer. Many web-based courses require students to install plug-ins to experience interactive content. Consider your access privileges to currently installed technology. Without technology for production or ready access to web servers, WBT will be difficult to implement. Finally, consider the presence of corporate firewalls. It's not unusual for web-based course participation to require access to materials out on the Internet. Some organizations do not allow its employees access to the Internet.

When the Teaching Takes Place

When is the training needed in your organization? Training that must be provided just-in-time or on demand is well suited for WBT. Training that must be available anytime is also well suited for WBT. Consider how rapidly your courses must be distributed. While development time of on-line courses may not be quick, the distribution time (how fast the data travels from the web server to the desktop) is. Also, consider the locations of your offices. If they are spread over multiple time zones, the anytime nature of on-line learning can be a benefit. Consider the frequency with which your courses are taught (repetitive vs. one-shot). If training classes are typically just taught once, a more traditional training medium might be a better solution.

How the Teaching Is Supported

What kind of technical support is available? Consider the technical support your organization currently has to assist learners with connection problems, computer problems, etc. Computer help desks will be a necessity to accommodate the potentially thousands of employees who will be logging on for training. Does your organization have 24-hour-a-day toll-free technical support by phone? If your WBT will truly be utilized anytime and anywhere, the learners will need that level of support. Also consider the kind and amount of in-house expertise your organization has for both course maintenance and updates. Someone must have the responsibility to quickly and efficiently maintain and update the on-line courses.

What level of corporate support do you have for a web-based training delivery solution? Consider whether on-line course delivery is aligned with your corporate vision or mission. Some organizations have a more 'cutting-edge' or forward-thinking philosophy than others do. Consider the kind of commitment management will provide, especially in terms of funding. Consider your organization's view of evolving technology. Internet technologies are certainly evolving, and will be for some time. If your organization tends to be fickle when it comes to funding technology that has a relatively short shelf life, WBT may not be a wise initiative. Also consider your organization's previous experience with CBT. Many see WBT as nothing more than CBT through a browser, so if there was a terrible past experience with a CBT venture, count on plenty of resistance to on-line learning.

Consider your organization's feelings toward high development costs versus delivery costs. Technology mediated instruction tends to be much more costly to develop than to deliver. If the employees at your organization are unionized, consider the level of union/labor support you have. Labor union contracts dictate not only who gets training, but also where and when that training takes place. Consider how much time has been made available to you in relation to when training must be launched. If management will support a web-based training initiative, but only gives you one month to implement it, short of changing their minds, WBT may not be the best choice. Naturally, consider the number of designers and "techies" you have in-house for development. If there are none, you may not be a good candidate for WBT until you rectify that situation. Finally, carefully consider your team's spirit. If there is a lack of enthusiasm or interest among those who are responsible for initiating the WBT, you might want to reconsider.

Concluding that an organization is not ready for WBT is not the end of the world. Some institutions or businesses do very well in a low-tech environment. The nature of their business and learners does not necessitate utilizing technology to deliver their training. There is nothing wrong with your institution or business if you don't need WBT!

For organizations that are candidates for WBT, remember you must be comfortable using technology. You must have the funds and technical support readily available to meet today's needs and the resources available to expand your technical capabilities for tomorrow.

References

Driscoll, M. (1998). *Web-based training: Using technology to design adult learning experiences.* San Francisco: Jossey-Bass/Pfeiffer.

Fister, S. (2000, April 1). At your service. *Inside Technology Training,* online, http://www.trainingsupersite.com/ittrain/pastissues/April00/apr00feature2.htm.

McGee, M. (1999). Train on the Web. *InformationWeek,* No. 1718, 101-105.

Sitze, A., Kiser, K, and Oas, B. (2000). Six for the century. *Inside Technology Training,* 4(1), 13-19.

Torode, C. (1999). More band for the buck in Internet training. *Computer Reseller News,* No. 833, 191, 196.

Dr. Gary C. Powell—the Multimedia Guru®—is an e-learning and CBT consultant in Grosse Pointe Woods, Michigan. You can contact him at multimedia-gurus@home.com.

How Digital Learning Differs in Europe

Jane Massy

It's a different world over in the EU—right down to the terminology. This article looks at Europe's unique take on e-learning—and provides advice for Americans seeking to do business there.

I s Europe different in the way technology is supporting learning and, if so, how? Let me start by answering the question. Yes, it's different, probably more so than many Americans might expect, but not as different as many Europeans would like to think.

My intention is to suggest what needs to be considered when looking at the European training market. I'll try not to spend too long explaining the origins and context of the differences; putting things in context is a European habit that's described by my American friends and collaborators as an excuse not to get to the point. But you're going to have to get used to that if you want to do business in Europe. Providing the context allows better consideration to be given to why and how any change might take place. So, the importance of explaining the differences lies in whether there is something to learn from those differences. I think there is.

Technology-supported learning is learning supported in some way by technology, including electronic tools for designing, delivering, and managing learning, as well as content in the form of resources and courses. Two terms—ICTs (information and communication technologies) and TSL (technology-supported learning)—are considered in Europe to be the least contentious and most likely to have shared meaning in every language. Terminology is hugely important in Europe, not least because there are 11 major languages in the European Union, with several more on the way as new Eastern European countries join. With different languages and new terms comes the challenge of finding shared meaning. The solution is not, at least in the short to medium run, to have one dominant language (most likely English) and expect everyone to accept imposed terminology. That's the quickest way to encounter resistance. Language and meaning are complex cultural identifiers. Though English increases in importance, especially with Internet growth, the solution for Europe lies in working towards harmonious understanding of different identifiers with shared meaning.

So, when the French and other Europeans talk about telematics and distance learning, it's important to understand what they mean by those terms and not expect them to use Anglo American terminology, such as computer-based training, Web-based training, and instructional design. Such terms tend to be perceived negatively in Europe, largely because of their association with old forms of instruction which, let's face it, were pretty awful. Two words that do have important meaning and shared resonance across languages in Europe are *learning* and *pedagogy*.

The Differences

There are several main differences in technology-supported learning between Europe and the United States.

- **Fundamental and contextual.** There are different patterns of education and training in Europe—not only different from the United States and Canada, but also widely different within the European Union.
- **Economic.** The take-up of ICTs in general in Europe has been at a slower pace and pattern than in North America, although parts of Europe are now catching up rapidly both in terms of installed IT base and Internet access.
- **Attitudes and expectations.** These differences are directly related to training professionals and planners. Attitudes and expectations of the potential of ICTs in education and training vary hugely across Europe. The great divide is not along country lines but more along sector lines: ICT industries embrace and generate TSL; other industries do not. Resistance is highest in the traditional sectors and in the education and training community, especially where the public sector has the strongest role.
- **Limited range of expertise.** The level of TSL skills among education and training practitioners in Europe is low, and there's an absence of significant attempts within the education and training community to identify and prepare appropriate education and training programs in TSL to drive the development of new applications and large-scale usage.

The Systems

I'll try to keep the contextual explanation short, but it is important to understand that there are and will remain significant differences in education and training systems across the Member States of the EU. The twin area of education and training is one that the Member States hold dear. Early hopes of standardization and harmonization have largely been recognized as futile, and have been abandoned in favor of seeking cooperation and mutual recognition.

Not only does each country have its own system, but also the education and training establishment is, in general, extremely conservative. There has also been—as a result of economic, political and demographic change—enormous pressure on education and training systems to provide more training within tighter budgets and, in real terms, decrease public expenditure. The result has been resistance to any change, aversion to any risk and innovation, and behavior that's typical of an industry in decline. Only in the past months have governments and education and training systems awakened to the fact that education and training are, in fact, industries in growth. They're (mostly by law) two of the most highly regulated industries in Europe, typified by two examples: France and Germany.

In France, as in a number of other European countries, education and initial vocational and professional training are the responsibility of the state, and there's little or no involvement of enterprises or the private sector. At the heart of the French philosophy is the idea that education and training should be for developing citizens with political, social, cultural, and economic knowledge and skills. The title of the most recent Education and Training White Paper, *Towards a Europe of Knowledge*, produced by the European Commission, is strongly influenced by French thinking.

In addition, adopting ICTs in education and training has been slow, partly because the agenda was seen to be set by the industries and not by the wider needs of society. And partly because most of the industries driving change were perceived to be American or Anglo in origin and not appropriate to French learning needs and methods.

The other example of the European context is Germany, where years of social partnerships and close involvement of employers in the education and training systems have led to the model of the Dual System, of which Germany is justifiably proud. Germany has been slow to adopt ICTs, to some extent because it believes that the existing system is best for meeting its needs.

The challenge for both of those philosophies is how to adapt to the rapid changes that have taken place. There's little doubt that the structures of the education and training systems in both countries are powerful and well established, but slow to change. The point is that if the education and training systems are unable to plan and implement TSL, then the supply of good quality human and digital resources for learning is going to be low. That's now changing, and some of the credit must go to the European Commission and the huge number of funded programs and projects that have over the past decade or so attempted to bring together players from research, education, training, and industry to develop and pilot TSL across the Member States.

Regarding use of ICTs in general and the Internet in particular, it's well known that companies, public sector organizations, and consumers in European countries generally have been slow to recognize the potential of the Internet for business, education, and consumer usage. Unlike in the United States, European political and business leaders have really only in the last 12 months started to realize and articulate visions and policies to capture the potential of learning technologies.

Nicholas Negroponte, speaking at the Confederation of British Industry conference in November 1999, commented that after all his years of presenting at conferences, he felt it had only been in the previous six months that Europe's industry leaders had started to demonstrate that they believed what he was saying about ICTs was for real and not in some vague future.

Five years ago, I was commissioned by a Danish organization to research the question of sustainability in technology-supported learning in full-time education. At that stage, not one single European government had articulated a policy or plans to prepare their young citizens for the information age. That has changed, and most European countries now have policies and large public spending programs to bring ICTs into the education, public administration, and business communities.

There have also been huge changes in the telecomms sector, with deregulation accelerating in the past decade, resulting in more competition, much lower prices, and expanded services. The biggest impact has been in mobile telephony. Some European countries, especially in Scandinavia, have a greater penetration than in the United States. In terrestrial services, there are still de facto monopolies and excessive local charges for consumers and small businesses in particular. Even those companies that have decoupled charges on Internet use from other services still impose local charges on a time basis. The effect is discouraging continuous online usage.

That picture differs widely across European countries and even within countries. In 1999, the UK saw a massive increase in Internet signups with the huge success of Freeserve, the first major ISP to provide Internet access without signup fees or annual charges—demonstrating that removing the cost barrier increases massive use. It's only a matter of time before the telecomms industry in Europe learns the same lesson about call charges. That will probably be the case by the time you read this, at least in the UK.

Slower Acceptance

At a recent conference in the UK, Gary Hamel said that no company board member should be allowed to keep his or her position without having direct personal experience using the Internet and also, preferably, e-commerce. On that basis, most European companies would retain only a few of their current board members. That also applies to senior management in all types of European companies, few of whom have direct knowledge or experience using the Internet and are unlikely to. This conservatism and lack of direct engagement with technology at senior levels means that investment is slow and difficult to achieve in knowledge and resources to integrate technologies into formal corporate learning and training systems. Even more worrying is the lack of expertise and knowledge, and the resistance, among teachers and corporate trainers.

The seats of learning—colleges, universities, and training institutions—have, except in rare cases, been some of the most vociferous opponents of TSL. When asked why technology isn't being integrated into education and training, Europeans educators will argue ad nauseam about low-quality pedagogy, linear mechanistic and boring learning materials, and technology never replacing teachers—all quite reasonable and acceptable arguments about traditional CBT.

Sadly, it must be admitted that the opponents to TSL have a certain weight to their case, as much of what passes as technology-supported learning is exactly as they describe. The problem is that the naysayers haven't noticed that significant change has taken place and that new TSL is varied, dynamic, and actually driving the development of new pedagogy.

The most conservative voices are found in traditional sectors, where occupational profiles are the most developed and haven't changed a great deal. The most active industries in terms of embracing technology tend to be those in which fixed occupational profiles are either new or nonexistent. The difficulty is that in countries with highly regulated training systems and employment, companies without qualifications that are certified by formal systems players (vocational and academic authorities) find themselves without official recognition.

A great irony, not lost on many Europeans, is that a new dual system is emerging that recognizes two types of certifying authorities: the traditional national and professional authorities and the major global industries such as Oracle, Microsoft, and Cisco. It has been difficult, if not impossible, at both national and European levels to find accommodation for accreditation and recognition between countries. Now, there emerges a forceful third player—the global company—and no one seems sure how to deal with it.

What that means for TSL is that integrating new technologies and new approaches in powerful education and training systems is slow because change of any kind is difficult to achieve. Coupled with that is people's fear of being made redundant through technology, which is a complete misunderstanding of the potential and impact of technologies in learning. What's more, the tendency of technology advocates to use a cost-savings argument reinforces people's fears, which is also a misunderstanding and seriously underestimates the investment required.

The "forces of conservatism" that UK Prime Minister Tony Blair describes in the education sector are still alive and well across all Member States. The picture, however, isn't all gloomy. A huge amount of public funds at European and national levels has been going into researching and piloting new TSL tools, methods, and content in the past few years. The level of knowledge and awareness of the potential for TSL is growing, mainly in full-time education at secondary and primary levels and then feeding through into higher education and vocational and professional training.

One of the challenges Europe now faces is how to provide the tools, services, and content that burgeoning users are demanding. Failure by the education and training systems to recognize and anticipate the need for skilled designers, authors, developers, mediators, and assemblers of TSL has meant that there are almost no trained professionals. Most who have TSL expertise gained it through experience, often achieved at great expense through publicly funded projects that have produced only a few usable results. There are barely a handful of European universities teaching master's degree programs or supporting Ph.D. students in instructional design, and those precious few graduates are snapped up quickly by large, mainly ICT industries and consulting firms.

That means that the trained professionals are not going back into the education and training systems of organizations that are attempting to design and develop new TSL programs and content, albeit inexpertly and inefficiently. To compound matters, the term "instructional design" is perceived by most teachers and trainers in Europe in a negative light.

I often advise U.S. organizations wanting to market TSL in Europe to find other terms to describe the functions of instructional design. The European attitude towards instructional designers can be ascribed to the performance and quality of CBT from the 1980s and early 1990s, some of which is still in evidence in linear, purely expositive, and noninteractive presentations. In short, the instructional designer is seen to be the devil behind low-quality learning material.

A few years ago, the European Commission agreed to a call for project proposals that would establish skill profiles and training programs in the whole field of technology-supported learning design and development—from initial training and undergraduate programs to post-graduate and doctoral courses. At the launch in Brussels, one rather hostile university representative asked me whether I seriously thought universities should have instructional designers in teams that develop TSL, a sentiment that was applauded by others in the audience. Not surprisingly, the attempt to elicit proposals for funding was a failure; the subject simply didn't seem to interest education and training organizations.

In the current huge upsurge in demand, European universities may now rue their lack of foresight. Europe desperately needs highly skilled people with multidisciplinary skills and knowledge in technology, graphics, semiotics, education, sociology, psychology, business development, and project management for designing and developing technology supported-learning.

Pedagogy and the Importance of Culture

Before looking at what is being done in TSL in European companies and training institutions, I'd like to return to the issue of pedagogy, as it sometimes puzzles my U.S. colleagues. Why the concern about pedagogical values? Don't we all share the same concerns? Yes, but the concerns of Europeans are heightened by their view that there are particular pedagogical approaches that have a more natural fit with certain European cultures.

Perhaps that's best illustrated by a French colleague, Bernard Blandin, a senior adviser at CESI in Paris, and a major influence on TSL in France. He sees the model of TSL that has emerged in the Anglo American culture as one that categorizes trainees as a target group that shares the same training needs and is given the same training provision. To him, that explains the large-scale, expository type of TSL provided by U.S. universities in their distance delivery of lectures and course materials, and remote and often automated assessment—heavy on broadcasting activities, low on interaction. That model, with its high-volume, low-cost strategy, provides an economic example for widespread take-up of TSL.

Blandin argues that the French model is based on an approach to learning that is about developing people's skills and knowledge, based on personal learning paths and individual support and within which constructivism plays a key role. The economic model for that cannot be based on large-scale, high-volume usage. He further suggests that the Internet offers advantages over broadcasting through personalization, interactivity, and shared communication and learning spaces. It lets his model, a French model, be economically viable and demonstrate that a learner-centered approach is more holistically effective than one that is teacher-driven.

I empathize strongly with Blandin's view, having run an open-learning business school for some years. At the time, I developed, with some European colleagues, an open-learning program in supervisory management for the retail sector. We ran trials with exactly the same materials in Ireland, the UK, France, and Spain. The most learning-independent group was in the UK, where little interaction with the tutor was sought. The group with the highest dependency on the tutor and heaviest demand for direct one-to-one support was in France. The evaluation of the results suggested that the effectiveness of the training in terms of performance was highest in France, but the cost of the training (same materials cost but higher tutor cost) was significantly higher than elsewhere. France exemplifies a particular approach, but the views expressed by French educators and trainers are shared across many European countries.

It is now felt in Europe that the Internet enables more individualized learning paths and a greater focus on individual learning needs. Those can be done at a reasonable cost, with smart use of technology. France has excelled particularly in using technology in learning for disadvantaged groups. The reason may be because it started from a base of giving each person individual help and focus, and the expectation was that the resource requirement would be high if it were to be effective. France has also produced some of the best TSL science and mathematical resources—mainly, tools for simulations and exercises and excellent language training resources. But, in France, you rarely find TSL courses with any preset learning pathway.

Germany provides a different example. Students and trainees spend much longer in training and education. The curriculum, teaching, training, and work experience components are highly planned and are the result of many years' refinement by educators and industrialists. Few Germans expect to learn in their own time, and traditional open-learning or correspondence courses have always had a notoriously high attrition rate.

In particular, TSL in the form of traditional CBT hasn't proved popular in Germany. However, Germany has some of the most advanced TSL applications available—applications that focus on developing innovative solutions to technical training and that, again, apply constructivist principles. Currently in the pilot stage are applications that aim to use technology to develop skills in physical constructive processes, such as learning how to build electronic equipment or developing surgical skills. These applications also aim to simultaneously improve knowledge through combining real and virtual reality.

Where TSL *is* being applied, the highest usage is for ICT skills, as is the case in the rest of the world. Next come soft skills, communication, people management, and personal development. European directives in health, safety, and environmental protection have stimulated the demand for training in recent years. There has been a strong focus on developing new resources and new learning methods in those subjects, and many of the experts are consultants in the private sector who have developed software for managing processes and extended the applications into training and performance support.

Language training is inevitably a significant aspect of the European training industry, and some of the best and most advanced programs and resources have been developed in that field. One of the best-known pioneers in TSL for language learning, Auralog, is producing highly interactive resources and is now marketing successfully in the United States.

In Germany, Denmark, Sweden, and Finland, there's a strong demand for high-quality TSL to support technical training, and some of the best resources are being developed as simulations for mechanics, electronics, materials science, industrial processing, GIS, and other technical subjects. Sales, marketing, and communication programs (highly popular in the United States) are less favored, and there's strong resistance to U.S. products in those fields.

The Internet has shown itself to be an extremely important medium for broader training and education services. In the UK, some of the most advanced applications are in the field of guidance and career development, primarily for young people but also for adults needing to adapt or upgrade skills at a time of change. Performance support systems haven't had the same level of attraction in Europe as in the United

States—at least not in the manufacturing sector. But ERPs such as SAP have been extremely successful in Europe, as in the United States.

It should be noted that the concept of a performance support system is rarely understood by European training professionals. If systems are in place, they're more likely to have been driven from another department in the firm.

The Response of Training Professionals and Policy Makers

Training and business consultants (excluding the heavyweight players) and sector training firms in Europe have tended to be unaware and uninterested in adding TSL to their portfolio of services. When asked why they don't innovate using ICTs, the response tends to be that their clients don't necessarily have direct access to the technology or confidence in using it.

My own view is that most European consultants receive little stimulus from their customers to change and don't really understand the potential of the technology. When customers come looking for services that integrate new technologies, these consultants will be out of date and easily displaced. Large public training organizations (very often operating at a national level, such as FAS in Ireland and VDAB in Belgium) have participated in research and pilot projects in TSL but haven't yet embraced the potential of the Internet to revolutionize their industries. TSL is seen as a peripheral activity, and few national training organizations have invested in either the infrastructure or internal skills development needed to take full advantage of the sudden upturn in customer awareness and demand.

One of the most innovative and potentially important initiatives in TSL is the UK government's University for Industry. This initiative intends to foster the use of ICTs in learning and is aimed mainly at stimulating the interest of new learners and small-enterprise managers and brokering skill needs and the technology-supported learning supply. The initiative will endorse a high-quality supply, disseminate information about courses and resources, and in some cases directly fund the development of TSL. It shares similar objectives to America's Learning Xchange, although there are important differences in approach.

For example, approved suppliers must provide support for learners; unsupported self-learning programs won't be approved. In the first phase, the focus is on learning programs for information and technology skills, basic literacy and numeracy, skills for small and medium-sized businesses and the business sectors automotive components, multimedia, environmental technology and services, and distributive and retail trades. It's hoped to have 1,000 local learning centers by March 2001, to be providing information on learning to 2.5 million users by 2002, and by 2004 to have 1 million courses and packages available. It's anticipated that most of those will be delivered in part or wholly through the Internet.

While there's a clear intention to have widespread geographical presence, many of the local learning centers are expected to have a sector—and even company-specific base. Qualified supplier processes have been set up, learning center applications are being processed, and pilots will run throughout the winter and spring until the official launch in autumn 2000. University for Industry, or UFI as it's known, is the single biggest TSL initiative of any European country, and TSL providers and users will watch its development with great interest.

The European Commission's Role

The European Commission has been a major contributor to the development of TSL. Participation in EU pilot and research projects has provided opportunities for valuable learning for almost everyone involved in TSL in Europe. Millions of Euros and hundreds of person-years have been expended on projects through programs such as Leonardo da Vinci, Socrates, ADAPT, and the Research and Development Framework programs. Hundreds of prototypes have been developed and piloted, but little commercial success has emerged. Exceptions include the learning platform TopClass, which is widely distributed in the United States and Europe. It received yearly development funds under the R&D Framework program and language resources from Auralog, which received funding under the Leonardo da Vinci program and one of its predecessors, Lingua.

So, what are the lessons for TSL providers and training professionals looking at offering TSL in Europe?

- **Watch your language.** Terms such as "instructional design" may be perceived negatively. Secondly, remember that the people whom you expect to deliver training may not have the TSL expertise needed to provide the highest-quality learner and business support.
- **Use high-quality media and navigation.** They will be appreciated, but if the pedagogy is straight down-the-line expository material, most learners will decline. Europeans expect sophisticated pedagogical design, clearly geared towards the target group, keeping in mind the subject matter and the type of support to be provided.
- **Systems are important.** In particular, local and national education and training systems are essential. Flexible resources that can be used within a training program for specific job profiles or linked to curricula for particular competencies will have a much better chance than courses that are only partially relevant. You'll need to demonstrate the range and quality of the skills of the people involved in the design and development.

Jane Massy is a consultant in technology-supported learning based in Cambridge, the United Kingdom. In addition to private practice, she works for the European Commission and conducts workshops worldwide. E-mail her at jane@jmassy.freeserve.co.uk.

The E-Learning Revolution

Patricia A. Galagan

In this article by the editor of Training & Development, *we learn more about what she contends is the future of training and, by not-so-subtle implication, the future of trainers as well. Traditional trainers still have important roles to play, but technology is changing things dramatically. Traditional classroom learning is under siege, and appropriately so, as increasingly sophisticated technology becomes a one-to-one teacher, always available when and where needed.*

"Let me lay my cards on the table face up," says Peter Drucker, venerable author, consultant, and professor of management, when asked if e-learning is changing the training profession. "I am the author of several online learning tools."

That piece of news says it all. Drucker, born well before World War I, recently worked with Corpedia Training Technologies to offer some of his management courses online. That move hastened his appreciation of two of e-learning's most compelling features: accessibility and scalability. Drucker, now 91 and still one of the most sought-after teachers of our time, knows he can reach only so many people through the classroom.

But e-learning has done far more than make knowledge easy to access by a large number of people. Its effects on the training profession are nothing short of revolutionary, challenging most of its basic tenets—from the classic instructional model, to who "owns" learning in an organization, to its strategic role. The profession is in the midst of a revolution generated not from within but by new players from other disciplines, by forces in the supplier market, and by the kind of learning that technology makes possible. Those are the tough truths facing training's fundamentalists.

Drucker agrees, cautioning that "as things are going, the trainer will be left high and dry. There will, of course, still be training as we have traditionally understood it—training in skills. But it is not a growth sector. The growth sector is learning, especially concept learning." Drucker maintains that his own foray into the e-learning world is based on the assumption that the trainer is obsolete. "The trainer is built into the teaching (or learning) device."

No more pencils, no more books, no more teachers' dirty looks. That old song lyric by the 1970s group Alice Cooper could be the revolution's anthem. Goodbye and good riddance to the classroom and its artifacts—the test, the lecture, and the semester system, says Roger C. Schank, a vocal critic of traditional teaching methods. Schank is director of the Institute for Learning Sciences at Northwestern University and founder of Cognitive Arts, a company that pursues the commercial use of software-based teaching. He's also the author of *Coloring Outside the Lines: How to Raise a Smarter Kid by Breaking All the Rules.*

"Classrooms couldn't possibly work today," says Schank. "Centuries ago, they made sense: one literate person reading to the illiterate from what might have been the town's only book." But technology and times have changed. The ideal of one-on-one instruction is not practical in today's classrooms. "A computer can give you more one-on-one interaction than a human can when that human has 30 other humans to deal with," he says. "In a classroom, people who are curious, inquisitive, and questioning take up too much time."

The best things that technology has given training, says Schank, are "the possibility of one-on-one for every learner, the ability to simulate, and the chance to try stuff out and fail in private without the fear of ridicule from other students."

Schank believes that the strongest impetus for effective learning comes not from schools but from business organizations. "It doesn't matter to the school if you learn the Pythagorean Theorem, but it really does matter to your company that you learn to do your job," he says. It is corporate learning programs, many made possible on a large scale by e-learning, that are finding new ways to put human interaction into computer-based programs.

"Corporate trainers better figure out how to be part of that," warns Schank. "The ones who are part of the ancient system [of classroom training] are going to watch that ancient system disappear on them."

Clark Aldrich, a training market analyst for the GartnerGroup [see his review of the state of e-learning in Part One of this yearbook], has a different perspective on the origins of the classroom, but reaches the same conclusion: Trainers need to move on.

"The modern classroom is based on tenets of the Industrial Revolution," says Aldrich. "In that industrial model, instructors are the blue-collar line workers and students are the widgets moving through the assembly line." But, the GartnerGroup predicts, the traditional classroom model will represent less than 30 percent of all formal corporate learning programs by 2003.

Aldrich has been an early herald of a sea change in the role of training in business organizations. When e-learning and outsourcing began to change the training topography, Aldrich articulated this warning: "Companies must reexamine their core processes, including customer service and employee management, through the lens of an e-learning strategy. Primary responsibility for the execution against those goals cannot be the sole responsibility of the traditional training organization. CKOs, CLOs, and even COOs will have to drive the activities."

Strategic at Last

The rise of e-learning is dividing training into two streams: corporate learning—usually owned by HR or corporate training departments—and training for a variety of strategic purposes, usually owned at a level just below the CEO. The strategy-linked learning programs may target people beyond the company such as partners, suppliers, and hoped-for customers. But companies are also using e-learning to change direction quickly, such as going from a traditional business to an e-business.

A hallmark of such strategic learning initiatives is that they are companywide and built onto existing technology systems at great cost. That makes them different in scope and visibility from most other training. Consequently, they are high-stakes and high-risk projects whose owners are reluctant to entrust them to traditional training units. That has produced a booming line of business for large consulting firms poised to guide a strategic initiative with a major e-learning component.

Jeff Schwartz, a partner at PricewaterhouseCoopers and global leader of e-learning services, confirms that such strategic initiatives are his unit's fastest-growing business area. "We're seeing more major supply-chain projects and lots of e-business projects, especially around building e-marketplaces. Increasingly, the foundations of those learning programs are e-learning based." At PWC, such projects are labeled "extended enterprise solutions."

Although solutions is an overused buzzword, it does convey one important characteristic of such programs: They address real business issues and do what training programs of the past have often failed to achieve, which is to help deliver value that a CEO can appreciate—such as new customers, additional business channels, or rapid product rollouts. In corporate-speak, they are known as value plays.

By contrast, says Schwartz, "Corporate learning focuses on efficiency and effectiveness in implementing learning. There's no question that in helping to administer learning and develop and deliver content, e-learning is a huge efficiency and a very effective way to go. But it's a cost-based argument."

The status boost for e-learning, says Schwartz, stems in part from the explosion during the 1990s of such companywide processes as enterprise resource planning (ERP) and customer resource management (CRM). "Companies are now in the second and third generation of those projects, and they're looking for e-learning platforms to support ongoing training for them."

For one such company, PricewaterhouseCoopers is helping piece together a learning platform to support an ERP overhaul that includes the installation of SAP (an ERP package), I2 (a supply chain package), and Siebel (a CRM package). The e-learning platform is a combination of KP2000, a learning management system from KnowledgePlanet.com, and Knowledge Warehouse, which is SAP's content management system. A learning portal, created with Knowledge Warehouse, is hosted on KnowledgePlanet's learning management system.

"This is a good example of a companywide strategic initiative that's leading a major learning effort," says Schwartz. "We expect to see a lot more of that."

Strangers in a Strange Land

What do a former junk bond king, a real estate tycoon, and a Wayne Huzenga wannabe have in common? They're all major stakeholders in new companies that have entered the training market in the past five years. And they are just the tip of the iceberg. A flood of entrepreneurs and their management teams are emigrating from formerly hot market niches in the industrial economy to superheated niches in the knowledge economy.

In the United States, the education enterprise, from cradle to gray hair, is the second-largest segment of the economy after health care. The education market is estimated by the investment firm W.R. Hambrecht + Company to total $772 billion.

Hardly anything is more telling of the new face of the learning market than a visit to a corporate training industry trade show. The Levittown-like booths of five years ago—a table, a chair, some brochures, and a guy in a nice blue suit—have disappeared from expo floors. In their place are towering constructions that feature espresso bars, leather sofas, second stories, and enough electronics to dim the lights of Las Vegas. They're staffed by Gen Xers in khakis and company-monogrammed polo shirts. With hastily acquired training lingo and sales skills honed at other dot.coms, these men and women are reaping the generous commissions that come with the sale of "enterprise-wide, end-to-end solutions." Front and center are companies that wouldn't have exhibited at a training show a few years ago—IBM, Intel, Oracle—and other companies that have changed their names so often you need a skip tracer to figure out who they really are.

Behind the scenes, you'll find some of training's founding fathers serving as discreet tour guides to the newcomers. Their management teams rarely include training pros. Instead, you'll find execs from other fields: toys, games, publishing, soft-drink bottling—all old-economy moneymakers. But as any geneticist knows, marrying outside of the clan enriches the gene pool.

Is Nothing Sacred?

What could be more sacrosanct to a trainer than the instructional systems design process? Yet, it too is being challenged by e-learning, whose essence is speed—the antithesis of ISD's cover-all-bases approach.

"The way we were taught to implement ISD 20 years ago often doesn't work anymore," says Diane Gayeski, principal in Omnicom Associates and professor in the Park School of Communications at Ithaca College. "It's too slow. By the time you find master performers and attempt to clone them, or by the time you write exquisitely detailed behavioral objectives, the business problem has changed. Trainers are trying to achieve a kind of perfection, and in that slow process you can miss the business opportunity."

The Internet has blurred the distinction between who is a content user and who is a content provider, throwing off balance another pillar of training—the role of instructor. "A lot of e-learning is a collaborative sharing of knowledge rather than an information dump," says Gayeski.

ISD models don't address the task of managing conversation and collaboration, she notes. "They are meant for something very different—project management and problem solving, which are applied very rigidly. It's not that ISD models are bad but that, typically, they are applied badly and their limitations aren't acknowledged. They may be good aids in learning instructional design, but master designers tend to be more fluid and rapid in the processes they use.

"In new training approaches, you should be able to address emerging problems and expect that some of your participants are actually the content experts. The just-in-time capability of the e-learning medium allows us to capitalize on new ideas."

E-learning also allows learners to displace the trainer at the center of the learning experience, says Joe Miller, president and chief learning officer at KnowledgePlanet.com. "The science and the instructional methodology and the standards are emerging now for an individual to be at the center of the experience, instead of being at the end of a flow of information from a subject matter expert or a trainer. That not only energizes the learner, but also shortens the time to mastery, making training time more efficient."

Miller continues, "I think the training industry will embrace that over the next 10 years and that it will appear in multiple modalities of training, not just e-learning, because trainers will see it as both valuable and doable."

"Technology is the great enabler," says Karen Vander Linde, a PricewaterhouseCoopers partner and the lead for outsourcing learning for PWC's clients. "It's creating new opportunities for learning professionals in how we can deliver learning." She sees knowledge management systems as prime examples of how technology can make learning continual rather than event-based. "CBT promised to do that, but it was really just a book on a screen. Now there is the capability to do much more."

Jeff Schwartz also sees technology enabling new things, but says the more important point for the profession is that "what we're doing in the learning space mirrors what businesses are doing as they restructure around the Internet."

Adds Schwartz, "We're seeing a much more pronounced interest in learning from senior executives beyond the HR or training worlds. In boardrooms around the world, the same question is being asked: How can I reinvent my company around the Internet before some Internet company takes me out?" E-learning enters the picture when CEOs realize they must transform their companies in 12 to 18 months, not in the three to five years it typically takes with a classroom model of learning.

Few CEOs, or their training advisors, choose a cold-turkey move away from classroom training. Most efforts are a blend of c-learning and e-learning. Yet, Schwartz still sees many training execs looking for ways to complement large instructor-led approaches with technology instead of looking at how things could be done differently with e-learning. "We encourage our [trainer] clients to really focus on the technology part," says Schwartz.

Counting What Matters

It has always been tough to isolate and measure the results of training. The decades-old Kirkpatrick evaluation model is still the blueprint for many trainers, even those who admit that its Level 4 (measuring the return-on-investment) is a nirvana seldom reached. The GartnerGroup has found that doing a Level 4 analysis costs at least twice as much as the training it measures. Will such classic measures as student reaction and even ROI be swept aside by the e-learning revolution?

KnowledgePlanet's Miller sees traditional measures of ROI changing "as we move toward knowledge-based businesses and a workforce that is measured by its ability to convert ideas into services, not products. But it's not happening yet." Pressure will come when companies have "mission-critical issues they really want driven by individuals, not by a corporate-mandated training program. Then you may see companies rewarding people for taking the initiative to acquire and use new skills and for aligning that effort with corporate goals."

Some of the most interesting developments in corporate learning are coming from new entrants to the training supplier market, especially those with lots of capital and corporate officers who come from fields other than training, such as games, systems development, and entrepreneuralism. As these new players rush to brand themselves and fight off competitors, they are attempting to invent better learning models, give learners more control, and integrate learning management into other business systems.

In the process, they're questioning many of training's oldest assumptions. Everything from what constitutes a basic unit of instruction to how to evaluate the success of learning programs is being reexamined in the light of what technology permits,

The Long View

Comments by Peter F. Drucker

I see the new technologies as only the trigger for the changes taking place in training. The root causes are elsewhere. One is the radical shift in the structure of the workforce.

Another root cause is the rapid restructuring of traditional work, whether in the factory or in large-scale repetitive clerical operations, which are actually production work. The application of systems analysis to mass production underlies the rapid decline in the number and proportion of blue-collar manufacturing workers in the U.S. labor force. It also underlies the upgrading of the blue-collar worker—something that traditional training does not yet understand and does not so far handle well.

A third root cause is new learning theory. Let me explain: Traditional training is a product of World War I, perfected in World War II. It arose out of the application of the basic concepts of Frederick Taylor's scientific management to the German invention around 1840 of apprenticeship. The first modern training was developed by Henry Ford's early partner, James Couzens, about 1914.

That kind of training hasn't become obsolete-far from it. But it is being transformed by the application of learning theories developed in the past 30 to 40 years, particularly in connection with Deming's total quality management. I could summarize that by saying that learning as we practice it still puts the teaching process at the center. Increasingly, we must instead put the learning process at the center.

There will, of course, still be training as we have traditionally understood it—predominantly for blue-collar and clerical people. But the growth sector is learning—still skills but, increasingly, concepts that must be learned by knowledge workers at all levels. GE's Crotonville, which I helped found 50 years ago, is the prototype for this new kind of learning for managers.

Now, new technologies make it possible to reach learners wherever they are and whenever they find it convenient, instead of bringing inadequately small groups to a central location away from their work. The learning devices we need for the new learning aren't first-rate college courses or even the first-rate seminars that so many universities are trying to market. They have to be designed for the new learning, which is what Corpedia and I tried to do with my online modules.

There will still be a need for skills training and for skills training that must be delivered where the workers' machines are. My knowledgeable friends say that can already be simulated, and I am certain that such developments will radically change the role and the performance of the skills trainer.

But more and more of learning will be concept learning, and even more of that will be on the part of knowledge workers whether they are blue-collar or white-collar. So far, new learning is not being left to trainers, and as far as I can tell, traditional trainers are not reaching for it. In many institutions, both businesses and large nonprofits that I know, learning is the province of either the CEO or the senior HR executive.

There is one thing that should be said loudly and clearly: Trainers need to realize that things are going on that don't fit their assumptions, their own training backgrounds, and the way they typically have been doing their jobs.

and what matters to the business. That is bound to produce some innovations, and some discomfort, for training fundamentalists.

GartnerGroup's Aldrich notes the parallels with IT departments of five years ago and warns that history may repeat itself for training units. "Top officers are paying attention to strategic learning initiatives but not to training departments," he says. "Virtually none of the IT innovations of that period, such as supply-chain management, intranets, ERP implementation, salesforce automation, and data warehousing, to name just a few, was introduced or championed effectively by the IT department. Instead, they were pushed by product vendors, systems integrators, and the consulting community. IT's involvement, if any, became maintenance."

He adds, "That upheaval is not unique to training departments. Trainers face the same revolutionary challenges as do banks, retailers, and even governments.

"Training is not going away, especially group training for customers. The part of the curriculum that is the same for all groups will be automated, freeing up trainers to be more like consultants."

Aldrich foresees a day when high-profile training, such as that which supports a new product or sets a new corporate direction, will be broadcast, not rolled out.

"The training organization will resemble CNN covering a war, working 24 hours a day for two to three weeks," he says. "If part of the program falls flat at 6 in the evening in Paris, it will be fixed in real time so that it's ready for the people on the East Coast of the United States when they get up."

When a profession finds its cherished practices under close scrutiny, there's often a tendency to circle the wagons and repel innovation. But for many trainers, that could be a career-limiting move. While traditionalists wring their hands about preserving instructional integrity, the new guard will forge ahead to reinvent learning so that it works with technology and supports corporate goals.

In the end, what trainers want may not matter. The growth of online high schools and colleges, plus the abundant opportunities to pursue learning online from Staples to Powered, may shape the expectations of the next generation of learners and the companies that employ them. Even in the knowledge economy, the market speaks.

Patricia A. Galagan is editor-in-chief of ASTD Magazines Group, pgalagan@astd.org.

Blending Traditional Classroom Training and E-Learning Technologies

Long Live C-Learning

James N. Farrell

It's true that Web-based delivery is becoming more and more important, but classroom training isn't going away. What we will have for a while is blended learning. Learn more about this approach in this article from Training & Development.

Happy New Year: Innovate or Die! I read those words as I clicked through *RedHerring.com*, an online magazine specializing in cutting-edge technology. As I set my iced mocha down, I began to ponder what that chilling warning meant for training and development professionals.

As visions of an online training paradise danced through my head, I began to wonder whether the days of instructor-led training were coming to an end. After all, the 1999 ASTD State of the Industry Report showed that instructor-led training is on the decline in leading-edge firms, while use of digital instructional technology continues to rise. Should that have stand-up trainers worried? Perhaps not.

The State of the Industry Report also shows that classroom training remains the dominant form of instructional delivery among the leading-edge firms (58 percent) and among benchmark companies (77 percent), despite the continued rise of instruc-

tional technologies such as CBT and Web-based training. In fact, instructor-led training is likely to remain the dominant form of instruction for most types of training, due
in part to the unique qualities a trainer brings to the instructional relationship. A brief
look into the past will explain why instructor-led training is here to stay.

Back to the Future

The movement in training toward increased use of technology parallels a similar movement that occurred in distributed communication systems. During the l990s, companies implemented a variety of new communication media such as electronic messaging and teleconferencing, in order to increase the efficiency of management decision
making through distributed communication. However, the projected cost savings, such
as reduced travel expenses, were never achieved. Managers still preferred to communicate face-to-face, even if it involved travel expense.

   The research of Richard Daft provided a straightforward explanation for why distributed communication didn't achieve its projected cost savings: Technology used for
distributed communication didn't allow managers to exchange the right type or quantity of information needed to reach a decision. More specifically, in situations in which
managers had to choose between competing solutions—such as when there was no
established policy to deal with a problem—distributed communication was inadequate.
Simply put, in difficult decision-making situations, managers couldn't reach consensus
through e-mail or teleconferencing. They needed to communicate face-to-face.

   Daft concluded that in difficult decision-making situations, in which information-
processing demands were high, managers selected face-to-face communication
because it provided the exchange of a wider variety of information such as voice inflection and body language. The managers preferred face-to-face communication over
email and teleconferencing due to its capacity to impart information richness.

   Training and development professionals should take heed of the findings of communication systems research for a variety of reasons. One, training is a specialized
form of communication and uses many of the same technologies found in communications systems. A second, more compelling reason is that when such concepts as
information richness and information processing demands are considered within the
instructional relationship, useful predictions can be made about how effective training
delivery systems will be under various learning situations.

The Instructional Relationship

Vygotsky noted that the instructional relationship is a highly specialized form of communication, in which the student and teacher assume specific roles. The role of the
teacher was considered to be complex, involving the assessment of student potential,
administration of instruction, monitoring of feedback, and adjustment of instruction

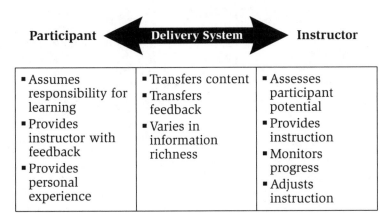

Figure 1. The instructional relationship

to meet the student needs. Participants performed an essential role by providing the instructor with feedback on how they were progressing.

With the advent of such new instructional technologies as distance learning, the instructional relationship has evolved to the point at which some training isn't in the same room as the participants are and may be hundreds or thousands of miles away. Although such situations typically provide two-way communication via cameras and microphones, some provide only one-way communication; others provide no live instruction at all. As with communication systems of the 1990s, the movement toward increasing distance between participants and the instructor is believed to result in more employees being trained while cutting travel cost.

The move to distributed learning does present interesting possibilities for enhancing the instructional relationship and achieving cost savings, but will it enable trainers to reach their instructional objectives in all training situations? Consider this example, albeit extreme: You're in a hospital emergency room, and a nurse says you need immediate brain surgery. Two physicians are available, and you must choose. One has undergone traditional one-on-one training with an experienced surgeon. The other has been trained through the hospital's revolutionary new distance learning program for brain surgeons, which included the completion of a 12-step CD-ROM course. Which surgeon do you want to operate on you?

Although medical training is a farfetched example, it does illustrate a critical point about applying distance learning technology to training. There are situations in which distance learning has a negative impact on the instructional relationship, by making the achievement of instructional objectives more difficult or even impossible. Another look at communication systems of the 1990s might provide some answers why that's the case.

Information richness. Experience and research in communication systems have shown that nonverbal cues such as posture and facial expression can be as important

Information Characteristic	Description
Feedback	How immediate the feedback is for participants and the instructor; enables participants to communicate lack of understanding; allows instructor to assess learner progress.
Multiple Cues	Body language, voice inflection, pictures, and various nonverbal cues that lead to more accurate communication.
Language Variety	Range of meaning that can be conveyed with symbols. Some symbols can convey precise meaning better; others are better suited to convey broad concepts such as natural language.
Personal Focus	How much emotion and personal meaning can be brought into the situation. The instructor can express emotion, talk about personal experiences, and use personal experiences of participants.

Figure 2. Information richness

as words or numbers. As any trainer who has looked out over a class and experienced blank stares can tell you, there's a lot more to communicating with trainees than the strict content of the course. Furthermore, it's often a good idea to personalize instruction by having learners share personal experiences related to the topic.

When instruction is provided through distance learning, many nonverbal clues are lost. When there's only one-way communication, the instructor can't view participants' expressions or receive questions. In those situations, it's difficult—if not impossible—for the instructor to assess each participant's potential and provide developmental feedback. For participants, the instruction can be impersonal, with no way to provide the instructor with information on their progress. In order for training goals to be reached, the instructional relationship must be dynamic and have access to a rich variety of information from the instructor and the participants.

Information-processing demands. Distance learning isn't ideal for all learning situations, but it can meet instructional objectives while reducing travel time and expenses as well as other costs. Daft's work in communication showed that when the information processing demands on managers were high, they preferred face-to-face communication. The flip side of that coin is that when information-processing demands were low, managers favored less rich communication media, such as email and teleconferencing. Information processing demands can lead to similar scenarios in training.

Learning Mode	Description
Accretion	Adding new information to an existing skill set. Example: A nurse learning how to administer a new type of drug.
Tuning	Significantly modifying a set of learned procedures and skills. Example: A nurse learning a new procedure for registering patients in an IS system.
Restructuring	Learning a complete set of new skills. Example: A nurse learning how to conduct training.

Figure 3. Three modes of learning

Cognitive learning research has shown that learning situations vary in the demands placed on learners. Some situations require the addition of information to existing knowledge and skills (accretion)—such as a slight modification to a command in an information system. Other situations, in contrast, require the complete learning of a new set of skills and procedures (restructuring)—such as the learning of a new information systems and business process.

If learning situations differ in the demands placed on learners—as decision-making situations differed in their demands on managers in Daft's study—then it's reasonable to conclude that the type of communication system used by trainers should vary depending on the unique information-processing demands required to attain instructional objectives. In situations in which a great deal of new information and procedures has to be learned, it makes sense to have the instructor in the classroom with the trainees. In those situations, participants are likely to need more feedback and personalized attention in order to achieve mastery.

When learning involves a slight modification to old skills or there's only a small amount of information to learn, distance learning is probably appropriate. In such situations, participants should be able to learn the information on their own. A hotline or online coach can be included.

What's Next?

What does all this talk about e-learning mean for training and development professionals? You may find yourself between various delivery systems. Your choice, its impact on achieving instructional objectives, and its eventual impact on bottom-line business goals, will likely be the measure by which your performance is evaluated. Understanding the effect of instructional technologies on various learning situations

Delivery System	Capacity for Information Richness
Face-to-face instruction Distance learning Stand-alone PC Video Print	High ↕ Low

Figure 4. Delivery systems for information richness

will help you justify your cost estimates to senior-level managers.

Learning technologies are attractive in speed and ongoing low cost, but consider whether they are appropriate for the training situation. When selecting a delivery system, consider the unique information-processing requirements along with a communication system's ability to provide meaningful information to the instructional relationship.

The most efficient instruction occurs when a training system's capacity for information richness is matched with the information-processing demands placed on learners. Some situations will benefit from the use of distance learning, but many still will require the extra benefits that the presence of an instructor can provide.

Therefore, despite the rise in e-learning, it appears that classroom training is here to stay.

James N. Farrell is an independent consultant specializing in Web-enabled HR applications; jnfphd@aol.com.

Mixing Media for Continuous Learning

Diana L. Mungai

Blended learning proved to be an Rx for organizational change at this health-care risk management firm. Learn how they balanced e-learning with classroom learning to meet their training goals.

Integrating new employees into an organization in a way that's both consistent with and supportive of the organizational culture and strategy is a huge challenge. When an organization experiences rapid, large-scale growth through acquisition, the challenge looms even larger. Yet, for companies to thrive in constant change brought on by acquisitions, mergers, rightsizing, and downsizing, they must develop proactive, innovative ways to communicate and support the organizational culture to cultivate their most valuable asset—their people. MMI Companies confronted this challenge several years ago when its employee base nearly doubled, largely through acquisition.

Before going public in 1993, MMI Companies had an employee population of approximately 200 located primarily in the corporate office, with smaller offices in eight to 10 locations across the United States. Growth was gradual, so the challenge of inculcating the company's vision and mission to new and existing employees was relatively modest. That changed in 1996 when MMI merged with or acquired seven niche U.S. and European companies. In fewer than 18 months, the company almost doubled in size. With the January 1999 acquisition of a 200-person company, the employee base grew by another 40 percent.

In 1997 the company launched MMI Insights University, a corporate university that supported organizational learning and cultural transformation through synchronous and asynchronous media. It was through the university that we created an organizational learning initiative called The Harvard Series. The program evolved during several years, but its purpose, goals, and vision remained constant. The program was designed to

- use a selected *Harvard Business Review* article as the basis for a shared learning experience facilitated by MMI thought leaders
- provide a forum for employees to explore our business and culture in an interactive format
- support our integration efforts
- support our continuing transformation through learning.

The program was designed initially as a monthly, one-hour learning experience open to all employees. The corporate office served as the origination site, with five videoconference sites around the continental United States. We also made the programs available to remote locations via audioconference or videotape. Prework activities often were developed and delivered using email and hyperlinks to Websites that supported the monthly program themes.

The first program was conducted in January, 1998, and featured an *HBR* article, "Building Your Company's Vision" by James Collins and Jerry Porras. To demonstrate high-level support for the program, our featured guest was Rick Becker, MMI's chairman and CEO. He integrated themes of core purpose and values from the article into a discussion on the importance of understanding and perpetuating MMI's vision and mission internally and externally.

Subsequent programs featured leaders of our various core businesses and, beginning in the second year of the program, external customers and suppliers. Regardless of the speaker or the featured article, common themes emerged around building and sustaining strong customer relationships, developing professionally in a learning organization, thinking strategically about our work, and defining and sustaining corporate values.

Other articles featured included

- Henry Minzberg's "Musings on Management." This program facilitated greater awareness of the ways we could best mobilize around organizational strategy by demonstrating "spirit of the hive" behaviors.
- Thomas Jones and Earl Sasser Jr.'s article, "Why Satisfied Customers Defect." This discussion was on the importance of maintaining customer relationships.
- Ralph Nichols' article, "Listening to People." This program was the basis for a highly interactive session among a family practice physician and MMI customer, a long-term MMI supplier, and the president of our insurance company who discussed the importance of really listening to customers, suppliers, and each other.
- Chris Argyris's classic 1994 article, "Good Communication That Blocks Learning." In this program, we explored ways in which "defensive reasoning"

and "theories-in-use" can inhibit our personal growth and professional relationships.

Building collaborative learning relationships with several key suppliers was essential to the success of the program. Curt Peoples, a consultant with many years of experience in the communications and public relations field, helped us establish a prototype for the program structure, interactivity, and creative development. He guided us in the design and development of each program and served as the moderator of the live sessions. Joel Shayman developed the program's look and feel by creating presentation templates and stage signs. Gene Hartman and his staff served as our behind-the-scenes technical support. Hartman was able to draw on his experience and knowledge of videoconference systems when using our somewhat outdated videoconferencing technology.

In 1999, we began delivering programs every other month. We found that this sequencing helped us build greater momentum between programs. The cost to produce a one-hour program was approximately $3,000 to $4,000, so we felt it was important to reserve a greater portion of our budget for new program development. All scripting, creative planning, and hosting were brought in-house, and our technical consultants were able to provide more sophisticated hands-on support because they didn't have to devote so much time to troubleshooting. They had greater freedom to help us develop creative program design.

For instance, we asked our telecommunications partners to help create interactivity among audioconference participants. We gave audioconference, live, and videoconference attendees an article quote and asked them to discuss whether they agreed or disagreed with it. Audio-only participants, who had not been able to engage in program interactions, were placed in a "subconference" by the telecommunications operator. There, they collaborated with fellow audio participants to arrive at a group response. The format enabled them to contribute to the learning in real time.

The Harvard Series became an integral part of the culture. Level-1 program evaluations improved steadily, and written evaluation comments, follow-up emails, and informal comments indicated the program resonated strongly with employees on many levels. The average attendance for the live program remained consistent, with approximately 25 percent of U.S. employees in attendance for any given program. Program videotapes were distributed to all MMI offices, but we did not track how they were used.

This program proved to be a success on several fronts because it
- served as a timely forum to educate employees about our business
- connected more employees to the learning than a traditional, face-to-face experience
- helped build learning relationships along the customer-supplier chain
- allowed us to showcase internal talent and leadership and to hear from external clients

- provided an opportunity for employees to reflect upon, discuss, and translate for our customers key learning from business thought leaders
- demonstrated the creativity and innovation we considered essential to our success.

Most important, perhaps, is that it provided a living, learning legacy for our work.

Diana L. Mungai (dmungai@execpc.com) is the former assistant vice president of organizational development at MMI Companies in Deerfield, Illinois. The company was acquired by The St. Paul Companies in April 2000.

Imagine That: Hybridizing Training

Wendy Webb

This article looks at the process of creating blended training programs and the move from strictly classroom instruction to the blended approach. As an example, it looks at how US West did this.

Imagine, for a moment, all of the ways you can use a computer to enhance job performance. Take a critical look at how we use technology now—training, performance support, knowledge management. Then imagine all three blended into an integrated system that does it all: up-front training, on-the-job support, and instant access to the collective corporate mind.

If it sounds futuristic, take a gander at the double zeros you're writing on the date line of your checks these days. The future is now. And the future of training just might look something like the new $3 million knowledge management system at Denver-based US West.

The system is a hybrid—part training, part performance support, part knowledge management. Like the new millennium, it's just a few months old. And like the future, it's a brave new world.

Making It Better

Employees get their first look at the system in new-hire training. It accompanies them into the classroom, where they learn sales skills, customer service skills and the like—knowledge that's reinforced through Web-based modules and role playing. The system also provides self-paced Web-based training (WBT) courses that work in tandem with instructor-led training. The WBT covers the basics before class begins, and in-person classroom time is spent on advanced topics.

When new-hire training is completed, the system acts as a Web-based performance support tool and a database of corporate knowledge. Employees can bookmark, organize and collect the information they'll use most often in their jobs.

The knowledge management system is the brainchild of a team of forward thinkers at US West. They believed training just wasn't what it should be in one of the company's retail divisions, and they wanted to make it better. It's a story about return on investment (ROI), full CEO support and the power of imagination in the workplace.

In the Beginning

It all began a little more than a year ago, when three US West training colleagues at the company's Phoenix office—June Maul, senior regional director for retail markets knowledge and performance solutions, Jonathan Jones, special projects multimedia development manager, and David Thomas, training technology architecture manager—saw a need to update the training for 13,000 employees scattered across the nation in US West's retail marketing and sales division.

As it was, new hires would complete reams of self-paced reading, then hop online for some Web-based training courses, which accounted for about 20 percent of their overall training. They did the rest of their learning in the classroom.

Although the training was effective and made good use of technology—US West is a telecommunications company, after all, and WBT was nothing new to them—Maul and her colleagues thought the current system could stand a little improvement. "We wanted to improve our new product training cycle time, and shorten the time between hiring and 100 percent job performance," Maul says.

In addition, they sought to shift the focus from training to performance. It's a subtle but important distinction—and one that many training experts believe is vital. When it comes right down to it, most companies don't really care about the training of their employees. Companies care about the performance of those employees, and training is a means to that end.

For Maul and her team, this subtle shift in focus meant aligning their objectives for a new training system with the overall business goals of US West. And that alignment, as any ROI guru will tell you, is gold when you're trying to open your company's purse strings. "It's not just about training," Thomas says. "We needed to find out what keeps people up at night, and then use training to fix it. We had to ask, 'How can we help you do your business better?'"

In the case of the retail marketing and sales division, people tossed and turned over new product training cycle time—or put more simply, how long it took employees to get up to speed on new products. The logical fix, as Maul's team saw it, was a training performance support tool.

"We sell hundreds of products and services," says Maul. "With this new system, employees have instant access to information about every one of them. It shows how each product works, how to sell it, and the technology behind it."

When Maul says "instant access," she means just that. "It's up and running in the background all the time," says Jones. For example, if employees are stumped by a customer question or need additional information during a sales call, they're only a keystroke away from the answer. Problem solved. Customer satisfied.

"When the employees are in training, they're also learning how to gain new information and knowledge quickly, and how to access it exactly when they need it," Jones says.

Get Out the Checkbook

This wasn't a system to be developed on a shoestring. To do it right, US West would have to spend $3 million. Half of that was spent on architecture, including servers, support and infrastructure. The other half covered the development of the programs themselves. Facing a multi-million dollar price tag, Maul and her team knew that solid ROI figures were mandatory.

"People will respond to a big investment if you show them a big return," says Thomas. Her team did just that. They included the usual ROI elements: savings on printing costs, decreased training time, less time away from the job, increased employee retention. But what's just as significant is what they didn't include. "We didn't use any estimates on increased sales results," she says. "We hoped the sales results would be better with this system, but we just didn't know."

Though Maul won't have the exact sales figures until quarter's end, she says sales are significantly higher now than before the knowledge management system came along. "That was just gravy," Thomas notes, with more than a hint of satisfaction in his voice.

Even without the figures from increased sales, the team estimates that the system will pay for itself within one year. That was through shortened cycle time and salary savings alone, says Maul. Along with those killer ROI figures, Maul and her team had something that is vital to any proposal. "These ideas have full CEO support," she notes. "US West believes that the Internet is the future."

Still, the idea of millions of dollars riding on this project was a bit daunting for the trio. "If you're going to propose a project like this," says Thomas, "you'd better make sure to deliver."

With the green light from above, Maul, Jones and Thomas put together a team to develop the system's heart and soul. They worked with outside vendors for multimedia production, but did the design themselves. The entire process took about a year.

"One thing you absolutely need for a project like this is one or two staff members

---

Sage Advice

To other trainers chomping at the bit to design their own knowledge management systems, the team at US West offers this advice:

- Don't attempt it without the resources. "Access to the necessary resources for a project like this is the most important thing," says David Thomas, training technology architecture manager. "It can only be accomplished with big, big resources. If you're going to build a 747, you need to be able to build the whole thing." In other words, if your company won't fork over the funds, forget it.
- Everything is harder than it seems. "Technology changes every few months," says Thomas. "It's like farming, really. You're never done."
- Market your efforts internally. "You constantly have to push the internal sell," says June Maul, senior regional director for retail markets knowledge and performance solutions. "If it's successful, communicate it. Show your results."
- Get strategic buy-in early. Involve key people in your efforts, and have them be your internal cheerleaders. "This is more than just slapping a module onto the intranet," says Maul. "You need to sell it from a strategic point of view. You must let people know it's the right thing to do, not because it's cool to use this technology, but because it's based on performance results and business strategy."
- Lose the training jargon. When you're in the midst of selling this project internally, don't use training lingo. Always use business terms and corporate vocabulary.

---

who really understand training technology," Maul says. "David and Jonathan were the instructional technologists. That allowed us—not the vendors—to be the experts."

And that was important to achieving the best result possible, Jones says, because these types of systems aren't simply about technology. For people to really use the system, it must be designed with the company's culture in mind. And outside vendors may not understand the subtle nuances of that culture.

Jones and his team have since created their own multimedia development group. "It helps to have people in place internally for maintenance, because the content changes quickly," he says. "It allows us to keep the information current."

The Result

The knowledge management system has been up and running for a few months—and according to Maul, team members couldn't be more pleased with their creation.

The system has shortened the length of new-hire training by 30 percent. In other words, employees are out of training and on the job 30 percent faster. Follow-up training is now 100 percent Web-based, and employees have instant access to information whenever they need it. Sales results are significantly higher, too. In addition, all of US West's paper-based training is now on the Web, eliminating those printing costs. Right now, 13,000 US West employees use the system, and it's on track to pay for itself within the year.

Next on the docket is live Web-based training to replace the company's satellite training. And remember Maul's goal of improving new product training cycle time? "Before, it took weeks and months," she says. "Now, it's a half hour."

Wendy Webb is a technology freelance writer in Duluth, Minn. She can be reached at wkwebb@bresnanlink.net.

Delivering Instruction at a Distance Using a Blended Approach: A Case Study in Higher Education

Simone Conceição-Runlee

In this original article, the author explains how her school, the University of Wisconsin-Milwaukee, developed its distance learning program and how it blends technology with classroom instruction.

I n the rapidly expanding and transforming world of higher education, the use of technology for instruction and training has become a challenge for colleges and universities that try to serve a changing learner population and workforce. In part these challenges have been due to the inability of higher education institutions to respond to change in a timely fashion (Duderstadt, 1999). Therefore, higher education is faced with pressure from a competitive market. This pressure has forced institutions to strategically rethink ways of delivering instruction.

Some of the approaches that have been used by colleges and universities to meet the market needs and maintain a competitive edge involve the creation of partnerships with other institutions, use of blended technologies, and development of unique curriculum to deliver instruction through collaboration. This case study describes a collaborative approach using blended technologies to successfully plan and implement a course at the higher education level. The case study illustrates the key issues related to the planning and implementation process of a distance education course using a blended approach, as well as the benefits and outcomes derived from it.

Setting the Stage

One of the needs identified for the development of an early childhood special education (ECSE) course focusing on children ages birth to eight with special needs and their families (Hains, Conceição-Runlee, Caro, & Marchel, 1999) was reaching learners in remote areas. The course involved six Wisconsin institutions of higher education, 12 faculty members, over 90 learners, and it was based on the idea that if one capitalizes on the collective expertise of a group of faculty from a variety of subjects within a field, learners in remote areas can be better served. These institutions created a partnership to provide undergraduate and graduate training to learners seeking ECSE certification.

This partnership was made successful through the use of blended technologies. Blended technologies means a combination of resources, the selection of the best technology to integrate with instruction. A blend of web-based, text-based, video-based, and Internet-based technologies were employed to design this course, to prepare faculty members for teaching, and to deliver instruction (Conceição-Runlee, Hains, Caro, Lehman, & Dewey, 1999).

Selecting the best technology for this course was not an easy task. It depended on factors such as time, funding, instructional technologies, and expertise. Time was an important issue because there was a deadline for promoting the course to perspective learners. Time was also a factor in planning the distance education course because it required lots of pre-planning. Funding was an important element for the success of this initiative because it was needed to pay for faculty time, videoconferencing connections, an instructional design consultant, and travel expenses. The availability of instructional technologies in each site was an important factor in selecting the appropriate medium of delivery. The six sites had to have compatible technologies. Expertise of an instructional designer was very important because it was the "power behind the wheel." The instructional designer facilitated every step of the planning and implementation phases.

Due to the collaborative nature of the initiative, learning how to use the technologies for instruction was part of the process. The outcomes of the project resulted in an environment where faculty learned how to teach with technology in a non-threatening way (Conceição-Runlee, Hains, Caro, Lehman, & Dewey, 1999).

The focus of the course development was not exclusively on the technology, rather the instructional strategies that were used with it. An important aspect of the blended technologies is to think in terms of efficiency, effectiveness, and appeal of each technology before making a decision.

In the ECSE course, each campus had at least one faculty member responsible for program development and implementation. Program development and implementation involved selecting the appropriate technology to meet the needs of the learners and match with the teaching style of the faculty members.

With the use of a blended approach to communication, faculty-developed course content, instructional strategies, and delivery methods during the planning phase. During the implementation phase, the course was delivered using video-based and Internet-based technologies. Blended technologies were used to assist in developing the course as a communication tool and to create interactivity among learners and instructors as a delivery tool.

Planning Phase

The instructional design process characterizes the planning phase. Planning involved making decisions about the methods of instruction that best fit the learners' knowledge and skills. During this phase, faculty interacted with each other via videoconferencing, telephone, and email technologies to define learner characteristics, identify the learning environment, develop course format and instructional strategies, create interactive activities, and determine course evaluation approaches (Conceição-Runlee, Hains, Caro, Lehman, & Dewey, 1999). The outcome of this phase was a blueprint of instruction, which included the content to be delivered, technology to be used, stategies and activities to be used, when to use them, and how to structure them (Newby, Stepich, Lehman, & Russell, 2000).

Throughout the planning phase, faculty members had to maintain a proactive position in the development of the course modules. For example, a course developed for a traditional format such as lecture may not be effective in a video or web-based format. Even though the course objectives may remain the same, the instructional strategies and learner activities are very different.

The first step in the course development was to select the core content areas to be addressed during the course. The next step was to divide faculty into small teams to work on specific topics. The content planning of each module involved collaborative decisions on the overall framework, scope, and sequence of the course (Conceição-Runlee, Hains, Caro, Lehman, & Dewey, 1999). After designing the course content, faculty determined the instructional strategies to be used with a specific technology. Table 1 provides the combination of instructional strategies and technologies used in the course. Tables 2 and 3 provide definitions for each strategy and technology.

Many of the formats and strategies used for each module were dependent on the development of visuals, their applicability to the technology in order to be effective for the learner, and the teaching style of the faculty member. Faculty members needed to know how to create and use visuals and the best way was to create a simulation of the instructional method by having faculty to participate in a real-life videoconferencing activity (Conceição-Runlee, Hains, Caro, Lehman, & Dewey, 1999).

The design of instruction is best described by the organization of the module structure. A module was comprised of a class session (two and a half hours of class meeting, 80 minutes via videoconferencing and the remainder face-to-face). Each module had specific components, including a course overview, readings, actions/protocol, and assignments. Figure 1 shows the general module schedule. Figure 2 provides an example of a module structure.

If you look at the sample module in Figure 2, you will see the module overview, the reading materials, the actions that took place during the videoconferencing session, and the assignments for the week following the videoconferencing meeting. In this module, a variety of strategies were used. Learners had to access the Electronic Reserve area of the University library to download course readings, visit web sites related to the module, participate in a two-way videoconferencing session, and post answers to discussion questions in the online forum entitled, "Early Brain Development Forum."

An instructional designer was hired as a consultant to develop the course web site and facilitate the design of each module by assisting faculty members with the selection of format and instructional strategies (Conceição-Runlee, Hains, Caro, Lehman, & Dewey, 1999).

Each module had an online discussion forum. The online discussion forums were part of the web-based management system "Web Course in a Box" and they were restricted to learners enrolled in the course and faculty. Since the time allocated for videoconferencing interaction was limited, the online forums provided an opportunity for learners to interact with each other and instructors outside the whole group meeting. Figure 3 shows how the online discussion forums were arranged.

Implementation Phase

The delivery of instruction characterizes the implementation phase. This was the time when instructors prepared the instructional materials, the learning environment, and the learners in order to proceed with the modules. Preparing the instructional materials involved selecting, modifying, and/or developing the materials for the modules in their final format. This required reserving the equipment and the facility in advance and gathering the materials. Preparing the learning environment involved setting up the videoconferencing unit and giving course participants access to restricted areas of the course web site. Preparing learners meant providing orientation on the use of the technologies, supplying an outline of the content, course activities, and other pre-instructional information (Newby, Stepich, Lehman, & Russell, 2000).

One or two faculty members performed the role of coordinators for each site. Proceeding with the modules every week required a set script to be followed by faculty members at all sites. The script contained the actions to be taken during a session and the handouts to be distributed to learners in class (description of the instructional activities, PowerPoint presentations, case studies, etc.). The script was located in a separate web site restricted to faculty in the discussion forum area of Web Course in a Box. The discussion forums were organized by module. Figure 4 shows the faculty discussion forum within Web Course in a Box.

1999 Seminar Modules		
Date	**Module**	**Faculty**
1/25/99	Orientation: Overview of course, introduction to field and classmates, hands-on experiences with technologies, discussion of structured observations using rating scales	Faculty Coordinator at each site and Instructional Designer
2/1/99	Legislation and Policy: IDEA and Welfare Reform	Team Leader, Faculty Contributor
2/8/99	Eligibility, Identification, and Assessment	Team Leader, Faculty Contributor
2/15/99	**Individual Study 1:** Structured observation using selected rating scale	Faculty Coordinator at each site
2/22/99	Families as Members of IFSP, Part 1	Team Leader
3/1/99	Families as Members of IFSP, Part 2	Team Leader
3/8/99	**Individual Study 2:** Projects and potential meetings at individual continuing education sites	Faculty Coordinator at each site
3/15/99	Recommended Practices and Curriculum	Team Leader, Faculty Contributors
3/22/99	Recommended Practices and Curriculum	Team Leader, Faculty Contributors
3/29/99	Early Brain Development	Team Leader, Faculty Contributors
4/5/99	**Individual Study 3**	Faculty Coordinator at each site
4/12/99	Data-Based Decision Making	Team Leader, Faculty Contributors
4/19/99	**Individual Study 4**	Faculty Coordinator at each site
4/26/99	Resources for Early Childhood Programs	Team Leader, Faculty Contributors
5/3/99	Project Presentations	Faculty Coordinator at each site
5/10/99	Project Presentations, Course Evaluation, and Final Comments	Faculty Coordinator at each site

Figure 1. Modules schedule

Early Brain Development

The Importance of the First Three Years of Life as Revealed by the Most Recent Research on the Brain

I. Overview

Due to advances in medical technology, far more is known about the activity of the brain than even five years ago. An avalanche of material is available focusing on the development of the brain during the first three years of life and the activation of sub-components of the brain in response to varying activities. In this session, information about the development milestones that have arisen as a result of this research will be described.

II. Readings

Gunnar, M. R. & Barr, R. G. (1998). Stress, early brain development and behavior. *Infants and Young Children*, 11(1), 1-14.

Mack, K. J. (1996). *Nature, nurture, brains and behavior.* Appeared in the World and I, The Washington Times Corporation.

Shore, R. (1997). *Rethinking the brain: New insights into early development*. New York: Families and Work Institute.

Electronic Reserve:

http://www.uwm.edu/Library/ERES/hains/360-589.html

Supplemental Readings:

Crook, G. (1998). Balanced beginnings. (http://www.unol.org).

Greenspan, S. I. (1998). *The growth of the mind: And the endangered origins of intelligence*. Reading, MA: Addison-Wesley Publishing.

I Am Your Child Campaign (1998). (http://www.iamyourchild.org).

Pribman, K. & Rozman, D. (1998). Early childhood development and learning: What new research on the heart and brain tell us about our youngest children. (http://www.web-com.com/hrtmath/IHM).

Ramsburg, D. (1997). Brain development in young children: The early years ARE learning years. (http://ericps.ed.uiuc.edu/npin/pnews).

Simmons, T. & Sheehan, R. (1998). *Too little, too late: The first years last forever*. (http://www.news-observer.com/2little2late).

Great Beginnings.

III. Actions

4:30 - 4:40 Introduction of guest speaker from Wisconsin Council on Children and Families

4:40 - 4:50 Give each student a small piece of playdoh. In small groups, students will respond to this question, "What are the qualities of elasticity found in your playdoh?"

4:50 - 5:30 Interview resumes

5:30 - 5:45 Question and answer period

5:45 - 5:50 Wrap up

5:50 - 6:00 Break

Figure 2. Example of a module

6:00 - 6:50 Discussion questions (see below) and possible visit to web sites

IV. Assignment

Discussion Questions

- Given research and knowledge base about brain development, how do you think early childhood interventionists should be integrating this information into their practice?
- What role do you think early interventionists can have involving the use of the latest brain research with the families who have children with special needs (already in birth to three, three to five, and five to eight year old programs) within their community?
- One could visit the web sites mentioned under supplemental readings.

Figure 2. (continued)

Spring, 1999 Exceptional Education 360-589 Section 001 Discussion Forums & Learning Links

Discussion Forums

01 Legislation & Policy Forum

02 Eligibility, Identification, & Assessment Forum

03 Families as Members of IFSP Forum

04 Recommended Practices & Curriculum Forum

05 Early Brain Development Forum

06 Data-Based Decision Making Forum

07 Resources for Early Childhood Programs Forum

08 Student Lounge

This forum is for you to share informal personal accounts, social events, and other information not essential to the class but of general interest to everyone.

09 On-line Help Desk

This forum is designed for you to post questions or comments on the use of the technologies used in this course (e.g., Web Course in a Box, compressed video, etc.)—what you like about it, how to use it, what you don't like about it.

Figure 3. Online discussion forums for learners (note: each listing is a link to forum)

During the implementation phase real-time communication was blended with delayed technology. Half of the course was done in two-way video format and the other half was done via email and asynchronous online discussions. Within a particular class module, technologies were combined. Learners used the course web site to download a case study before the class meeting. During the class meeting they discussed the case study in small groups at remote sites and presented the case study to the whole group via videoconferencing. The week following the class meeting, learners continued the discussion in the online discussion forum.

The role of the instructional designer was essential to keep the course operational.

Spring, 1999 Faculty Development 350-999 Section 001 Discussion Forums

Discussion Forums

Data-Based Decision Making (Access Restricted)

   The purpose of this forum is to discuss the Research Techniques and Efficacy of Instruction, Therapeutic Practice and Accountability Module.

Early Brain Development (Access Restricted)

   The purpose of this forum is to discuss the Medical and Technological Module.

Eligibility, Identification, and Assessment (Access Restricted)

   The purpose of this forum is to discuss the Eligibility, Identification, and Assessment Module.

Faculty Autobiography (Access Restricted)

   The purpose of this forum is to collect biographical information about faculty and staff members who are participating in this collaborative course.

IFSP & IEP Teams (Access Restricted)

   The purpose of this forum is to discuss the Families as Members of IFSP and IEP Teams, the Role of Special and General Educators Module.

Legislation & Policy (Access Restricted)

   The purpose of this forum is to discuss the Legislation & Policy Module.

Orientation

Recommended Practices & Curriculum (Access Restricted)

   The purpose of this forum is to discuss the Recommended Practices and Curriculum Module.

Resources for Early Childhood Programs (Access Restricted)

   The purpose of this forum is to discuss the Resources for Early Childhood Programs Module (including third-party payer concerns, relationship to policy, landcape of funding for early childhood and finance).

Figure 4. Online discussion forums for faculty (note: each item is a link to forum)

The instructional designer provided support, maintained the course web site, and gave constant feedback regarding the use of the instructional technologies and strategies for student learning throughout the course delivery.

   Using the blended approach demanded organization, clear instructions, and constant feedback to learners about the process (Newby, Stepich, Lehman, & Russell, 2000). As part of the evaluation of student learning, at the end of each module learners were asked to complete a learning journal. The learning journal asked learners to provide information about their understanding of the content along with questions that they still had about the module. This procedure was a way to assist faculty in tailoring the course to meet learners' needs and provide support to learners.

On a couple of occasions the technology failed in one or two sites for short periods of time. The technology failure did not affect the course delivery because instructors were prepared. They had a well thought out plan, even though establishing an environment for learning, maintaining learners' attention, questioning, providing feedback, and making smooth transitions were challenging (Newby, Stepich, Lehman, & Russell, 2000).

The best way to achieve success while increasing efficiency and effectiveness of the learning environment for the learners was to blend technologies by selecting the best tools and techniques for each learning situation. Looking back at the technologies selected for the ECSE course, videoconferencing was very intense and prescribed, while email provided flexibility. Even though videoconferencing provided the capability of two-way interaction, it was costly; conversely, the use of Internet-based tools was inexpensive.

The question still remains on which instructional method is the best and what technology is most effective when blended together. These are challenging questions. Live communication is no more effective than delayed communication. However, interaction is more effective than passive observation in learning. Thus it is the interactive nature of learning, not the live character of distance learning, that may be the key to learning. No matter how good the technology being used, learners still need a good instructor who can act as a guide, mentor, or facilitator.

The following box and table provide additional information for understanding blended training approaches.

Instructional Strategies: Definitions

Active Experimentation Learners conduct surveys; perform tests or experiments, site visits, etc.

Case Study Learners work through authentic or fictitious narratives of problems or situations, which require a variety of thinking skills to resolve.

Class Handouts Reading materials developed by the instructor to be distributed to learners.

Collaborative Learning Learners work together in groups to teach each other new material and produce group documents or projects, which may include group and individual assessment.

Colloquy is a technique in which experts interact with the audience.

Debates Learners are asked to take sides of an issue and argue for them; may include arguing against one's own point of view.

Guest Lecture Guests make presentations.

Interrupted Lecture Instructors regularly interrupt lecture to pose problems, encourage questions, ask for feedback; may involve learner-to-learner interaction.

Interviews Interrogators ask resource people for information.

Lecture/Mini-lecture Instructors make presentations. Mini-lectures are short presentations.

Peer Teaching Learners present information or lead discussion in class; may also involve peer critiquing.

Question and Answer Learners or instructors ask questions; answers may be individual/group, written/verbal.

Quizzes Instructors pose questions to learners, which require individual/group, written/verbal responses for evaluation purposes.

Role-playing, Performance Learners act out issues, positions, literature, etc., in order to demonstrate understanding of important concepts; also includes mock interview or clinical practice.

Simulations Learners work through "What if?" scenarios to practice formulating hypotheses and examining outcomes.

Small Group Discussion Learners work together in groups of 3-5 for a variety of purposes.

Instructional Technologies: Definitions

Course Web Site (http://www.uwm.edu/Dept/early-childhood/): Environment where text-based information about the course is available for faculty and learners.

Electronic Reserve (E-Reserve) Web-based environment that allows learners to use a computer to view or print course materials (lecture notes, journal articles and book chapters) that faculty have placed on the University Library Reserve area.

Electronic Mail (E-mail) Messages sent from one person to another via computer.

World Wide Web (WWW) Graphical interface to the Internet. It provides an orderly set of choices for navigating through Internet resources. A user may enter the Internet via a home page. The WWW has multimedia capabilities. It is best oriented to support multimedia files: sound, video, photos, and graphics.

Online Forum Bulletin board on the Internet using a web-based management tool where participants post a message and/or respond to messages posted by others.

Two-Way Videoconferencing Uses **ISDN** (**I**ntegrated **S**ervices **D**igital **N**etwork) telephone lines to send and receive sound and images. When sites are connected via videoconferencing technology, video and audio signals are changed so that they can be transmitted over the ISDN telephone lines by the CODEC (coder/decoder) device.

Videotape Storage of visuals and their display on a television screen.

Electronic Presentations Software designed to assist and enhance lecture presentations, outline lecture notes, etc. Examples of software programs include PowerPoint, ClarisWorks, Presentations, etc.

Instructional Strategies	Instructional Technologies							
	Course Web Site	Electronic Reserve	E-mail	WWW	Online Forums	2-way Videoconferencing	Video-tape	Electronic Presentations
Active Experimentation						✔	✔	
Case Study	✔			✔		✔	✔	
Class Handouts	✔	✔		✔				
Collaborative Learning			✔	✔	✔	✔	✔	
Colloquy						✔	✔	
Debates					✔	✔		
Guest Lecture					✔	✔		✔
Interrupted Lecture						✔		✔
Interviews			✔		✔	✔		
Lecture/Mini-lecture						✔		
Peer Presentation						✔		✔
Question and Answer			✔		✔	✔		
Quizzes			✔	✔				
Role-playing, Performance						✔		
Simulations						✔	✔	✔
Small Group Discussions					✔	✔		

Table 1. Matrix matching instructional strategies and instructional technologies

References

Conceição-Runlee, S., Hains, A., Caro, P., Lehman, R., & Dewey, B. (August, 1999). "Using a collaborative model of instructional design for the development of a distance education course and faculty training." 15th Annual Distance Teaching & Learning Conference. Madison, Wisconsin.

Duderstadt, J. J. (1999). "Can colleges and universities survive in the information age?" In Richard N. Katz & Associates, *Dancing with the Devil: Information Technology and the New Competition in Higher Education.* San Francisco: Jossey-Bass.

Hains, A. H., Conceição-Runlee, S., Caro, P., & Marchel, M. A. (1999). "Collaborative course development in early childhood special education through distance learning." *Early Childhood Research & Practice,* 1(1).

Newby, T. J., Stepich, D. A., Lehman, J., & Russell, J. D. (2000). *Instructional technology for teaching and learning: Designing instruction, integrating computers, and using media.* 2nd edition. Englewood Cliffs, New Jersey: Merrill.

Simone Conceição-Runlee is an instructional design/technology consultant for the University of Wisconsin-Milwaukee School of Education. She is co-author of 147 Practical Tips for Teaching Online Groups: Essentials of Web-Based Education. *You can reach her at simpass@uwm.edu.*

Video/Teleconferencing and Synchronous Techniques

Choosing a Synchronous Learning Solution

Jennifer Hofmann

Before choosing a synchronous learning product, take the time to analyze your needs, capabilities, and budget. This article gives you a heads-up on what to consider.

There are more than two dozen synchronous learning products on the market, and more coming out all of the time. Each has its own special features and limitations. How do you choose the package that is right for your organization? Make sure you have done your homework before inviting vendors to the table.

Your Assignment

Include the key players. A synchronous implementation will affect more than the training department. Make sure that the training, information technology, and content development areas are represented. You may also want to include members of your compliance, human resources, and marketing departments. And make sure the project sponsor is involved throughout the process.

Conduct an audience analysis. What is the makeup of your target audience? What's the mix of employees, customers, and partners? The answer to this question can affect your technology, support, and content decisions.

Conduct a technical analysis. Determine the minimum end-user platforms of your audience. Document Internet connectivity (dial-up, ISDN, T1), operating systems, standardized browsers, acceptable plug-ins, firewall configurations, and available onsite technical support. Synchronous applications have different hardware, software, and connectivity requirements—and some require substantial technical support. Knowing your limitations up front can help to identify the products to consider.

Determine the use of the software. Some products lend themselves to specific training situations, so you need to determine what you want to do. Will you be using your synchronous product for application training, soft-skill training, large group seminars, marketing announcements, workgroup collaboration, virtual consulting, or other tasks? Will you be teaching 10 people at a time or 100? Is it important that individuals be able to create virtual meeting rooms at their own discretion?

Determine the true budget. There is a lot more involved than the cost of software and IT hardware. Is your organization willing to dedicate bandwidth, invest in audio/visual equipment, and train trainers and technical support staff? Content will need to be redesigned. Are those resources available? The reason some implementations fail is the lack of understanding of the true cost of implementation.

Determine the capability or desire to manage the technology. Do you want to manage the technology yourself, or do you want to outsource such things as software hosting, content development, and registration?

Discuss portability. Are you willing to change software providers as technology advances, or do you want your first tool to be your last tool? If you are open to change, who will be responsible for monitoring the industry?

Identify where synchronous fits in your training mix. Is the synchronous component part of a larger portal or virtual university initiative? Find out what knowledge management, asynchronous, and Web-based tools are being used across your organization so you can be sure of compatibility and integration later on.

Discuss desired features. Create a matrix of synchronous features. With your team, make "Must Have," "Nice To Have," and "Don't Want" determinations. Identify what you might use each feature for, and create a short business case for your results. Knowing this up front will keep you getting lost in a bells and whistles pitch when attending software demonstrations.

If you do the research up front, you will be armed with the information you need to make the right choice for your organization, for now and for the future.

Jennifer Hofmann is the principal of InSync Training Synergy (www.insynctraining.com), which provides consulting services to organizations interested in adopting synchronous WBT. She currently teaches the Certified Online Instructor program for the Walden Institute for Learning and Leadership. She can be reached at jennifer@insynctraining.com.

Making Synchronous Training a Success

Jennifer Hofmann

How do you prepare to conduct a live training session over the Internet? This article by synchronous learning expert Jennifer Hofmann offers some do's and don'ts for organizations interested in applying the technology.

For many organizations, synchronous Web-based training (WBT) is the killer app that balances their self-paced online learning with the benefits of classroom instruction. But before jumping headlong into using a synchronous application, it's worth doing some homework to ensure that it's the right fit for your needs.

First, how do you distinguish synchronous delivery from other forms of WBT? Here are some basic working definitions.

- Self-paced WBT is learner-directed and not conducted in real time.
- Asynchronous WBT is facilitator-directed, but not conducted in real time.
- Synchronous WBT is facilitator-directed and is conducted in real time.

The next issue involves determining when it's appropriate to use synchronous WBT. Typically, synchronous tools make sense when

- real-time interaction with instructors or subject-matter experts is critical
- face-to-face interaction is not critical
- your audience is geographically dispersed
- you must ensure that participants complete the training and grasp key learning concepts

- you need to update your workforce quickly or frequently (for instance, for new product releases).

When putting together your implementation plan, you should think of additional uses for synchronous technology. For example, you can implement a synchronous technology to

- supplement self-paced training (WBT or otherwise)
- implement a cyber-mentoring program
- boost your help-desk efficiency and reach
- implement a cyber-consulting initiative.

Who Needs to Be Involved?

Once you've done some research, you'll find that synchronous software vendors use television and radio metaphors to define their products. Terms like "on-air" and "passing the microphone" are common.

Indeed, a synchronous class should be treated as a live broadcast event. We need to coordinate remote participants, various media (video, audio, graphics), technology, facilitators, sponsors, and, of course, content. Ask any television producer if this model seems familiar.

Figure 1 illustrates the roles involved in getting a live learning event on-air.

The project manager, often an instructional designer, is responsible for the content, participant materials, rollout schedule, trainer selection, and working with SMEs, project sponsors, and content developers to ensure that learning and business objectives are met. The project manager also manages the project budget and timeline. In short, the project manager is responsible for making sure the project goals are identified and met.

The producer, often someone skilled in IT implementations, is responsible for making sure the trainers and technical support team are trained from a software perspective. The producer assists participants in setting up, testing, and troubleshooting the synchronous software prior to the live event and manages the technical-support process during the event. The producer also manages registration. In sum, the producer is responsible for making the live event work.

In most instances, members of the project team will juggle multiple roles. The producer might be the registrar and technical-support manager, and the project manager might also be the SME and trainer. The critical point is that a team member be assigned to play each role represented by the model.

The success of this model hinges on the relationship between the producer and the project manager. The project manager needs to communicate any special needs (required plug-ins, connectivity limitations, and so forth), and the producer is responsible for the technical implementation of these requirements. Working together, the producer and project manager can ensure a successful learning event.

Figure 1. People who need to be involved in a live event

Things to Consider

Following is a checklist of issues to consider when creating your online content and your project plan.

How Will You Design Your Program?

Use instructional design. Always review your goals and performance objectives. Ask, "Can these objectives be met in an online format?"

Plan your program. Create a detailed instructor plan that includes instructional strategies, helpful anecdotes, and other pertinent information. Remember that there is a lot to manage in a synchronous session, and you need to be prepared.

Maximize your use of the technology. Use asynchronous methods for "content dumps," and use valuable synchronous time for collaboration, problem solving, case studies, and role-playing.

Extend the classroom experience. Maximize your online time by scheduling chunks of learning before and after the real-time event. Stress to your participants that pre-work is essential.

Maximize interactivity. Design interactive exercises based on the desired performance outcome. If the objective calls for the ability to interact with a customer, then a customer situation should be modeled and practiced.

Design with available tools in mind. There are many tools available via the Internet that aren't available in the traditional classroom. Learn what they are, and use a variety of them.

Vary your instructional strategies. Try different approaches to maximize engagement. A one-hour lecture is not a good use of synchronous applications.

Select your first training course carefully. The first course should be information that's of interest to a large group, but not mission-critical. New users will likely be fascinated by the technology and distracted from the content.

Design breaks in the program. We recommend a 10-minute break for a 90-minute program.

Keep it human. Make sure the design doesn't imply that you are taking people out of the process. Learning is a social activity, and participants benefit from a personal touch. What type of media should you use?

Build for the content, not the technology. It's tempting to use all the bells and whistles available, but if the media does not support the goal and objectives, it may be superfluous and distracting.

Know and design for your technical environment. Conduct a technical audit ahead of time. Who is your audience? What's the connection speed? Are plug-ins allowable? Are there firewall issues? The best program can be a flop if your audience cannot easily use the content.

Create a storyboard. Use a detailed storyboard to communicate with your graphic designer. Don't miss deadlines because of insufficient planning.

Get collateral material ahead of time. If logos, corporate colors, video clips, or other materials are required, provide them to the graphic artist with the storyboard.

Make it visual. Too much text can be tedious, and your participants will tune out. Take advantage of color, graphics, sound, animation, and other media when you can.

Don't let the graphic artist manage the program. Remember that this is a learning initiative—not a commercial Website. The instructional designer needs to stay in control of the content and interface design.

Keep up with changes. In the world of online training, the media used to deliver or enhance the online class changes frequently. It's up to the designer to stay in touch with those changes and incorporate them when they would enhance the learning experience. And it's up to the online instructor to utilize the changing media to enrich the instruction.

What Do You Need to Know About Online Facilitation?

Participate before you facilitate. Anyone expected to facilitate or train in a synchronous WBT environment should first experience a synchronous event as a participant. Doing so provides needed perspective for the facilitator that will aid in his or her turn at the controls.

Be an advocate. Virtual classroom instructors must support the initiative and be advocates within the organization. If the instructors don't like their new roles, the participants will know it, and the success of the initiative will suffer.

Practice, practice, practice. Don't try a synchronous session without a rehearsal or two.

Learn the technology. Provide ample time and resources for the instructors to learn how to manage the technology in a low-risk situation.

Keep tuned in to the participants. In order for learning to stay active, listen and "feel" for the atmosphere of the participants. Just because eye contact and body language aren't available doesn't mean the participants are not sending signals. Avoid letting the session become a passive experience for learners.

Prompt some form of interaction every 3 to 5 minutes. From raising hands, to talking, to chatting, to asynchronous exercises—connect with your audience as often as possible.

Record questions that are asked in the session's chat function. To make sure you get back to everyone with complete answers, have participants log questions in the chat room and save the chat file for later reference. Remember that spelling doesn't count in a chat!

Use a teaching assistant. An assistant can help participants with technical issues, monitor chat rooms, and assist subject matter experts. How can you take advantage of collaboration tools?

Collaborate. Online learning is a collaborative event. In a live environment, participants should be encouraged to interact with each other and view each other as resources.

Encourage coaching. Set up classrooms where employees can coach each other, practice important presentations, and discuss work issues.

Expand the virtual classroom model. Use synchronous tools for sales meetings, workgroups, company announcements, and whatever else you can dream up.

What Pedagogy Applies?

Apply pedagogical theories to synchronous class design; it's a must. Recognize your audience and specific learning styles and set goals and objectives to meet those learning styles and ensure the successful design of an online class.

Be judicious with live time; it's at a premium. Decide in the design phase which exercises can be asynchronous, or self-paced, in nature.

Keep it active. Synchronous delivery lends itself to a constructivist mode. While instructive methods are sometimes appropriate, remember to keep the learning active.

Apply the tenets of adult learning theory and accelerated learning. What technology issues do you need to consider?

Watch out for firewalls. Firewall issues can bring the best program to a dead stop. Application sharing and other features often cannot be managed through a firewall without working with the technical support staff ahead of time.

Do a tech check prior to each session. If you can ensure that the participants' technology works prior to the program, it will make the experience better for everyone.

Check audio at the beginning of each program. Even if you implemented a tech check, you should perform an audio check prior to each class.

See biography for Jennifer Hofmann on page 147.

A Glossary of Synchronous Tool Features

Jennifer Hofmann

This is our third piece by Jennifer Hofmann. Here she provides more background on what's involved in setting up synchronous Web-based training. This is a kind of glossary, but in addition to definitions, it includes questions to ask about these tools when considering them and what their best uses are.

Synchronous Web-based training features mean different things depending on which vendor you're talking with. What follows are some cold, hard definitions—and questions to ask to make sure a synchronous product does what you want it to.

Attending a synchronous classroom software demonstration can be exciting—and overwhelming. Software vendors razzle and dazzle prospects by demonstrating feature after feature. Some features are ubiquitous across various products; others are unique. But, even those that are common don't work the same way from product to product.

For example, in some synchronous products, learners and instructor can use a whiteboard at the same time. In others, only one person can or only an instructor can access it. All of these products can accurately claim they have whiteboard capabilities. It's up to you to ask the right questions that get to the heart of each feature.

The list below defines major features of synchronous training packages and offers some questions you might want to ask a vendor. It also suggests some instructional uses for each feature that you may not have thought about.

Audio

The most common synchronous medium. One-way or two-way audio is available in most synchronous packages. It can be delivered via the Internet (VOIP) or by a phone bridge (audioconferencing).

Questions to Ask
- Is it one-way or two-way audio?
- Is the audio unicast (slower), multicast (faster), or can you alternate between these modes?
- Can the instructor and learner speak privately?

Instructional Uses and Methods
- Use audio like you do in a classroom. Lectures, group discussions, and Q&A sessions are all effective in a synchronous classroom—once facilitation techniques are mastered.
- The instructor's voice is perhaps the most important content delivery method available in a synchronous classroom. Instructors should be cautious about depending too much on technology-based tools.

Text-Based Chat

Another avenue for interaction among and between participants and an instructor. Private messaging allows learners to signal difficulties without disrupting a session. Chat dialogues can be saved for future reference.

Questions to Ask
- Can learners send private notes to the instructor? To other learners?
- Can the chat be saved?
- Can chat be disabled by an instructor during a session?

Instructional Uses and Methods
- Participants who are shy and reserved are more likely to interact when text chat options are available.
- Questions can be "parked" to be answered later during or after class. Brainstorming sessions can be conducted and the results saved for later use.
- A technical support person can monitor the chat to identify and fix technical problems without interrupting the class.
- A subject matter expert can monitor a classroom in order to answer content-related questions that may be out of the scope of the current lecture.
- Independent or group exercise instructions can be pasted into a chat area for students to review during an exercise.

Breakout Room

Feature that allows individuals or small groups to share information in a larger synchronous session.

Questions to Ask
- Is there a limit to the number of breakout rooms?
- What features (whiteboards, application sharing, and so forth) are available in breakout rooms?
- What results of a breakout session (a whiteboard, for example) can be shared with an entire class?
- Can breakout rooms be set up ahead of class and assigned separate content modules?

Instructional Uses and Methods
- Breakout rooms are ideal for training sessions in which separate teams or groups can share specific content.
- Students can be assigned to individual breakout rooms in order to complete a self-paced exercise or assessment.
- Team competitions can be conducted.
- The instructor can work with groups or individuals on an as-needed basis.
- Different groups can work with different content or on different exercises.
- If there are differing levels of expertise in a class, a program can be divided and different instructors can moderate the breakout rooms.

Shared Whiteboard

The synchronous equivalent of a traditional flipchart, allowing instructors and participants to post ideas. Images can be placed on prepared whiteboards ahead of time or pasted on the fly.

Questions to Ask
- Is the whiteboard object-oriented?
- Can learners write on the whiteboard?
- Can multiple people write on the whiteboard simultaneously?
- What whiteboarding tools are available to the instructor and students?
- Can whiteboards be created ahead of time?
- Can whiteboard results be saved for later use in class?
- Can graphics be pasted or imported to the whiteboard? What graphic formats are acceptable?

Instructional Uses and Methods
- Use a whiteboard for anything you would use a flipchart or marker board in a traditional classroom setting.
- Expectations can be captured at the beginning of a class and revisited at the end of the program.
- Content changes and additions can be captured and used to revise the program.
- The instructor can capture participant ideas flipchart-style.
- Whiteboards can often be archived for reuse in asynchronous applications or emailed to class participants.
- Content can be highlighted as it's discussed—making lectures more meaningful.
- Icebreakers and games can be created using the whiteboard.

Survey/Poll

A quick way to check the pulse of the class. These can be true and false, multiple-choice, or other formats.

Questions to Ask
- Can questions be created ahead of time and sequenced into the agenda?
- Can questions be created on the fly?
- Can the results be shared with the class? Can they be displayed graphically (bar or pie charts)?

- Can the instructor identify how individual users answered a question during a live class?
- Are results archived in a database for later review?

Instructional Uses and Methods

- Use surveys to determine whether the students comprehend the material, and to keep them tuned in to the lesson.
- Use surveys to switch to a new topic.
- Create icebreakers and introductory exercises by polling the audience.
- Share results with the class to foster a sense of community.

Pacing/Comprehension

Element that allows students to continually appraise the instructor on the pace and clarity of the content.

Questions to Ask

- Is this feature available to students at all times or must it be prompted by the instructor?
- How is this feature accessed?
- Is feedback confidential?

Instructional Uses and Methods

- Asking users to provide feedback will act as a re-engagement technique if the instructor feels the audience isn't participative.
- Anonymous feedback allows the students to be honest without being concerned with repercussions.
- If the instructor is not comfortable with receiving and responding to constant feedback, this feature should be introduced slowly.

Evaluation

Feature that helps an instructor conduct pre- and post-session assessments and tests, the results of which can be automatically tabulated and saved.

Questions to Ask

- What type of evaluation questions can be created?
- Can evaluations be graded as tests?
- How are saved results reported? (Ask to see a sample report.)
- Can the instructor see the evaluation results while a class is in session?
- Can evaluation results be shared with the class?

Instructional Uses and Methods

If these built-in solutions aren't robust enough, savvy users can create assessments in HTML and post them to participants over the application window.

Video

One-way or two-way video (live or canned) offered as an option by more sophisticated synchronous applications. It's the most bandwidth- and technology-intensive tool, limiting its use to audiences with broadband connections. The exception is the use of streaming media in one-way video configurations, which can be fed to participants on connections as slow as 56 Kbps.

Questions to Ask
- Is the live video one-way or two-way?
- How much bandwidth is required for live video?
- How and where is the live video shown on the student screen?
- What are the hardware and software requirements for live video?
- In what formats can prerecorded video be created?
- What are the hardware and software requirements for prerecorded video?

Instructional Uses and Methods
- Use live video for Q&A sessions in which the instructor can look directly at the camera.
- Using live video throughout an entire session can be very distracting—design your content (voice, media, application tours) to be the focus of the program.
- If face-to-face interactions are critical, consider using a traditional teaching approach.

Discussion Board
An asynchronous feature of some synchronous products.

Questions to Ask
- Are discussion boards integrated into the product, or are they a separate Website?
- Can discussion boards be accessed outside of class?
- Can discussions from one class be imported into another?
- Can multiple learners use discussion boards simultaneously during a live session?

Instructional Uses and Methods
- Discussion boards are used to post class information, FAQs, pre- or post-session assignments, SME insights, and other information relevant to the synchronous session.
- For multi-session classes, encourage use of the discussion area to stimulate knowledge sharing and community building. The instructor needs to stay involved to make sure this is successful.
- Often, classes that include such asynchronous activities as discussion boards and short synchronous online sessions are more effective than using just one delivery methodology.

Application Sharing
Feature that allows an instructor to share software applications (such as spreadsheets) with participants using a synchronous application. There are many varieties of this feature, ranging from "view only" on the client side to the ability of learners to upload and use applications from the synchronous tool server.

Questions to Ask
- Are there any restrictions on what type of applications can be shared?

- Can multiple applications be shared at the same time?
- Can users share an application?
- Can students access a shared application?
- What are the bandwidth requirements for application sharing?
- Is there a maximum number of users that can participate in an application-sharing session?

Instructional Uses and Methods

- Use application sharing to demonstrate software features.
- Small groups can collaborate by sharing common office software packages.
- Individuals can be walked through software packages with which they're having difficulty.
- Individuals can use shared applications in breakout rooms if they have that software installed on their individual computer. The instructor can then privately assist individuals with assigned exercises.

Synchronized Web Browsing

Element that allows instructors or participants to bring the class to the Internet site or corporate intranet. A variation of the feature allows the use of browsers to run short, self-paced exercises as part of a synchronous session.

Questions to Ask

- Is synchronized browsing a separate feature, or part of application sharing?
- Can a learner bring the class to a Website?
- Once the instructor brings the class to a site, can participants navigate the links independently?
- Can bookmarks be created prior to class to speed navigation?
- Does this function require a specific browser?

Instructional Uses and Methods

- Instead of re-creating content that already exists, instructors can use the Internet or corporate intranet as a content source.
- Students can share related content by leading the class to a Website.
- Independent exercises can be initiated for the entire group—including Web-enabled, self-paced exercises created in authoring applications.
- Last-minute content can be added to an existing program by placing it on the Web.

Record/Playback

Feature that allows the instructor and student to record synchronous events, play them back later, and edit them into asynchronous sessions. This feature benefits individuals who miss sessions and allows quick creation of asynchronous training content.

Questions to Ask

- Are chat messages (public and private) saved with the recording?
- Are breakout-room interactions recorded?

- Are recordings editable?
- Is client software required to view the recordings?

Instructional Uses and Methods

- Instructors can use the Record/Playback feature to practice and review their performance.
- New instructors can preview existing programs in order to familiarize themselves with the content.
- Learners can use recordings to preview or review course material.
- If a student misses a session from a multisession offering, he or she need not miss the content.
- This is a relatively inexpensive way to create self-paced "videotaped" classes.

Assistant Instructor

Feature that allows a second individual to take some of the burden of facilitating a synchronous session. Assistant instructors don't need to be at the same location as the instructor, but they use an instructor version of the application to conduct various tasks—from technical support to helping field questions.

Questions to Ask

- How many assistant instructors can be used at one time?
- Do assistants need to be identified ahead of time?
- What can a lead instructor do that an assistant can't do (create breakout rooms, launch applications, and so forth)?
- Can an assistant receive private chat messages usually sent to the instructor?

Instructional Uses and Methods

- The assistant instructor is the perfect role for an instructor in training. He or she can participate as a student and assist the instructor at the same time.
- If there's a subject matter expert involved in the delivery, he or she can manage the assistant role and take some of the pressure off of the lead instructor by answering chat questions and providing lecture assistance.
- If you have a special guest instructor that doesn't know how to manage a synchronous classroom, the lead instructor can facilitate the discussion and manage the technology while the guest acts as the assistant and leads the discussion.

Content

Common to all synchronous applications, content windows are used by instructors to display content in HTML, PowerPoint, or other Web-ready media. Some products limit the types of file formats that can be displayed via content windows.

Questions to Ask

- Can content be added on the fly?
- What type of content can be used (HTML, for example)?
- How are plug-ins managed?

Instructional Uses and Methods

- Remember that synchronous classrooms are a very visual medium. What's shown in the content area needs to be relevant and engaging.
- Don't include slides that the instructor will read verbatim. If that's the nature of the content, consider an asynchronous or self-paced delivery method.
- Use multiple media types when it makes sense—not just to use them. Remember that every time you add a new technology, you are also adding a potential technical obstacle.

One final, critical issue to consider when evaluating synchronous applications is the number of learners the system can accommodate. Some tools, like InterVu's NetPodium, are designed for one-way streaming of audio and video to an audience of hundreds; others use more interactive two-way audio and video features but are more limited in the number of users.

See biography for Jennifer Hofmann on page 147.

Online Learning Goes Synchronous

Tom Barron

A surge of technologies that allow trainers to conduct "virtual classes" over the Web—at a fraction of the cost of previous systems—is expanding WBT in bold new directions. This article explains these expansions and changes.

J ust when you were getting used to the idea of Web-based training (WBT), with its easy content distribution, electronic bulletin boards, and self-paced learning model, the Web's technological juggernaut has thrown the workplace learning field a new curve: synchronicity.

The ability to join instructor and remote learners together in a virtual classroom, which called for custom hardware and pricey satellite network services scarcely two years ago, has become the training field's equivalent of the iMac. An explosion of synchronous developers, some with satellite-based videoconferencing credentials, others tracing their roots to collaborative computing technology, and still others attacking the market with freshly minted streaming-media technologies, are converging on the learning arena with unprecedented ardor. The swelling number of products, combined with steady Web technology advances leveraged over standard PCs and Web browsers, are pushing costs of synchronous WBT within reach of mainstream training organizations.

Another driver: the standard learning-software business model, in which training organizations purchase software licenses and product support, is being joined by a new approach in which developers or third parties provide WBT hosting services, extending the technology's reach to less sophisticated users.

The pace at which these developments are occurring has astounded WBT enthusiasts and industry analysts alike.

"It's huge, absolutely huge," says Cushing Anderson, a senior market analyst who tracks development of learning technologies for technology research firm International Data Corporation (IDC). He's referring not to the current size of the synchronous market, but its potential to become a major form of online learning over the next few years.

"It's gone from 'unmeasured' to a large blip on the radar screen practically overnight," says Anderson, adding that IDC has only just begun to focus on the synchronous segment.

"We don't have numbers yet, but we expect it to be the hottest growth area for Web-based training," he says.

David Collins, who heads a consulting practice specializing in synchronous WBT, says his years working for one synchronous developer, LearnLinc, gave him an inkling of the technology's potential. But even he admits surprise at the swift growth of the synchronous market. "It's moved from potential to reality with incredible speed," he says. Bandwidth issues that seemed a significant hindrance to the technology are evaporating both from growing availability of broadband networks and from advances in using streaming media for slow Internet connections, he notes.

Growing, too, is the sophistication of trainers researching synchronous technologies, says Collins. "The technology has such a huge 'wow factor' that people used to want to buy the first product they saw. Now when they approach me, they say they've got specific return-on-investment goals and want help narrowing down the choices," he says.

But the technology's appeal has thrown many training organizations into a tizzy. "What I see happening all too often is that the sales function will jump all over it—they can see the ROI and they have the money to spend. So they buy a [synchronous] product without even inviting training to the party—then ask training to help implement it," says Lillian Swider, a training technology consultant based in Cranford, New Jersey.

Like all technologies that are being harnessed for learning, synchronous WBT products typically call for a healthy dose of collaboration with in-house information technology (IT) expertise. "Unless you're talking about having it hosted for you, you need to approach these tools strategically, with IT's support," says Swider.

A bewildering array of products that span every niche from full-on videoconferencing to simple text-based chat make wading into synchronous WBT especially daunting. What used to be a fairly simple analysis—Can we afford two-way videoconferencing or not?—has turned into a game of matching the right technology to current and forecasted training needs.

Technology Underpinnings

It's the combination of several technologies that is fueling the push into synchronous WBT delivery. But a key driver is a move away from proprietary hardware and software to the Windows/Intel platform, which has cut the costs of synchronous systems dramatically. New systems are all designed to function on a PC, with little to no additional hardware outside the addition of a sound card. Most call for a Pentium chip and room on the hard drive, an issue only for organizations more than a generation or two behind current processor speeds.

Most synchronous products are also designed to run over a standard Web browser and make use of its Java capabilities for various functions. And the majority are written to function on either of the two dominant browser platforms. A small handful continue to use a proprietary software application.

Beyond those platform standards, four core Web technologies are behind the growth of synchronous WBT tools. They include the following:

Voice-Over-IP (VOIP), which allows audio to run over the same pipelines as Internet data, enabling one-way or two-way voice interaction among users. While some synchronous products continue to use a separate phone line for two-way audio (known as an audio bridge), more are taking advantage of the cost savings of VOIP. Labeled a "pivotal technology" for the growth of the Web by IDC, several versions of the technology are being employed by synchronous vendors. The speed with which standards are minted for VOIP will be a key factor in the technology's growth, according to IDC.

Streaming Media, which allows audio, video, and other data to be delivered in a continuous flow to an end-user's PC. The technology allows large data files to be streamed to end users on lower-bandwidth connections, a key requirement in making synchronous WBT available to target audiences in the field. A handful of competing technologies led by RealNetworks' RealPlayer and Microsoft's Windows Streaming Media provide the ability to stream synchronous data to multiple users.

Document Sharing, which allows multiple users to view and/or edit the same documents in real time. The contribution of collaborative software or "groupware," these tools provide the platform for content used in synchronous training.

Text-Based Chat, which allows users to share their thoughts during a session, or in some implementations, send private messages to the instructor.

In various combinations, these technologies form the basis for new synchronous WBT systems. And the degree of emphasis on one or more of these tools often forms the paradigm that synchronous products use to distinguish themselves. For instance, NetPodium, described by its developers as a Webcasting product, makes use of one-way streaming audio and video together with document viewing to provide a presentation to participants; their link back to the instructor is limited to text-based chat. The product follows a talk-show paradigm, allowing polling of participants—with lightning-fast results displayed in the application's document window.

Other products emphasize the two-way audio capabilities provided by VOIP or a separate audio-conferencing line, which allows the instructor to ask questions and engage in dialogue with individual participants in a traditional classroom paradigm. Systems from Centra Software and Interwise, neither of which provide video capabilities, are examples of the approach.

High-end systems provide the full suite of capabilities, including two-way video that allows participants to see the instructor or other participants. Such high-bandwidth implementations call for broadband connections among all participants, although some products allow those on slower connections to participate without bandwidth-gobbling video.

Other features offered include the ability to record, edit, and repackage synchronous sessions for asynchronous playback (so much for skipping class); a button that allows participants to notify the instructor when they must step away without interrupting the class; and breakout rooms where participants can share information—or gossip—as the class progresses.

In all synchronous products, the instructor and/or assistants use an enabled version of the tool that gives them the control needed to conduct the session. Their end, also PC-based, may call for a PC or two and multiple monitors to keep things flowing.

Of course, a hefty serving of back-office requirements—enough to mesmerize many an IT manager—are needed to cast a synchronous spell. Consultants agree that putting those items in place is not for IT rookies. "Let's just say they're getting a little easier to configure," quips Collins.

Bandwidth Solutions

Bandwidth limitations have been among the biggest obstacles to synchronous WBT, which inherently calls for moving large amounts of data between instructor and participants. The problem is being addressed on two fronts. Gains in compression technologies for video and audio together with clever streaming methods are allowing synchronous products to function over dialup connections as slow as 28.8 Kbps.

At the same time, broadband services, including digital subscriber line (DSL), cable-modem services, and home satellite connections are allowing more users to connect to high-speed Internet services.

Both developments are seen as critical for synchronous WBT, because a dominant audience for WBT is sales staff and field personnel that often use dial-up connections.

"One of our criteria was that if we couldn't do it through a regular phone line, it wasn't a solution," says Rick Huber, manager of learning technologies for GE Medical Systems, Waukesha, Wisconsin. Huber has tested a variety of systems over the past four years as capabilities have evolved; the organization currently uses a DataBeam system and an audio bridge to conduct synchronous training of its 5,000 field workers.

Though most of its field force is able to connect to GE's intranet at speeds of 56 Kbps, Huber says actual transmission speeds often hover "in the mid-30s."

"We have to design our materials to be very low in bandwidth," he says of documents that are shared over the system. "We're looking forward to the day when everyone has access to higher speed connections."

"As high-bandwidth networks continue to grow and are linked with intranets that already have high-bandwidth capabilities, we'll be able to take advantage of enhanced services such as video," says Eric Newman, former product manager for DataBeam who now represents Lotus collaboration products. "There's a tremendous amount of movement toward that goal," he adds.

Synchronous WBT products differ widely in the size of the software application required by end-users. The more complex products that feature two-way VOIP audio, video, or document sharing are typically large, "thick-client" applications of 10 MB or more. On the other end of the spectrum are thin-client applications that rely on one-way (instructor-to-student) audio, two-way text-based chat, and Java-based controls. Many of these sleeker client-side applications can be downloaded over a dial-up connection in minutes.

Sorting Synchronous Options

A question consultants increasingly hear is how to choose among a broad array of synchronous WBT products, no two of which offer the same suite of capabilities. Where a handful of companies offered custom hardware-based systems a few years ago, more than a dozen now offer PC-based synchronous learning products. Synchronous veterans including One Touch Systems and Arel Communications have shifted from proprietary hardware to the desktop, joining a crop of Web-savvy upstarts that include Centra Software, Horizon Live Distance Learning, Interwise, Intervu, and Liveware5, to name just a few. With the exception of Interwise, which dates its origins to 1994, the bulk of these Web-based synchronous providers are less than three years old.

Software developers from other arenas, including collaboration software maker Lotus Development Corporation, which last year acquired DataBeam, have also entered the synchronous learning field. And rumors continually swirl over an expected move by Microsoft into the synchronous arena.

The crowded field has analysts predicting consolidation in the long term, though how large the synchronous market will grow before then is anybody's guess. "At this point, it seems that the sky's the limit," says Collins.

One likely scenario is the folding of synchronous capabilities into larger learning-management systems (LMS) that allow electronic management of online and classroom training. That's the tack being taken by Lotus, which acquired Macromedia's Pathware LMS division last year and is expected to release an integrated synchronous/asynchronous/LMS system early this year. The latest version of LearnLinc's synchronous product, released late last year, also includes LMS features. Other products currently lack the assessment and reporting features that are among the chief benefits of asynchronous WBT.

"That's the logical next step—the addition of these feedback tools that indicate more than simply whether someone has taken a class," notes IDC's Anderson.

In the meantime, consultants suggest that organizations study how they might want to incorporate synchronous WBT into their repertoire of delivery options.

"Identify the key players—which of course includes IT—and bring them together to find out what major obstacles need to be overcome," says Swider, principal of LLS Associates. "You want an integrated strategy—not different departments going off on their own," a situation she says she encounters far too often.

How quickly the training community adopts synchronous tools remains to be seen, but vendors and consultants say interest is skyrocketing. Large organizations with distributed workforces have begun incorporating synchronous delivery; firms from Ernst & Young to Aetna U.S. Healthcare to Raytheon are reporting good results.

And training providers are also harnessing synchronous delivery to offer training to corporate clients and free agent learners. IT training provider Global Knowledge Network recently launched a synchronous IT training program that uses Centra's product, and UNext.com, which provides Web-based financial training, is using Lotus LearningSpace in a similar manner. FlightSafety Boeing Training International recently piloted a system by Liveware5 for its aircraft-maintenance training services.

"ROI data and anecdotal accounts are beginning to come in on these tools, and that's going to fuel investigation by more organizations," predicts Anderson. "It's going to be a big year for synchronous."

Tom Barron is editor of Learning Circuits *(tbarron@astd.org).*

Part Three

State of the Art: Corporate Distance Learning

D istance learning now appears in nearly every venue that involves the delivery of instruction, whether for practical skills or basic knowledge. Certainly distance learning is increasingly popular in private enterprise as an effective and economical training method. The purpose of Part Three is to examine in some detail how distance learning is being implemented and used in corporations today. To do so, we've selected seven articles that examine this methodology from different perspectives.

To start this part, we have two pieces from a special section in *Forbes* that was devoted to e-learning. The first, "Corporate Drivers of E-Learning," is brief but makes the point that distance and e-learning are a less expensive yet still sound way to deliver training, especially when employees are in many different locations. The second, "Corporate E-Learning Economies," documents in some detail, with specific company examples, the economic benefits of e-learning over more traditional training approaches.

We next include e-learning pioneer Brooke Broadbent's helpful "Tips to Help Decide if Your Organization Is Ready for E-Learning." You have to think carefully about how and whether e-learning is appropriate for your organization. This article lays out several factors to consider in making this determination.

The American Industrial Hygiene Association (AIHA) is just one of hundreds of professional organizations that offer their members training. This article documents AIHA's approach to distance learning and what they've done to make it work in their organization.

One of the largest consulting companies, Ernst & Young, has embraced DL to help it deliver training to its far-flung geographically dispersed employees. The company has garnered an Excellence in Practice Citation from ASTD. The article "Teletraining Distance Learning at Ernst & Young" explains the approach this company has taken with its partner Intellinex that has garnered them this recognition from ASTD.

Another large company that has embraced distance learning is BellSouth. In the article, "Online Performance and Learning at BellSouth" by Darin E. Hartley, you'll learn how e-learning fits into the organization's strategy to help it meet its performance goals. You'll learn the specifics of how this company implemented its e-learning program.

Lotus LearningSpace is a program that facilitates distance learning over the Web. The article "Asynchronous Distance Learning for Corporate Education" by Lisa Neal and Debbie Ingram explains how one company selected and then used Lotus LearningSpace in their distance education efforts in an asynchronous situation.

We hope we have whetted your appetite for what's to follow. What we hope you'll find is a nice blend of principles, practices, and examples, enough to help you get your program moving or improve on it.

Corporate Drivers of E-Learning

Brandon Hall

From Forbes Magazine'*s special section on distance and e-learning, this piece examines what factors are causing corporations to look at and adopt electronic technology to deliver their training.*

The Corporate University

If knowledge is a corporate asset, then training must be viewed as both a strategic initiative and competitive advantage. One sign that training has come of age is the advent of the corporate university and the CLO (chief learning officer). In many cases, the CLO reports to the chief executive officer, is a lateral position to the chief financial officer and participates when the executive team plans future strategy. In 1988, there were approximately 400 corporate universities. Today there are approximately 1,600, and if the trend continues, they will exceed the number of traditional universities in the U.S. by 2010. In addition to training employees, corporate universities are also becoming profit centers that are responsible for training a corporation's complete ecosystem or supply chain—including customers, partners, channel partners and suppliers. Serving the value chain ensures proper representation of the corporation's products and services, garners mind share in nonexclusive relationships and captures future e-commerce revenues in various other cases.

The Global Economy

Since corporate employees around the world work either from the office or from home, learning resources and knowledge databases must be available 24/7 to cover every

171

Terminology Confusion

When I talk to training groups within an enterprise to help them define e-learning strategies, they most often complain that they are confused by all the technology options. Walk the aisles at a training conference expo and everything sounds the same. This difficulty is only going to increase, and is due to a number of factors:

Terminology. In our new e-learning industry, there are few agreed-upon terms. Many are simply buzzwords—generalized terms meaning different things to different people.

New Categories of Software. With a continual flow of new products that offer unique ways to solve training and performance problems, it is hard to understand the new capabilities, or how one program differs from another.

Limited Experience Selecting Software. Human resource training professionals—unlike IT professionals—have limited experience with a rigorous process for selecting big software packages. Trainers are trained to deal with people, not software.

All-Encompassing Claims. The next time you hear a vendor offering a "Total Training Solution," don't be misled. This phrase says nothing, claims everything, and only contributes confusion to the marketplace. What the vendor is really saying is, "We haven't found out yet how to describe our product, or what differentiates it. Just trust us."

time zone. Language and cultural differences, sometimes called localizations, also must be taken into consideration. By using the corporate intranet, students can access e-learning content whenever they need it. Some suppliers in the e-learning space have been working to establish a global presence.

Time-to-Market

Time-to-market is also a major driver for corporations. When your company is global and product-launch information needs to reach thousands of sales, support and management professionals who are decentralized—perhaps around of the world—instructor-led training just can't provide the speed necessary to maximize return on investment. The product may be available for sale, but if salespeople are not made aware, that is opportunity lost and an open door for a faster competitor to react. Product development cycle times are diminishing most visibly in the technology industries. Field organizations within high-tech companies experience a tremendous amount of pressure to keep up with the constant barrage of information. Resolving any enterprise-wide issues via e-learning strategies and tools will quite often provide the greatest visibility and the most substantial rewards.

In the knowledge economy, corporate universities and learning organizations are playing mission-critical roles within the corporation. Cost containment, downsizing and strategic change, are factors that affect who we train and how we train. While some learning organizations may take traditional classroom approaches, others are using the benefits of e-learning to meet corporate objectives. Examples of other e-learning implementations within the enterprise include using technology to train technology, new product introductions, tracking regulatory compliance, on-demand task or skill references, degree programs from online universities and IT certifications.

Cost Savings

According to *Training Magazine* corporations save between 50% to 70% when they replace instructor-led training with alternative electronic delivery. Housing and travel costs account for the majority of the savings. Lost productivity and revenue can actually be higher if you consider that classroom days include not only travel time, but also total time away from the office.

What is the cost of looking for information? Savings from just-in-time reference tools may be difficult to accurately assess, but should be considered in the cost-saving mix.

Modular e-learning is another source of cost savings that allows training to be spread out over a period of several days. This flexibility allows the student to attend to business and then learn when he/she has the time to concentrate. The company benefits as the employee keeps work on schedule, and the student benefits by being able to progress with valuable course work.

The last cost-saving strategy involves strategic training, as opposed to just-in-case training that is not necessarily tied to specific corporate objectives. Training in this category simply becomes an event. While some information will be retained immediately following the course, over longer periods of time, knowledge retention dissipates. The Research Institute of America found that 33 minutes after a lecture is completed, students usually retain only 58% of the material covered. By the second day, 33% is retained, and three weeks after the course is completed, only 15% of the knowledge is retained.

See biography of Brandon Hall, information about brandon-hall.com, and contact information on page 439.

Corporate E-Learning Economies

Brandon Hall

This article comes from Forbes *and was part of the special section devoted to distance and e-learning. It looks at the economic benefits of delivering training using e-learning techniques.*

Consistency

Instructor-led training does not always guarantee that the same information or quality of instruction is provided to all students. Class dynamics can often provide different outcomes. Instructors and students engage in the class with differing levels of competency about the topic. *Training Magazine* reported 50% to 60% improved consistency using some form of e-learning. Because business moves at Internet speed, content needs to be updated frequently to avoid obsolescence. The scalability of e-learning allows one course to train thousands of students, as opposed to the ratios of 1 to 20 in the more traditional classes. Both consistency of information and content integrity can be maintained efficiently.

Time Savings

Depending on the complexity of the topic and the individual skill level, some students will learn faster or slower than others will. E-learning allows students to learn at their own pace. The slower student can review course material as often as necessary, redoing exercises or simulations until the information converts to knowledge. An average of 50% time savings has been found when comparing time-to-learn in a classroom versus on a computer.[1]

174

Compliance Training

If your industry is regulated, the importance of being able to provide timely, consistent and accurate training for your employees is crucial. The ability to assess, test and track the results of perhaps thousands of students is also mandatory. Failure to do both might result in expensive fines and settlements from lost lawsuits. Fortunately, there are a combination of e-learning content, tools and vendors to assist you. Vendors are beginning to specialize in providing compliance training to the insurance, banking, securities, health care, law and real estate professions. One vendor in this field is eMind.com, which offers a "Knowledge Portal" to attract and serve financial professionals.

The Free Agent

Many individuals in the workforce today have probably worked for companies that have experienced downturns in business. Even the most people-centric organizations will downsize, reorganize or right-size to survive. Workers often display very little loyalty to their organization. One of the highest-priority issues for corporations today is retaining skilled workers. Add to this equation the value of intellectual capital and the characteristics of the knowledge economy discussed earlier, and the result is a free-agent mentality when it comes to pursuing employment. Employees may very well choose the highest bidder, the one with the best benefits, the one that allows the most flexible working conditions or the one that offers the most potential for development of valuable, marketable skill sets. Skilled workers know their value to the organization, but they also know that they are responsible for their own growth. Those employees have a position of strength when negotiating with their prospective employer. When talent is scarce, corporations are forced to compete for the best people. A leading-edge company that offers new experiences and training will be attractive to the free agent. Training is a benefit.

Who Has Time for Training?

As a knowledge worker, if you are able to keep up with the advances and changes in your industry, and master the products and services your company produces, you are very valuable. In the Knowledge Age, this combination is rare. Learning must be accessible at anytime, anywhere, in the right amount, and suited to the individual's needs. If you have to dig for an answer and get back to a customer who is on the phone, nine times out of 10 you'll probably get voice mail. At the same time, you can't afford to spend extended amounts of time in the classroom at the expense of personal productivity.

Technology Is Not a Panacea

Applying technology to learning is not yet a pure science. Classroom learning provides the human touch that many business-skill topics require to transfer new skills. And some learners need the face-to-face interaction in order to attain those new skills. Learning is fundamentally a social process. The right solution might be to provide a combination of appropriate high tech and high touch. High touch may mean that a learner is in the classroom, online or both.

Building the Business Case

As with any new technology, e-learning may be met with skepticism from those who don't have a clear understanding of its benefits. Launching an online learning initiative must be viewed as an investment for the business that is cost-justified.

A study by brandon-hall.com to determine the return-on-investment value of moving courses from the classroom to the computer showed substantial savings in student time and the organization's money.[2]

Every person who has risked his or her reputation as an internal champion of a new initiative knows that organizational changes don't come easily. Launching e-learning effectively, which involves staff training, software and course development services, often requires spending in excess of the usual amounts that are budgeted for training.

Like any investment for an organization, there's a process that needs to be followed. First, one needs to build the business case, showing where and how such new procedures will be paid for. Then, one must outline the benefits to the company when it moves to these new training methods.

Enterprise-Wide E-Learning

While adding e-learning piecemeal to the existing training structure may be attractive, companies that set the bar for training excellence—and are reaping the most benefits—are creating enterprise-wide e-learning strategies. They identify how e-learning can be used by the entire workforce as a component of the overall training plan.

Strategic, enterprise-wide implementation of e-learning typically comprises one-third to one-half of the total training budget. Employees who need to learn new software solutions all at one time don't have to be dragged, group by group, into packed classrooms. Rather, they can find training on their desktops when they need it.

Companies that have successfully put into place enterprise-wide e-learning strategies have a few characteristics in common. A recent study by brandon-hall.com of e-learning across the enterprise shows that top-management support is key, as these senior executives must see that e-learning is a way to meet corporate priorities and close business-critical knowledge gaps.[3] Then a team needs to be assembled that will implement the plan. Finance and human resource departments should be included in the discussions so the budget as well as the tracking system can be taken into account from the start. The IT network services group also should be represented early on to address issues of bandwidth and network compatibility. HR trainers need to solicit support from IT if online learning is to be a reality at a company.

Once the enterprise-wide e-learning team is in place, the members will need to create comprehensive strategies that include planning around staffing, budget, technology and metrics considerations.

IBM Integrates E-Learning into Management Development

Management training is a critical business issue at IBM, and is part of its strategy for adapting to the New Economy. Subsequently, e-learning is a crucial component of the company's overall training approach.

"We have been able to provide five times as much content, at one-third the cost, with e-learning," says Nancy Lewis, director of worldwide management development at IBM's corporate headquarters in Armonk, N.Y.

For more than 30,000 IBM managers, e-learning is essential to the management training program. All first-line managers take part in a four-tiered strategy for training. The first six months of the program are almost exclusively online.

IBM invited researchers from Harvard University to conduct a preference study of its training program. When the managers were asked prior to taking part in the training program which method they wanted, most of them selected classroom, or face-to-face, learning. After participating in the e-learning-based training, however, most of the managers selected the e-learning model as their favorite. "The response has been better than we expected," says Lewis. "Users do not want to leave the collaboration area online when they are done with the last phase of our program." Managers learn to take advantage of the opportunity to ask for advice from colleagues and to share common challenges.

IBM's four-tiered e-learning program begins with groups of 24 managers entering the first tier of the program simultaneously, although the learners do not meet face-to-face. Content is offered online at any time and delivered via the company intranet. A key component of the program is the transfer of information and communication of basic concepts regarding what it takes to be an IBM manager.

The tools in this tier are just-in-time performance support, with access to a massive database of questions, answers and sample scenarios to address common concerns such as evaluation, retention and conflict resolution.

The second tier presents interactive learning models with more than a dozen situation simulations. Here, more seasoned IBM managers coach the new managers online. Simulations give the learners an opportunity to interactively experience topics such as business conduct, compensation and benefits, and employee skill-building. Within a handful of simulations, there are more than 5,000 screens of action. Further simulations dip into areas like multicultural issues and retaining talent. Harvard Business School Publishing provided some of the content for this area and Cognitive Arts of Chicago helped create the scenarios.

Collaboration begins as the manager enters the third tier. Using Lotus Learning Space, the groups of managers that have been moving up through the tiers interact and solve problems as a team. At any given time, many groups of 24 will be learning simultaneously.

The fourth tier assembles colleagues from a particular management class for a week of in-class lab activities. The difference is that there are no lectures. Anything that previously would have been delivered as a lecture or pure content will have been delivered online, and learners will have passed an online test on that content. Learners also have to complete work prior to attending the lab. The lab time is spent in activities that require the managers to solve problems as a team, face-to-face. This fourth tier typically follows six months of e-learning experiences.

Before the e-learning program, managers had to travel to attend in-class training courses during the first six months of management development. Now all of it occurs online, when and where the student desires to learn.

According to IBM's Lewis, students comment that they will never again "suffer through a workshop where the purpose is basic information transfer." Information transfer takes place online. The training development team at IBM took a thoughtful look at the audience, topics and organizational needs, and created a system that provides a great balance of content and interaction. The bottom-line benefit is that IBM has saved two-thirds of the money previously spent on traditional training.

Cisco Systems Walks the Talk

In a major speech at last year's fall Comdex show, John Chambers, chief executive officer of Cisco Systems, said that he believes e-learning usage will grow bigger than the use of e-mail. *The New York Times* picked up the story the next day, and overnight Cisco became a high-profile advocate for e-learning. Cisco spent tens of millions of dollars on its "Are You Ready?" advertising campaign, and one of the current themes is e-learning: "One day, training for every job on Earth will be available over the Internet," a young girl predicts in one of the commercials.

Not only do companies need faster, cheaper development of online training, but employees want the information in small chunks of training materials online when they need them. At Cisco, Chambers helped drive e-learning as a corporate directive from the top down. "If you think about Cisco's internal learning challenges, we need to train over 5,000 salespeople and account managers worldwide. We have to train them for literally hundreds and hundreds of new products annually," explains Tom Kelly, vice president of worldwide training at Cisco Systems in San Jose, Calif.

From an e-commerce perspective, nearly 80% of all orders that come into Cisco for networking gear are handled entirely over the Internet, Kelly says. That provides cost savings of an enormous scale and the ability to handle much larger volumes than manual order taking. With that lesson learned, it was only a step farther to use the power of the Internet to help train Cisco's employees, and educate its customers and partners.

Because it is an Internet networking company, Cisco clearly pays more attention to e-learning than some other companies might. "If we were selling widgets, we might not start from the bottom layer and ask questions, such as what is the optimal network infrastructure to support an e-learning solution. But that's going to be a fundamental area that gets covered, just because of the nature of who Cisco is," says Kelly.

"We've made something like 50 new acquisitions over the last two years," he adds. "Our account executives and salespeople have to be up to speed and able to communicate intelligently about these new products and technologies that the acquisitions bring in almost on a daily basis." Before e-learning mailings went out regularly, there were communications meetings, CD-ROMs packaged with course information and training classes. "Those sorts of old-world learning mechanisms simply don't scale to the Internet era," Kelly explains.

To keep the business running fast, Cisco is moving 100% of its courses online. The topic is hot at department meetings, and there is a constant review at the executive level. For example, Kelly notes a recent operational review featuring a two-hour assessment of e-learning operations by corporate executives.

To implement the enterprise-wide e-learning strategy, Cisco put together a program that stores each part of a lesson in a reusable format on a database. Small chunks of information can be pulled out on demand to serve training needs. The program uses XML megadata tagging, which is based on the emerging IMS standard (www.imsproject.com), to ensure it is user-compatible with the other programs and systems in the industry.

This system allows for the creation of a single repository of information that can be used in training, documentation and other capacities. "We are constantly on the lookout for new ways to implement Internet solutions that can change for the better the way we run our business," says Kelly.

Helping Smaller Companies Meet Training Needs

The cost of online courses is sometimes 50% to 75% less than instructor-led training. It is convenient because people don't need to travel or block out several days for a class. It is efficient because a course can be completed in half the time. And retention can be just as good as or better than with instructor-led training. These benefits are available to organizations of any size, and learning portals make it easy to access thousands of courses.

Peter Mellen is the chief executive officer and cofounder of Headlight.com, an e-learning application service provider. Headlight.com is one of several companies that provide training services for small and medium-size businesses that lack the resources or infrastructure a large company might have to create its own program. Think of these learning portals as an Amazon.com for online learning.

"When we meet with these companies, we find that most of them spend about $700 per year on training for one employee. So if the employee takes one instructor-led course for $500 and buys a few books or videos, that's it," says Mellen. At a learning portal, one can purchase five to 10 courses for $700. It is much more cost effective for employees. These e-learning sites also offer assessments, transcripts and even management reports. Other sites include Trainingnet.com, eMind.com, GeoLearning.com and Click2Learn.com. (There are links to two dozen learning portals from www.brandon-hall.com.)

"The history of e-learning is really very archaic," states Mellen. "The way it has often been done is to provide a solution behind the firewall. You had to buy lots of licenses and big servers, and it was really expensive." The Web has made everything easier and less expensive in the training realm. "We can really take e-learning to the companies. We accelerate the value people get from e-learning products and services. It really boils down to being an application service provider," says Mellen.

Learning portals have found a niche by partnering with companies to provide training to businesses and individuals when they need it, however they need it. One such partnership is with Compaq. Through a learning portal partnership, computers are delivered with training that is easily accessible through a few mouse clicks on the company's Web site. "Compaq has solutions that simplify business computing, and by offering complimentary Windows 2000 online training, we are making the transition simpler for our customers," says Ray Frigo, vice president, Services Division of Compaq.

Learning portals are a technology solution category that is a cornerstone in e-learning training plans for companies of all sizes. Whether your company is large or small, taking advantage of tools that are available makes sense. The challenge is to make sense of what is available.

The Tail That Wags the Dog

The most important foundation for e-learning in your organization is a learning management system (LMS). A learning management system provides the infrastructure and database from which employees may quickly tap e-learning courses, registration and needs assessment, as well as receive just-in-time training. Once a learning management system is in place, it can include all members of an extended enterprise, from employees to vendors to customers.

The infrastructure for e-learning gives managers the ability to track usage and scores, enable online registration, deliver courses and update calendars as needed. Learning management systems also can incorporate e-commerce to track payments from customers or bill back to an internal department.

As companies strive to manage the knowledge of their workforce, learning management systems emerge as a tool that can assist with skill-gap analysis and development plans for future learning needs.

A recent study on learning management systems conducted by brandon-hall.com showed Docent, Phoenix Pathlore and SocratEase to be highly rated learning management systems, with strong customer satisfaction.[4]

A learning management system links to your human resources database, provides custom options and must incorporate technology for e-learning transactions. The e-commerce capability often includes an account management component that will allow students and organizations to maintain specific accounts on the system. An LMS will track purchase orders and can accept payment in the form of tokens or training units as well as checks and credit cards.

Any LMS you select should be AICC-certified, which is an existing standard for tracking users and scores across different courses. (AICC stands for Aviation Industry CBT [computer-based training] Committee.) Software licensing and implementation can run from $10,000 to more than $1 million, and can take months to complete an in-depth analysis, but the cost savings is so substantial that the investment is worth it.

An LMS sometimes has a competency management system that encourages organizations to define skill profiles based on a built-in or add-on module. Individual skills are assessed against the skill profiles to identify skill gaps and to personalize learning plans for each student. Profiles can be used to match people with job openings. An LMS also provides catalog search capabilities and built-in e-mail notification for things like waiting list openings.

A learning management system should be an open, scalable system that provides a foundation for e-learning. Products allow companies to assess, plan, deliver, manage and improve both the self-paced and the instructor-led learning process. Courses can be created once, then distributed to thousands of students simultaneously using LANs, WANs or the Internet. There is another option, which is much less expensive than these others and yet retains tremendous functionality.

An Inexpensive LMS and Authoring Tool

John Blagdon, education manager for Eastman Software (a subsidiary of Kodak), was on a mission to improve training for corporate partners. "I knew what we had to do. Our business model involves partners; we certify these partners, then they will package and resell the product," says Blagdon.

Customers who resell the software must first pass a certification exam. "When we first created these exams, it was a manual process. Diskettes went out and were returned. We had to evaluate the test results and send responses to the people to say whether they had been certified. It was a cumbersome process," says Blagdon.

SocratEase made it possible for these tests to be conducted online with scores tallied immediately. Both Eastman Software and the learners know in a short time frame whether they have passed. Depending on the access rights that are prescribed, however, an Eastman Software executive, for example, may be able to view more data than individual learners.

Internally at Eastman Software, Blagdon works with a team of traditional course developers. He needed to develop a program that ensured the traditional instructors would stay happy amid a changing environment.

"I needed to use the instructors we had, but move what people were learning to the Web. I had to be careful that the authoring software wouldn't require too much time and effort to make it work," he notes. Blagdon is pleased that registration and administration of training can be handled online with SocratEase.

For an initial investment of about $1,500, you can offer a server full of courses to an unlimited number of students. The system has been implemented at a number of organizations, including several large ones, and it seems to be working well. (Keep in mind, however, that some other organizations have not been able to implement it.) People who have used SocratEase with success appreciate the ability to create classes very quickly using commonly available formats. Its Java-based, multi-platform capability is another advantage.

David Wilson, manager of training for Aventail, a builder of extranets for business-to-business communications, recently chose SocratEase to serve an international group of about 175 employees in small offices throughout the U.S. and England.

Wilson implemented SocratEase with his previous company, where it proved successful. Wilson demonstrated to his peers that you could create a learning module in one afternoon, with no specific product training. If you had the text and the graphics already, it might take only about three hours to create a course. "I never read the manual," says Wilson. "Everything was well documented online. It was pretty intuitive." Wilson took months working with consultants, thinking about the appropriate learning management system. Once he reviewed SocratEase, however, the decision to purchase it took just two days. "I've been impressed with the fact that the product is not that old. Eutectics, creator of SocratEase, continues to improve it dramatically with every version that comes out," says Wilson. "This brings excellent online training capabilities into the hands of smaller training departments and companies that can't afford $80,000 to $250,000 for a system."

Notes

1. brandon-hall.com, "Return on Investment and Multimedia Training" (1995).
2. brandon-hall.com, "Return on Investment and Multimedia Training" (1995).
3. brandon-hall.com, "E-Learning Across the Enterprise: The Benchmarking Study of Best Practices" (2000).
4. brandon-hall.com, "Integrated Learning Systems: How to Choose an 'All in One' System for Your Organization" (1999).

See biography of Brandon Hall, information about brandon-hall.com, and contact information on page 439.

Tips to Help Decide if Your Organization Is Ready for E-Learning

Brooke Broadbent

You just don't decide one day to institute e-learning as your mode of training. It requires careful consideration and preparation. This article lays out several factors to think about before moving ahead in your company.

E-learning. Has a training term ever caught on like e-learning has in the year 2000? Is it because training has caught dot com fever or is it because e-learning is a superior way to conduct training? Frankly, we don't know yet. One thing is certain, however: e-learning is not the perfect fit in every organization. To implement e-learning successfully in an organization you need the right people, place and resources. Does your organization have the right mix of people, place and resources?

The purpose of this article is to help organizations decide if they are ready for e-learning. We offer a checklist and strongly recommend that you adapt it to individual situations. Every day, instructional designers, consultants, trainers and training managers make recommendations to use e-learning or not to use it. The approach of this article will help them give reasoned advice and help organizations make wise decisions.

Introduction

In the first few months of the new millennium, e-learning looms large. The term e-learning pops up in advertisements for training and education services, conference presentations, and it seems to be quite popular among marketers of technology-assisted learning products. Is e-learning just a marketing device? Or is this a new word to describe a new reality? What does it mean to add an 'e' to the word learning?

At e-LearningHub.com, we view the moniker "e-learning" broadly. It represents convergence in the education, training and information fields. As we see it, the term e-learning includes education, training and structured information delivered by computers, through the Internet, or the Web, or from the hard drive of the computer—or an organization's network. This definition of e-learning includes CBT, WBT electronic performance support systems, webcasts, listservs, knowledge management undertakings and other discussions on the Internet, threaded and unthreaded.

In this environment that is supportive of e-learning, stakeholders are wondering if it could be the right approach for them. After all, e-learning promises to offer training that is just in time, just enough and just the way you like it.

Ready for E-Learning?

Learning consultants from Canada, the US and the UK have identified best practices associated with e-learning. They uncovered three factors that contribute to readiness of organizations to embrace e-learning: people, place and resources. Within these three areas there are a number of variables. For example, in the *people* variable there is commitment and skill, for *place* there is stability and infrastructure, under the *resources* category we identified funds and knowledge. These are sample variables, cited to kick-start your thinking process so that you will identify the criteria that are the most important in your situation. When you make your list of criteria, keep it short, with key criteria—the ones that will have the greatest impact on the success of e-learning in your organization. You might decide, for example, to develop criteria that assess whether there is enough time to develop the training in an e-learning format and whether e-learning will offer enough personal interactions for the type of training that is required.

Our goal is to help you think systematically about whether e-learning will help your organization meet its performance targets. Here are the six variables, two under each of people, place and resources.

People

An international e-learning consortium team selected the following two people variables as critical indicators of readiness of an organization to embrace e-learning: commitment and skill.

Commitment. One way to measure commitment is by considering whether key decision-makers in the organization are serious about investigating the use of e-learning. It is a positive sign if this commitment is rooted in an understanding of what e-learning can do and what it cannot do. It's an ominous sign if the commitment is based on a flavor-of-the month approach to training.

Skill. Can your organization tap into a supply of people skilled in all the aspects of e-learning? If you are going to develop your own e-learning program, you may require a project manager, instructional developers, software programmers, multimedia experts, graphics experts, and others, including information systems experts. Experienced people have had opportunities to develop their skills, so experience with e-learning is a very desirable quality to seek.

Introducing e-learning challenges project management skills. Managing e-learning demands the ability to scope work, assign resources, manage expectations, monitor progress and revise plans as required. Your project manager will need to skillfully communicate with stakeholders throughout the e-learning project.

If an organization decides to develop e-learning, it will need to have either the employees with the required skills or a direct line to reliable consultants. And once the materials are developed or off-the-shelf materials are purchased, your users will need to be comfortable using the hardware and software that surround your e-learning, including using your operating system and navigating in your learning package.

Place

The two factors under "place" that are critical indicators of readiness of an organization to embrace to e-learning are flexibility and infrastructure.

Flexibility. Today's organizations are spelled c-h-a-n-g-e. The corporate landscape is a panorama of new companies, merged companies, new roles, new technologies, and new knowledge to learn. We need flexibility to adjust to change. In order to meet change effectively, diverse groups must work together effectively. Training project leaders must foster team spirit. People assigned to training projects must put the accomplishments of the team before their individual successes. Team members must help each other complete work on time and within budget.

Infrastructure. E-learning does not necessarily require a huge infrastructure. Some successful programs are simple add-ons to the enterprise-wide intranet. However, many organizations build e-learning on an infrastructure of powerful multimedia computers, and the e-learning you adopt may also require Web access and an enterprise-wide intranet.

Resources

Under "resources," the key variables selected by the team as critical indicators of readiness of an organization to embrace e-learning are funds and knowledge.

Funds. The initial costs of developing e-learning are higher than most equivalent leader-led interventions. So, deep pockets help. Faced with high costs, you might be tempted to cut corners. In the long run, however, a well-designed e-learning package shrinks high costs associated with travel, accommodation, and instructors.

Knowledge. When deciding whether your organization is ready for e-learning, you will need to assess whether there is sufficient knowledge about the range of e-learning options, knowledge about the impact that using e-learning will have on your organization and the people who work there. Knowledge goes hand-in-hand with all the factors examined above. It is probably the most important of all the factors we have listed. And remember: a little knowledge can be a dangerous thing.

Challenges and Responses

Every day, instructional designers, consultants, trainers and training managers make recommendations and decisions to use e-learning or not to use it. The following scenarios tell the stories of two organizations making e-learning decisions.

Case Study: A Decision to Use E-Learning in the Insurance Industry

At a meeting of senior executives, the V-P of Human Resources of an insurance corporation learns that in nine months' time over 1,000 employees will start to use a new computer system for registering and tracking insurance claims. After considering the technology the corporation has now and working with a consultant to investigate factors similar to the six explored above, the insurance corporation decided to use e-learning. They selected a self-directed Web-based training application that allows employees to learn the new computer system from their own computers on the job, at their own pace. Super-users of the new computer system are stationed at each office, and a help-desk is established to provide personalized assistance.

Let's look at how the insurance corporation evaluated the six factors. We used a scoring key of 0 for no evidence of meeting the criteria, 1 for low compliance, 2 for medium, 3 for high. Our rating scale is examined further in the table below.

Commitment. The key decision-makers are somewhat committed to investigating the use of e-learning. They have attended presentations about it in other organizations and they have a vague idea of what e-learning is. On our scale of 0 to 3, they score 2.

Skill. The insurance corporation has produced a few videos in the past and they have developed expertise in multimedia as a result. Past projects have offered opportunities to develop skills in project management and crafting training materials. In summary, the corporation has a few skilled people in e-learning related matters but no directly related skills. Score: 1.

Flexibility. The company merged with another three years ago. Employees demonstrated considerable flexibility during the merger. People work relatively well together. The training organization has had some successes and some mild failures when working closely with operational and administrative groups. Let's give them the benefit of the doubt and score 3.

	0	1	2	3
People				
Commitment	No decision-makers are committed to online learning.	Some decision-makers are committed to online learning.	Most decision-makers are committed to online learning.	All decision-makers are committed to online learning. Their commitment is rooted in an understanding of what online learning can do and what it cannot do.
Skill	Your organization does not have skilled people in any of the aspects of online learning: a project manager, instructional developers, software programmers, multimedia experts, graphics experts, and others including information systems experts. Nor do you have access to consultants.	Your organization has a few skilled people in online learning matters or knows consultants in some of the areas.	Your organization covers most of the online learning skill requirements either internally or through consultants.	You have all the skills in your organization to develop online learning or you have identified consultants who can help.
Place				
Flexibility	Diverse groups do not work well together. Leaders do not foster team spirit.	There are examples of people working together but there is conflict among diverse units in the organization that would be involved in online learning.	Most of the people assigned to the project will put the project before their individual successes.	People assigned to training projects always put the accomplishments of the team before their individual successes. Team members help each other complete work on time and within budget.

Table 1. Decision-making matrix (continued on next page)

	0	1	2	3
Place				
Infrastructure	You have none of the required technology: multimedia computers, Web access, or an organization-wide intranet.	You have some of the required technology.	You have most of the required technology.	You have all of the required technology, know how to use it, and have an effective 24x7 help service.
Resources				
Funds	Your organization does not have sufficient funds.	Your organization has most of the required money. A few stakeholders realize the importance of committing sufficient resources.	Your organization has the required money. Most stakeholders realize the importance of committing sufficient resources.	The organization has sufficient resources and all stakeholders are committed to using those resources to develop a quality product.
Knowledge	People are misinformed about online learning and about the range of online learning options, about the impact that using online learning will have on your organization and the people who work there.	Some people are well-informed about online learning. But most are not well-informed.	Most people are well-informed about online learning.	Everyone is well-informed about online learning.

Table 1. Continued

Infrastructure. Most people have access to the technology required for e-learning. They use it competently. There is a good support system for people who have questions about the new technology. Score: 3.

Funds. The organization has always been cautious about spending money on training. However, in this case it seems that stakeholders have decided that e-learning is a priority. They realize that costs are higher than most equivalent leader-led interventions. They also acknowledge that the initial outlay could be substantial and skimping on the quality of the design phase will end up costing more in the long run. Score: 3.

Knowledge. Employees are comfortable using their computers. Some operational and administrative employees have used e-learning and CBT successfully. There is not, however, much knowledge of e-learning in the training group or elsewhere in the organization. Score: 2.

The Decision. Adding up all the points from above gives a total of 14. Accordingly, this insurance company is fairly well-suited for e-learning. The combined score of 14 out of 18 tends to emphasize this. Also, the high scores in flexibility, infrastructure, and funds augur well for introducing e-learning. These strong areas will continue to need some work, as will the weak areas. All shortfalls need to be addressed, especially commitment, skill and knowledge.

Case Study: A Decision to Not Use E-Learning

You might think that an organization that has many years' experience with e-learning would readily adopt e-learning for a new major training program. We will see below that an organization heavily committed to e-learning still needs to look at each case individually. And indeed after studying a situation they might even decide to not adopt e-learning—even when they score high on our factors.

This resource industry leader uses WBT (a form of e-learning) extensively. The company has found that the e-learning is a cost-effective way to provide a consistent, up-to-date message to employees just-in-time. They have used e-learning for many years extensively in their training programs for safety, operational procedures and employee orientation. In the existing e-learning programs, employees use a computer to obtain background facts. For example they use a Web-based training program to learn the theory of driving a fork truck. After the online training, the student drives the fork truck under the guidance of an instructor. They refer to the technical knowledge gathered in the e-learning lesson as required. An added bonus: after the training, employees can access the company Web-site and use the WBT modules as a reference manual. There is no longer a need to print manuals and worry about updating them. The updated version of materials is always available on the company intranet site. E-learning modules have replaced thousands of pages of training manuals.

With strong support for e-learning in the company, experience, expertise, commitment and other positive signs, we might assume that e-learning would be used for new training programs as they come along. After considerable soul-searching, the company decided to shun e-learning. Let's examine why.

Although the company scored high on the six criteria of our decision table, with several threes, they are missing key ingredients. First of all, there are 2,000 people to train in a short period of time. They must learn how to use the new enterprise-wide management (ERP) software the company is introducing to all employees. To learn to use the software in an online mode, every learner requires access to a personal computer. However, in a production environment there are few desks and fewer desktop computers. Making computers available to these people and ensuring that they have the time to practice in the workplace is inconceivable. In addition, the design team had only two months to develop the training program and it is feared there will not be enough time to develop WBT modules.

The final nail in the e-learning coffin is the ERP project leaders' concerns about the quality of training. They feel that classroom training offers the best option for ensuring that people taking the training learn what is required. Instructors and classroom coaches will monitor participants as they complete exercise and help them when they have problems. Also, classroom training offers opportunities to discuss the difference between the legacy systems and the new ERP, to deal with resistance to the new system—and to point out the advantages of the new software.

In the end, the company did use its intranet to support classroom training. Information about the new software and the training program was distributed via the company intranet—as well as up-to-date manuals and job aids. These uses of the Web represent effective uses of Web technology to support classroom learning.

Using the E-Learning Score Card

You can assess your organization's readiness for e-learning in the way that we assessed the two organizations above. Using the table below, read each of the six items and select one answer that most closely maps to your situation. If you realize that the replies are going to be different for various units in your organization, you should complete more than one survey. For example, an administrative unit might score differently from an operational one. To score your organization against the grid, add the weighted totals from the four columns. This total score represents the readiness of your organization to use e-learning.

Table Talk

The main use of the e-learning report card is to assess where you are, and to gain insight into what you need for moving ahead with e-learning. After you have calculated the readiness of your organization for e-learning, you will need to interpret your results. The table will reveal the areas where your organization is most vulnerable. The low scores on the six variables, for example the zeros and ones, indicate where you might run into roadblocks if you implement e-learning. If you take action to raise your scores in these areas, your organization will be better prepared to implement e-learning.

How should we interpret scores? Will it be a snap to implement e-learning if your organization scores 18 out of 18? Probably not. Introducing change to any organization is a complex matter and it requires careful planning at the best of times. What does it mean if your organization scores 6 out of 18? Will it be impossible to implement e-learning? Any organization can implement e-learning, but you face more risk if you have a low score on this table. It's best to attenuate risks before embarking on e-learning. In other words, you should develop ways to address your low scores very early in your project.

Summary

Implementing e-learning can be challenging. You could experience setbacks, even failure. To succeed you need to think critically about the ability of your organization to implement e-learning successfully. You need to address the weaknesses. Successful implementers of e-learning think systematically about people, place and resources, as well as other factors in their individual situations.

Some thought-leaders and marketers are positioning e-learning as a panacea. This is misleading. E-learning is not a universal solution. It is complex. It demands the right mix of people, place and resources. Or a concerted effort to improve that mix.

Brooke Broadbent is an independent e-learning analyst and the founder of e-LearningHub.com, a center for e-learning excellence. He is writing a book about e-learning to be co-published by ASTD and Jossey-Bass. He may be reached at brooke.broadbent@ottawa.com.

Go the Distance!
It May Be Your Answer

Jim Parsons

This article originally appeared in the journal published by the American Industrial Hygiene Association, which has embraced distance learning as a way to deliver training to its members. This article reviews AIHA's perspective on distance learning and its perspective has relevance to any organization that wants to include this approach in its training program.

Ask anybody who has ever organized a training class to rank the biggest obstacles to making the program successful, and you'll likely see "logistics" near the top of the list every time. Finding a convenient time, date and location that satisfies every participant's schedule is never easy, particularly if the trainers and/or students are located many miles apart. Even if you do manage to get everybody together in one place, there may be any number of distractions to deal with: an insufficient number of handouts, faulty ventilation or audio/visual equipment or jingling cell phones.

Nobody expects to see the traditional classroom setting disappear anytime soon. But given these and other limitations, plus the ever-expanding range of technology options, industrial hygienists (IHs) are increasingly looking for other ways to exchange much needed information and expertise with employees and each other. The answer for many is distance learning, or DL.

Although DL sounds new, the concept has been around for a long time. Correspondence courses have been advertised in everything from respected professional journals to the backs of matchbooks for years. Many IHs of the baby boomer generation got their first taste of DL in school when they watched science and history programs beamed from the nearby educational TV station. Others may have purchased an AIHA video on a particular technical issue, or taken a "telecourse" conducted by satellite or cable hook-up from an instructor across town or across the country.

DL in the Internet Age

More recently, DL has evolved into the age of the Internet, with a variety of online programs and formats that range from posting text on websites to real-time streaming of audio and video. To put it simply, Carol Tobin, AIHA's director of education and meetings, says, "DL is any organized learning program that doesn't take place in a traditional classroom."

Dan Markiewicz, the owner of a Toledo, Ohio-based environmental health and safety (EH&S) consulting firm, agrees that DL is right for the times. "Our very busy, highly mobile society has also spawned an ever-increasing volume of information that we need to do our jobs better," he says. "DL frees us from the traditional constraints of time and geography. We can learn wherever we go."

For example, Markiewicz points to an interactive training program for forklift operators that's currently available on OSHA's website. "Obviously, you still need a 'hands-on' component to complete the training," he says, "but employees can study the written portions when they want to, and at their own pace." Markiewicz adds that he uses Internet sources instead of textbooks when he teaches a class in industrial hygiene at the University of Toledo. "All the references can be found on various government and university websites," he says. "It's much easier for the students to download what they need. The sites also lead them to other information sources for project research."

Studies of Internet DL courses conducted at colleges and universities reveal many other advantages. Professors report that some students who are reluctant to participate in class often become more active when the discussion is conducted in cyberspace. Other research indicates that because students have an increased responsibility to locate and learn material, DL may actually foster a more productive learning environment than traditional classroom settings.

Perhaps the biggest advantage of web-based DL is that the information is always there when trainers and students need it. Chuck Heindrichs, corporate safety manager at Eaton Corp., Cleveland, has developed a website dedicated to EH&S issues. The site provides the company's safety managers with information from a variety of online sources.

"The users can search the site for the topics they're interested in, download software or text, then edit the material as appropriate to suit their needs," Heindrichs says. "There's no need to 'reinvent the wheel' and come up with something new all over again."

Back to Earth

While DL has a lot to offer today's time-crunched, information-hungry IH professionals and the workers they serve, it isn't perfect. Not all subjects lend themselves to self-paced learning, and even those that do may require some kind of "live" supervision from an instructor or facilitator. "Surveys of AIHA members have found that DL works best for technical and regulatory topics," Tobin says. "Traditional classroom environments are preferred for more complex subjects that would likely require extensive discussion."

In addition, companies and organizations that conduct in-house DL programs must be prepared to make a sizable investment in equipment, space and technical support to keep the system running. There may also be a need to retrain the trainers and acquaint them with the DL format; a speaker who's a hit in a room full of people may come across much differently in a teleconference or online.

Heindrichs also questions whether we're ready to make EH&S training programs so dependent on computers. "Many people are not comfortable with technology because they have difficulty using the software, or fear that personal information will be compromised if they put it on the Internet," he says. "Then there are others who simply prefer interacting with another human being in the same room."

Markiewicz adds that there's also a lingering credibility issue regarding some Internet sources. "There's a lot of material on the web, and it's being posted faster than it can be verified," he says. "I don't pass along any sources to my students until I have confirmed their credibility. Until there are system-wide quality controls, I would be very leery of anyone who claimed the web as the sole source for his or her continuing education."

Making It Work

Developing quality DL courses and materials has long been one of AIHA's objectives for professional development. "This organization has been very proactive when it comes to DL," Tobin notes. "We began in 1992 with the self-study correspondence packages, which were very popular. Our DL offerings have now evolved to a mix of correspondence courses and videos."

What's more, AIHA's leadership has also been willing to make the necessary investment to help the DL program evolve with both technology and member needs. The organization is one of the few national professional associations to have a full-time staff member whose sole responsibility is to oversee the development of DL programs.

"The PDCs [professional development courses] offered at our annual conference and exhibition remain the backbone of AIHA's continuing education program," says AIHA's Continuing Education Committee Chairman Dennis Bridge, "but not everybody has the luxury of being able to attend and take the courses. DL, on the other hand, allows members to take classes from nearly anywhere. We may well see the day when DL is the accepted—and preferred—method of continuing education."

In fact, AIHA-sponsored telephone seminars have proven to be very successful. One such program, *Setting Cartridge Replacement Schedules*, attracted 161 participants at 34 different locations. The instructor, Thomas Nelson, president of NIHS Inc. in Wilmington, Del., has taught this course as a PDC for four years, and says that familiarity made it easier to transition his presentation to the telephone format. "The most challenging thing about this kind of course was getting immediate feedback," he says. "In a room full of people, I can use visual cues to see if I'm connecting with the participants. There were also some points that I felt could be better illustrated on a chalkboard, but you can't do that over the telephone."

On the other hand, Nelson believes the telephone format provided ample opportunity for participants to ask questions. "You don't always have that luxury in a classroom setting," he says.

Many of the telephone seminar's participants agree. One called it "an excellent method—not only because it is cheap and accessible, but also because AIHA did an excellent job of providing handouts prior to the course so we could follow along easily."

Another participant noted some of its limitations: "I suspect this would not be a pleasant experience for an eight-hour course because it might be too easy to get distracted during such a long time frame. I also found it difficult to stay focused without a speaker being in the room."

Taking the Next Step

Although increased reliance on DL for training and professional development seems certain, IHs should be cautious as they explore various technology options. Credibility and cost are just the start; IHs—particularly those who are considering using DL at their workplace or for their clients—must plan their approach very carefully, much as they would formulate a research study or prepare a presentation.

The first step is to consider the needs of the learners. As we have seen, not everybody is comfortable with computers or the Internet, nor may it be possible to arrange on-site facilities to conduct such programs. Even using tried-and-true methods such as videotapes can be cumbersome and inconvenient.

And web-based DL may not be as impersonal as some people believe. One IH who has taken professional development courses by mail and online prefers the interaction afforded by the web. "Although the correspondence courses were convenient, the feedback from the instructor was limited; I never knew whether I was one student out of 10 or 10,000. On the web, I get immediate feedback from the instructor. And while I was separated from most of the other students, I still felt like I was part of a class."

IHs who work for firms with multiple plants should remember that DL is not always a "one-size-fits-all" proposition. Heindrichs notes that many training programs required for OSHA standards have two components—a "generic" part that is applicable to all workers and a "local" part that covers issues specific to the particular location. "The generic portion can be done easily, either through a video, a handout or a website," Heindrichs says. "The local component requires more thought and development to make the generic information relevant to specific situations and local conditions. Depending on the issues or locations, that can be an expensive, complicated process."

Also remember that no two DL programs are alike. Every hour of online time requires literally days' worth of preparation by the instructor, human resources and training coordinators and technical support specialists. "Each hour of a basic class—one with very little interaction from the instructor—requires between 30 and 60 hours of preparation," Tobin says. "A more complex course that has two-way audio/video streaming, special programming and other features could easily require up to 5,000 hours of preparation per hour of instruction."

Nor are all web users alike. "Individual access is a definite consideration," Bridge says. "Not everybody has the same data speed. Some people may have a T1 line as opposed to a dial-up modem. These and other technical considerations alone can make the cost of a DL program cost-prohibitive."

The Best Teacher

Fortunately, IHs are not alone when it comes to figuring out the hows and whys of DL. "As with any rapidly evolving field, the only way to see if something works is through trial and error," says Tobin, who also suggests that IHs can learn more about DL technologies through professional organizations such as the American Society for Training and Development (www.astd.org or (703) 683-8100). "AIHA has also joined a DL coalition of other professional associations," Tobin says. "It's a good opportunity to share stories, discuss various DL options and learn things we can apply to our own programs."

Such experiences have helped clear the way for AIHA to introduce its first web-based courses. "We want to be involved in ensuring quality DL programs, while avoiding some of the bottlenecks and problems that may limit their effectiveness," Bridge says. "We are particularly eager to use web-based DL for time-sensitive issues such as OSHA announcements, technology or medical developments or major events that have a significant impact on our profession."

The bottom line on DL appears to be that anything can happen, and probably will. "I can see the day when I'll be able to teach my IH course from my office, at home or on the road, and all interaction is conducted online," Markiewicz says. "Some people may feel that's placing too much emphasis on technology. But as systems become more reliable and users become more comfortable with these methods, using the web for training will be second nature. As health and safety professionals, it's our mission to share important information with workers or clients in the most effective way possible. DL is another tool to help us fulfill that responsibility."

Jim Parsons is a freelance writer based in the Washington, D.C., area.

TeleTraining Distance Learning at Ernst & Young

Paul Ishimaru

This article documents the teletraining initiatives at Ernst & Young that have garnered the company an Excellence in Practice Citation from ASTD.

Background
Description

TeleTraining is an interactive instructor-led program that connects virtual learners through the telephone for a period not exceeding 60 minutes. A certified TeleTrainer handles up to eight learners on a single call. TeleTrainers conduct the sessions with their laptops connected to the firm's wide-area network via direct or remote connection. Participants' set-up of the system can include some or all of the following:

- telephone
- laptop or desktop computer
- wide-area network connection (directly or via remote connection)
- remote-control software to allow for control of the participants' computers by the TeleTrainer.

TeleTraining topics range from foundation skills to proprietary knowledge applications. Sessions are scheduled in advance based on discussions with the internal clients, information from the national help desk, input from the network of national trainers, and feedback from the online evaluation database. Each client can request registration for these sessions through a national registration system. All participants confirmed to be in attendance at the beginning and end of the TeleTraining session receive Continuing Professional Credits.

As an adjunct to the instructor-led sessions, trainees can access several prerecorded sessions 24 hours a day through a teleconferencing center. These sessions are five to ten minutes long, with an integrated voice response system providing the navigation through the menu selections.

Purpose

Acknowledging the evolving global, knowledge-based environment in which we work, the challenge to our company was one of delivering highly focused, just-in-time training to a widely distributed workforce. Traditional instructor-led programs were hugely successful for those individuals based in the main office or capable of attending. Web-based solutions were also viable alternatives but did not address individual preferences for facilitated learning. With 75 percent of the workforce being virtual workers, classroom instruction was not a viable or cost-effective alternative.

To meet this challenge proactively, Ernst & Young (the firm) contracted with Intellinex, the company that designed, developed, and implemented a global Tele-Training program that offers its members opportunities to

- enhance understanding of knowledge-based tools
- specifically target and strengthen foundation technology skills
- receive highly focused training in an interactive personal environment
- easily access (via telephone) firm subject matter experts
- continue their personal development while managing a busy personal and professional life.

Sources of TeleTraining development include discussions with clients, input from national instructors, online evaluations, and data from the national help desk. A national registration system makes TeleTraining accessible to all members of the firm. Certified TeleTrainers conduct TeleTraining sessions several times a day (before, during, and after work hours), using customized courseware designed and developed in conjunction with the firm's subject-matter experts.

Implementation

This is the second year of the TeleTraining program, with full deployment to the U.S. firm (35,000 people) and selected global deployments (the United Kingdom, Canada, Australia, and the Far East). The company anticipates continued global deployment as countries catch up technologically and are able to leverage the TeleTraining program.

TeleTraining combines the best of instructor-led interactive training with the ability to service remote individuals in a short intensive timeframe across a global, geographically dispersed area. To provide even greater access, the company has made prerecorded TeleTraining sessions available 24 hours a day, seven days a week, through a toll-free number.

Target Audience

Although TeleTraining is available to the entire firm, it is specifically targeted to the virtual user who requires just-in-time training on knowledge-related applications. In this knowledge-enabled environment, the firm expects all levels from partner through administrative staff to be performance-ready on its technology. Annually, about 6,000 internal clients receive learning through TeleTraining solutions. The company anticipates that this number will increase to over 10,000 clients, or 30 percent of the firm's population, in the next year.

Resources Committed

TeleTraining was designed, developed, and implemented by a core group of 10 individuals at the company who represented senior management, management, and senior staff. Senior management completed the needs assessments, while management and senior staff primarily performed design, development, and delivery with input from 30 national instructors. The company implemented the rollout of TeleTraining with a national communication campaign, creating a high level of interest among the virtual community. Two full-time and three part-time TeleTrainers service 500 to 700 learners each month.

Costs incurred for this practice include professional consulting program development and delivery and the teleconferencing costs for the interactive and prerecorded sessions. Costs of providing this service have historically run about $225,000 annually ($450,000 since inception), with future costs expected to increase variably with the addition of certified TeleTrainers.

State of the Art

On a very basic level, lack of training limits sound learning and performance improvement. Also, time spent obtaining training is time taken away from servicing external clients. TeleTraining has provided an option that significantly reduces the time commitment needed to obtain training, provides the training just in time, and allows the trainee to receive this anywhere there is a telephone. In addition, thanks to the prerecorded sessions, this training can be received 24 hours a day.

TeleTraining is a highly focused, intensive training on a very specific set of learning criteria. This hands-on training takes place with a certified instructor in the comfort of one's home, at a client site, or in an office. TeleTraining bridges the gap between traditional instructor-led training and nonfacilitated learning solutions (such as computer-based training, Internet/intranet-based training, etc.). TeleTraining achieves a balance between the firm's desire to use more "pull" learning solutions and the internal clients' surveyed responses that indicate a need to have facilitated training. TeleTraining offers the advantage of interactivity between participant and instructor while removing the requirement of being in a single physical location. It truly brings the best of the classroom world into an interactive session that has few limitations on accessibility and availability.

Documentation
Needs Identification

1. Describe the problem or need for which this practice is designed and implemented. How was this problem identified, and how was it determined that this practice is an appropriate response?

TeleTraining resulted in direct response to the following issues:

- Members of the virtual community could not avail themselves of the traditional location-based instructor-led classroom training.
- Firm-wide survey results indicated a strong preference for additional training and the desire to have that training be in a facilitated, interactive learning environment.
- Trainees wanted a solution that would balance their personal and professional lives.
- The firm wanted a solution that would accomplish the needed training without taking too much time from the higher priorities of serving clients and generating revenues.
- There was a need for just-in-time training to solidify' learning concepts.

The firm first identified the need for such training in 1997 when the first metrics were gathered on technology training. In-house assessments showed favorable results for those who attended instructor-led programs and, not surprisingly, unfavorable results for those who did not take advantage of these offerings. Further investigation resulted in identification of the above issues.

Although there were many solutions on the market that allowed the individual to increase learning in self-paced unmediated environments, none satisfied the desire for a facilitated learning environment. After reviewing internal training alternatives, the firm determined that none would be able to meet all the criteria set forth by the user community. Thus, the company conceived of TeleTraining in January 1998, with initial pilot testing beginning a few months thereafter. TeleTraining satisfied the need for facilitated learning while catering to the virtual worker.

Although results appear below, it is interesting to note that both virtual and office-based workers take frequent advantage of the TeleTraining program, as it provides a higher-intensity, focused learning opportunity compared to other alternatives. Learners have commented that they were able to take advantage of this type of learning given its shorter timeframe and greater availability.

Design Values

2. Please describe how this practice takes into account the best interests of both the organization and the employees targeted.

The firm has aggressively moved into a knowledge-based environment, releasing new tools, on average, once every eight weeks. Proficient use of these tools helps maintain our competitive advantage. With up to 75 percent of the employees being virtual workers, the need for training has not diminished but has increased, given our rapidly changing business environment. Internal clients can ill afford to expend the time and energy required to leave their off-site client locations to travel to the office for traditional instructor-led training. Should an individual choose the instructor-led alternative, he/she must make up the time missed or be penalized with lower utilization/revenue statistics when compared to peers. Thus, attending classroom-based training may have a negative impact on one's personal life and work/life balance.

For the firm as a whole, continuation along this path could result in higher organizational turnover, greater recruiting costs, mandatory renewed investment in the training of the new hires, and a forced steeper learning curve. None of these outcomes are desirable.

TeleTraining solves many of these issues since

- the virtual worker does not have to travel to an office location.
- the time commitment is less than 60 minutes.
- the training is available before, during, and after normal work hours (and 24 hours a day if one is accessing the prerecorded sessions).
- the training occurs near the time when the knowledge is required, thus enhancing retention and the overall learning experience.

With the more efficient use of time, firm professionals are able to focus on servicing the external clients while still reaping the benefits of educating themselves on firm foundation or knowledge tools.

Alignment

3. How is this practice in alignment with the performance problem identified, as described in your answer to question 1?

TeleTraining provides an ideal solution to meeting the stated desires of the learner for facilitated learning while moving to a more virtual environment. It is the best mix between a virtual learning experience and one that allows the learner to receive personal attention in a situation where interactivity between the learner and instructor still exists. Pure Web-based solutions (even with audio, streaming video, or simulation) cannot take into consideration the multitude of different questions that arise in each session.

TeleTraining provides immediate response by a certified expert to any questions. Other interactive solutions that provide screenshots of the application or, at best, simulations of the application fall short on demonstrating the full capabilities of the tool. TeleTrainers are capable of structuring their responses specifically to each learner, resulting in a more relevant learning experience and one that promotes a higher degree of learning and retention.

4. Please describe how this practice integrates other training, learning, and perform-

ance improvement practices, and aligns itself with organizational goals to achieve the desired outcomes.

TeleTraining is an integral part of the overall education plan for the firm. The company has developed "learning maps" for every individual in the firm that indicate the required learning one must undertake to be successful. Performance management, compensation, and human resources systems incorporate all or part of these learning maps into their processes.

Traditional instructor-led classroom training still provides a majority of the primary learning within the firm, with computer-based, Web-based, video-based, and satellite distance learning being other alternatives offered to employees.

The goal has always been to raise the bar on technology and knowledge-based skills for every member of the firm, from administrative assistant to partner. It is this high-level proficiency (performance readiness) that gives the firm its competitive advantage, an edge that would not be possible without continuous education on the firm's technology and knowledge toolset.

The challenge is to improve training in a global, knowledge-intensive environment where the demands of education can meet those of the job. Training today must meet the anytime, anywhere paradigm.

5. What evidence is there of partnerships within and outside the organization (e.g., with senior management, frontline supervisors, unions, external training suppliers consortia)?

TeleTraining was a direct response to the request for interactive training delivered to virtual clients in the firm. During the phased implementation, the monthly data gathered indicated that a mix of office-based participants and virtual participants have taken advantage of this training alternative. Participants have ranged from employees in entry-level positions to senior partners within the firm. TeleTraining has quickly become a preferred alternative during deployments and whenever the firm has specific training needs. Since its implementation, the company has provided TeleTraining to both internal and external clients with great success. External clients frequently request information on the firm's TeleTraining. Typical comments from TeleTraining participants include the following:

- "I liked [the] ability to attend training without leaving my desk."
- "The short timeframe for the training kept my interest while still [allowing time for] covering the information in great detail."
- "I have not been able to attend any instructor-led training due to conflicts with my schedule, [so] offering it before and after work has allowed me to take advantage of the training opportunity."

Evaluation Strategy

6. How is this practice evaluated? What factors are included in your calculations (e.g., time, costs, staff count, lost phone calls, customer satisfaction)? Are the financial costs of this practice calculated? If so, how? How often is this practice evaluated?

Participants evaluate every TeleTraining session through an online evaluation database (Level 1). Company management read these evaluations monthly. The design, development, and implementation core team meets on a regular basis to discuss the results of the evaluations and to address any issues and make any modifications.

Financial costs are mostly fixed, with a smaller portion of the cost related to variable, volume-dependent aspects. On a monthly basis, the company captures analyses of time saved as a result of attending the training and uses these data to prepare an opportunity revenue analysis, which is distributed to firm upper management.

Historical data have shown that participants view time spent in training as being recouped in less than eight weeks. The break-even point of TeleTraining, as compared with all costs associated with traditional classroom training, is 1.4 participants per session. On the basis of a maximum class size of eight participants, the company recovers costs of TeleTraining five times faster than it does the costs of traditional classroom training.

A development-to-implementation ratio of 10:1 hours is several times more efficient than other alternatives, including instructor-led, Web-based, video, satellite, etc. As a result, the company can design, develop, and deliver TeleTraining programs faster, allowing the company to be more responsive to the needs of the firm.

Results

7. What specific participant behaviors are observed as a result of this practice, and how do these behaviors contribute to the goals of the practice? Are the impacts of these behaviors short-term or long-term? How do these behaviors differ from the results of previous practices?

The most significant result observed to date is the willingness of individuals to obtain the training through the TeleTraining alternative, as opposed to forgoing training when only traditional classroom instruction was available. This directly addresses the goals of the TeleTraining program, as it is accomplishing what was set forth as its primary objective (to train remote professionals who could not avail themselves of the classroom training).

The company anticipates that results will be long term, as the impetus for developing TeleTraining appears to grow stronger each year, resulting in a greater need for highly focused training that can be delivered to a growing population of remote professionals. Data show that in traditional classroom training only 15 percent of the participants are remote clients. With TeleTraining, this figure increases to 40 percent. This percentage has remained consistent, resulting in our being able to reach 20 percent more virtual clients through TeleTraining as compared with classroom training.

It is anticipated that 10,000 learners will take advantage of the TeleTraining opportunity in the next fiscal year, representing 30 percent of the firm. In most cases, TeleTraining is reaching a population that otherwise would not have received training, or at best, would have received the training much too late. Ease of use and overall greater availability are two of the major reasons why TeleTraining is continuing to grow.

The firm's edge over our competitors is a superior knowledge environment with a multitude of tools being available to all members of the firm. Knowing how to leverage the tools properly provides the difference between winning and losing sales opportunities or keeping its existing external clients updated with the latest information. TeleTraining is a powerful tool to help maintain this advantage in an environment that is fast paced and constantly changing.

8. What was the impact of the practice on your organization? Are the impacts of these behaviors short-term or long-term? Wherever possible please include actual figures related to the practice.

The impacts of the TeleTraining program are forecast to be long term as the need for continuous training becomes greater. This is especially true with knowledge-based tools that are being deployed rapidly and frequently. To retain its competitive advantage, the firm encourages proficient use of the knowledge tools. If TeleTraining did not exist, employees could gain proficiency only through self-paced alternatives or traditional classroom training. Firm measurements indicate that TeleTraining has become a viable alternative, and it expects this trend to continue.

Following the logic that better-trained individuals are more proficient in the use of technology, the firm would expect a direct impact on the its bottom line. As employees become more efficient, the firm can redeploy resources to other engagements, and we win a higher percentage of proposals.

Shared Learning

9. What have been some of the specific lessons learned from designing and implementing this practice for the purposes of continuous internal improvement? Please discuss whether and how this practice might be transferred and replicated both internally and external to your organization.

The most significant lesson learned is that traditional methods of training are fine as long as the environment in which one is training remains traditional. With the pace of the business world quickening and the demands for knowledge growing exponentially, companies must design and implement nontraditional alternatives in order to meet the needs of the business, the firm, and its people. TeleTraining has been very successful. Several new benefits have become available to the members of the firm without any perceived losses. The company will continue to offer more traditional training alternatives, thus allowing our employees to obtain more comprehensive training. In the meantime, TeleTraining is reaching a subset of the firm's population that received no training in the past, and this is helping to raise the bar on foundation and knowledge learning.

As noted above, other groups within the firm have expressed great interest in TeleTraining. As it is the firm's objective to disseminate training to the same groups (but usually with different content), this practice can be easily transferred and replicated. The requirements would be to identify the qualified TeleTraining instructor, to design and develop the course materials, and then to include the program in the national registration system. Beyond that, the technical aspects have already been tested and have proved to be workable.

Paul Ishimaru is manager, Professional Services at Intellinex LLC. Contact him at paul.ishimaru@ey.com.

Online Performance and Learning at BellSouth

Darin E. Hartley

This article is excerpted from the book On-Demand Learning *and describes how BellSouth is using distance learning and other technologies to move corporate goals forward.*

Online Performance and Learning at BellSouth

Online Performance and Learning at BellSouth

BellSouth is a $23 billion international communications company, headquartered in Atlanta, Georgia, providing telecommunications, wireless communications, cable and digital TV, directory advertising and publishing, and Internet and data services to nearly 31 million customers in 19 countries worldwide. The BellSouth Leadership Institute (BSLI) is responsible for providing high-quality management and executive education across the BellSouth companies. Management development courses supplement on-the-job training and technical job training courses, and play an important role in the overall development of management employees.

In the fall of 1998, two circumstances arose simultaneously at BellSouth, prompting the need for an online coaching and leadership development system. The two driving issues, and the solution the BellSouth Leadership Institute implemented to address them, are discussed below.

The Challenge

During a management needs assessment process, performed by the BellSouth Leadership Institute, a new learning need became evident: the need for a just-in-time coaching resource to supplement classroom training experiences and supervisory support.

To ensure it's meeting the needs of its management employees, BSLI carefully gathers needs assessment data approximately every 18 months. During the latest assessment, which started in the spring of 1998 and was completed later that fall, BSLI sent surveys to a statistically valid random sample of first- and second-level supervisors, and followed these surveys up with focus groups to discuss findings in more detail.

One of the key findings was that supervisory managers need just-in-time learning resources to address critical problems and issues. The managers reported that they still value the face-to-face training programs offered by BSLI, but they are unable to participate in group classroom sessions for *all* of their learning needs, and the classroom sessions are not always timely enough to meet immediate needs.

This need was exacerbated by the fact that BellSouth is hiring first-level managers at a fast rate to prepare for a significant volume of expected retirements in the first few years of the next century. BSLI believes that just-in-time learning resources for these new managers will be critical, because their learning curve is steep.

The second factor driving BellSouth to the implementation of an online learning system occurred at about the same time. BellSouth's senior leadership team reassessed organizational goals to bring them in line with the company's vision for the future. As a result, they devised three organizational aspirations:

- A Great Place to Work: Top 100 Employer
- Tops in Customer Loyalty
- Financial Excellence

BellSouth recognizes that a significant factor in employee satisfaction is the opportunity to learn and develop. The 1998 BellSouth Employee Satisfaction survey revealed that 68 percent of employees would like more opportunities for training.

"We want to meet our managers' needs for training opportunities," said Scott Boston, Director—Management Training and Development, BSLI. "We believe that if our employees are satisfied, then they'll work harder to satisfy our customers. Our new online coaching system helps support our company's first and second aspirations."

The Solution

At first, Boston and team believed they would offer a medley of online courses to meet the just-in-time learning needs of leaders. They planned to offer a wide selection of online courseware, some developed internally and some externally, from which managers could select learning tools. They then realized that a more appropriate response to the stated needs of supervisory managers was an Electronic Performance Support System (EPSS) that provides easily searched and retrieved, small bytes of learning. The managers didn't need to complete a structured online course for every learning need. Rather, they needed fast coaching resources and job-transfer tools for quick skill application. People are smart enough to use smaller bits of knowledge to perform a new skill without knowing all of the theory and background behind a topical area.

BSLI found a solution in OPAL℠, *Online Performance and Learning*, from Development Dimensions International (DDI), headquartered in Pittsburgh, Pennsylvania. OPAL is a rare example of an EPSS for human performance skills, also called soft skills, and it dovetails nicely with the classroom training offered by BSLI (some of which also comes from DDI). It is made up of three components: *Advisor*, which offers just-in-time coaching arranged by work situation; *Developer*, which provides competency-based skill development resources; and *Assessor*, which provides learners with a fast and easy, individually driven method for collecting feedback on competencies to drive development activities. Developer and Assessor are described more fully at the end of this chapter.

To meet employees' immediate needs, BSLI chose to implement OPAL Advisor for the entire management population in all thirty-six BellSouth companies. Several companies also opted to promote OPAL to their non-management employees.

OPAL Advisor provides a range of learning resources that employees can access on a just-in-time basis. Employees get practical tips, guidelines, pointers, and pitfalls with a click of the mouse. In addition, there are more than 200 skill-building tools, such as checklists, road maps, guidelines for action, planners, tip sheets, and intervention techniques, that are designed to be used on the job to help people use what they learn. Also included are sell-assessments, which help employees determine where to focus their learning. The topics in Advisor cover a wide variety of job situations, from rescuing difficult meetings to being a good team member to developing ideas in a discussion.

The topics are grouped under thirteen skill areas:

- Change
- Coaching
- Collaborating
- Conflict
- Core Interpersonal Skills
- Customer Service
- Delegating
- Interviewing
- Meetings
- Performance Management
- Productivity
- Stress Management
- Teams

BSLI found that these topics support the learning needs most requested by BellSouth supervisory managers, and that the content is relevant and comprehensive. "BSLI is impressed with the variety of suggestions and performance tools offered with each situation, and has found OPAL to be as beneficial to managers who have only a few minutes, as to those who need more comprehensive coaching and guidance," said Boston.

The Implementation

BSLI analyzed OPAL's content to ensure it supported BellSouth's policies and language/terminology. They also put OPAL through usability tests and a pilot to make sure that it would be valuable and user-friendly to their target population. OPAL was seen by the test and pilot participants to be an effective and usable tool. The results helped drive communication strategy and positioning, as well as customization of the system for greater ease-of-use and clarity. BSLI performed some simple customization, while DDI helped with more advanced applications.

BSLI conducted usability studies on six management employees from different BellSouth entities. Employees were given sample tough work scenarios and asked to solve problems through advice found in OPAL. The participants found the site easy to navigate and the content helpful.

After receiving the favorable usability study results, BSLI conducted a pilot on 3,000 management and nonmanagement employees at BellSouth Advertising and Publishing Company (BAPCO), in early spring 1999. During this pilot, communication and orientation materials, as well as OPAL itself, were evaluated. Feedback from the management employees was positive.

BSLI decided to target management employees with the new online training package. The staff sent a communications package, complete with a cover letter, brochure, and a laminated helpful hints card, to all BellSouth first- and second-level managers in June 1999.

BSLI has recently identified an additional application for OPAL at BellSouth, which is currently under consideration. Future management employees at BellSouth go through an assessment before being considered for a management role. BellSouth believes OPAL can help prepare the test participants for the evaluation, and enhance pass ratios.

The Early Results and Future Measurement

Although long-term impact has yet to be measured, BellSouth has received positive survey and anecdotal feedback from BAPCO employees. Management users found that OPAL is particularly helpful when they face a discussion with an employee or co-worker of a challenging nature, such as poor performance, work habits, or personal problems that interfere with productivity.

BAPCO employees also found that OPAL's performance support tools are very valuable. One tool in particular, a Meeting Planner found in the Leading Successful Meetings portion of Advisor, was reported by numerous managers to cut meeting time in half, which can obviously lead to significant pay-off in productivity gains across large numbers of people. Users additionally reported that OPAL is easy to learn and navigate without formal training.

These early results are positive indicators for a successful ongoing OPAL implementation. BSLI plans to continue to gather feedback from several sources and create monthly reports on the progress of the OPAL program. Users will have three ways to offer feedback on OPAL to BSLI: a "feedback icon," a hotline, and the next needs assessment survey during which feedback for OPAL will be queried specifically. The BSLI measurement team will analyze results from all these sources, and evaluate usage via a web tracking system to drive the monthly reports.

The ultimate goal is for supervisory managers to report improvements in managerial effectiveness and greater availability of appropriate, just-in-time learning opportunities. "We look forward to analyzing the monthly reports," Boston said. "Based on the results, we may further customize OPAL to meet our employees' needs."

More About OPAL

In addition to OPAL Advisor, OPAL offers two other components, each of which offers different types of online development support.

Providing time-efficient, just-what's-needed learning, OPAL Developer helps employees understand and gain skill in a variety of business competencies. Employees select the competency they want to develop; they can then read a complete, concise definition of the competency, and click to Quick Tips for on-the-spot help. They can thoroughly investigate each of the competency's key behaviors to learn exactly what's expected on the job, including off-key actions and over-actions, behaviors that either fall short of the mark or go too far. To further reinforce their knowledge and transfer it to the job, they can work through a range of over 300 capacity-building exercises.

Developer fosters both intellectual understanding as well as the skills to put that knowledge into practice. To develop their skills, learners can explore OPAL Developer's thirty-two competencies, which are customizable to reflect an organization's existing competency models:

- Adaptability
- Aligning Performance for Success
- Building a Successful Team
- Building Customer Loyalty
- Building Partnerships
- Building Strategic Working Relationships
- Building Trust
- Coaching
- Sales Ability/Persuasiveness
- Collaboration
- Contributing to Team Success
- Continuous Improvement
- Continuous Learning
- Customer Focus
- Decision Making
- Delegating Responsibility

- Developing Others
- Follow-up
- Formal Presentation
- Gaining Commitment
- Impact
- Information Monitoring
- Initiating Action
- Innovation
- Leading through Vision and Values
- Managing Conflict
- Managing Work
- Oral Communication
- Negotiation
- Planning and Organizing
- Tenacity
- Written Communication

OPAL Assessor is an online tool employees can use to create flexible assessment surveys designed to target strengths and development areas within a broad range of competencies and associated key actions, the specific behaviors that make up the competency. Users create their own self- or self-plus-other surveys by clicking through OPAL's easy-to-follow prompts. They choose what competencies and key actions they'll be evaluated on, and indicate who will receive the survey. OPAL does the rest. It sends the survey out, logs who has or has not responded, and creates easy-to-read reports of the results. Survey respondents are anonymous; the employee initiating the survey doesn't see individual ratings, only compiled results from all respondents.

The employee can view detailed ratings of all the competencies and key actions, a prioritized list of strengths and weaknesses, and a self-versus-others comparison of all the competencies and key actions. The survey reports also have hyperlinks that take the learner instantly to OPAL Developer for immediate online help with strengthening specific competencies.

BellSouth is considering OPAL Developer and Assessor for future implementation.

Darin E. Hartley, a ten-plus-year training veteran, has undergraduate and graduate degrees in Corporate Training and Training Management. Darin manages the Dell Learning Technology Services Department of Dell Computer Corporation's training organization. Prior to Dell, Darin worked for Lockheed Martin, EG&G, General Physics Corporation, and the U.S. Navy as a nuclear power plant operator for eight years. Darin has also authored Job Analysis at the Speed of Reality. *He has presented at many conferences on both on-demand learning and the JASR method.*

Asynchronous Distance Learning for Corporate Education: Experiences with Lotus LearningSpace

Lisa Neal and Debbie Ingram

This article by two practitioners explains how they used technology in an asynchronous distance learning course. They discuss the technology they chose, why the asynchronous mode worked for them, and what lessons they learned in doing this course.

We used Lotus LearningSpace to teach an asynchronous distance learning class on human-computer interaction (HCI) to employees at EDS, a global information-technology services company. Based on this experience, we suggest that asynchronous distance learning presents significant potential for delivering training in a corporate setting and that LearningSpace is a powerful resource for course delivery. More importantly, however, we argue for wider recognition of instructor-led asynchronous distance learning as fundamentally discontinuous with other delivery models since it demands entirely different approaches in the dimensions of course development, pedagogical behaviors, and student expectations than are used for the classroom or synchronous distance learning.

Course Planning and Selection of LearningSpace

We selected Lotus LearningSpace 2.5 to deliver a course on HCI at EDS, basing our selection on an existing EDS-Lotus relationship rather than on a systematic evaluation of authoring tools or distance learning packages. The project began in response to EDS' interest in migrating certain classroom-delivered training to the Web. Web-based training is becoming common in corporate training programs due to cost effectiveness, maturation of IT infrastructures to accommodate Web-based training, and advancements in Internet technologies and access (Julian and Capozzi, 1998). Asynchronous distance learning has the advantages of time zone independence and, once developed, it can be reused much more easily than the synchronous or classroom versions, with a knowledgeable facilitator to replace or assist the instructor. There is also the pedagogical advantage that students have time to think about points made in class and their contributions (Laurillard, 1993), as well as to relate what they learn to their jobs. The opportunity to pursue the HCI course's delivery via LearningSpace provided us a point of departure for examining asynchronous distance learning, as well as the LearningSpace tool. Further, this opportunity enabled EDS' training organization a basis upon which to evaluate Web-based education. To our use of LearningSpace, we brought extensive expertise with Lotus Notes/Domino development, traditional classroom teaching, and synchronous distance learning (Neal 1997, Neal 1998a, and Neal 1998b).

LearningSpace includes five modules, a schedule, a repository for course content, a threaded discussion area, personal home pages, and tools used by the instructor for creating and grading exams. We intentionally strove to use all of LearningSpace's capabilities in order to fully experience its potential as a course delivery mechanism. As part of our preparation, we took Lotus Education's LearningSpace classes to ensure that we leveraged the tool as much as possible. While helpful, especially since we hosted the class internally and provided all technical support, these classes focused on the mechanics of using LearningSpace rather than on strategies and methods for developing course materials for an asynchronous-learning environment. Contrary to our expectations, our professional networks and pertinent newsgroups yielded sparse information that guided our course design and content development efforts.

Synchronicity vs. Asynchronicity: A Fundamental Discontinuity

Although we had taught HCI many times previously, we found that preparing an asynchronous class was a different and difficult process. We learned that asynchronous distance learning classes are often developed by teams, in which instructional designers, multimedia specialists, and technical experts obtain information from subject matter experts. This has advantages over our approach since it narrows each contributor's focus; we had two people playing all roles as well as providing technical support. Planning and developing the class top-down necessitated having a clearer picture of the class activities—as translated into LearningSpace—than we started with. We worked instead in a more linear fashion, developing content while planning what the student interactions with the material and each other should be like in order to create an engaging learning experience. We were surprised at the time and attention that were essential to ensure the quality of the course's content.

Writing text was the most striking and time-consuming difference from the preparation of previous classes, since they had been delivered orally and fairly spontaneously, aided by PowerPoint slides. Creating content was ultimately like writing a book, with more consideration for pacing, exercises, and multimedia than most books necessitate, as well as more opportunities to personalize and update it than a printed book allows. Another difficulty in preparing the class was that we were accustomed to giving live presentations, in which materials were presented differently based on the presenter's mood and the audience makeup, feedback, and reactions. Writing text seemed static in comparison. There was also the perceived need to accurately reference or attribute text, which is generally not an issue in a verbal presentation since the reference is less important than the point being made.

In teaching HCI, like most topics, there is a recitation of facts supplemented by rich examples that serve to illustrate the facts as well as pace the class. Many of these examples are presented differently based on a variety of factors; for example, the humorous or frustrating aspects of a consulting engagement might be exaggerated, especially in a class occurring after lunch. In developing an asynchronous class, we felt self-conscious capturing this informal information, whether as text or audio, without an audience and with less control over materials since people besides the actual students might have access to the class. In addition to the streaming audio used for informal information, we added other multimedia, mainly relevant cartoons and graphics, to break up the text and URLs to link to resources.

The class required two hours a day from each student for a two-week period. To make students' class time more compelling, we choreographed the segments with multiple activities, such as reading, discussion participation, and exams. Using the LearningSpace environment for preparation of the class proved fairly straightforward; the main difficulties were in developing the content and determining the content and structure that would make the class most effective. We started the class with an e-mail message that welcomed students, followed by a one-hour conference call on the first day. We added a closing conference call, as well as individual phone calls that we made to each student halfway through the class to check on their progress and prospect for questions. These were the only synchronous activities, since we wanted to fully experience the LearningSpace environment. When the class began, there were some administrative and technical problems that were not anticipated and were primarily circumstance-dependent. We spent the first days of the class trying to correct these problems; about half of the class of seventeen, including most of the non-U.S. students, were impacted. Lost start-up time was a problem in a class of such short duration. Students were in four countries, and time zone differences meant technical support had to be available beyond typical work hours. In LearningSpace, discussions were built into the class by presenting topics and hoping students would have lively and evocative responses. There was less ability for us to gauge, from immediate feedback or prior knowledge of student job experience or interests, that it was a good time or topic for a discussion. Many postings were self-contained, rather than responses to other postings or dialogues, and some students contributed heavily to the discussions while others did very little. This resulted in fewer opportunities for students to learn from each other's experiences and insights and to network, which are valuable parts of any class and particularly valuable in corporate training. Interestingly, there were more complaints about time zone differences than there had been in previous synchronous distance learning classes; students were frustrated when no one responded immediately to their postings or when project teams had trouble meeting.

Lessons Learned and Student Feedback

In both phone conversations and class evaluations, student feedback was largely positive, especially when students were asked to discuss the initial technical and administrative difficulties separately. We learned an enormous amount from the student feedback and from our own perceptions about the design of our course, the use of LearningSpace, and asynchronicity. We learned, for example, that the exams were not constructive as designed, either for the students to use for self-evaluation or for us to use to gauge their progress. Discussion participation was lower than expected, in part, because of navigation between the class notes and a discussion area. Students unanimously suggested that subsequent classes start off with a hands-on introduction to LearningSpace, in addition to the textual tutorial we included, so that no time is lost gaining comfort with the tool.

We were confident of our abilities to keep students motivated and engaged in a classroom or a synchronous distance learning class, but concerned about how to do so in an asynchronous environment. It was hard to gauge how much the students were learning: the threaded discussions and tests did not provide as much feedback on student's grasp of the concepts as did real-time discussions. Although our students' positive feedback was gratifying, we were nevertheless surprised by the amount of adaptation that was necessary because of the absence of traditional classroom behaviors that teachers and students take for granted. For example, the comparatively simple teacher-student feedback loops that enable teachers to evaluate how the class and particular individuals are progressing are largely absent. Essential questions, such as the efficiency with which students learn and how satisfied they are with the course, go largely unanswered until end-of-class class evaluations are available.

Conclusions

Our experiences suggest that asynchronous distance learning carries substantial potential and that LearningSpace is a powerful and effective delivery tool. However, we need approaches that will manage both teachers' and learners' expectations about what to expect in asynchronously delivered instruction while highlighting the advantages of this delivery method, as well as methods and strategies that will enable teachers to more effectively develop courses for asynchronous delivery. We also suggest refinement of LearningSpace and other tools to the end of facilitating navigation and overcoming such challenges as are specific to asynchronous learning, such as developing relationships electronically. Undoubtedly, additional synchronous activities would have changed the nature of our class and enhanced the communication, as many students commented in their evaluations. Facilitating live discussions is a developed skill, but we found it much easier than the facilitation of asynchronous discussions, where it is challenging to draw out people who are not contributing, quiet others, and comment appropriately and constructively on contributions. Integration of real-time discussions and chats, as will be available in subsequent releases of LearningSpace, benefit the students and instructor, since they learn more from, and are more of a resource to, each other.

References

Julian, E., and Capozzi, M., *The Emerging Market for Web-Based Training, 1996–2002,* IDC Document #15602, March 1998.

Laurillard, D., *Rethinking University Teaching: A Framework for the Effective Use of Educational Technology.* London: Routledge, 1993.

Neal, L. (1998a), "A Comparison of Two Distance Learning Classes," in *Teleteaching '98 Distance Learning, Training and Education, Proceedings of the XV. IFIP World Computer Congress,* Vienna, Austria and Budapest, Hungary, August 31-September 4, 1998.

Neal, L. (1998b), "Issues in the Development and Delivery of Distance Learning Classes," in *Proceedings of ED-MEDIA & ED-TELECOM 98,* Freiburg, Germany, June 20-25, 1998.

Neal, L., "Virtual Classrooms and Communities," in *Proceedings of GROUP 97,* Phoenix, Arizona, November 16-19, 1997.

Lisa Neal is a senior research engineer at Electronic Data Systems. She consults on e-learning projects with corporate and academic clients and has been developing and delivering e-learning classes at EDS for more than five years. She is editor-in-chief of eLearn, *ACM's new online newsletter. She received her Ph.D. in computer science from Harvard University.*

Debbie Ingram was a systems engineer and e-learning consultant for EDS for ten years and is currently an independent software developer/consultant.

Part Four

State of the Art: Distance Learning in Government

I n the past few years, government has become a leading advocate of distance learning. It has also become a leading practitioner in many agencies and departments, especially the military. The purpose of Part Four is to look at what the government is doing in distance and e-learning and how different groups are going about it.

This part of the book includes three articles that we believe give a good sense of distance learning in government. The first, "From Sea to Shining Sea" by Todd W. Carter, examines how the U.S. Navy is using distance learning technology to deliver training to personnel stationed around the world. Using the Web, the navy can continuously update its offerings and these can be accessed from anywhere when needed, including at sea.

The second reading in Part Four, "Distance Learning Takes Root at Government Agencies" by Ed McKenna, looks at how distance learning is being adopted as a practical and economical way to train people. The article includes examples from the General Services Administration and the Social Security Administration and introduces the Advanced Distributed Learning (ADL) sponsored by the White House to come up with common standards for DL in government.

This leads us to the third article in this part, "All About ADL" by J.D.Fletcher and Philip Dodds. This explains why the ADL was established and how it works.

We believe these three articles will give you a basic sense of how government is adopting DL to meet its training needs. Of course, the methods the government is using may indeed have application in other sectors, and if you don't work in the public sector, we urge you to read these articles from that perspective.

From Sea to Shining Sea: Navy Online Training

Todd W. Carter

Training people who are scattered across the globe has long been a challenge for the Army and Navy. They are looking to online courses to help change that. Here's how.

As a Navy electrician in Norfolk, Va., master chief David Burnette knows a little bit about wires. And he's finding that a wired world can help him learn about new technologies without spending a minute in the classroom. Burnette already has spent several months learning the deep, dark secrets of Microsoft software from his home computer. The Navy's library of about 350 online courses allows him to study Word, Excel and other applications at his own pace. At the same time, he's gathering the knowledge he needs to become a certified expert in these programs.

"It's the best thing I've seen in a long time as far as online training," he says from his office at the Navy's Shore Intermediate Maintenance Activity facility. "You can go in and set up your own training program."

Technology Is the Tool

Burnette is one of thousands of military employees using Web-based training (WBT) to conveniently increase their technology skills from nearly anywhere in the world. In addition, military trainers are finding that WBT may encourage more people to take classes while allowing the military's dwindling funds to stretch further.

"What we've been doing for the last couple of years is looking at learning strategies to determine how we can improve our learning with our reduced resources," says Phyllis Ferguson, deputy director for education and training strategies in the Navy's Pensacola, Fla., education and training office. "Manpower is going down and dollars are going down. So we have to come up with some creative ways to teach people what they need to know in order to do their jobs more efficiently. And obviously, technology is the tool."

Thousands of the Navy's 1.2 million civilian and military employees visit the organization's online training site every day. Some of those users are looking to learn specific skills, while others want to complete an entire course. Overall, the Navy has more than 4,000 courses that it offers in various mediums. WBT courses and classes transmitted over closed-circuit television networks are among those that eschew traditional classroom settings in favor of technology. Students can also take advantage of an around-the-clock help desk.

"In the past five years, we've made some movement away from the traditional classroom setting or made efforts to augment it," Ferguson says. "We may still teach people in the classroom, but we'll also send the CD-ROM courses out to where the sailors are working."

For Navy employees who have Internet access, some classes are scheduled so that groups of students move through the material together, using Internet chat functions to communicate with each other. Beginning as early as this summer, the Navy will host some of those collaborative functions on its Web servers. "People have opportunities to study together or to discuss things that they're not real comfortable or familiar with," Ferguson says.

But the Navy definitely isn't ready to move all of its training to the Internet. "We're not closing our schoolhouses by any stretch," she says. "We have to selectively determine what gets taught in a schoolhouse, what gets taught totally outside the schoolhouse, and what gets taught in multiple locations."

Training at Sea

Of course, with ships and sailors spread out across the world, often in the middle of large masses of water, the Navy has some problems with WBT that other military branches don't experience. "The other services certainly have their people dispersed all over the world, but they're typically land-based," Ferguson says. "[Accessing] the Internet on a ship is a little more challenging than it is at certain land bases. We've been trying to figure out the best way of tackling the bandwidth issue."

Satellites provide Internet access to the Navy's aircraft carriers and other large ships. Some midsize ships also have access, Ferguson says, but they don't have enough bandwidth to handle live video and audio. For smaller vessels without Internet access, technicians install the courses directly onto computer servers, eliminating the need for a live connection. Information about students and the courses they've completed are stored on the servers just as they would be if the classes were taken online.

But even when online courses are available on board ships, Navy personnel often don't have time to take them. Sailors regularly work 18 hours a day, six days a week. With that schedule, even combat might seem easy compared with finding time for training.

When sailors find they can't perform their jobs without training, though, making time for it gets a little easier. "Say someone is working on a boiler and something goes wrong with it," Ferguson says. "They don't know how to fix it, and the expert is on leave that week. They can go and pull down that courseware if it's available. It's an 'I need it right now,' just-in-time kind of training."

Navy employees can choose from about 350 off-the-shelf courses that have been licensed from several vendors, including NETg and Cisco. Most of the technology-based classes focus on IT topics. Navy officials hope to add some custom, Navy-specific online classes in the future for example, corrosion control, fire control and surface warfare.

For the most part, the move to WBT has been a smooth process for the Navy, though no system is bug-free, Ferguson warns. "Keep in mind that mostly what we're using are commercially procured products that have been on the market awhile. They have been used by literally millions of people, not just military people," she says. "When we introduce our new network with newly developed courses, we expect we will run into some bugs." She says the Navy plans to do extensive pre-testing so they can catch some of those bugs before launching the commercial courses.

While the military's acceptance of online classes is growing, there still are hurdles. Next to bandwidth issues, the biggest challenge is the cultural change, says Ferguson. Older students and traditional classroom instructors may need more education about WBT. "It's a real cultural change to have a wealth of information available to you when you want it," she says. "It's difficult to get the people who are used to teaching in the formal schoolhouse setting to accept that there's another way of training people and educating people."

Long-Term Training

Meanwhile, the Army started offering technology-delivered courses in November 1998. At the time, they had about 800 online classes. Today, that number has grown to more than 1,100. Soldiers and Army civilians can take Web-based courses or request a set of 32 CD-ROMs containing all of the classes.

More than 120,000 people have enrolled in the Army's courses since November 1998. The Army spent about $800,000 to license the courses, according to Col. John Grobmeier, director of acquisition for the Army's command, control, communications and computers office. To make sure they continue to get funding, officials are making the training a part of the service's long-range planning and budgeting process, he says.

"It's an important aspect that we're offering to our young soldiers now in order to incentivize them to consider the Army as a long-term career," says Grobmeier. Most of the IT classes use off-the-shelf courseware from Reston, Va.-based SmartForce.

"To have had 117,000 people sign up this quickly, it's almost a grassroots-type thing," Grobmeier says. "Soldiers and civilians have learned through our publicity that it's available, and the response has been great."

Despite the initial success, the Army's classroom learning won't be phased out anytime soon. While computer-based courseware has some strong advantages, he says, "the human factor is also important when you want to enrich somebody and develop an individual as a total person. I think it's a complementary approach."

No Limits

Military officials seem to shun any suggestion that trainees may take online courses to make themselves more marketable in non-military careers. But with the high demand for information technology workers, and the focus of so many online courses on technical subjects, it seems plausible that many are doing so.

"We find that a better-trained sailor, given more opportunity for learning and education, has a tendency to stay in the Navy," Ferguson says. "All [courses] are to help them in their Navy careers, not to help them in their [post-Navy] careers." Still, she acknowledges that "some of that might happen."

Grobmeier agrees. "Yes, some people are going to receive education of this type in the military and then use that as a springboard when they retire, or if they decide to leave the service early and enter into the private sector," he says. "But either way, computer-based training in these types of initiatives is an investment in the American resource."

If the military enlisted the Navy's Burnette as its poster sailor for online learning, there's a good chance that thousands of civilian and military workers would follow his lead. "There's really no limit as far as what you can do," he says.

Todd W. Carter is a freelance writer in Jenison, Mich, specializing in business and technology. He can be reached at todd@toddcarter.com.

Distance Learning Takes Root at Government Agencies

Ed McKenna

Goverment has been promoting the use of distance learning in many venues. This article, however, explains how various federal government agencies are using distance learning to more efficiently deliver training to employees in many different locations.

Federal agencies are in a bind. As they deploy advanced technology to improve delivery of services amid flat or declining budgets, they also are ratcheting up the pressure on their downsized work force to adjust quickly to new systems and responsibilities.

The government is in the middle of a technology movement where job responsibilities are changing rapidly, said Elaine Lowry, program manager for the General Services Administration Online University. "We have to be able to learn much quicker [and] do more with less."

To avert a skills gap and still keep costs down, government organizations are launching distance-learning initiatives—often called e-learning when involving the Internet—using Web-based, satellite and videoconferencing technologies to deliver critical training to their employees.

E-learning in the professional training market is booming. Revenue from e-learning, including solely Internet or intranet-based initiatives for both the private and public sector, will surge from about $550 million in 1998 to about $11.4 billion in 2003—

a robust 84 percent annual growth rate, said Ellen Julian, an analyst with the market research company International Data Corp. of Framingham, Mass.

A mix of workplace and cost-cutting issues is sparking that growth in the government sector.

In today's busier work environment, these programs give employees who find it difficult to get away from their desks an opportunity to learn new IT skills or even polish their office skills, Lowry said. Using Web-based courses offered by the GSA Online University, they can "spend maybe an hour one day or two the next on the courses ... or work over a weekend or in the evening." This allows them to complete their mission for their organization and learn at the same time, she added.

Since the online university opened for business in April 1999, GSA employees have taken about 3,000 courses, noted Lowry, who said that GSA offers a catalog of 250 courses covering IT and office skills, all published or licensed through the project's contractor, Vcampus Corp. of Reston, Va.

Vcampus is an application service provider that not only provides off-the-shelf and custom-designed courseware, but also hosts the programs on its own servers, noted Firuzeh McLean, director of business development at Vcampus. Plans are afoot to open the offerings of GSA to other federal organizations, McLean added.

These programs give the agencies "a logistical boost for training an increasingly mobile and distributed work force," said Clark Aldrich, an analyst with the GartnerGroup, Stamford, Conn.

With the advent of distributed computing, telecommuting and telecenters, "our whole operation at the federal government has changed dramatically," said Marc Santini, program director of the GSA Federal Technology Service's federal learning technology program, or Fed Learn—a program begun late last year to help agencies develop distance learning programs.

"In my organization, people are distributed all over the country, so they can be closer to the clients and for them to get any training they have to get on a plane," Santini said. Using the Internet makes "it very easy to access online courses and very inexpensive," he said, citing the cost of all GSA online courses at $100 or under.

FAA and SSA

Having that distance learning accessibility also translates into savings in per diem and transportation costs for users of the satellite-based program at the Federal Aviation Administration Academy, according to Rich Schrum, interactive video teletraining operations manager at the academy based in Oklahoma City. From there, the system reaches 65 sites around the country.

"Aviation security folks are one of our big users because they have field agents at every airport all over the world," he said. "We [also] are a quick means of getting information out," including new laws and congressional mandates, he added.

The Social Security Administration gets similar benefits from its satellite-based learning program, according to Jim Noble, senior technology adviser for the interactive video teletraining system at SSA. The program began as a pilot project in 1995 and has been managed since 1997 by Electronic Data Systems Corp., Plano, Texas, under the Department of Energy's Telecommunications Integrator Services contract, valued at $600 million over five years.

At present, the system comprises 830 facilities and five broadcast studios around the country. It will add another 670 sites and a studio in the next two years, said Noble. SSA has invested about $13 million in the program so far and the agency likely will begin some Web-based training during that time frame, he added.

FAA and SSA are two of 10 agencies, including the Internal Revenue Service and the Department of Veterans Affairs, that use technology from San Jose, Calif.-based One Touch Systems Inc., according to Kevin Lawrence, government regional manager for the company in Washington. The company offers distance learning systems for satellite, videoconferencing and the Web, said John Futrell, One Touch vice president for North American sales.

All the initiatives are being acquired off the GSA schedule, said Futrell, who noted that the company takes part in several schedules of other companies, including Hughes Global Systems, which owns 51 percent of One Touch.

Programs such as those offered by One Touch offer a way to deal with the thorny issue of employee retention by providing an easier outlet for continuing education. "The government is having a bear of a time retaining good IT [personnel]," Aldrich said. "It takes three years to train them and then they leave."

Since it cannot hope to compete on a salary basis with private-sector employers, the government has to adopt a long-term plan that provides continual training to keep ever-changing employees up to date, Aldrich added.

Variable Standards

There are only a couple of dark clouds in this otherwise bright picture and one of them is the lack of standards.

No standards for interoperability have been developed despite more than two years of work by various standards bodies as well as a White House-sponsored Advanced Distributed Learning initiative, or ADL, that was tasked to facilitate development of common standards.

To date, the ADL has produced a publication called SCORM—Shareable Courseware Objects Reference Model—said Raye Newman, director of human performance at Science Applications International Corp., San Diego. "The emphasis right now for SCORM is metadata and how you can describe the learning objects in ways that make them easy to find and use and reuse," he said. While that has gotten a lot of press, the standards it is based on are still evolving, according to Newman.

But Aldrich argued that standards are not particularly relevant at this point. "Right now we are in a best of breeds world [with] de facto standards. When you look at formal standards bodies in the learning area, they are kind of lowest common denominator," he said.

It has been more effective to allow top companies to build custom bridges between their systems, he maintained. "Once the technology stabilizes a little bit, then standards will come into play," he said. But that may not occur for three to four years.

Another challenge that is surfacing is the substantial market potential for distance learning. The promise of a possible financial windfall has spawned a confusing, crowded marketplace. "Every month there are new companies and new technologies and you can't keep up with [the pace]. ... It is the next revolution in IT," Santini said.

Yet all that growth "is confusing for our customers because there is a lot of hype and things are changing rapidly," said Newman. "It is not only the new products, but all the new releases with new architectures from companies that have been in the market for some time—everybody wants to be for everybody," he said.

Fed Learn offers one solution to this problem in the public sector, according to Santini. "My market niche is to provide IT solutions for traditional training issues that agencies have," he said. "I take care of their project, contract and financial management and any legal support—the whole soup to nuts."

In the meantime, government organizations have adopted a number of strategies on their own.

Many organizations are vesting their trust in traditional systems integrators. The Army National Guard and Air Force National Guard respectively have tapped EDS and Murray Hill, N.J.-based Lucent Technologies Inc. to manage their expansive video-conferencing-based programs. Begun in 1996 under a GSA blanket purchase order, the Army Guard's Distributive Training Technology Project now reaches 151 classrooms located in every state and territory and is still growing, said Gary Yenser, vice president of distance learning solutions for EDS' federal business in Herndon, Va.

"They've deployed a nationwide telecommunications backbone that is capable of supporting two-way full interactive voice data and video," Yenser said, adding that "Internet access is embedded in the [network] architecture." A variety of technologies are used in the project, including videoconferencing systems such as VTEL, PictureTel and First Virtual.

The Air Guard uses the PictureTel system to reach 170 classrooms across the country, said Chief Master Sgt. Bill Moore, who manages the systems for the Guard at Andrews Air Force Base, Md. The Air Force has invested about $15 million over the five years it has been in place, according to Moore, who said the service is looking to deploy desktop video and voice via the Internet over the next two years. "We have our own contract with Lucent and now are in the process of negotiating a new contract with the same support," he said.

Along with working with the Chief of Naval Education and Training office on the service's broad-based distance learning initiatives, SAIC is shepherding the Naval School of Health Sciences' efforts to transition its CD-ROM training system to the Web. "We are providing a reality check to keep smaller agencies [such as Health Sciences] apprised of where big Navy is going so they will end up being consistent," Newman said.

The school is test piloting the Accredix distance learning system from Alameda, Calif.-based Knowledge360. "If that is successful it will presumably take the next step and find a way to go worldwide with this capability," said Newman of the Navy. That would mean an estimated 15,000 to 20,000 medical professionals all over the world would be using the system, said Josh Berson, vice president of marketing at Knowledge360.

Similarly, General Dynamics Corp.'s Taunton, Mass.-based Communication Systems unit is managing a pilot project for the Department of Agriculture designed to reach an estimated 2 million disadvantaged farmers, said Richard Semon, director of distance learning for the company. General Dynamics is offering its own distance learning product, the Pathways Platform, which uses streaming video technology from Akamai Technologies Inc., Cambridge, Mass., and mGen Inc.'s learning management system, he said.

Some agencies are eschewing the traditional contractor route and launching their own test programs or simply filling niche needs.

NASA's Ames Research Center in Mountain View, Calif., has engineered a multi-vendor vehicle, awarding contracts in April to DigitalThink Inc.; Skillsoft; Mindleaders.com Inc.; Knowlgy Corp.; and Network Automation Technology Inc., said Jeff Brown, a contract specialist at Ames. The contracts are part of NASA's Consolidated Contracting Initiative under which one center initiates a contract and makes it available to all NASA Centers. Valued at up to $600,000, contracts are limited to one year after which the agency plans to do an evaluation, he said. "If we do another procurement next year, we will probably consider including options in it so that we can extend it," he said.

The agency opted for a multivendor contract this year because it was believed that "no one vendor was going to make everyone happy," said Brown.

"NASA is a very distributed organization and every location is a little bit different," agreed Sally Turner, director of the government sector for DigitalThink. An application service provider based in San Francisco, DigitalThink hosts its own classes, which cost from $99 to $325 per person depending on the courses. Prices also vary when bought in volume off its GSA schedule, Turner added.

The Environmental Protection Agency is using technology from AdvanceOnline Inc., Seattle, to help train its personnel and customers on how to deal with hazardous waste. Also working with the U.S. Army Corps of Engineers, AdvanceOnline's focus "is related primarily to OSHA safety training, environmental compliance and transportation of hazardous materials and related topics," said Monte Rosen, vice president for business development and marketing at the company.

The Army's Aberdeen Test Center in Aberdeen, Md., is looking at Scottsdale, Ariz.-based KnowledgeNet's online learning program to provide training for its network employees, said Robert Stastny, an engineer at the facility. KnowledgeNet's focus is IT training providing online courses from the most complicated Cisco Systems' training to Microsoft certification down to commercial end-user products, said Tom Graunke, chief executive officer at KnowledgeNet.

The following table gives further insight into the future of e-learning in both the public and private sectors.

	1998	1999	2000	2001	2002	2003	Annual Growth Rate
Content	$391M	$735M	$1.33B	$2.27B	$3.91B	$6.16B	73.6%
Learning Services	$99M	$201M	$533M	$1.22B	$2.42B	$4.11B	110.7%
Delivery Solutions	$61M	$178M	$356M	$567M	$782M	$1.14B	79.7%
Total	$550M	$1.11B	$2.22B	$4.05B	$7.11B	$11.41B	83.4%

Figure 1. E-learning forecast: The U.S. corporate market for e-learning, which includes the public and private sectors but not the academic sector, is expected to top $11 billion by 2003. Source: IDC

A frequent contributor to Washington Technology, *Ed McKenna has also written about information technology, public policy, and transportation issues for publications including* Federal Computer Week, Aviation Week, Aviation Daily, *and* Air Cargo World. *He splits his time between the San Francisco Bay area and Washington D.C. and can be reached at edward_mckenna@hotmail.com.*

All About ADL

J.D. Fletcher and Philip Dodds

This article looks at the federal government's effort to foster interoperability of learning courseware, known as the Advanced Distributed Learning initiative.

The Advanced Distributed Learning initiative is a technology development effort sponsored by the U.S. Department of Defense (DoD) in coordination with the White House Office of Science and Technology Policy (OSTP). It's motivated by a vision of the future—one in which shareable courseware objects are assembled in real time from a global information network to create on-the-fly instructional or performance-aiding interactions with learners.

With the rapid growth of electronic commerce and the World Wide Web, much of this vision will occur without DoD or OSTP involvement. The ADL initiative is intended to take advantage of this global activity, accelerate it, and apply it to the needs of the DoD and other federal agencies. It will help provide the learning resources that the DoD needs to ensure the operational effectiveness of its forces. It will help provide similar resources to all federal agencies, which also depend on human performance and competence. Cooperative development among economic sectors—government, private industry, and academic—is needed and is being used to achieve the ADL initiative goals.

Few enterprises touch the lives of as many people as those concerned with education and training. High-quality education and training benefit individuals whose knowledge and skills are upgraded, businesses seeking a competitive edge, and nations in their overall productivity and increased global competitiveness. The ADL initiative is intended to ensure that all individuals have access to the education and training they need and that the teaching and learning enterprise becomes a high-performance activity.

We envision a future in which everyone will have an electronic personal learning associate. This device will be able to assemble learning or mentor presentations on demand and in real time—any time, anywhere. The presentations will be tailored to the needs, capabilities, intentions, and learning state of each individual or group (for example, crew, team, or staff) of individuals. Communication with the device will be based on natural language dialogue initiated by the device or by its users. The device will be portable, perhaps small enough to be carried in a shirt pocket.

Most of the technology needed to build such a device exists now. Though we cannot yet fit it into a shirt pocket, we expect advances in electronics to take care of that. What's lacking is content—in the form of instructional objects that we call "shareable courseware objects." These objects include a wide variety of skills, shown on the left side of Figure 1 as shareable courseware, must be readily accessible across the Web, or whatever future form our global information network takes. Once these objects exist, they can be assembled in real time and sent to our personal learning associates.

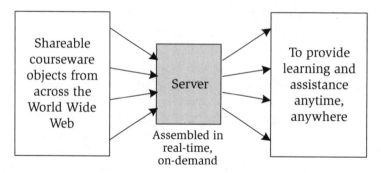

Figure 1. The ADL future

The ADL initiative is focused primarily on the design and development of shareable courseware objects—and on fostering an instructional-object economy.

Computers Are Key

The initiative is based on a host of learning technologies. It focuses mostly on asynchronous technologies that can deliver instruction and mentoring without requiring learners to gather in specific places at specific times. These technologies depend on computer technology for delivery and presentation. They include the following:

- computer-based instruction
- interactive multimedia instruction
- intelligent tutoring systems

- networked tutorial simulation
- Web-based training.

Why have we chosen to focus on these computer-based technologies? Computers allow us to adjust the pace, content, difficulty, and sequencing of instructional material to the people or groups who need it. Just as books made instructional content widely and inexpensively available, computers have made both the content and the interactions of instruction widely and inexpensively available. Does this added, individualizing capability matter? Empirical research with students in real learning situations suggests that it does.

Figure 2 shows the combined results from three studies that compared one-on-one teaching (one instructor with one learner) with one-on-many teaching (one instructor with a classroom of 25 to 30 students). We might expect such a difference in instructional presentation to matter—and to favor one-on-one teaching. What's surprising is how much it matters. The difference in student achievement from these two approaches amounts to two standard deviations. It's roughly equivalent to raising the achievement of 50th percentile students to the 98th level of achievement.

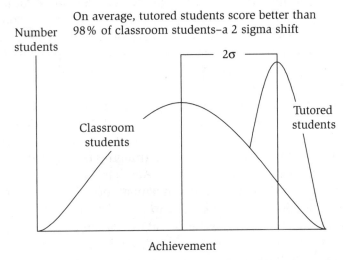

Figure 2. Why technology-based instruction? ADL technologies makes this instructional imperative affordable

Adapted from Bloom, B.S., "The Two Sigma Problem: The Search for Methods of Group Instruction as Effective as One-to-One Tutoring," *Educational Researcher*, 13, 4-16 (1984)

Then why don't we provide one-on-one instruction to all our learners? The answer is simple: We can't afford it. Although one-on-one teaching may be an instructional imperative, it's also an economic impossibility.

Enter computer technology. Because computers can interact with users and tailor presentations to their needs—and because the necessary computer capabilities are less expensive than people—some of the gaps between one-on-one and one-on-many instruction can be filled affordably by computer technology.

Support for applying the tutorial capabilities that technology-based instruction allows is found also in other research. For instance, how much are learners in a typical classroom likely to differ in the rates that they master instructional material? It turns out that, over a range of material and settings, the rate with which the fastest 10 percent of students can progress compared to the rate of the slowest 10 percent of students varies by a ratio of about five to one. That means some students are able to master in a day what requires others five days to master. Even in highly selected instructional institutions, such as our best research universities, the ratio can be as high as seven to one. There are, then, significant economies and substantial effectiveness to be gained by adjusting for pace in instruction. This is something that technology-based instruction does well.

Is there research evidence that using technology to instruct reduces learning time? In more than 40 assessments performed since the 1960s, we've found time savings to average about 30 percent. This seems to have occurred without any particular effort to reduce instructional time. Much more might be gained if we tried harder.

The value of technology-based approaches may also be seen in comparisons with classroom interactivity—the frequency with which questions are asked and answered. Research shows that this frequency increases by about 4,000 percent—a ratio of 40 to 1—with technology-based instruction. The increased intensity of technology-based instruction seems hard to deny.

We also find significant improvements in knowledge and skills gained through using technology-based instruction. We are not yet at the two standard deviation level, or "two sigma," but during the course of 233 assessments of computer-based instruction, we found an improvement of 0.39 sigma (roughly raising achievement from the 50th percentile level to the 65th percentile). Another 44 assessments of interactive multimedia instruction produced an improvement of 0.50 sigma (roughly raising achievement from the 50th percentile level to the 69th percentile), and five assessments of recent intelligent tutoring systems that directly mimic one-on-one instruction produced an improvement of 1.05 sigma (roughly raising achievement from the 50th percentile level to the 85th percentile).

Cost reductions are also notable. We've found that reductions in operating and support costs average about 63 percent.

Overall, we have assumed a rule of "thirds" in our assessments of technology-based instruction. That means that use of these technologies—our ADL technologies—reduces the cost of instruction by about one-third and it either reduces time of instruction by about one-third or it increases the amount of skills and knowledge acquired by about one-third.

The real payoff for the U.S. military is that by increasing the effectiveness and accessibility of instruction and by reducing instructional costs, the ADL initiative will significantly enhance the military's operational effectiveness. The operational military payoffs of education, training, and mentoring remain difficult to quantify and assess, but they are the real and ultimate objective of our efforts. Similar increases in operational capability and productivity should result from application of ADL technologies in civilian education.

ADL "ilities"

To meet our functional requirements, the shareable courseware objects at the heart of the ADL initiative must meet certain criteria, which we loosely call ADL "ilities." Among the "ilities," four seem most prominent:

- It must be possible to find needed and shareable courseware objects. They must be *accessible*. Basically, we need widely accepted and standard ways to store objects so that widely accepted and standard ways can be used to find and retrieve them.
- Once found, the objects should be *usable*. This means that they must be interoperable and portable across most—if not all—platforms, operating systems, browsers, and courseware tools.
- Once implemented, the objects should continue to operate *reliably*. If the underlying platform, operating system, or browser is modified (for instance, when a new version is released and installed), courseware objects should continue to operate as before. They should also be *durable*.
- Courseware objects should be *reusable*. Other platforms, operating systems, browsers, and courseware tools should be able to reuse, and perhaps modify as needed, the original courseware objects.

What must we do to achieve these "ilities"? Primarily, we must agree on and use common guidelines to develop courseware objects and make them available. Within the ADL initiative, we use the term *guidelines* because we're not yet certain what form they'll eventually take, although we're working with both national and international standards bodies to shape them. The guidelines are likely to end up as standards, but that's an issue to be considered later, after we've developed, tested, and revised our initial guidelines.

To discuss guidelines and, most important, make them implementable so they can be used in everyday practice to develop instructional objects, we need to refer to a model. This model isn't intended to replace other models for developing courseware, but it is intended only to provide a foundation so that we can accurately express our guidelines and make them usable. For these reasons, we call it a reference model. The product of this effort is a shareable courseware objects reference model (SCORM).

As the Figure 3 details, SCORM is a software model that defines the interrelationship of course components, data models, and protocols so that courseware objects are shareable across systems that conform with the same model. It remains a reference

The SCORM Initiative
The SCORM initiative is less about technical standards than: • Building consensus among users, developers, and industry • Bringing together key players • Forging alliances and agreements • Accelerating the adoption of ADL technology to make learning accessible anytime, anywhere Promoting "enlightened self-interest" among all stakeholders

Figure 3. The SCORM initiative

model. We have shown that other models of courseware development can be mapped into our reference model.

Fortunately, businesses in the courseware tool development industry have as much of a stake in the production of shareable courseware objects as we do. So, much of the work required to create the SCORM is being done by them. The primary function of the ADL initiative in this process is to organize, encourage, orchestrate, and document their development efforts—and to ensure that defense education and training requirements are reflected in their work.

A successful shareable courseware objects reference model must meet three primary criteria:

■ It must support full articulation of guidelines that can be understood and implemented in the production of shareable courseware objects.

■ It must be adopted, understood, and used by as wide a variety of stakeholders as possible (courseware developers, courseware tool developers, and courseware customers, for example).

■ It must permit mapping of any stakeholder's model for instructional systems design and development into itself.

With so many current and potential stakeholders in the ADL initiative, developing a SCORM is as much an organizational challenge as anything else. Any organization concerned with learning through education, training, or performance monitoring is a likely stakeholder. These organizations include U.S. military services and those of other countries, businesses, academic institutions, and various laboratory activities concerned with ADL-type courseware development. Development under the ADL initiative is therefore cooperative and keyed to the promotion of each stakeholder's self-interest.

Many organizations have worked hard with the ADL initiative to build consensus. Draft versions of the ADL SCORM have been circulated for comment in hard copy and on the Web site.

We've helped establish co-laboratories that will test ideas for developing shareable courseware objects and assess courseware objects developed elsewhere for their conformance with current versions of the SCORM. The co-laboratories are also assessing the costs and effectiveness of different approaches to technology-based instruction; demonstrating the capabilities and value of ADL technologies applied to education, training, and mentoring; acting as clearinghouses for information generated by them and others; and performing additional ADL support functions. The family of cooperating co-laboratories formed to support the ADL initiative is growing. There's enough work to go around to keep all fully employed. And there is much more to be done.

What can other stakeholders do to participate in the ADL initiative? Here are five possibilities:

- Provide review and feedback to the ADL SCORM process.
- Start designing content in small, logical chunks with sharing and reuse in mind.
- Develop an organizational strategy that links your core competencies to ADL capabilities.
- Share data, processes, findings, lessons learned, and so forth with ADL co-laboratories.
- Participate in ADL efforts to build consensus and cooperation through demonstrations and sharing of findings.

All interested organizations are encouraged to join the ADL initiative. Coordination of ADL activities is necessarily kept loose, with an emphasis on cooperation and helping participants best serve their own self-interests. Insofar as ADL represents the awaiting future and our vision is correct, we all have a stake in the success of this initiative.

J.D. Fletcher is a research analyst with the Institute for Defense Analyses, which provides consulting services to the Department of Defense.

Philip Dodds is principal of Randall House Associates, which advises the Department of Defense on technology issues. Both are active participants in the ADL initiative.

Part Five

State of the Art: Distance Learning in Higher Education

Distance learning started in colleges, and it is in higher education that distance learning continues to be an important new trend. We examined this trend in one of the articles in Part One. In Part Five we look at distance learning as practiced in colleges and universities. We've included five articles that we think give a good overview of what's going on in higher education today.

We start with "An Overview of Some of the Leading Virtual and Online Universities" by Paul DeVeaux. An important trend today is the delivery of courses online and more and more universities are offering such courses and entire degree programs. Some universities, such as the University of Phoenix, offer all their courses online and are what the title calls "virtual universities." This article explains this important trend and how well these programs are working.

Next we include "An MBA Your Way" by Kim Kiser, editor of *Online Learning Magazine*. She describes how more and more employees are getting their MBA degrees through online distance education programs. Some are delivered by new colleges set up specifically to provide distance education programs. Others are from well-established universities setting up their own programs. This article provides some background on how this is working.

You'll next find the article "Dot-com or Dot-edu?" by Rebecca Ganzel. As universities move to develop online distance learning programs, she asks whether they are becoming more like for-profit businesses or retaining their educational mission. This is an intriguing question and this piece provides some useful insights into what's going on.

Next we include a short piece that further looks at how higher education is going online, but this piece, "Any Path Will Do" by Bob Heterick, suggests that if traditional universities do not offer online distance learning, they will lose students to those universities that do, including those that are devoted to this type of education.

Finally we've selected "How to Choose a College Partner for Distance Education" by Sylvia Vander Sluis. This article is aimed more at corporations seeking to align themselves with colleges to deliver training to employees. It lays out a series of steps you can use to do this effectively.

Higher education aimed at adult learners is a very large potential market, in business parlance. How that evolves is still being determined, and we hope that you benefit from the ideas that are being discussed, the implementation strategies that are presented, and the practical application possibilities for your own organization, even if you are not in higher education.

An Overview of Some of the Leading Virtual and Online Universities

Paul DeVeaux

Higher education is moving quickly into delivering courses at a distance. This article looks at some of the online university pioneers and leaders. It provides an overview of recent surveys looking at the growth of distance learning in colleges and universities and profiles some universities now doing this.

International Data Corp. (IDC; Framingham, Mass.) indicates that distance learning enrollments are growing by 33 percent and will reach 2.23 million in 2002. Distance learning is essential for ambitious types, says Glenn R. Jones, founder of Jones International University and CEO of Jones International Ltd. (Englewood, Colo.). "People definitely have the desire to advance themselves, but in today's fast-paced world, not being able to take time out for the traditional classroom can be a barrier to getting ahead." The number of institutions and organizations that provide "non-traditional" education is already escalating in order to meet the demand for continuing education, as several public and private higher education institutions are offering distance learning courses (see Figure 1). In this article I will discuss some of the different types of courses, programs and degrees offered on-line, including information about tuition, admissions and accreditation.

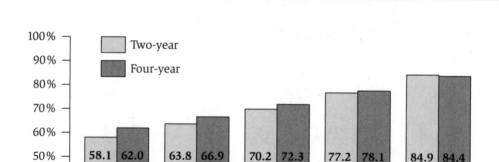

Figure 1. Percentages of public and private higher education institutions offering distance education courses

Virtually Without Walls

Capella University is far from the traditional university—it has no student center, no athletic teams or cheerleaders, nor any actual classrooms. Despite not looking like the typical alma mater, the Minneapolis-based school is fully accredited by the North Central Association of Colleges and Schools (NCA). (Regional Accreditation is the highest level of academic accreditation a college or university can obtain and is recognized throughout the United States.)

Once known as the Graduate School of America, the university is the principal enterprise of the Capella Education Co. Students can register, order books, submit papers and pay tuition on-line. Tuition that, according to school officials, is comparable at the master's level to that at similar private institutions, and approximately 10 to 20 percent less at the Ph.D level. Capella has several programs to choose from, including a School of Business, a School of Education and Professional Development, and a School of Human Services.

Which Course to Take

There are two different course formats at Capella University: online courses and "Directed Study" courses. Online courses are more structured and in some ways similar to traditional classes. They have specific beginning and ending dates and there is a professor and a class of 10 to 15 learners who cover specific material week by week. A learner in an online program who takes one or two courses per 12-week quarter should complete a master's degree in about a year and a half to two years, while Ph.D programs which use the online format can be completed in about three years.

Directed Study courses are more self-paced. They also make use of the Internet but are more of a partnership between the course instructor and the learner. The two plan the course together, but the learner is then free to complete the course in his or her own way, with the instructor serving as a tutor. The average completion time for the master's degree via Directed Study is 18 months, while the average completion time for the doctoral degree is about three years.

A Phoenix Rising

The University of Phoenix Online was among the first accredited universities to provide college degree programs via the Internet. Founded in 1989, the university offers complete degree programs in business, management, technology, education and nursing. Additionally, the University of Phoenix Online provides customized training programs to many of the world's leading corporations.

Courses typically require 10 to 20 hours of study each week, with each course lasting five weeks. Courses are taught sequentially, not concurrently, so that each course can build upon the previous one. The university estimates that a typical student will earn a degree in two or three years.

According to University of Phoenix Online officials, 100 percent of the school's curriculum can be completed via the Internet, the only exception being the school's doctoral degree, which requires a few weeks of residency. Students use the Internet to retrieve lectures, questions and assignments from instructors. Students also have access to a vast online library of research materials.

The Online Campus vs. the Traditional Campus

Does the online format provide the same quality of education offered by a traditional campus? Yes, according to author Thomas L. Russell. In his book, *The No Significant Difference Phenomenon*, Russell cites 355 research reports, papers and summaries dating back to 1928 that found no significant difference between distance learning and in-class learning. Where a difference was identified, it generally favored the distance learning student.

The University of Phoenix conducted its own study comparing campus-based students to distance learners and came to the same conclusion. In addition, it identified the current online format as the most effective vehicle for distance education.

A Call from the Governors

Western Governors University (WGU; Salt Lake City) is somewhat different from other virtual universities. WGU is a competency-based institution. The university's philosophy is that learners should be able to earn degrees by focusing on the skills and knowl-edge areas that they need. Competency-based education is not based on the number of credits that students have accumulated; rather, according to WGU, competencies are skills or knowledge identified by professionals in a particular field as being essential for mastery of that field. The school recognizes that students may have gained skills and knowledge on the job through years of life experience.

"Now more than ever, people need to find affordable, practical education that will give them skills and knowledge they can take directly into the workplace," says Bob Mendenhall, president of WGU. To help give people a leg up in the job market, WGU offers more than 500 distance education courses from over 40 universities and col-leges. WGU has the backing of governors from 19 states, and offers several degrees, including a master's degree in Learning and Technology and associate degrees in Network Administration and Electronic Manufacturing Technology.

Admissions and Accreditation

Enrollment in WGU classes is open to everyone. There is no admission process for stu-dents wishing to take classes available through WGU; however, students wishing to earn a degree or certificate must apply and be accepted by the institution. WGU pro-gram tuition varies depending upon the level of the degree or certificate. Tuition for an undergraduate degree is $1,500, while tuition for a master's degree is $3,850.

WGU has a distributed faculty, which means that it does not hire its own teaching faculty. Classes are taught by the faculty of education providers associated with WGU. The university currently is in the process of seeking "Candidate for Accreditation" sta-tus by the Inter-Regional Accrediting Committee (IRAC).

Thinking About Distance Learning?

Distance learning isn't for everyone, as some people need or want the structure and discipline provided by a classroom. Western Governors University includes a ques-tionnaire on its Web site to help prospective candidates decide if they should enroll in a course or program. Listed below are some of these questions.

Having face-to-face interaction with my instructors and fellow students is:
- not particularly important to me
- somewhat important to me
- very important to me

When it comes to assessing my own progress, I
- feel as if I can keep tabs on my own progress, even without immediate or fre-quent feedback from my instructor
- prefer to receive regular feedback from my instructor, but don't mind if I can't get that feedback immediately after turning in a test or assignment
- need feedback from my instructor immediately and often

If I had to describe my predominant learning style/preference, I would say it is:
- Auditory—I learn best when I can listen to an explanation of a concept
- Visual—I learn best when I can read the course materials or view graphics and other visuals
- Tactile—I learn best by "doing" (for instance, conducting an experiment in a lab)

Jones International University (JIU)

JIU also exists entirely online. According to its mission statement, Jones International University is an institution of higher education that offers courses and degrees at the undergraduate and graduate levels through sound curricula, innovative delivery of instruction through technology, and a commitment to relevant, readily available and student-centered service for a geographically dispersed adult student body.

Founded in 1995 as International University, JIU is the first 100 percent online university to receive accreditation from a nationally recognized accrediting body (the university received regional accreditation from the NCA in March 1999). Professors from several leading schools, including Columbia University, Stanford University and Michigan State University, help develop each JIU course.

Degrees and Certificates

JIU currently offers the following fully accredited degree programs:
- Bachelor of Arts in Business Communication;
- Master of Arts in Business Communication; and
- Master of Business Administration.

Additionally, JIU offers a range of shorter-term certificate programs that focus on specific business issues. JIU offers more than 20 certificates, each comprised of two to four JIU courses. Current certificate programs online include:
- Public Relations and Marketing;
- Global Communication;
- Using the Internet in Education;
- Leadership and Communication Skills; and
- New Communication Technologies.

Corporate Training

JIU offers adult workers an established and effective method for continuing their education, says Pamela Pease, president of JIU. "Our model is outcome-driven, it combines the theoretical with the practical, enabling working adults to immediately apply what they're learning on the job as well as in the online learning community they and their classmates create."

Survey Says: Yes to Lifelong Learning

A 1999 survey conducted for Jones International University (JIU) by Market Facts' TeleNation found that 70 percent of Americans say they have considered taking a class or course to help further their career or pursue a skill or topic of interest. The survey, which consisted of more than 1,000 interviews with adults 18 years of age or older, also found that among respondents, younger Americans were even more likely to be interested in furthering their education than their elders.

Other Key Findings from the Survey Revealed:
- The majority (82 percent) of those who would consider taking a course to further their career or to pursue a skill were in the 18-to-24 age range.
- Barriers to pursuing this interest included time constraints (mentioned by 36 percent) and cost issues (mentioned by 23 percent).
- When considering online class or course study: 26 percent favored classes that fit into their own schedules, 18 percent cited no transportation as a requirement of learning online, and 13 percent favored learning methods that let students work at their own pace.

Developing World Embraces Virtual Universities

Virtual education is making quite a mark both domestically and globally. New technology is making it possible for those in some of the most rural areas and developing nations have access to higher education. What follows is a description of some of the more unique distance learning programs.

The African Virtual University

The African Virtual University (AVU) contends that it uses modern information and communication technologies to give the countries of sub-Saharan Africa direct access to some of the highest quality academic faculty and learning resources throughout the world. The AVU services 16 countries in Africa using professors from the continent, Europe and North America via video tape, the Internet or live satellite broadcasts.

Since the launch of its pilot phase in 1997, AVU has provided students and professionals with more than 2,500 hours of interactive instruction in English and in French. More than 12,000 students have completed semester-long courses in engineering and in the sciences, while more than 2,500 professionals have attended executive and professional management seminars. AVU also provides students with access to an online digital library with more than 1,000 full-text journals.

Connecting Turkey and California

Located in Eskisehir, Turkey, Anadolu University is considered one of the world's mega-universities. The institution has 12 faculties, three of which use distance education, and also has one of the largest distance education programs in the world, with approximately 60,000 students enrolled.

In an effort to increase the number and diversity of students studying abroad, Anadolu University and San Diego State University (SDSU) have forged ties through an educational exchange agreement between the two institutions. "Providing our students with a global education and study abroad opportunities is one of the most important charges at SDSU," says Stephen Weber, president. "With an excellent distance education program that has students throughout Turkey and Europe, we can exchange a wealth of ideas that will benefit both universities and their students."

The Open University

The Open University (OU) is a British public university that awards UK degrees. The university, which began admitting students in 1971, is currently the largest in the United Kingdom. Courses are available throughout Europe and by means of partnership agreements with institutions in other parts of the world. The school estimates that it delivers degree-credit programs to 180,000 students in more than 40 countries, and a further 10,000 in various continuing professional development courses.

Earlier this year, the Open University announced the establishment of a sister institution: the United States Open University (USOU). The USOU is offering versions of Open University courses adapted for American students, but is expected to develop its own courses in future years. "Until the creation of USOU, the OU tended to keep its various international partnerships in separate compartments," says USOU President Sir John Daniel. "Thanks to the USOU the OU is now thinking of itself much more as a confederation of partner institutions that could develop into a multinational university."

Parting Shots

The exponential growth of the Internet has opened higher education to new diverse audiences and allowed institutions to establish fresh markets in geographically distant locations. Online programs eliminate several concerns that students might have regarding time and distance, while costing less than most traditional universities. Virtual universities are not only here to stay, but they have the potential to revolutionize the practice of all those involved in the educational process.

Paul DeVeaux is editor of Teleconference *magazine. He may be reached via e-mail at pdeveaux@advanstar.com.*

An MBA Your Way

Kim Kiser

Internet technology is allowing corporations and universities to customize MBA degrees. This article looks at some of these programs and how well they are meeting student needs.

When Karen Calabrese took a job with Honeywell's Western Region Learning Center in Phoenix in 1998, one of her first assignments was to help employees earn their master's in business administration (MBA) degrees. She needed a local university that could bring evening classes to the learning center, and found a willing partner in the University of Phoenix.

But when Calabrese, a senior educational consultant and program manager for academic alliances, started marketing the opportunity to Honeywell employees, she got an unexpected response. Sure, people at the high-tech engineering firm's three Phoenix business units liked the idea of earning a degree while working. However, attending class at the learning center every Monday or Wednesday night was impossible for many.

"We were getting calls from people saying, 'I'd love to get an MBA degree, but I travel,'" she recalls. "Our folks are on the road constantly. We needed to find a way to meet the needs of people who couldn't attend a bricks-and-mortar facility."

Calabrese went back on the research trail. This time, she looked for a school that would offer an MBA over the Internet, tailor the content and schedule to Honeywell's specifications, and have it ready by the fall of 1999. Although she found schools that offered distance learning MBA programs, most required students to spend several weeks on campus each year. "That was a difficult thing for me to sell Honeywell management on," she says. "I needed a program that was cost-effective, that had no residency requirement, that met our accreditation requirements, and that met the needs of this group of employees."

Calabrese found another willing partner in Susan Rud, business school dean at Capella University(www.capellauniversity.edu) in Minneapolis. In exchange for a guarantee of 15 students who would go through the program as a group, Rud agreed to create a pilot for a customized MBA degree.

After their initial meeting in July, Calabrese and Rud worked by phone and email to draft the blueprints for the program. The curriculum had to include the basic MBA framework: courses in finance, operations and information technology management. However, Calabrese was able to add electives—such as global financial management and ebusiness—that were important to Honeywell. In addition, instructors would allow students to tackle work projects, rather than academic exercises, for some of their assignments.

Calabrese and Rud configured the schedule so students completed one course at a time. But to get the group through all 13 courses in time for a November 2001 graduation, they had to cut the number of weeks per course from 12 to eight, eliminate a break midway through each class, and do away with some of the getting-to-know-your-classmates activities normally built into the start of each class.

By September, the instructors were up to speed on how to work with the Honeywell cohort, the class Web site was up, and the 17 students from the company's Western region were ready to log on to their first class.

The Custom-Fit Degree

Since creating the pilot for the Honeywell MBA, Rud has talked to several other organizations that are interested in developing similar programs. "Companies realize they have to do this to keep their retention rates high and to attract great people," she says.

Universities are warming to the idea, too. A number of schools have created specialized training and executive programs for employers, but until recently, few have been willing to wrap company or job-related skills training into degree programs. "When the whole concept of degrees came about 200 years ago, people believed everyone had to learn the same core things," says Vicky Phillips, CEO of geteducated.com (www.geteducated.com), a distance learning consulting firm in Waterbury, Vt. "So like it or not, we had a one-size-fits-all model."

But because of the way the Internet has changed business, we no longer live in a one-size-fits-all economy. That's forced business schools to incorporate lessons on topics such as ecommerce into degree programs, and it's also changed their approach to designing courses. Where it used to take two years to write and publish a textbook that would be used for several years, Internet technology now allows course materials to be updated and customized instantly.

Phillips, who is also co-author of *The Best Distance Learning Graduate Schools 1999: Earning Your Degree Without Leaving Home* (Princeton Review 1998), says employers shopping for MBA programs are looking for a curriculum that can respond to the short shelf-life of knowledge. That's particularly true in fields such as business and IT, where what you learn today may be outdated in six months. "When it comes to Internet degrees, the whole idea of customizing them is becoming pervasive. It's not a minor trend," she says.

An observer of the distance education industry for the last decade, Phillips has been watching the move toward customization play out in three ways.

By corporation. Honeywell isn't the first organization to want a company-specific MBA. In 1993, the University of Michigan Business School developed a distance MBA program especially for managers at Cathay Pacific Airways in Hong Kong; the university crafted a similar program for Daewoo Corporation in Korea two years later. In 1998, the accounting and consulting firm PricewaterhouseCoopers partnered with the University of Georgia Terry College of Business to launch a consulting-focused MBA program that combines classroom and distance education. More recently, University Access, a Los Angeles online learning company, closed a deal with the University of North Carolina's Kenan-Flagler business school to build a global executive MBA program for five companies.

By specialty. Last month, Unexus University, which was created by Canadian IT training company Learnsoft Corp., launched an online MBA program for technology professionals. The program, which is awaiting accreditation, is an outgrowth of Learnsoft's certificate program in advanced technology management.

By content. Several for-profit education corporations are using Internet technology to create "superstar" MBA programs. UNext.com in Deerfield, Ill., has formed alliances with Columbia University, the University of Chicago, Stanford University and the London School of Economics and Political Science. The company wants to create an Internet school that will offer an MBA made up of the best courses from those universities. Late last year, Pensare in Los Altos, Calif., signed a deal with Duke University's Fuqua School of Business to license its MBA curriculum. The company also has developed an Internet platform that lets universities create MBA programs using some or all of the Duke curriculum. Senior vice president Dean Hovey says corporations will be able to use the platform to create "certificate MBA programs."

Too Narrow a Focus?

But as education becomes yet another fast product in our white-hot e-economy, is the move toward have-it-your-way MBAs shortchanging students? Will those who hold IT or consulting MBAs find themselves at a disadvantage when they change industries? Will employees who enroll in programs designed to corporate specs end up with a degree that's meaningless outside the company they work for?

Some are concerned that students won't get the schooling they really need. "Part of higher education is understanding issues in a larger context," says Mark F. Smith, associate director of government relations for the American Association of University Professors in Washington, D.C.

Smith, who staffs the association's committee on distance education, is especially troubled by the idea of repackaging and selling university courses and customizing them to meet corporations' needs. "In some ways, it's a good thing for a company to tailor training for its own particular use and circumstances. But is it a broad enough educational experience to warrant an MBA? What might be good practice in a particular case might not be good practice if it's applied to more general education."

But Stuart Crainer and Des Dearlove, authors of *Gravy Training: Inside the Business of Business Schools* (Jossey-Bass 1999), say business schools have to be more responsive to the needs of corporations—especially as they go up against for-profit education companies, consulting firms and training programs that can deliver exactly what a company orders.

"Business schools are vulnerable because they are an expensive solution," say the British business writers, who have seen MBA programs designed for businesses or consortiums of businesses catch on in the United Kingdom.

Hadley Baas, a consultant with PricewaterhouseCoopers in Chicago, admits she was concerned that being in a class made up entirely of her colleagues would expose her to too narrow a range of experiences. "Other MBA programs attract people from all different companies," she says.

A year into the program, her doubts have vanished. Baas, who started out in the company's IT group and moved into financial cost management, says the very nature of her fellow consultants' work gives them an unvarnished look at the challenges faced by companies in a host of industries—a view that employees of those corporations may never be exposed to. "Even though we all work for the same company, we bring a lot of different perspectives," she says.

Chris Thaxton, a product data management systems developer at Honeywell and a student in the Capella MBA program, also likes being in a class full of people from the same company. "Even if others in the class don't understand the particulars of your job, if they understand the company's culture and vision, you can talk a lot more openly," he says.

Although he's only taken a couple of the bread-and-butter MBA courses so far, he says he has compared notes with friends going through traditional programs and finds they're learning the same material. "These subjects are required for accreditation," he says.

Education for E-People

Baas and Thaxton aren't unusual in their desire to take advantage of online degree programs. According to International Data Corp., a Framingham, Mass., research firm, the number of students enrolled in distance education courses is expected to rise from 710,000 in 1998 to 2.2 million by 2002.

"This is an era where we're seeing more fast-trackers or what I call 'e-people' come along," says Capella's Rud. "They're very talented, and they come into companies and move very quickly. They want education more and more but their time is becoming less and less."

For businesses to attract and hold on to those people, they will have to offer them the chance to improve their skills and education. And they'll have to do it in a way that allows employees to attend class in their own space and time and provides them with knowledge that directly applies to what they're doing. "When I talk to my staffing people, they say the MBA program is one thing people look at when considering a job offer," says Honeywell's Calabrese.

Calabrese, who is also a student in the Capella-Honeywell program, believes this is only the beginning for customized online programs. "I see more and more companies looking into this," she says. "These programs provide flexibility, and that's so important right now because of the fact that our work is changing greatly and our lifestyles are so busy."

Building a Corporate MBA

Karen Calabrese, Hadley Baas and Chris Thaxton have one thing in common: They're busy people. Calabrese, a trainer and program manager for Honeywell in Phoenix, and Baas, a consultant for PricewaterhouseCoopers in Chicago, have jobs that can take them any place at any time. Thaxton, a product data management systems developer at Honeywell in Phoenix, enjoys spending evenings and weekends being dad to his five children and leading his oldest son's Boy Scout troop.

Despite their demanding schedules, all three are also working on their master's of business administration (MBA) degrees—although not in a traditional way.

Calabrese and Thaxton are enrolled in a customized online MBA program offered by Honeywell and Capella University. Baas is taking part in a customized program that combines classroom and online learning though the University of Georgia Terry College of Business and PricewaterhouseCoopers.

Their companies created these programs for employees who live nowhere near a university, who might face a corporate transfer or whose schedules don't permit them to spend a couple nights a week in class. Because they're tailored to the corporations' needs, the degree programs also ensure that students learn about topics that are relevant to their work.

If your training department is thinking about creating such a program, consider the following words of advice from those who've done it:

Make sure the university issuing the degree is accredited. Accreditation gives a university credibility. "You can have a degree from a university that's not accredited and what is it worth?" says Susan Rud, dean of the school of business at Capella University in Minneapolis, which is accredited by the North Central Association of Colleges and Schools.

Make sure enough employees are interested. When working with PricewaterhouseCoopers to develop a custom MBA program, the University of Georgia required the consulting firm to have at least 40 people enrolled to make the effort worthwhile. Honeywell had to guarantee Capella a cohort of at least 15. "If you don't have enough people, it might work better to get a consortium of companies together," says Don Burkhard, a director with PricewaterhouseCoopers' learning and professional development group in Tampa, Fla.

Have the right technology in place. Students enrolled in the Honeywell-Capella program need at least a 486 computer with a 50 MHz hard drive and 16 MB of RAM that is capable of running multimedia programs. They also need a 4X CD-ROM, a 28.8 kbps modem, Windows 95, Microsoft Internet Explorer 4.0 or Netscape Navigator 3.0, and email capability. (A Pentium processor, 12X CD-ROM and 56 kbps modem are recommended, however.) In addition, be sure the university is able to deliver the courses online and provide technical support when needed.

Create a balance. "You have to remember that people are still working full time," says Burkhard. When developing the program with the University of Georgia, Burkhard asked faculty to balance the workload so PricewaterhouseCoopers students wouldn't get hit with multiple exams or projects due the same week. Capella's program is structured so students are enrolled in only one class at a time, thus eliminating problems with conflicting deadlines.

Provide face time when possible. Although the students enrolled in the Honeywell-Capella program don't gather on campus, some who live in the Phoenix area have formed a study group that meets in person. PricewaterhouseCoopers' Burkhard found that small groups of students who work together virtually on projects need time for team building when they come back to campus. "Being able to spend time getting to know people and working with them on campus makes it easier when we have to work together over the phone or by computer," says Baas.

Kim Kiser is managing editor of Online Learning Magazine. *She can be reached by e-mail at kkiser@onlinelearning.com.*

Dot-com or Dot-edu?

Rebecca Ganzel

As the Internet puts its stamp on the way people learn, traditional universities are taking on the characteristics of dot-com companies. This article asks whether this is a good thing.

That crackling noise you've been hearing lately just might be the sound of high-speed wires penetrating ivied walls. Every day, it seems, brings news of another big-name university that's moved into e-learning. And it isn't just that academics are putting their courses online to reach students in faraway places. They're taking a page from the breakneck dot-com world and creating separate companies that not only move at Internet speed, but sell courses to knowledge-hungry corporations—thus giving their corporate-training counterparts a run for their money.

Such happenings are blurring the lines not just between the academic and for-profit worlds, but between higher education and training. So why are institutions that traditionally have been more interested in expanding minds than improving the bottom line entering into these ventures? And is it a good idea for universities to move so far beyond their traditional scope?

We posed those questions to professors and administrators across the country who are intimately involved in such programs. Their answers, as expected, were varied. Some are jumping at the chance to market what they see as a particularly good program or course to a wider audience, including the corporate-training market. Others believe that creating an in-house program is the only way to protect the university's "brand" from being siphoned off by others.

Where It Began

New York University led the way in 1998, when it created a for-profit subsidiary, NYUonline, to build, market and distribute Web-based courses. The organization, which worked with e-learning vendor click2learn.com to put those courses online, is currently marketing instruction that leads to a certificate in management techniques. "We're focused on what will become a $20 billion market in the next three years," says NYUonline's CEO and president, Gordon Macomber.

Similar for-profit spin-offs are either in place or in the works at dozens of other private schools, including Cornell, Duke and Temple universities. Last December, the University of Maryland became the first public school to formally approve such a plan. George Washington University (GWU), which developed its Prometheus online course-ware for on-campus use in 1996, created a for-profit company last year to license the system to other colleges and universities.

Moreover, professors are increasingly being courted by outside companies, such as UNext.com in Deerfield, Ill., and Pensare in Los Altos, Calif., that want to package their courses for Web distribution. "There are a number of programs specific to Cornell, including our hotel school and our industrial and labor relations school, that could be money-making ventures if offered in an executive-education format," says Barry Carpenter, professor of chemistry and chemical biology at Cornell in Ithaca, N.Y. Professors in these schools, he says, are constantly being approached by outside vendors who want to sign them up.

Vendors that have developed online training courses are also looking for other ways to partner with colleges. Since 1997, Pima Community College in Tucson, Ariz., has been working with the Industry Training Credit Approval Process (ITCAP) program to offer credit for information technology certification courses created and sold by commercial training vendors such as Redwood City, Calif.-based SmartForce and Naperville, Ill.-based NETg. A student who completes a NETg course from the Microsoft Certified Systems Engineer curriculum and passes the related exam, for example, can earn credit toward an associate of applied science degree from the school.

"For Pima, they saw an opportunity to boost enrollment, to get access to a new kind of student," says Paul Sturm, manager of program development for ITCAP, which reviews courses for their academic rigor. Sturm adds that his organization is in discussions with other schools that are considering similar arrangements.

The Need for Speed

Why court the for-profit world? There are several factors to consider, says Bo Davis, the lead developer of GWU's Prometheus software, a distance education platform that allows professors to post lecture notes, make Web-based presentations and hold online discussions.

GWU, in Washington, D.C., is unusual in that it is marketing its product not to corporate training departments, but to public and private universities that might be considered its competitors. So far, nine have bought it, including Vanderbilt University, the University of Michigan's school of engineering and the University of Toronto's school of continuing studies.

Raising capital is a primary reason for spinning off a for-profit venture, Davis says. And one thing that money goes toward is the infrastructure needed to distribute online courses, which can be prohibitively expensive. "Most experts say that the entry fee into this game is in the tens of millions of dollars," Cornell's Carpenter says. (A February *Wall Street Journal* article puts it at a minimum of $25 million.)

Some might charge that, in creating a for-profit subsidiary, GWU is exposing faculty members to the demands of business, rather than leaving them alone to focus on research and teaching. But Davis doesn't buy this. "Universities have always been profit-motivated; they have to be," he says. "GW is the second-largest employer in the D.C. area, behind the federal government—and 7,000 employees is a lot of mouths to feed." He says they could have gone out and bought an online delivery platform but decided instead to use the talents in house to develop their own.

Gerald Heeger, president of the University of Maryland University College (UMUC) in Adelphi, Md., points out that universities aren't exactly protected from commercialism now. Taco Bell sells burritos in university food courts, Barnes & Noble runs college bookstores, and long-distance phone companies such as AT&T produce combined student I.D./calling cards. Still, he says, universities that make their online learning for-profit have to guard against the tail wagging the dog—in other words, against stockholders' concerns trumping a university's core mission.

"That's my job," says Heeger, who helped launch NYUonline before joining UMUC. "With or without a for-profit, as universities start to compete on a worldwide scale, there's always the danger they might think too much about marketing, and not enough about academics."

The profit motive is definitely there, but Davis and others insist it's not the only incentive. Davis predicts Prometheus will be profitable, "but it just doesn't need to be insanely profitable. Our mission is to develop a quality product, not to make lots of money," he says.

Training or Education?

Given the importance that universities are placing on maintaining their "brand," the issue of quality becomes paramount. Some, like Denise Marie Tanguay, professor of management and industrial relations at Eastern Michigan University in Ypsilanti, are concerned about universities' rush to enter the online education market. And, since she serves on the accreditation committee of the American Association of University Professors (AAUP), her opinion carries some weight.

The AAUP has so far refused to accredit any institution that does not have at least some classroom component. In an editorial she co-wrote last year for *The Chronicle of Higher Education*, Tanguay spoke out against the North Central Association of Colleges and Schools' accreditation of Jones International University, the all-cyberspace school founded by a cable entrepreneur in 1995.

In a subsequent interview, Tanguay does, however, draw a broad line between degree programs and corporate training. The latter, she says, can be just as good online as in the classroom—maybe better. She says she would encourage her 20-year-old son, a computer engineering major, to go online to get Microsoft certification, "just not to get an online undergraduate degree."

In fact, most of the coursework that's offered online qualifies as training, not education, in her book. "That's fine—we need good training," Tanguay says. "The problem is that the current market, especially on the profit-making side, is moving toward providing credentials and calling them the same thing as a degree. When you introduce the profit ethic, you start to look at the product as a commodity—as something that satisfies a student's short-term needs. Sure, a lot of people will get a promotion, a raise or a job because they have a degree, but that's not the business higher education has been in. We're into educating students," she says.

But administrators of community colleges don't necessarily agree. "Community colleges in general take advantage of the opportunity to serve students in whatever way they possibly can," says Chris Lamar, director of telecommunications and production services at Pima Community College. "Universities have a different mission; their students come to them. They have standards for admission, for instance, that community colleges don't have." Consequently, corporations often look to community colleges to pick up where their training departments leave off.

"Corporate training really is not interested in a course or a program," says NYUonline's Macomber. "They have distinct, real needs. We [at NYUonline] can develop courses [for corporations] in a modular form, link them to assessment technology, and ascertain who needs what learning, then deliver it just-in-time."

Training like this may fall under the same brand name as NYU's degree program, but companies understand the difference between addressing skills gaps and enrolling in, say, a master's program. "We're not claiming it's certified education, but we're saying it's coming from an accredited university," he says.

Those Pesky Professors

Once you've separated training courses from degree programs, some serious questions of academic freedom and intellectual property remain. As for-profit ventures try to license content from well-known professors, universities are hashing out who, exactly, owns a professor's classes. Is a course like a book, which a professor can write (even on the university's time, using an office computer) and send to a publisher while keeping the copyright and the royalties? Or is it like the patent on a machine or a laboratory process, created by the professor but owned by the university?

This problem surfaced last year when Arthur Miller, a professor at Harvard University's law school who had parlayed his distinctive classroom style (some claim he was the inspiration for the terrifying law professor in the 1970s movie "The Paper Chase") into a television career on WBGH's "Miller's Court," was prevented by Harvard from selling a course to an outside online law school. Miller argued that, since he taped the 11 Internet lectures during his summer vacation, he should be allowed to sell them to the Concord University School of Law.

"This is not about a professor waking up one morning and saying, 'I'm going to do a course online,'" says UMUC's Heeger about the Miller case. "If a faculty member does research that has commercial possibilities, it's been historically understood that this piece of research is not simply created or owned by the faculty member. We all sense that there's a difference between a professor producing a book and a professor producing a course that might compete with the university that he's a part of."

People have likened this situation to the superstar phenomenon in sports, he says. "I think Michael Jordan would have become the greatest basketball player in the world regardless of what team he was on. But would Arthur Miller have become as famous as he is without Harvard? I'm not so sure about academic superstars."

But when a university does take control over its own e-learning program, the ownership problem doesn't go away. In an online course, "the faculty member is going to be more dependent on the university" than in a traditional classroom, Heeger says. Professors have to work with software designers and other content providers to create and distribute the class, and as a result the course itself might not be flexible enough to meet some students'—and professors'—needs.

Extra Compensation

In part to make up for this loss of freedom, many universities pay professors extra for developing and teaching online classes. NYUonline compensates NYU faculty members separately for contracting with them, as does Cornell.

Still, even when professors are adequately compensated, the idea of selling their courses through a for-profit entity doesn't always sit well. Last winter, a brouhaha erupted at Cornell when administrators announced plans to create e-Cornell. The corporation's for-profit status with the prospect of it requiring external capital troubled a number of instructors. "In an educational venture, any loss of control [over course content] is a source of concern," says Cornell's Carpenter.

Indeed, a hallmark of a traditional college or university is its ability to spend money, not make it. "Traditional universities are not in the business of making money; they're in the business of providing services," says Tanguay.

But the proponents of these brave new ventures say that if they're going to compete with the Jones Internationals of the world, they have to take on the characteristics of other dot-com companies. They have to move quickly, and they have to attract new capital. Even when the corporation is wholly owned by the university (as is NYUonline and, so far, e-Cornell), no one is ruling out the possibility of an initial public offering down the road.

Money and Values

Going public is a big gamble, one that's likely to pay off only as long as e-business stays the darling of the stock market—and there are signs that Wall Street may be losing its patience here. Still, universities remain sanguine about having thrown their hat into the for-profit e-learning ring.

"Why do people want to go to any university? Because of its reputation and brand image," Macomber says. "NYU is a top research university, it has world-class faculty, and through NYUonline it works to benefit both the university and employees of a corporation." He says they could have worked with an outside company to develop NYUonline, but instead chose to keep the company—and its profits—in house.

But having a good business plan and a recognized name aren't the only ingredients to success. Macomber believes the institutions that will thrive are those that make the students' education their primary concern.

Make your content "compelling and engaging," he says, and the money will follow. It remains to be seen whether universities' venture into dot-com territory will justify such a high-stakes investment—or turn into a costly bust.

Rebecca Ganzel (thomp144@tc.umn.edu) is a freelance writer who lives in St. Paul, Minn., and frequently writes about technology, training, and educational issues.

Any Path Will Do

Bob Heterick

This article provides a brief overview of the direction higher education may take. It suggests that a focus on the learner will gradually take over, with funding actually going to learners rather than institutions. The author suggests that private and public educators will compete for these funds, with asynchronous on-demand distance learning playing a bigger and bigger role.

As traditional colleges and universities feint, dodge, weave, stumble and sometimes fumble in their move toward the incorporation of technology-based learning strategies, a sort of Alice in Wonderland aura permeates the educational landscape—if you don't know where you are going, any path will do.

We sometimes wonder if our traditional institutions of higher learning have seriously stopped to consider the likely outcomes of the increasingly significant infusion of computer and communications technology into the teaching/learning process. If they had, it would be difficult to explain some of the choices being made. There is an element of wisdom in the old technology maxim, "It only took God six days to make the heavens and the earth because he didn't have an installed base to worry about." New, commercial entrants in the higher education market currently have the edge precisely because they don't have an installed base to worry about. Our long-established institutions, while not necessarily moribund, suffer from the inertia of several hundred years of tradition that make change on any significant scale exceedingly difficult.

As the focus shifts from teaching to learning, a number of changes will become increasingly obvious. Just as the student will become more responsible for his or her learning outcomes, we can expect the student to become responsible for setting his or her educational agenda.

There are certainly historical antecedents for this. It was well into the 19th century before an established curriculum, leading to a four-year undergraduate degree, became the norm. Prior to that time, and even into the 20th century, it was not uncommon for students to pick and choose courses at the university and, when they felt themselves ready, to leave with letters of recommendation from various faculty that they felt would open the necessary doors to a long and rewarding career. In today's world, the number of university dropouts who have created the engine that fuels our booming economy is legend. It hasn't escaped observation that Microsoft has created many more millionaires from its staff roster than has the National Football League from its.

All this may signal the resurgence of the professorate. Educational institutions have long struggled with the limited allegiance of their faculty who, especially in the case of research institutions, have been focused more on their professional discipline than on their employer of record. New organizational structures to deliver learning opportunities with technology seem likely to further exacerbate this long standing concern. Just as the marginal farmer, who could provide subsistence for his family and a few others, has shrunk to near invisibility, so too will the lecturer who can provide a learning opportunity for only 50 or 100 students at a time. Those faculty (more likely teams of faculty) who can provide compelling learning experiences for literally thousands of students may become like successful researchers and football coaches and their staffs—greatly in demand and following the money.

As the student takes increasing responsibility for his or her education, it seems likely that the funding, which has been directed to the institution, will begin to shift to the student. We have a little taste of this with the beginning of state scholarship funds directed to the student and with the rise of state support for secondary students in charter and private schools. We hear rumblings in the legislatures of several states about funding the consumer rather than the provider and there is clear evidence that significant amounts of federal educational support are beginning to follow this model.

Directing support to students rather than institutions will increase the aggressiveness of potential commercial competitors. Unencumbered with the inertia confronting our traditional institutions, they will be formidable competitors. Unlinking financial support from a formal degree would further pressure educational institutions who eschew learning opportunities outside their degree curricula. Enrollment competition—which has generally been an issue only for second-tier, high-cost, private institutions and institutions in states with declining or only marginally growing populations—will become a major issue for all but a few high-prestige institutions. Many traditional institutions will find themselves "over-built" in terms of bricks and mortar. Maintenance of an under-utilized physical plant could become a significant competitive deterrent for some.

The more significant issue may be the potentially precipitous decline in the number of students actually seeking the four-year undergraduate degree. Life-long learning and job re-skilling are likely to be the goals of the vast majority of people pursuing post-secondary learning experiences. It seems likely that three-quarters of the enrollment in post-secondary learning will not have degree expectations or intentions. Fewer than one-fourth of all current students are seeking the "undergraduate experience" as a full-time, residential student. That percentage can be expected to continue to diminish.

For the majority of students, credit-for-contact is of little import, but certification of learning is critical. To accommodate this majority, we can expect to see an increased emphasis on outcomes assessment and a decreased focus on seat time. As more and more regional and statewide asynchronous learning institutions such as the Western Governors and Kentucky Virtual universities come into existence, the rise of credit banks and transfer-of-credit agreements should be expected. While conferring a degree on a student who has never set foot on the campus, or possibly never completed a course taught by the institution, is a specter that haunts most traditional institutions, new providers can be expected to emerge to meet student demand for certification.

The comfortable rhythm of the 15-week semester will be shattered. Students will begin the study of a "course" at anytime and will finish at anytime. Traditional institutions of higher learning will be confronted with scheduling issues that boggle the mind. Student progress and "eligibility" will require new definitions. These are not new problems to the dot.com world, but our traditional institutions of higher learning are not necessarily adept at operating in Internet time.

If you think you know where you are going, the path really does make a difference.

Bob Heterick is former President and CEO of EDUCOM and Vice President Emeritus of Virginia Polytechnic Institute and State University. He is the author of a dozen monographs and book chapters and more than 60 articles.

How to Choose a College Partner for Distance Education

Sylvia Vander Sluis

Selecting a higher-education alliance for management-level e-learning shouldn't be a guessing game. This article lays out a plan that helps you choose partners in these endeavors.

You're a corporate training manager responsible for training first-level managers (both new managers and those already in the job) and country-level managers. Perhaps half of the latter have bachelor's degrees. Your audience is dispersed around the globe, and they're busy people. Your company has excellent programs in place for providing training on tools, systems, and procedures, but that's not what this audience needs.

They need undergraduate- or graduate-level college courses. In addition, they need to work with people from other corporations to expand their experience. Your company offers a program to help workers earn college degrees, but most of the burden of selecting a school and enrolling in a degree program is placed on the employee, and there's no mechanism in place to ensure that such training supports related business goals.

You decide on a Web-based solution that leverages the corporate intranet by linking to college partner sites. Employees are already using the intranet for job- and education-related information, services, communication, and marketing, and such a program will provide a reasonably priced global solution without the travel requirements.

So, how do you select an experienced college or university that can provide quality distance education and associated services and meet both employee and corporate needs?

What We Did

As a training manager at Digital Equipment Corporation, I established such a Web-based program—DIGITAL Online University—in the fall of 1997. During the pilot program, Compaq Computer Corporation acquired DIGITAL and the name of the program changed to Compaq College Link (CCL).

The pilot program was completed with an accredited college in the spring of 1998. An international group participated in two Web-based courses, working with an instructor and other course participants over the Internet. Based on what we learned from the pilot experience and our research on distance learning, I created a comprehensive set of business practices to support ongoing program implementation. The following three-step method documented in our Business Practices Guide allowed us to select and evaluate potential college partners.

Step 1: Screening. The preliminary screening criteria are: What are the company's most important program requirements? What does an educational institution need to offer to be considered?

To determine whether an institution meets your requirements, you need to do research. An institution's ability to communicate well over the Web is a critical success factor, so you may base your initial screening on information gathered from a review of the college's Website. You may also want to sample an online course at the site to review its instructional design.

For CCL, baseline requirements fell into the following categories that we organized into an online questionnaire template:

- *Academic criteria.* Does the institution have regional accreditation? Does it have demonstrated experience with an international adult population? Do the courses include content and resources that reflect current theory and practice in international business?
- *Distance learning criteria.* Does the institution demonstrate experience with delivering instructor-led, Web-based courses? Is an orientation program available to acquaint participants with online processes and the online environment? Is there responsive academic and technical support for course participants?
- *Online course criteria.* Are courses designed specifically for the online environment with a consistent approach to design and functionality? Are communication and delivery mechanisms primarily asynchronous and text-based to make access as inclusive as possible and independent of a participant's location or time zone? Is communication between participants and with the instructor enabled by the following technologies: asynchronous text, email, and fax?

■ *Systems criteria.* Do the courses make minimal use of tools and technologies that may require excessive bandwidth or that may pose technical problems for the corporate intranet?

After completing a screening and an initial review of online courses, you'll be able to determine which institutions meet your baseline requirements. You can then select several for a more thorough assessment.

We screened 24 U.S. distance learning colleges—chosen from *Forbes*'s list of top cyber universities and other resources—on their ability to meet our corporate requirements and function successfully as partners. We ranked the 24 on the screening criteria, and five were identified for more in-depth assessment. Non-U.S. colleges were also screened, but only a small number looked like immediate partner prospects. To establish and maintain a database of information on current and potential college partners, it's useful to make the screening process an ongoing activity.

Step 2: Assessment. Colleges that meet your baseline requirements move on to assessment. Assessment requires personal contact with an appropriate person at the institution, such as the director of distance education or continuing education. Call him or her to introduce yourself, describe your business needs, and determine the college's potential interest in becoming a partner. If the college expresses an interest, you'll need to provide information on your program requirements and expectations in terms of college courses and support services.

We sent interested colleges a descriptive introduction covering CCL's purpose, strategy, values, and baseline program requirements. For example, in the design category, we stated a need for flexibility in course length and start dates to accommodate the demands of a quarterly business cycle and to support a variety of employee needs. We also stated our expectations for evaluation methodologies, administrative support, and program management, as well as our expectations for other academic services.

Forms, such as a request for information (RFI), are essential for gathering information. We sent an electronic RFI questionnaire to each college contact. The college's potential as a CCL partner was assessed by reviewing the completed RFI and by holding follow-up conversations with appropriate college staff.

Step 3: Proposal review and evaluation. At this point, you're looking for colleges' responses to specific business training needs in a request for proposal. Send RFPs to colleges that have passed your initial screening and in-depth assessment and that have also expressed interest in becoming a partner. Each proposal you receive from a college or university holds a wealth of information, and the success of your program depends on careful analysis. This is the time to include input from business consultants in the organization to make sure the program will meet corporate business needs. Now's also the time to perform a more thorough analysis of the sample courses offered by each college and evaluate each school's method of orienting students to online learning.

We developed a decision matrix for proposal reviewers. It organized data into the following broad categories with a rating scale of weak, solid, and exemplary:

- *Proposal submission.* Is the proposal complete, timely, and easy to comprehend? Is information presented clearly?
- *Content and structure.* Is the proposal consistent with the RFP? Does it present relevant information? Is the college ready to deliver the needed course content? Can the college deliver a program with the proposed structure?
- *Services.* Does the college offer academic advising, enrollment administration, support for English as a second language, and other services?
- *Instructors.* Does the proposal indicate the academic and professional profiles of the instructors and do those profiles meet the program's needs? Are the instructors trained to deliver online courses? Are they ready to deliver the proposed content or is additional development time needed?
- *Evaluation.* What are the college's existing processes and tools for evaluating courses? What process is proposed for the program?
- *Technology.* Is the college able to meet the program requirements? For example, does it make minimal use of high-bandwidth tools?
- *Costs and timeframes.* What will be your investment in course development? What will be the per-employee tuition cost? Is the college able to meet your time constraints?
- *Overall.* Summary results from all categories.

In addition to these ratings, we performed a second, more comprehensive evaluation of the sample online college courses using a similar matrix. Evaluation criteria for online course design were organized using the same rating scale in the following categories:

- *System.* What's the overall look, feel, and operation of the online courses?
- *Technology.* What's the platform? What applications, hardware, and software are required for successful completion of the courses?
- *Integrity.* Are the courses instructionally sound?
- *Support.* What processes and materials are provided to assist learners and instructors?

After analysis came negotiation. We were interested in offering business certificate programs made up of several related, credit-bearing courses. Most colleges that responded to the proposal had the content we desired, but their proposals raised new, substantive questions that forced further discussions and exploration. For example, one of the two colleges we were most interested in required admission to either their undergraduate or graduate school to enroll in the business certificate programs—whether the employee wanted to apply the credit toward a degree or not. In addition, both of the colleges required the equivalent of a U.S. bachelor's degree for admission to the graduate-level certificate program.

These academic admission requirements were a concern to Compaq because we believed the majority of employees would prefer focused certificate programs to degree programs, and we felt that the substantive admissions hurdles could be a negative motivator, particularly for those who lacked a bachelor's degree. The colleges were convinced that people enrolling in the graduate-level classes needed a bachelor's degree in order to ensure an even level of preparation for all students, as well as to adhere to academic policies.

This experience highlighted the fact that businesses often need flexibility in academic policies for their employees. Flexibility, of course, must be weighed against many other factors. It may be worthwhile to take an investment approach with colleges that offer greater academic flexibility. As long as their curriculum content and services are basically on target, they may be the best choice for a long-term, evolving partnership.

For us, two universities were standout preferences. Interestingly, they had significantly different course structures and, in some cases, admission requirements. We decided to offer certificate programs through both universities so that employees could complete the college program that offered the best fit.

A Manager's Work Is Never Done

After college selection, there's still significant work to be done. In the case of CCL, we created an internal Website for marketing the program, communicating with potential learners, and linking employees to the college Websites. We also added Webpages on each college site to welcome Compaq employees and direct them to Compaq-specific programs and enrollment information.

The process of managing and evaluating a program like CCL and the college partnerships that support it is an iterative process. You need a valid selection process with a robust, consistent set of criteria and assessment tools to identify the best potential educational partners. Documenting the steps in the process and formalizing tools and sample implementations of those tools makes an efficient process over time.

Sylvia Vander Sluis (sylvia.vandersluis@compaq.com) is a training program manager in Customer Services Training and Development, Compaq Computer Corporation.

Part Six

Instructional Design for Distance Learning

Y̶ou want to develop online distance learning courses. How can you make sure you're creating courses that will actually deliver the goods for your students and organizations? Of course, trial and error is involved, but there are ways to design effective content and delivery approaches, and that's what the five articles in Part Six address.

We start off with "Some Design Strategies for Developing an Online Course" by Nancy Harrison and Carole Bergen. This is mainly aimed at those in higher education, and it includes a whole variety of tips and techniques for structure, course outlines, weekly modules, papers, testing, and more. While most ideas are presented for college courses, there will also be some useful ideas for those developing online training programs as well.

You'll next find the article with the important title, "Building Effective Interaction in Distance Education: A Review of the Literature" by Kim Flottemesch. It provides a useful review of findings from various researchers on what they've discovered about the nature of interactions between students and between students and the instructor to make sure the course is successful. This has equal application both in higher education and in other sector training programs.

From a rather academic though still practical article, we move to one that is explicitly practical: "Checklists for Developing Web-Based Courses" by Ann Yakimovicz. Here you'll find four detailed checklists aimed at different types of Web-based courses. Think of these checklists as reminders of all the things you need to consider as you design and develop your course(s).

Next we offer another article with practical advice: "Effective User Interface Design: The Four Rules" by Kevin Kruse. Making your online course easy to navigate is very important, and in this article, you'll find plenty of useful ideas, some of which are relevant, no matter whether you're designing an online course or just an easy-to-find-things Web site.

We conclude with "Developing Courses for Online Delivery: One Strategy" by Ann Luck, senior instructional designer at Penn State's World Campus. In it she describes the steps they go through in developing a course for their online university, and she usefully includes how they deal with problems, when the steps in the process break down for one reason or another.

As in the other parts of this book, this one blends principles and applications, but we think this selection of articles should help you with sound action ideas as you begin to design and develop your online distance learning courses.

Some Design Strategies for Developing an Online Course

Nancy Harrison and Carole Bergen

This article provides a whole series of helpful ideas and plans for setting up a successful online distance learning course. The authors include tips for structure, course outlines, weekly modules, papers, testing, and more. This will be most useful to those planning courses in higher education.

Higher education is certainly in the throes of change; one of the key ways in which it is changing is in the area of distance learning. In fact, many institutions allow students to complete entire programs or degree requirements working exclusively online.

For certain categories of students, this is a real plus or even a necessity. Some students need such courses because of their work schedules; when students work different shifts or must travel as part of their jobs, they are unable to attend a class at a specific time and location. Students who have young children, full-time jobs, or disabilities which make it difficult to attend class on a regular basis really appreciate the flexibility of a distance learning class. Also, students who move when they are within a few courses of completing the requirements for a degree find that distance learning classes enable them to continue at the same university rather than taking courses at a different university and maneuvering through the red tape of trying to match up courses or get credits transferred. However, it is true that these classes are not for everyone. To be successful, students must be *self-motivated* and *independent* learners. Students who choose a distance learning class because they feel that it will be easier than a traditional class are almost always disappointed. Distance learning students must complete the same assignments as in the traditional class *and* have the discipline to complete the course requirements on a weekly basis even though there are no real-time classes to attend.

Our college uses TopClass, which is one of many Web-based instructional products currently on the market. However, this article concentrates on *general design aspects* of a distance education course rather than the features of a particular product.

Preparation

Before the semester starts, it is recommended that all faculty planning to teach a distance-learning course receive training in both the specific course management and delivery system being used and in the techniques of designing an effective online course. Many instructors who have previously taught distance-learning classes are willing to serve as mentors to faculty inexperienced with this modality. The first time a course is presented online, it may be similar in format to its traditional counterpart, but developing a successful online course is an ongoing process. As instructors gain experience using the new technology, they become aware of more effective ways to present the material, such as graphics, video, audio, testing software, etc. Also, links to Web sites must be updated regularly, since previously used links are not always active and new links will be added as additional relevant Web sites are discovered. Often, students in the class will alert instructors and class members to Web sites that they have found helpful while doing research for an assignment or project.

Structure

Teaching in this format requires that the instructor be more organized than in a regular classroom. A "welcome" message to the students is a good place to explain the broad structure of the course. The differences between the major components of the software should be made clear. Most systems distinguish an area for announcements, a place for class discussion, and a way to send and receive private e-mail messages. Students should be clear on the function of each area.

Depending on the particular course delivery system being used, instructor messages and/or course materials are usually posted in read-only announcement areas. Instructor postings contain pertinent course information, such as the course outline, testing procedures, guidelines for any required papers, due dates, etc. In some course delivery systems, the actual course materials, usually organized as weekly modules, are also posted in this area, while other systems contain an area specifically designated for that purpose. Usually, students read and print out the information in this area but do not post any messages here.

Another important component is a discussion list, which is basically a public bulletin board where students and the instructor post messages for everyone in the class to see. This is the area where class "discussions" take place, questions can be posted and answered, etc. Usually, the discussion is organized into folders, with a separate folder used for each topic. There are a variety of ways that these folders could be organized; some faculty organize them around chapters in the textbook, others around weekly discussion questions, and some around assignments. It is recommended that the organization be worked out before the class begins, to enable students to follow more easily the participation component of the class.

Lastly, everyone in the class has the ability to receive and send private e-mail messages. It is important that students understand the difference between sending a public message to the full discussion list and a private e-mail message to one other person.

In addition to providing an explanation of each of the above areas, the welcome message should also direct the student how to start the course. Typically, this would include the steps necessary to find the course outline and print it for reference throughout the course.

Course Outline

It is preferable to have a copy of the course outline available even before the class begins, in order to give students an overview of what to expect. As in a traditional course, the course outline should contain any prerequisites for the class, the objectives, a brief listing of the topics to be covered, the required materials such as texts, specific grading criteria for the course, participation requirements for the course, and a bibliography. Students must know ahead of time how all tests will be administered, what percent the tests count toward their final course grades, what percent online postings will count, etc. In fact, it is a good idea to assign weights to all the various components of the course.

Having this information available prior to the start of the semester enables students to decide whether this course really is for them.

Most faculty organize the presentation of their course around weekly modules, which are discussed in the next section.

Weekly Modules

If possible, it is helpful to have the entire course organized into weekly modules before the students actually come online. At the very least, the underlying structure of the modules as well as the first three weeks should be already prepared. Each weekly module contains a number of components. The first part contains reminders such as "Don't forget that you must submit the topic of your paper as an e-mail message to the instructor by February 26th at midnight."

The second and most important section is the presentation of new material. Depending on the technology available, instructors have a variety of options, ranging from a predominantly text-based presentation to linked Web pages, which may incorporate graphics, video, and audio components.

For example, a module on a course in American Literature might include information about a particular author, questions to think about while doing the readings, and links to various Web sites related to the author and/or his or her works. Students would be expected to read the materials and visit the Web sites indicated to prepare for the discussion questions.

In a mathematics course, this area would include the main mathematical concepts of the week together with examples. Also, warnings about common mistakes would be appropriate in this section as well as links to related Web sites.

The third component is simply a detailed listing of the assignments for the week, in particular the pages to read, questions to answer, and problems to solve.

The material for the online discussions constitutes the fourth component. It is important to be quite specific here. In addition to giving the question(s) to be discussed online for a particular week, the instructor should indicate where the answers should be posted in the discussion area. A specific folder should be designated in the discussion area for each discussion question that is given. This will help to keep the discussion area well organized and easy to follow.

Fostering a Community of Learners

In the absence of traditional class meetings, it is important to foster a learning community among the members of the class. For example, it is helpful to require the students to post an introduction of themselves to the class as part of the first online assignment. This allows students to informally get to know a little about others in the class. Often, students will share information, such as why they are taking the course, their career goals, their family responsibilities, etc. Students in similar situations, such as mothers at home with young children, are pleased to find online classmates who share the same challenges of balancing school and family life. This serves to break down some of the isolation that students may feel when they first start the online course.

Distance education is neither a private tutorial nor a traditional classroom experience. Consequently, students must participate in the class by posting regularly in the class discussion area. In assigning weights to the various components of the course, we recommend that a minimum of 20 percent of the grade be allocated to the online discussion part of the course. All students are expected to post at least two messages in the discussion area every week of the course. In addition to general reminders in the class announcements or in the weekly modules at least a couple of times during the semester, individual e-mail messages are sent to students who are not regular contributors to the discussion.

Papers

Many college level courses, online or not, have a paper or a series of papers as a requirement. Along with the course outline, information about such papers should be posted at the start of the semester. It is also helpful to include links to Web sites that students may find helpful as they begin to prepare their paper.

In order to encourage students to work regularly on the papers, specific steps along with deadlines may be posted.

In a traditional class, students are expected to present the highlights of their papers to the class in oral presentations. However since this is not possible in online courses, we include a folder in the discussion area titled "Tidbits from My Research" to allow students to share interesting information uncovered in their paper research. Contributions to this folder count as part of the required two messages a week. In our experience, students enjoy contributing to this folder and have posted some interesting observations in this area. Sometimes students will find that they are doing similar topics and will suggest books or Internet resources to each other.

Testing

We use a combination of online quizzes and proctored tests to determine if the students are in fact learning the material that is required in the course. Each type of test achieves a different purpose. The online quizzes can be posted by the instructor and then taken by the students at a time convenient for them. We usually post our quizzes on a Wednesday and require that they be completed by the following Sunday. This schedule seems to work well for all students, since it gives them days and evenings as well as weekends to work on the quiz. Usually, students will print out a copy of the quiz and then send an e-mail to the instructor with the answers. The instructor can then correct the quiz and e-mail the results back with very little time lapse. Many distance learning systems have a testing feature which allows students to fill in the answers to test items online and then click a submit button when all items are complete. If tests are submitted this way, instructors may comment on each answer and indicate the number of points earned on each question. The first online quiz is given after the third week of class and is a good way to spot students who are having difficulty. These students are given some guidelines as to how to improve their performance before it is too late in the semester. We usually give a second online quiz between the midsemester and the final exam.

The major disadvantage of the online quizzes is the inability to guarantee academic integrity. In order to assure that the students are in fact learning the material and doing the assignments themselves, we require that all students take a proctored midterm and final exam.

Students who live near one of the college's campuses go there for the exams. Students have the choice of taking the exam on Friday evening or Saturday morning.

Students who live at a distance take the exam with an approved proctor. At our college, it is the responsibility of the individual student to locate an appropriate proctor. The main source used by such students is the assessment center at a college near them. The director of the center for learning and assessment services verifies the authenticity of the proctor. Such proctors are responsible for ensuring the integrity of the exam; they receive the exam packet, arrange an appropriate time for the student to take the exam, proctor the actual exam, and then mail the completed exam back to the college. Proctors are given a stipend for each exam administered. The major disadvantage of this system is the difficulty of arranging a testing schedule for every student. However, we feel that it is worth the inconvenience, since this helps to assure that students are getting credit for their own work.

Conclusion

Because of the advances in technology and the convenience for students, distance learning is a rapidly growing option in the field of education. As faculty members, we need to do the best job that we can to teach students who choose this method of delivery. A substantial amount of planning and preparation must go into the design of an online course, and the development of such a course is an ongoing process as we become more knowledgeable and the technologies continue to improve. It is our hope that the design strategies presented here will be helpful for faculty involved in the process of distance education.

Suggested Readings

Boettcher, J. (1999). Cyber course size: Pedagogy and politics. *Syllabus*, 12(8), 42-44.

Cini, M., and Vilie, B. (1999). Online teaching: Moving from risk to challenge. *Syllabus*, 12(10), 38-40.

Distance Learning in Higher Education. (1999). Special Publication for the Council for Higher Education Accreditation, Washington, DC.

Farrington, G.C. (1999, May 10). Learning is not downloading, but download we must. *Higher Education and National Affairs Newsletter*, 5.

Martin, M., and Taylor, S. (1997, September-October). The virtual classroom: The next steps. *Educational Technology*, 37(5), 51-55.

Serwatka, J.A. (1999). Internet distance learning: How do I put my course on the Web? *T.H.E. Journal*, 26(10), 71-74.

Nancy Harrison is Professor and Carole Bergen is Assistant Professor, Division of Mathematics and Computer Information Systems, Mercy College, Dobbs Ferry, New York (e-mail: nharrison@mercynet.edu, cbergen@mercynet.edu).

Building Effective Interaction in Distance Education: A Review of the Literature

Kim Flottemesch

There are plenty of ideas for developing distance learning programs, but what does the literature say about these ideas? That's what this article reviews in a systematic way. The author has taken the time to survey the literature and gives you some insight into what you need to remember as you plan or revise your current programs.

The quest for interactivity has become a necessary goal in the "design and provision" of distance education programs (Oliver and McLoughlin, 1996). Advanced technology can be used to enhance communication and overcome the isolation of distance. In the context of distance education, "any learning material or learning environment is usually said to be interactive" (Oliver and McLoughlin, 1996). Berge (1999) provides a broader description of interaction in a distance setting: "Interacting is two-way communication among two or more people within a learning context, with the purposes either task/instructional completion or social relationship-building, that includes a means for teacher and learner to receive feedback and for adaptation to occur based upon information and activities with which the participants are engaged."

Interactivity has been described as a fundamental aspect of conventional face-to-face teaching. In a distance education setting, it "provides a means to motivate and stimulate learners and provides a means [possibly through activities and the use of technology itself] for instructors to cause students to consider and reflect on the content and process of learning" (Juler, 1990).

Students, on the other hand, seem to view interaction by exploring how the technology was used rather than what type of technology was used (Jones, 1996). Students tend to define interaction "as a teacher's timely and consistent response to their needs rather than specific activities done" or technologies used by the instructor in the classroom (Jones, 1996).

This article will review current literature regarding interaction in distance education settings, specifically exploring its importance, perceptions of participants, and strategies to incorporate greater interaction in distance learning environments.

Why Is Interaction Important?

Teacher-to-Student Interaction

The literature reveals that creating interaction in the classroom is essential to student learning and to the overall success and effectiveness of distance education (Hodgson, 1999; Kearsley, 1995). Studies of traditional classrooms have shown a connection between classroom interaction and student learning and attitude. Simply having the ability to access information is not adequate. "Information must be shared, critically analyzed, and applied in order to become knowledge" (Garrison, 1990). Earlier research (Bloom, 1981) states that it is evident that "interaction between teachers and students in the classroom is the major factor in accounting for the cognitive learning of students, their interest in school subjects and learning, and their confidence in their own learning capabilities" (p. vi). Distance educators confirm that classroom interactions have positive educational outcomes. When students are actively learning, they learn more information, retain the information longer, are able to apply the information in a better manner, and continue the learning process (Weimer, 1993). Recent studies have found that interaction in distance learning environments may lead to increased academic achievement (Lenning and Ebbers, 1999; Niebuhr and Niebuhr, 1999) and greater retention rates (Lenning and Ebbers, 1999).

The role of interaction in distance education settings is addressed specifically by Barker, Frisbie, and Patrick (1989): "...like (in) traditional classroom settings, students in distance education settings can seek on-the-spot clarification from the instructor. Opportunities for teacher-student interaction can promote greater spontaneity for all participants in the teaching/learning process" (p. 23).

Education, whether at a distance or not, is dependent upon two-way communication (Berge, 1999). "Quality distance education is dependent upon the interaction and participation of the learner, similarly as in traditional face-to-face instruction. It is essential that the distance educator purposefully designs this ingredient into the instructional program" (Kruh and Murphy, 1990).

Student-to-Student Interaction

"Like other social systems, the classroom is made up of a network of interpersonal relationships structured to facilitate the achievement of educational goals" (Johnson, 1970). While there are a variety of relationships within schools in general to achieve varied goals, the primary educational relationships are between teachers and students and among students themselves. Though much of the literature is devoted to teacher-student interaction, research indicates that student-student interaction is the important determinant of educational success (Johnson, 1981). When a cooperative structure is established in the classroom, promotion of positive interaction and increased student exchange of information fosters educational success (Johnson, 1981). Interaction enhances achievement (Lenning and Ebbers, 1999; Niebuhr and Niebuhr, 1999), motivation (Hornbeck, 1990), and students being actively involved in their own learning (Whitworth, 1998). Student-to-student interaction through active participation and feedback has been found to be positively linked to critical thinking and problem solving skills (Hart, 1990; Hornbeck, 1990).

Though student-student interaction is critical to a student's achievement in the classroom, distance education settings may encounter problems in facilitating student interaction. Research indicates that some problems that occur involve students at remote campuses unable to see or hear everything that is occurring in the main campus classroom (Wilson, 1994). The technology itself must be working properly in order for successful interaction to be facilitated.

Research also indicates that remote students very rarely interact without being asked, due to intimidation of using the technology to interact (Monson, Wolcott, and Seiter, 1999; Wilson, 1994). "The geographical distance can create interpersonal distance where students' perception of closeness and belonging to the group are diminished. The distance tends to lessen spontaneous interaction [and reflection (Lamy and Goodfellow, 1999)] as well as the frequency of interaction among students" (Wolcott, 1994). Students at remote sites report that they have less of an opportunity to develop peer relations (Regan and Tuchman, 1990) and therefore feel isolated from peers (Hecht and Klass, 1999). The sense of isolation can cause lack of attention or social/off-task interactions with peers at the remote site (Hertz-Lazarowitz, 1981; Sorensen and Baylen, 1999).

Perceptions of Interaction

Technology not only serves to influence types and amounts of interactions, but also affects students' perceptions of the class and the communication in it. Students tend to judge a distance education course based on how truly interactive they felt the teacher was (Jones, 1996). More specifically, students perceive the nature and quality of the interaction to be more critical in their satisfaction with the distance education course (Zhang and Fulford, 1994).

Instructors who used more interactive questioning (Jones, 1996) with a relaxed interpersonal style, focusing on the interaction across sites, and involving students directly in the course content (Comeaux, 1995) were perceived as more successful in the distance education setting. Instructors who used technological strategies (Jones, 1996) and humor in dealing with technical nuances (Comeaux, 1995) were also perceived as successful in instructing in distance settings. Lecture as a presentation style was perceived as less successful. However, this style of delivery was positively received by field-independent learners (Jones, 1996). Research also indicates that students who have been previously exposed to distance education and have been trained in the use of the interactive technology (Kirby, 1999) tend to have greater satisfaction with the interactivity than do novice users (DeBourgh, 1999; Monson, Wolcott, and Seiter, 1999).

Overall, research indicates that a student's perceptions and expectations of the course interactivity vary between on- and offsite locations (Schuster, Collins, Hall, and Giffen, 1999) and the age of the student (Hammond, 1999). Students on the main campus expect and seek out interaction with teachers as part of their learning experience, thus having a positive impression of interactions (Regan and Tuchman, 1990). Those students in remote locations tend to consider the teachers more as "inanimate sources of information" and initiate fewer interactions (Regan and Tuchman, 1990).

Faculty who teach over distances express concerns about the interrelationships between instructor and students (Yucha, 1996). Depending on the technology used, one common barrier expressed by instructors is difficulty in gauging students' reactions and monitoring in-class discussions (Rezabek, 1992). In addition to these concerns, instructors indicate their struggle with lack of student responsiveness and therefore a lack of relationship satisfaction (Mottet, 1998). Instructors initially perceive distance teaching to be a more difficult setting in which to develop the intimacy generally found in traditional face-to-face classrooms.

With these concerns, many facilitators in distance education have expressed many positive aspects of interactivity in distance education. Using a variety of technological media, students can find an avenue for their voice to be heard (Dede, 1999). Different learners with varied needs can find a variety of outlets to use to communicate their thoughts and ideas. The technology may be seen as a means to accommodate different learning styles (Leh and Som, 1999).

Suggestions for Teachers
Teacher-to-Student Interaction

There are a number of strategies that distance educators can implement in order to promote learning, acceptance, and overall interaction in the classroom. The following statements list strategies identified by researchers as effective means for improving interaction. Though this is not an exhaustive list, it provides strategies with which to begin.

- Students are more likely to interact when the instructor is physically present (Bauer and Rezabek, 1993). If you are unable to be onsite, use an onsite facilitator to stimulate interaction (Willis, 1993). Another option is to utilize teaching assistants whose major purpose is to facilitate interaction and handle administrative duties (Comeaux, 1995).
- Computer-based communication through use of electronic mail and computer networks seems to be a feasible approach to providing communication between faculty and distance education students (Hezel and Dirr, 1990).
- Use pre-class (Coutts, 1996) study questions and advance organizers to encourage critical thinking and informed participation on the part of all learners (Willis, 1993).
- Study characteristics of your students, such as age, employment status, and family situation. Discover why students have enrolled in the course, their educational experience, and their content-related interests. This can help the teacher build a role as facilitator in assisting in the creation of an atmosphere conducive to student interaction (University of Alaska, 1990).
- Early in the course, require students to contact the instructor via electronic mail to get accustomed to the technology (Willis, 1993) and to assist in building rapport with all students. Teach students to use the technology (McHenry and Bozik, 1995).
- Arrange for telephone and evening office hours (Willis, 1993). In addition to being available for offsite students, try to physically visit remote sites and teach from those locations.
- Send letters of welcome to students (University of Alaska, 1990).
- Provide immediate communication and feedback on course assignments and inquiries (Jansen and Lewis, 1996). In addition to feedback, organize the distribution of class materials (McHenry and Bozik, 1995).
- Integrate a variety of delivery systems for interaction and feedback (Willis, 1993). Use strategies that personalize the class setting (McHenry and Bozik, 1995).
- Call on students at remote sites to ensure that all participants have ample opportunity to interact (Willis, 1993).
- Be proactive in interactions (Jones, 1996).
- Be open to the new environment (Jones, 1996).

Student-to-Student Interaction

Though many instructors may find it challenging to "transcend the distance" and create a comfortable atmosphere which fosters student interaction, there are some general strategies which can be implemented at the beginning, during, and at the end of the course.

Initially, interaction can be fostered by having students introduce themselves to class members at other sites, learn their names, and their particular interests in the course (Comeaux, 1995). Another strategy is to work to encourage use of electronic mail, telephone, and computer networks (Gibbs and Fewell, 1997; Hezel and Dirr, 1990). This type of interaction can be encouraged through course-required journal entries and logs of interaction with peers (Willis, 1993).

Support/study groups and tutoring are other viable options to enhance student interaction at distant sites during the course. These options may either be conducted independently or jointly, depending on the student's needs and location. Research indicates that those students who participate in study groups and/or tutoring achieve more academically than do "regular," non-participating students (Enoch, 1989). The focus is to create a link between the material and the students' experiences/knowledge to assist in the retention and comprehension of material.

Enoch (1989) identified three effective types of study/support groups for distant sites. These include (1) regular groups that meet once a month, (2) intensively tutored groups which meet once a week, and (3) groups within organized frameworks, in which students take a number of courses together and receive intensive tutoring once a week (cohorts).

There are a number of additional techniques for improving student-student interaction and having students at all sites feel that they are an integral part of the classroom during the course. They include:

- Instruct students to provide information across distances in relatively short exchanges (Oliver and McLoughlin, 1996). Depending on the technological medium used, this can add greater attention to what is being said.
- Incorporate group presentations into course assignments and/or projects (Miller and Kumari, 1997). Group projects require students to interact with their peers/group members through organization, preparation, and presentation. Creating groups with members from different sites can demand utilization of the technology and interaction from all locations in the presentation.
- Instructor questioning can promote classroom interaction. The questions should be open-ended, challenging, and interpretational to maximize student interaction. Instructors should increase wait time after questioning to improve quality and quantity of student interaction (El-Koumy, 1997).
- Improvisational techniques force active participation among students (Yucha, 1996). These strategies can be done through questioning, small group/dyad discussion, or activities.
- Interactions can be facilitated by using small discussion groups. Sites could go off-line for brief discussions of particular issues and then return online to discuss their findings with the larger group (Comeaux, 1995).
- Research indicates that the number of student questions in student-student interaction is much greater than in teacher-student interaction (El-Koumy, 1997).

- When group work is being accomplished, individual task assignments influence interaction among group members (El-Koumy, 1997). If each group member has a task, equitable workloads and group focus can be enhanced (Comeaux, 1995).

At the end of class periods and courses, support for interaction is easily dismissed and not acknowledged. One of the most common teaching errors is to provide too brief a time for students to process the quality of their cooperation (Johnson, Johnson, and Smith, 1991). A goal to closure of a lesson or the course itself is to have students assess how they have worked with others (Maier and Panitz, 1996).

If students have worked in small groups for substantial periods of time, some formal activities could lend themselves to effectively concluding the activity or the course itself involving interaction. One activity has the instructor "ask students to write a separate letter to each group member, using sentence completion stems as a guide: 'The way I experienced your behavior in the group...'; and 'What I personally feel you contributed to the group...'" (Wagenheim and Gemmill, 1994). Wagenheim and Gemmill (1994) recommend that the letter writer "circle those things that are true about themselves so that students recognize the importance of projection. When students own their feedback, interpersonal defensiveness is decreased and learning is increased."

Another activity is to make the final exam a teaching tool by asking students to take it in two stages, first, individually, and then with help from other class members. This method of examination assesses how well students work together to solve problems.

Conclusions

Technology has the potential of bringing a new dimension to interaction in the classroom. Though technology is a part of the mechanics of the process of teaching in distance education settings, it also focuses the instructor on the interactive process which may or may not be occurring.

Interaction in the classroom (traditional or distance learning) plays a key role in a student's learning, retention, and overall perceptions of the course/instructor effectiveness. With the proper techniques and strategies to incorporate student-to-student interaction, students across distant sites and onsite can develop rapport and provide support to one another. It is critical that instructors in distance education settings utilize the technology and generally prepare and plan for interaction in the classroom, since the very nature of the technology serves to influence classroom interaction. The quality of distance education is dependent upon the interaction and participation of the learners (McHenry and Bozik, 1995).

Technology can enhance presentation, communication, and teacher-student interaction as the instructor and students determine how it works for them and learn to expand upon its possibilities. With the use of the technology, these relationships and interactions can not only be developed, but also maintained. Utilization of the technology can decrease interpersonal distance and create camaraderie among students to enhance learning.

References

Barker, B.O., Frisbie, A.G., and Patrick, K.R. (1989). Broadening the definition of distance education in light of the new telecommunication technologies. *The American Journal of Distance Education,* 3, 20-29.

Bauer, J.W., and Rezabek, L.L. (1993). Effects of two-way visual contact on verbal interaction during face-to-face and teleconferenced instruction. In *Art, Science, and Visual Literacy: Selected Readings* from the Annual Conference of the International Visual Literacy Association (24th), Pittsburgh, PA, September 30-October 4, 1992 [ERIC Database: ED 363299].

Berge, Z.L. (1999). Interaction in postsecondary Web-based learning. *Educational Technology,* 39(1), 5-11.

Bloom, B.S. (1981). Foreword. In T. Levin, *Effective instruction* (p. vi). Alexandria, VA: Association for Supervision and Curriculum Development.

Comeaux, P. (1995). The impact of an interactive distance learning network on classroom communication. *Communication Education,* 44(4), 353-361.

Coutts, J. (1996). *The effect of distance education technology on teaching and learning* [ERIC Database: ED 406964].

DeBourgh, G.A. (1999). Technology is the tool, teaching is the task: Student satisfaction in distance learning. Paper presented at the Society for Information Technology and Teacher Education International Conference (10th), San Antonio, TX, February 28-March 4 [ERIC Database: ED 432226].

Dede, C. (1999). The multiple media difference. *TECHNOS,* 8(1), 16-18.

El-Koumy, A.S.A. (1997). *Review of recent studies dealing with techniques for classroom interaction* [ERIC Database: ED 415688].

Enoch, Y. (1989). The key to success in distance education: Intensive tutoring, group support, or previous education. Compilation of papers from the International Conference presented by the International Council for Distance Education with the British Open University Regional Academic Services (3rd), Cambridge, England, September 19-22, 1989 [ERIC Database: ED 317188].

Garrison, D.R. (1990). An analysis and evaluation of audio teleconferencing to facilitate education at a distance. *The American Journal of Distance Education,* 4, 13-24.

Gibbs, W.J., and Fewell, P.J. (1997). Virtual courses and visual media [ERIC Database: ED 408965].

Hammond, R.J. (1999). Fine tuning interactive delivery for high school students in a rapidly growing college and distance learning system [ERIC Database: ED 429630].

Hart, K.A. (1990). Teacher thinking in college: Accent on improving college teaching and learning [ERIC Database: ED 332613].

Hecht, J.B., and Klass, P.H. (1999). The evolution of qualitative and quantitative research classes when delivered via distance education. Paper presented at the Annual Meeting of the

American Educational Research Association (Montreal, QC, April 19-23) [ERIC Database: ED 430480].

Hertz-Lazarowitz, R. (1981). Student-student interaction in the classroom: A naturalistic study. Paper presented at the Summer Workshop of the Association of Teacher Educators/Institute for Research on Teaching (East Lansing, MI, August 2-5, 1981) [ERIC Database: ED 206590].

Hezel, R.T., and Dirr, P.J. (1990). Understanding distance education: Identifying barriers to college attendance [ERIC Database: ED 340335].

Hodgson, P. (1999). How to teach in cyberspace. *Techniques, 74*(5), p. 34.

Hornbeck, D.W. (1990). Technology and students at risk of school failure [ERIC Database: ED 327175].

Jansen, D.G., and Lewis, W.B. (1996). Creating high levels of interaction in distance education courses. *ATEA Journal, 24*(1), 8-9.

Johnson, D.W. (1970). *The social psychology of education.* New York: Holt, Rinehart, & Winston.

Johnson, D.W. (1981). Student-student interaction: The neglected variable in education. *Educational Researcher, 10*(1), 5-10.

Johnson, D.W., Johnson, R.T., and Smith, K.A. (1991). *Active learning: Cooperation in the college classroom.* Edina, MN: Interaction Book Company.

Jones, T.C. (1996). Communicating skills necessary for success in a distance environment. Paper presented at the Annual Meeting of the Southern States Communication Association, Memphis, TN, March 27-31, 1996 [ERIC Database: ED 399577].

Juler, P. (1990). Promoting interaction: Maintaining independence—swallowing the mizture. *Open Learning, 5*(2), 24-33.

Kearsley, G. (1995). The nature and value of interaction in distance learning. In M. Koble (Ed.), *The American Center for the Study of Distance Education Invitational Research Conference in Distance Education: Toward Excellence in Distance Education.* University Park, PA: Pennsylvania State University.

Kirby, E. (1999). Building interaction in online and distance education courses. Paper presented at the Society for Information Technology & Teacher Education International Conference (10th), San Antonio, TX, February 28-March 4, 1999 [ERIC Database: ED 432230].

Kruh, J. and Murphy, K. (1990). Interaction in teleconferencing: The key to quality instruction. Paper presented at the Annual Rural and Small Schools Conference, Manhattan, KS [ERIC Database: ED 329418].

Lamy, M.N., and Goodfellow, R. (1999). Reflective conversation in the virtual classroom. *Language Learning & Technology, 2*(2), 43-61.

Leh, A.S.C., and Som, Y.M. (1999). Challenges and considerations when conducting an online course. Society for Information Technology & Teacher Education International

Conference (10th), San Antonio, TX, February 28-March 4, 1999 [ERIC Database: ED 428743].

Lenning, O.T., and Ebbers, L.H. (1999). The powerful potential of learning communities: Improving education for the future. *ASHE-ERIC Higher Education Report, 26*(16), 1-173.

Maier, M.H., and Panitz, T. (1996). End on a high note: Better endings for classes and courses. *College Teaching, 44*(4), 145-148.

McHenry, L., and Bozik, M. (1995). Communicating at a distance: A study of interaction in a distance education classroom. *Communication Education, 44*(4), 362-371.

Miller, L.M., and Kumari, S. (1997). Project OWLink: Distance learning in electronic studios. Paper presented at the Annual Distance Education Conference (4th), Corpus Christi, TX, January 29-31, 1997 [ERIC Database: ED420296].

Monson, S.J., Wolcott, L.L., and Seiter, J.S. (199). Communication apprehension in synchronous distance education. Paper presented at the Annual Meeting of the Western States Communication Association (70th), Vancouver, BC, February 19-23 [ERIC Database: ED 427371].

Mottet, T.P. (1998). Teaching from a distance: "Hello, is anyone out there?" Paper presented at the Annual Ethnography in Research Forum (19th), Philadelphia, PA, March 6, 1998 [ERIC Database: ED 417436].

Niebuhr, K.E., and Niebuhr, R.E. (1999). An empirical study of student relationships and academic achievement. *Education, 119*(4), p. 679.

Oliver, R., and McLoughlin, C. (1996). An investigation of the nature and form of interactions in live interactive television. *Learning Technologies: Prospects and Pathways.* Selected papers from EdTech '96 Biennial Conference of the Australian Society for Education Technology, Melbourne, Australia, July 7-10, 1996 [ERIC Database: ED 396738].

Regan, K., and Tuchman, S. (1990). The importance of authority and peer relations on the educational process of onsite and online students: An exploratory investigation. Paper presented at the International Conference on Technology and Education (7th), Brussels, Belgium, March 20-22, 1990 [ERIC Database: ED 327169].

Rezabek, L.L. (1992). Distance Education: Perspectives from all sides of the desk. Paper presented at the Annual Meeting of the Association for Education Communications and Technology, Washington, DC, February 5-9, 1992 [ERIC Database: ED 346822].

Schuster, J.W., Collins, B.C., Hall, M.G., and Giffen, A.B. (1999). Ten years of distance learning: Changing to meet geographic, institutional, and student characteristics. *Rural Special Education for the New Millennium.* Conference proceedings of the American Council on Rural Special Education (19th), Albuquerque, NM, March 25-27 [ERIC Database: ED 429776].

Sorensen, C., and Baylen, D.M. (1999). Interaction in interactive television instruction: Perception versus reality. Paper presented at the Annual Meeting of the American Educational Research Association, Montreal, QC, April 19-23, 1999 [ERIC Database: ED 429590].

University of Alaska (1990). *Distance Education Interaction and Feedback at a Glance* [ERIC Database: ED 343575].

Wagenheim, G., and Gemmill, G. (1994). Feedback exchange: Managing group closure. *Journal of Management Education, 18,* 265-269.

Weimer, M. (1993). *Improving Your Classroom Teaching.* Newbury Park, CA: Sage Publications.

Whitworth, J.M. (1998). Looking at distance education through both ends of the camera. Paper presented at the Annual Meeting of the National Association for Research in Science Teaching, San Diego, CA, April 19-22, 1998 [ERIC Database: ED 418853].

Willis, B. (1993). *Distance Education: A Practical Guide.* Englewood Cliffs, NJ: Educational Technology Publications.

Wilson, A. (1994). Instructional multimedia in the math classroom and beyond. Paper presented at the Annual Conference of the American Mathematical Association of Two-Year Colleges, Tulsa, OK, November 3-6, 1994 [ERIC Database: ED 385332].

Wolcott, L.L. (1994). Audio tools for distance education. In B. Willis (Ed.), *Distance Education Strategies and Tools.* Englewood Cliffs, NJ: Educational Technology Publications.

Yucha, C.B. (1996). Interactive distance education: Improvisation helps bridge the gap. *Journal of Biocommunication, 23*(1), 2-5.

Zhang, S., and Fulford, C. (1994, July-August). Are interaction time and psychological interactivity the same thing in the distance learning television classroom? *Educational Technology, 34*(6), 58-64.

Kim Flottemesch, Ph.D., is an Assistant Professor of Communication at Lewis-Clark State College in Lewiston, ID. She received her doctorate from the University of Idaho, where her dissertation examined communication behaviors between individuals with disabilities and their non-disabled peers in distance education classrooms. She presented a paper entitled "Distance Education and Teacher-Student Interactions: The Impact on Students with Disabilities" at the 1999 National Communication Association/Caucus on Disability Issues. She has also co-authored a number of educational publications, including Diverse Learners in the Schools *(2000),* Educational Leadership Through Service Learning *(2001), and two chapters in the book* Service Learning in Teacher Education: Enhancing the Growth of New Teachers, Their Students, and Communities *(2001).*

Checklists for Developing Web-Based Courses

Ann Yakimovicz

This article is really a series of very useful checklists and suggestions for creating effective Web-based courses. It gives you many things to consider as you plan and implement this approach to delivering training.

Checklist 1. Developing Instructor-Led Web-Based Courses

1. Identify assumptions about student access to technology, technical skills, and metacognitive skills in web-based learning.
2. If possible, develop pre-course survey of student experience with web-based learning, reasons for enrolling, course expectations; disseminate; collect and analyze.
3. Discuss purpose and goals of instruction with instructor.
4. Review learning objectives; develop additional objectives if necessary for online learning environment.
5. Collect existing learning materials and map to learning objectives.
6. Identify gaps in learning materials and obtain new materials.
7. Review instructor's usual teaching strategies for the course.
8. Determine teaching strategies which must be adapted or replaced for web-delivered learning.
9. Develop additional teaching, and learning, strategies appropriate for content and delivery method (such as games, online research, computer-mediated conferenc-

ing—moderated vs. unmoderated, instructor-moderated vs. student-moderated, small group activities).

10. Review financial and technology resources to determine when and how much a technology can be employed.

11. Select and adapt content for web-based delivery, including screen-by-screen text presentation, hypermedia link locations, banks of test questions, formative and summative evaluations, graphics to be scanned, multiple connections in presentation of knowledge components, and other properties of hypertext systems.

12. Ask for detailed information about instructor, materials, activities, student interaction, technology issues, and metacognitive strategies in both formative and summative evaluations.

13. Obtain copyright for online use of text and graphic materials if needed.

14. Select appropriate online technologies such as video and audio conferencing, computer mediated conferencing, Internet access, bulletin boards and news groups, e-mail, to support teaching and learning strategies.

15. Select appropriate offline communication media, such as printed materials, audio and video tapes, computer disks, to support teaching and learning strategies.

16. Create navigational strategies and user interface alternatives, including consideration of differently abled learners with instructor.

17. Determine with instructor most effective presentation of visual materials for digital environment.

18. Develop online materials—HTML markup, interaction programming, graphics, background colors, icons, etc.

19. Identify necessary connections to databases for registration, test score storage, etc., and database management limitations.

20. Install and test course materials for operability as designed.

21. Conduct short user testing to confirm assumptions of student skills and course flow understanding.

22. Revise student guide and course presentation to respond to learner characteristics, required hardware, software, methods of feedback, and other course features. Develop online learning tutorial as needed.

23. Prepare instructor by demonstrating techniques to encourage student interaction with course materials, instructor, and each other.

24. Provide information and practice about effective facilitation and moderating of computer-mediated conferencing and creating community, if used.

25. Provide information and examples of appropriate e-mail communication, typical communication pitfalls, and user styles, especially cultural and gender differences.

26. Select presentation type and develop paper-based, audio/video taped materials such as guides, manuals, syllabi, course evaluation.

27. During course delivery, review student test results with instructor to determine

what revisions should be made to materials and presentation.

28. During course delivery, use formative evaluation information to further adapt and revise course presentation and content if needed.
29. Provide alternative means of evaluation such as e-mail and mailed/faxed forms, especially for summative evaluation
30. Use summative evaluation information to revise and adapt course for future use.

Checklist 2. Developing Web-Based Training Courseware (Non-Instructor)

1. Identify assumptions about student access to technology, technical skills, and metacognitive skills in web-based learning.
2. If possible, develop pre-course survey of learner experience with web-based learning, reasons for enrolling, course expectations; disseminate; collect and analyze.
3. Discuss purpose and goals of instruction with stakeholders and SMEs.
4. With stakeholders, plan course rollout, including target group for beta testing, need for help desk support and local train-the-tech training.
5. Establish evaluation levels to be included.
6. Confirm that organizational data for evaluation comparison is available.
7. Confirm that desired performance goals, if any, can be measured using online format.
8. Review learning objectives; develop additional objectives if necessary for online learning environment.
9. Collect existing learning materials and map to learning objectives.
10. Identify gaps in learning materials and obtain new materials.
11. With stakeholders and SMEs, determine teaching strategies which must be adapted or replaced for web-delivered learning.
12. Develop additional teaching, and learning, strategies appropriate for content and delivery method (such as games, online research, computer-mediated conferencing—moderated vs. unmoderated, expert-moderated vs. student-moderated, small group activities).
13. Review financial, scheduling, and technology resources to determine when and how much a technology can be employed.
14. Select and adapt content for web-based delivery, including screen-by-screen text presentation, hypermedia link locations, banks of test questions, formative and summative evaluations, graphics to be scanned, multiple connections in presentation of knowledge components, and other properties of hypertext systems.
15. Ask for detailed information about instructional design, materials, activities, student interaction, technology issues, and metacognitive strategies in both formative and summative evaluations.

16. Obtain copyright for online use of text and graphic materials if needed.
17. Select appropriate online technologies such as video and audio conferencing, computer mediated conferencing, Internet access, bulletin boards and news groups, e-mail, to support teaching and learning strategies.
18. Select appropriate offline communication media, such as printed materials, audio and video tapes, computer disks, to support teaching and learning strategies.
19. Create navigational strategies and user interface alternatives, including consideration of differently abled learners and review with HCI experts.
20. Determine most effective presentation of visual materials for digital environment and review with interface experts.
21. Develop online materials—HTML markup, interaction programming, graphics, background colors, icons, etc.
22. Identify necessary connections to databases for registration, test score storage, etc., and database management limitations.
23. Work with stakeholders of organizational data to access necessary databases for evaluation results comparison.
24. Develop registration, testing and reporting procedure with local stakeholders, ie., training department and human resources staff.
25. Install and test course materials for operability as designed.
26. Conduct peer review of instructional design, user interface, and programming during alpha test process.
27. Conduct anonymous observer and think-aloud user testing and qualitative interviewing to confirm assumptions of student skills and course flow understanding.
28. Revise student guide and course presentation to respond to learner characteristics, required hardware, software, methods of feedback, and other course features. Develop online learning tutorial as needed.
29. Provide information and practice about effective facilitation and moderating of computer-mediated conferencing and creating community, if used.
30. Provide information and examples of appropriate e-mail communication, typical communication pitfalls, and user styles, especially cultural and gender differences.
31. Select presentation type and develop paper-based, audio/video taped materials such as guides, manuals, syllabi, course evaluation.
32. Conduct pilot (beta) test of courseware with target users.
33. Develop and deliver hands-on classroom training for telephone help desk support staff, if needed.
34. Develop and deliver hands-on classroom training for local on-the-job technical support staff, if needed.
35. During course delivery, review student test results with design team and stakeholders to determine what revisions should be made to materials and presentation.

36. During course delivery, use formative evaluation information to further adapt and revise course presentation and content if needed.
37. Provide alternative means of evaluation such as e-mail and mailed/faxed forms, especially for summative evaluation.
38. Use summative evaluation information to revise and adapt course for future use.
39. Analyze continuously reported data to track usage of course, completion, evaluation, and organizational impact.
40. Report courseware impact across the organization.

Checklist 3. Determining Organizational Readiness for Web-Based Learning

1. **Human Readiness**
   - Are your users comfortable with computers?
   - Are your users experienced with using a mouse and a browser?
   - Are your users experienced with e-mail?
   - Are your users experienced with browsers, hypertext, and search functions?
   - Are your users ready and eager to learn?
   - Is continuing education and training valued?

2. **Technological Readiness**
   - Do you have networked computers available for users?
   - Do you have an Internet connection?
   - Do you have a functioning intranet/extranet with enough file space for courseware?
   - Do you have server-side technical support staff?
   - Do you have desktop-side technical support staff?
   - Do you have browsers installed on the target computers?
   - Do you have CD-ROM, sound and video cards, and multimedia plug-ins installed on the target computers, when appropriate?
   - Do you have a courseware administration system installed or planned to handle registration and tracking?
   - Do you have a database to handle testing and file storage?
   - Do you have a development platform (hardware and software) in place if you are going to create and test your own courseware?
   - Is a telephone help desk established if necessary?
   - Is remote access and security assignment planned if necessary?

3. **Financial Readiness**
   - Do you have long-term budgets for upgrading computers, servers, and browser software?
   - Do you have budgets for purchase of courseware or hiring of contract custom developers?

- Do you have funding support for retraining staff to develop necessary technical and design skills to develop and/or support courseware?
- Has the ownership of budgets and responsibility for hardware and software purchase, upgrades, and technical support related to training been determined?
- Do all the affected parties agree on the budget allocations?

4. **Political Readiness**
   - Do you have support of senior management? Who is the sponsor?
   - Do you have support of supervisors and managers?
   - Do you have support of the training department (if you are not it)?
   - Do you have the support of employees?
   - If you do not have support, do you have a plan to build support?
   - Have you determined who has ownership of the courseware once it is operational?
   - Who determines when and how courseware will be updated?
   - Who has ownership of programming support, help desk support, database support for courseware?
   - Is there a commitment from Information Services to support courseware?
   - Is the organization ready to accept online learning?
   - Is the organization excited about online knowledge sharing and knowledge transfer?

5. **Skills Readiness**
   - Can your staff develop courseware—instructional design, multimedia, HTML markup, programming, computer graphics, database design and management?
   - Do you have telephone help-desk staff trained and ready?
   - Do you have on-site desktop technical support staff ready?
   - Can your staff evaluate off-the shelf courseware?
   - Can your staff lead alpha and beta testing?
   - Can your staff use statistical methods to analyze and report on detailed data from courseware use and testing?
   - Is the organization ready to conduct on-the-job observation of performance following training?
   - Can your staff lead train-the-trainer sessions on courseware use for supervisors and beta testers?
   - Can your staff moderate online discussion forums?
   - Do you have a retraining plan or a plan for developing the necessary skill mix for courseware development and use?

Checklist 4. Evaluating Off-the-Shelf CBT and WBT Courseware

Information Design / Instructional Design

1. Is the purpose of the training clear?
2. Is the purpose appropriate to your organization's needs?
3. Will learners be motivated to use the training?
4. Does the product contain measurable learning objectives?
5. If not, are learning objectives needed?
6. Does the content map back to the learning objectives?
7. Is there unnecessary content?
8. Are there content gaps?
9. Is the scope of the content clearly presented or mapped?
10. Is the content written clearly for your target users?
11. Is the content presented for different kinds of users?
12. What kinds? Visual, aural, kinesthetic learning styles?
13. Big-to-small and small-to-big thinkers?
14. Is the content presented in learnable "chunks"?

Interaction Design

1. Are learners encouraged to interact with content?
2. If practice material is included, is it appropriate?
3. Do learners get immediate feedback to correct errors?
4. Can learners take notes?
5. Are learners tested?
6. If tests are included, do questions tie to learning objectives?
7. Are learners tested on recall of information or application to work situations?
8. Will good test scores likely translate to desired change in knowledge or skills in the workplace?
9. Does learner know the credibility of the SME or instructor?
10. Can learner interact with instructor or other learners?
11. Is interaction an important activity to transfer this training into the workplace?
12. If interaction with others is not included but is important, can added training activities help?
13. Does product support added training activities with train-the-trainer programs or workbooks?
14. Are related job aids, references, and resources included?

Interface Design

1. Is product easy to operate in your technology environment?
2. Will included audio/video or database connections operate within your company system? Do you need to add equipment or plug-ins?

3. Is user interface visually pleasing?
4. Is color appropriate?
5. Are buttons and icons easy to understand and use?
6. Are buttons and icons located consistently throughout the program?
7. Are controls and functions similar to those found on household electronic equipment?
8. Will they be familiar to your users?
9. If games, metaphors or stories are used in a product, are they easy to understand?
10. Are they culturally appropriate for your employees?
11. Is navigation through the product easy to do?
12. Can users explore and return to main menus, maps, or sections they want to review?

Unique issues or concerns for your company:

Overall Rating:

Notes, Final Thoughts, Follow-Up Activities:

Ann Yakimovicz is president and CEO of Aprendío, Inc, a consulting and training company in Austin, Texas. Her Web site is at www.aprendio.com.

Effective User Interface Design: The Four Rules

Kevin Kruse

Nothing is more frustrating than a distance learning Web page that's hard to navigate. In this article, one of the columns written by Kevin Kruse for Learning Circuits, *the author gives several hints to help you make sure that your distance learning site is easy to use and takes the needs of the learner into account.*

I consider the design of user interfaces the most neglected topic in the discipline of online learning. Here we examine four rules that you can apply to new projects to ensure that learners are focused on the content rather than on navigation.

Rule #1: Help Them Remember

Following are several design objectives to keep in mind to help learners navigate an information-packed site.

Chunking Information and Organizing Menu Structure

Using what we know about short- and long-term memory, we can apply the following strategies to maximize the effectiveness of a program's menu system.

A menu should ideally have no more than seven items on it. If it does have more than seven, determine whether it can be split logically into a higher-level menu and a submenu. This helps learners remember which menus contain certain items.

The order or placement of menu items should match the structure of the tasks and subtasks. For example, a main menu for a sales training program might list the classic four-step sales call in chronological order:

- Lesson 1: Building Rapport with Customers
- Lesson 2: Presenting Product Information
- Lesson 3: Handling Objections
- Lesson 4: Closing the Deal.

In turn, when the learner selects Lesson 3, a submenu might be sequenced along the consecutive steps of Classifying Objections, Responding to Objections, and Confirming Satisfaction.

If there is no sequence associated with menu items, place the most commonly used options at the top of the menu and least used items on the bottom.

Submenus should have titles that reflect the selected option from the previous menu. For example, the submenu described above for "Handling Objections" should maintain those words as the submenu's title. The cleanest way to handle nesting menus is to use expanding menus where the learner never loses sight of the original menu structure.

Using Mental Models or Visual Metaphors

A mental model or visual metaphor is the internal picture we create to help us understand how things work. Though we're not conscious of our mental models, they help us to use computers effectively. Designers use visual metaphors to take advantage of what we already know when helping us understand something new.

A good example of a visual metaphor is the directory structure of a computer. While the computer actually stores files and data haphazardly on its hard drive, the visual metaphor presented to the user is that of file folders and a vertical ordering system. This metaphor gives an artificial but clear sense of order to the system. As users we imagine that our documents are being held in these little folders, and that there is some kind of depth to them.

Mental models and metaphors, however, are still subject to short-term memory restrictions. Most users begin to get lost when their model contains more than three layers or paths. Imagine a training program that has a main menu (the first level) from which students gain access to a specific lesson (the second level), and eventually click on a More Information hyperlink, which displays some additional text (the third level). At this point, most users will still have a clear understanding of where they are in the program, and how to retrace their steps, if necessary. But if they are again presented a link for more information, such as a case study from within the More Information section, they will begin to lose track of their location or the relationship of the onscreen content to the overall lesson.

Using Multiple Access Points

A simple way to relieve the burden on users' memory is to provide multiple ways to locate and access the content. Common methods are described below.

- **Main menu.** The primary access point is always the program's main menu, which should be well organized and descriptive. Rather than using generic names, such as Lesson 1 and Lesson 2, use descriptive headings such as "1: Overview to Customer Service" and "2: Dealing with Difficult Customers."

- **Index**. An index of key topics or all learning objectives helps users find specific information. A well-indexed system will enhance any training program's subsequent use as a just-in-time support tool.
- **Keyword search**. The keyword search enables users to type a word and have the program scan the entire text for all occurrences. While a powerful feature, a keyword search only looks at on-screen text and cannot identify information presented as audio narration or in pictures.
- **Site map or content map**. A visual representation of the order of the topics in the program, or content outline, is called a site map. Typically, it displays the entire menu system graphically, extending down to individual learning objectives.

Rule #2: Put the User in Control

An effective interface puts users in control of the program or, at the very least, lets them feel like they're in control. By giving users control, you ease their anxieties, minimize their confusion, and create an environment that's conducive to learning. Descriptions of a number of time-tested ways of putting the user in the driver's seat via status or warning messages follow.

- **Loading delays**. If a computer is busy for longer than three seconds, the program should display what's called a status message. If the delay is due to bandwidth limitations, there is little you can do to forewarn the user. However, if you're using streaming media or Flash animations, you should anticipate the preloading delay and provide a warning message of some type. This message alleviates users' concerns that the computer may have "frozen." Though the message in itself doesn't provide control to the user, the communication helps them to feel that they're still in control.
- **Taking a test**. Final exams are often timed and intentionally prevent learners from leaving the test module until they're finished with the test. This kind of program control is designed to keep users from looking for correct answers in the lessons. Before the test is started, a confirmation message should appear that advises the student, "You are about to begin the test. Once you start this test you will have to finish it in one sitting. You will not be able to take the test again. Are you sure you are ready to take this test now?" Action buttons should be clearly labeled Take Test or Return to Main Menu.
- **Previous page**. Perhaps the most obvious undo feature is the Previous Page button or Back button in a linear tutorial. In addition to giving learners the control to move forward in a program, an effective interface also enables them to move back to a previous page.

Rule #3: Use Consistent and Logical Designs

Users can quickly learn a new visual metaphor or a new mental model, but they also quickly create expectations that the interface they see will be consistent. A program's interface is the door between the student and the instruction. In order to facilitate access and reduce confusion, consistency in interface appearance and behavior is paramount.

Clear and Logical Screen Layouts

An intuitive interface begins with the overall layout and design of the screen. Four principles of screen layout include the following:

- Place screen objects together in a logical order.
- Place buttons where the user's eye can easily find them.
- Give buttons clear symbols or labels.
- Group buttons together based on their function and frequency of use.

Web-based training programs often have navigation bars running vertically down the left side of the screen, or horizontally across the top of the screen. This is because scrolling text windows are a common user interface element on the Internet, making horizontal buttons on the bottom of the screen—which are standard on CD-ROM programs—impractical. Buttons should always be given clear labels, with both text and graphical indicators, if possible. Common button-naming rules include

- Use *Menu* to label the button that accesses the main menu. Don't use the ambiguous *Main*.
- Use *Help* to access navigational guidance. Don't use *Hint* or *Panic*.
- Use *Exit* to end the program. Don't use *Quit, End,* or *Stop*, which might refer to quitting the immediate exercise or lesson.
- Use *Forward* or *Next* and *Back* or *Previous* to designate page turning. Don't use *Up* or *Down*.
- Use complete screen counters, such as "1 of 30," not partial counters, such as "Page 5," that don't indicate how much longer the lesson will last.
- If your program runs on Windows, refer to the keyboard Enter key as Enter, not as Return.

Consistency in Visual Cues

Early seafaring explorers used celestial navigation to make their way across the high seas. Like the North Star, the buttons your students use to navigate should never change in their appearance or location on the screen. Button identification is a fundamental part of a mental model. Changing a button's location or appearance will cause users to think they're seeing a new button with new functions.

Menus That Behave Predictably

Menus are the key structures for organizing and accessing information and must be planned with great care. In addition to logical sequencing and having no more than three layers of menus, the menu action must be consistent throughout the program. When a user clicks on a menu item, similar actions must occur for each item on the menu. Main menu items that are clicked can lead to submenus, or the buttons can directly launch a lesson or simulation. But don't mix the two actions on the same menu. For example, if clicking "Module 1: The Cardiovascular System" launches a submenu, but clicking "Module 2: The Nervous System" launches a 30-screen linear tutorial, students can get confused. They may think "Oops, where is that submenu? Did I accidentally click something to launch this tutorial?" or "What's going on? Will I get to the submenu *after* this tutorial?"

Rule #4: Provide Informative Guidance and Feedback

Web-based training has significantly transformed training, replacing many traditional classroom sessions. But students of all ages are still students and perform best when given guidance and feedback. Just as in personal relations, politeness and courtesy should be extended in all technology-based training situations.

Page Counters

Every linear tutorial should have an onscreen page counter that tells users which screen or page they're on and how many more are in the lesson. A simple message such as "Screen 5 of 25" clearly describes what's required to finish the lesson in the program and engenders learner confidence. With self-paced programs that can be taken at any time, this type of progress marker helps users answer such questions as "I have a meeting in 15 minutes—can I finish this lesson or should I quit now?"

Some designers recommend using time estimates rather than page counters. For example, "Lesson 1: Overview (10 to 15 minutes)." However, estimating the time needed for self-paced training is difficult. Be aware that although a range is given, some learners may feel anxiety from the implied time limitation.

GUI Evaluation Checklist

When reviewing and evaluating the computer interface of your technology-based training program, you should be able to answer yes to the questions below. This checklist is suitable for CD-ROM and online learning programs.

- ❏ Do all buttons and icons have a consistent and unique appearance?
- ❏ Are visual cues, such as mouse cursor changes and rollover highlights, used on all buttons consistently?
- ❏ Are buttons labeled with text descriptions (or with rollover text)?
- ❏ Do buttons "gray out" or disappear when they're inactive?
- ❏ Do nonbutton graphics have design properties distinct from that of buttons?
- ❏ Are navigation buttons displayed in exactly the same screen position every time they appear?
- ❏ Are buttons grouped logically and located where the user is likely to be looking?
- ❏ Do users have one-click access to help, exit, and the main menu?

❏ Are users returned to where they left off after closing the help window and canceling the exit screen?

❏ Does every menu have a title?

❏ Does every menu screen include an option to return to the previous or main menu?

❏ Are there fewer than three levels of menus?

❏ Do menus have seven or fewer items on them?

❏ Are items on menus descriptive rather than general?

❏ Are menu items listed in a sequential or logical order?

❏ Do menus indicate which items a learner has completed?

❏ Are confirmation messages used in such areas as student registration, exit, and final exams?

❏ Are there clear instructions associated with menus, questions, and other tasks?

❏ Are error messages written in plain language?

❏ Are status messages displayed during delays greater than four seconds?

❏ Are exclamation points and sound effects used sparingly?

❏ Is there a bookmarking feature that enables users to exit and resume later where they left off?

❏ Can users move backward and forward in linear tutorials?

❏ Are page or screen counters used to show progress in linear lessons?

❏ Is the visual metaphor consistent and intuitive in nonlinear simulations?

❏ Are all pop-up windows positioned on the screen so they don't cover up relevant information?

❏ Does text appear clearly and with normal margins and spacing?

❏ Do information input screens force all capital letters and is input evaluation case- insensitive?

❏ Can users interact with the program from either the keyboard or the mouse?

❏ Are text fonts used consistently?

❏ Are audio volume levels consistent?

❏ Do users have the option to replay video or audio narration?

Kevin Kruse (kkruse@raymondkarsan.com) is a principal of Kenexa (formerly Talent-Point, formerly Raymond Karsan Associates), a provider of custom technology-based training solutions. He is also the author of Technology-Based Training: The Art and Science of Design, Development, and Delivery. *More information on Kruse and his book, including three free chapters, can be found at www.TBTSuperSite.com.*

Developing Courses for Online Delivery: One Strategy

Ann Luck

This article reviews how Penn State's World Campus, its online university for delivering courses to students anywhere in the world, designs its courses. The author explains the process as it's laid out on paper, but she also looks at "the real vs. the ideal" and discusses what happens when things don't go as planned.

D eveloping college courses for delivery on the Internet can be a daunting task. At some institutions, faculty are on their own, which often means that only "technologically savvy" faculty can participate in the growing trend toward online course delivery. The benefit of such an approach, on the other hand, is the level of faculty control over course materials. Technologically savvy faculty members cannot only create online materials but can also design the course exactly as they see fit. At the other end of the spectrum, we see commercial course development "shops" where teams of programmers, instructional designers, graphic artists, and the like work at record-breaking speed to produce online course materials, using content from contracted "content experts." While the rapid turnaround of these commercially produced courses is enviable, such an approach typically meets with outcries from the instructional design community and higher education faculty. Both groups fear that "factory-produced" courses are often little more than the equivalent of an electronic page turner with an exam at the end, lacking meaningful learning activities and interactions within a learning community.

This article was orginally published in *The Technology Source* (http://horizon.unc.edu/TS) as Luck, A. (January/February 2001), "Developing Courses for Online Delivery: One Strategy," *The Technology Source*. This article is reprinted with permission of the publisher.

So what happens in the middle? Penn State's newest campus, the World Campus, uses an approach to online course development that falls somewhere in between. The World Campus is a virtual university that employs information technology to deliver top-quality, Penn State-signature academic programs to adult learners worldwide. Here the course development process is a team effort, using the strengths and resources of Penn State faculty, instructional and instructional materials designers, technology and production specialists, and graphic designers. While the process of developing a course in a team environment is likely to be foreign to most university faculty, most at Penn State are quite pleased with the results. The Penn State faculty are able to concentrate on course content and the design of learning activities and assessment but can call on the other members of the development team for input in those areas that are outside of the faculty's expertise.

In this paper, I review the general process that the World Campus's Instructional Design and Development unit uses to develop cohort courses. It should be noted that course development is only one piece of the puzzle. To get a course ready for online delivery, a much larger team is needed, including people responsible for marketing, academic advising, registration, materials distribution, and program management.

An Overview of the Development Process

World Campus "cohort courses" (courses that will be delivered in a semester format, with groups of students taking the courses together) are typically developed in a two-semester time frame. As we walk through our development process, it is important to keep in mind that each member of the team has responsibilities for projects beyond the course at hand. For example, a faculty member who is serving as the content expert will also be carrying a traditional (but perhaps reduced) teaching, research, and service load; a lead instructional designer will likely be carrying a large number of course development projects on his/her plate at any one time, each in varying stages of development and complexity.

Since courses are developed by teams of individuals as described above, it is important to clearly delineate individual roles and responsibilities as well as target dates assigned to each task in the development process. This ensures that development runs smoothly and that key administrative units, such as the World Campus Student Services group, which registers and advises students and handles materials distribution, have the information that they need.

The First Semester

The first semester is used to generate the raw content for the course. The majority of the effort expended during this semester falls on the course author. During that time, the course author works primarily with the lead instructional designer, meeting periodically to discuss the course and to review materials that the author has drafted. (The course author is a Penn State faculty member who has been selected by his/her academic college or department to serve as the content expert, bringing experience with the subject matter and effective learning strategies to the project. The instructional designer provides expertise in course design and development and adult and distance education. Instructional designers at the World Campus are required to have a master's degree in a related field of study as well as prior work experience.)

At first, these meetings orient the course author to the World Campus and its course development process. The instructional designer is also oriented to the course by studying the syllabus and any other relevant materials, such as handouts or Web site URLs. The author(s) and instructional designer then lay out a general instructional design strategy for the course—the scope and sequence of course content, learning activities, and learning assessments—and begin to discuss how the traditional campus-based course might be adapted for delivery through the World Campus. Thus begins an ongoing dialogue on how to transform the traditional face-to-face course into an effective, high-quality distance education offering.

When appropriate, course authors, with the help of instructional designers, spend time gaining the technical skills and pedagogical strategies necessary to develop a distance education learning environment. In addition to one-on-one and group training, course authors access an online World Campus faculty development resource, called "Fac Dev 101," that is designed to introduce World Campus faculty to issues involved in authoring and teaching a course in a distance education environment. Moreover, World Campus course authors are given access to a collection of examples, templates, and other resources for use during course design and development.

Shortly after the first meeting, the instructional designer initiates an intellectual property agreement that will be signed by the course author(s). The agreement

- sets up the time frame for delivery of materials;
- identifies a signoff point for quality control (by the academic department);
- describes the author's work as "work for hire" and indicates the amount of author compensation;
- establishes University ownership of the particular expression of an idea but allows the author to quote up to 10% of the work without requesting permission. The author maintains ownership of course content ideas if they are expressed in a substantially different manner than in the copyrighted work;
- identifies a date when course materials should be reviewed for currency; and
- identifies a date after which copyright reverts to the author.

The lead instructional designer also works with the author to draft a course development schedule that outlines specific milestones and "due dates" for each component of the course development process. That document serves as an informal contract among all members of the development team.

Once the author(s) and the instructional designer have met a few times to discuss the course, one of the first tasks for the author(s) is to generate a detailed course outline. The purpose of the outline is to convey to the instructional designer the author's thoughts on the general plan for the course (thereby making sure that everyone is on the same page). The outline addresses what will be covered in the course, the author's vision of how the course will be delivered, and similar issues. It also provides a listing of general resources that students will need for the course and information about course goals and objectives, course requirements, the overall course structure, and lessons and topics. The instructional designer reviews the outline with the author, and they work together to refine the document. A "final" outline then is forwarded to the academic department head for approval.

Next, the author is asked to generate a set of sample course materials (e.g., sample lessons, sample exams with answer keys) as agreed upon with the instructional designer. The instructional designer reviews these materials and drafts a prototype (e.g., Web pages, PDF documents, print materials, stand-alone CBI) to illustrate how the resulting World Campus course might be presented. The prototype then is shared with the author(s) to determine whether refinements to the initial instructional design model are necessary. Once a model is agreed upon and refinements are made, the sample content is forwarded to the academic department head for approval.

With a detailed course outline and sample course materials in hand, the lead instructional designer arranges a "course launch" meeting with all members of the course development team. At the meeting, team members are introduced to the course author and review an abbreviated development timeline and a course design document prepared by the lead instructional designer. This document outlines the proposed instructional design model for the course. The team also discusses design and development procedures (how materials will flow from one team member to the next). This initial team meeting is a key point in the development process, as the entire team influences the course design. Meetings can get quite lively as participants share ideas and brainstorm strategies.

For the remainder of the first semester, the author generates course content. Ongoing meetings are used to review progress, discuss issues that arise, or capture initial ideas for learning activities and assessments. These meetings generally involve only the lead instructional designer and the course author(s), but other team members often are included, depending on the complexity of the project.

By the end of the first semester, the course author(s) have generated all of the core course content, including "lectures" and learning activities and assessments, and identified a textbook, other required readings, and supplemental resources (such as online resources).

The Second Semester

During the second semester of the development process, the course development team finalizes the course materials and designs and integrates learning activities and assessment strategies into the course. This includes the development of the course welcome page site, a publicly accessible informational site for the course. The welcome page includes an online syllabus, a course checklist outlining the materials and technology that students need, information about the nature of the learning environment used in the course, and section-specific information, such as a detailed course schedule of activities and assignments. Much of the site is based on a standard World Campus template.

The majority of the effort during the second semester is expended by the instructional designer and other members of the development team. In some cases, however, individual authors may take on a portion of the actual technical development. As the instructional designer works through the draft content and puts it into its final form, she/he incorporates comments, questions, and suggestions pertaining to issues such as course content, learning activities, and assessment strategies. "Marked up" course materials then are given back to the course author for review and revision. This is typically an iterative process, with team members exchanging materials and revisions multiple times as items are finalized.

Real vs. Ideal

The process described above represents the ideal. In reality, things do not always go as smoothly as one would like. The most difficult and important lesson to be learned is that the process is prone to a domino effect: if one key point in the development process fails (e.g., a deadline is missed), subsequent steps in the process will likewise be adversely affected. For individuals who are not used to working in a team environment, that lesson can be painful to learn.

So what is the key to success? While many factors contribute to the success (or failure) of a project, a team development process requires excellent communication among team members to ensure that things run smoothly. How that communication takes place will vary from team to team, based on the preferences of the group. The key is not how communication takes place, but rather that it does take place. Take, for example, a scenario in which a course author and instructional designer decide to require students to use a non-standard piece of commercial software in a course. If this decision is not discussed with World Campus Technical Support in advance of the course opening, there will not be adequate time for technical support staff to learn the software in order to support the students effectively.

At the World Campus, we have found that the majority of course development pitfalls can be avoided if everyone on the team is aware of what is going on. That communication extends beyond the core development team to a broader group of people who support the course during its delivery. With more than 155 courses being offered through the World Campus in a given semester (as of August 2000), it is hard for everyone involved to keep track of every detail for every course! To help with the communications process, for each course the World Campus offers, an implementation meeting is held before the course is opened for registration. That meeting includes key staff from World Campus Student Services (including Technical Support) who advise, register, and support students during course delivery. At that meeting, the staff work through a formal "Activity Sheet" that outlines key logistical facts and features pertaining to the course. It is a final opportunity to make sure everything is in order and that everyone present is well-informed about the new offering.

Once a course has been developed and opened for enrollment, the development process is not complete. Every course goes through various stages of formative and summative evaluation. Minor revisions are made each semester (an estimate of 25% of a course is revised after its first offering, 15% after the second offering, and so on), and substantial revisions are planned as well at intervals that vary depending on course content. (For example, courses that cover "high-tech" content might require substantial revisions every year, whereas courses that address more static content might be revised only every three years.) The original development team typically is involved in all course revisions. In some cases, however, faculty who possess technical skills may be able to make minor revisions on their own.

The payoff for the course development process has been well worth the effort of all involved. Student experiences in the World Campus have been studied through individual interviews and end-of-course online surveys. Self-reports of learning gains indicate that students view the World Campus as an effective environment for learning and as a welcome aid in meeting their goals. For example, results from the Spring 2000 survey indicate that 91% of respondents were "satisfied" or "very satisfied" with the amount of new knowledge; 95% "agreed" or "strongly agreed" that their courses helped them meet their educational objectives; and 91% "agreed or "strongly agreed" that their courses helped them meet their professional objectives. Areas for improvement identified through the survey were ease of use of technology (81% "satisfied" or "very satisfied") and interactions with fellow students (71% "satisfied" or "very satisfied").

Penn State's Center for the Study of Higher Education has engaged in an ongoing study of the faculty experience of teaching in the World Campus. Data from faculty interviews indicate that faculty members have been satisfied with many aspects of their participation, particularly high levels of student-faculty interaction and positive spill-over into their face-to-face teaching. However, the same faculty members have pointed out two aspects of their experiences that were less than satisfactory: perceptions of an increased workload and a traditional institutional reward system that undervalues online teaching and stresses alternate priorities. An additional factor, the collaborative/shared authority work environment in which course development takes place, was identified by some respondents as an incentive and by others as a problem. It is this author's belief that the latter is due to the fact that traditional course development typically involves only an individual faculty member, who has sole control over the pace and structure of the development process. The process of developing a course with a team of individuals in a collaborative/shared authority work environment may be a new experience for these faculty members.

The process of developing online courses undoubtedly will vary from one institution to the next due to differences in staffing, resources, and time—things will not always work out as planned. But having a strategy in place helps guard against reinventing the wheel and helps ensure a smoother development process. In an environment that is changing as rapidly as distance education, having a standard course development strategy in place is useful in training an ever-growing staff.

Ann Luck is Senior Instructional Designer, World Campus, Center for Academic Computing, The Pennsylvania State University.

Part Seven

Teaching Strategies for Distance Learning

A fter you've designed and developed a distance learning course, you or others have to actually serve as teachers in one way or another. What are some effective distance learning teaching strategies? That's the question Part Seven seeks to answer. To do so, we've selected five more articles that will give you both ideas for teaching and an idea of what life is like in the trenches (or at the distance education teacher's computer).

Appropriately enough, we start with Amy Sitze's "Teachers at a Distance." This article describes some of the experiences of teachers who have taught distance learning courses and includes some tricks of the virtual trade to make things go successfully.

Next you'll find a contribution from co-editor Karen Mantyla: "Who Wants to Be a Distance Trainer?" In it she provides a set of guidelines for selecting distance learning instructors and then a checklist of items to keep in mind to prepare these instructors to succeed.

What's it like on the job for a distance learning instructor? Lesley Darling's "The Life and Times of an E-Trainer" looks at that question. She gives us an intimate view of what the days of two e-trainers are like. The article includes a useful set of tips for new online trainers.

"Ten Facts of Life for Distance Learning Courses" by Annette C. Lamb and William L. Smith is a kind of memory jogger for a whole set of things a distance learning teacher needs to remember, from "students are individuals" to "technology fails" to "active learning takes time."

The final chapter in Part Seven talks about the concept of "adaptive learning": "Have It Your Way: Adaptive Learning" by Bob Oas. Adaptive learning is about meeting individual student needs, something that is easier in the classroom than online. This article provides some ways teachers can be more aware of and address individual students in a distance education setting.

Teachers at a Distance

Amy Sitze

Online instructors say Web-based courses can be just as personal as classroom learning, but they require a whole new set of teaching skills. This article explains more.

When Nancy White is standing in front of a class, she knows exactly when she's lost her students. Some scratch their heads, some yawn and others just look puzzled. When that happens, White knows it's time to rephrase a question or explain a concept differently. Or maybe it's simply time for everyone to stand up, stretch and take a short break.

Such interpersonal strategies work well in the classroom, but what happens when successful stand-up trainers try to transfer their well-polished techniques to an online environment? On the Internet, you don't have those valuable nonverbal clues that tell you how well students are grasping the concepts you're teaching. So if you're facilitating an online course on business writing, for example, you have no idea if Sally is eagerly devouring a lesson, or if she's slumped in front of her monitor snoozing through your explanations of proper grammar and style.

White, who teaches online facilitation at Full Circle Associates, a consulting group in Seattle, says online courses don't have to be impersonal. She and other online instructors firmly believe Web-based courses can be just as intimate and immediate as classroom courses—but, they say, it takes extra work on the instructor's part to make that happen.

Reprinted with permission from *Inside Technology Training* (now *Online Learning Magazine*), April 2000. Copyright © 2000 Bill Communications, Inc. All rights reserved.

Getting Personal

One of the biggest challenges in teaching an online course—whether it's a history class at a university or a sales training course in a corporation—is building a personal connection with students you may never meet in person. Libby Roeger, who has been teaching Web-based courses at Shawnee Community College in Ullin, Ill., for two years, says humor can go a long way toward making that connection.

For Roeger, that might mean something as simple as using an animated GIF of skeleton heads cavorting across the screen when presenting a section on Edgar Allan Poe to her American literature class. Or it could be something more closely related to class discussions. During a philosophy and ethics class that took place against the backdrop of the impeachment hearings last year, Roeger asked students to answer the question, "What's the best theme song for Bill Clinton and Monica Lewinsky?" (The winner was "Devil with the Blue Dress On.")

These techniques do more than just make people laugh, says Roeger. They reveal something of the instructor's personality and help students feel like they're part of a community. "Some people may not like to hear this, but you have to be a little bit of an entertainer in this medium," Roeger says. "You can't count on students just dying to read your stuff and wanting to learn for the sheer joy of learning. It's a nice concept, but it's unrealistic. You have to think of creative ways to keep your students involved."

From his home base in Las Vegas, Rick Mathews teaches an online course at Boise State University in Boise, Idaho, and does online training for an American Express division in New York City. He agrees creativity is the key to making Internet-delivered classes personal. Mathews encourages his students to post bios on the group bulletin board. He then uses that information to get them talking to each other on a more personal level. "Things like birthdays, holidays, dogs and cats are shared and celebrated," he explains.

When students know something about each other and about the instructor, say online facilitators, they feel more connected and are more likely to participate in discussions. But despite instructors' best efforts, there will always be students who lurk in the background, reading other students' postings but not typing a single character. They're the online equivalent of the shy student who hides in the back of the classroom, intently examining the top of his desk to avoid being called on.

Online Connections

To make sure lurkers get involved in a course's online community, some instructors make participation a requirement, using special software that monitors a student's level of interactivity. What the software tells you can be a springboard for conversations with individual students, says Donna McIntire, Houston branch manager at IBT Technologies, a consulting group that helps companies convert training into a Web-based format (*www.tsp-support.com*).

If the tracking software reveals that a student is regularly reading postings but not writing any, for example, there's nothing wrong with sending an email to say, "It looks like you were online and you saw this discussion. Do you have anything to add?" And if a student starts the online course and then disappears, McIntire says, you might send an email saying, "I see that you started Module One 30 days ago. Your peers are on Module Three. Where did we jump off track, and how can I help you?"

But Mary Gordon, account manager at Raytheon Training LLC in Arlington, Texas, a branch of Raytheon Corp., a diversified technology company, warns that if you're monitoring student participation, you'd better keep it up throughout the course. "Once you set up the expectation for interactivity at the beginning, you have to follow through," she says. "I've seen it happen where an instructor sets up an expectation for interactivity, but then forgets and goes back into lecture mode." And if instructors are lecturing instead of encouraging participation, students have no choice but to listen passively.

Another challenge for online instructors is overcoming email's lack of tone. Anyone who's ever sent or received an email message knows how easily a casual joke can blow up into a huge misunderstanding—all because the physical clues we normally use to determine someone's intentions (a wry smile, a shrug of the shoulders, a wink) disappear online.

White makes a strong effort to use what she calls "online body language." The term may sound like an oxymoron, but White claims it is possible to communicate expression and tone in an email. Emoticons, those little sideways faces— :-) for a smile and ;-) for a wink—are a start, she says, but sometimes they aren't enough.

One way to help prevent misunderstandings is to discuss online body language at the beginning of the course. In White's online classes, she emphasizes to students that it's easy to make incorrect assumptions about the tone of an email message. To make her point, she asks students to read the statement "If I thought you understood me, I wouldn't be wasting all this time talking to you" as if a good friend were saying it in a friendly, teasing tone of voice. Then she asks them to read it in the voice of their worst boss. Sounds a little different, doesn't it?

Practice Makes Perfect

If you've decided you're ready to take on the challenge of facilitating an online class, be prepared to make mistakes and learn from them, say instructors who have been there. Resources for people who want to learn more about online instruction are available, but often trainers find themselves on their own.

Gordon's company, Raytheon Training, recently conducted a benchmarking study of 11 organizations (five academic institutions and six corporations) and their Web-based training practices. None of the organizations had mandated programs to qualify instructors, but all of the academic institutions had some type of support for online

Tricks of the Virtual Trade

One sunny weekend in the spring of 1997, Judith Boettcher found herself stuck indoors sifting through the contents of her email inbox instead of enjoying the beautiful weather. As a newbie online instructor, the Florida State professor was overwhelmed by the number of messages she had received from students. Even worse, some of the messages were infected by viruses, others were sent in unreadable formats, and all of them had different file names, making them difficult to sort.

"I learned that actually doing this type of teaching is definitely more challenging than just talking about doing it," she writes in *Faculty Guide to Moving Teaching and Learning to the Web* (1999, League for Innovation in the Community College). Boettcher, who is currently executive director of the Corporation for Research and Educational Networking, a non-profit that supports IT professionals in research and education, offers some guidelines on managing email communications with students. Although she and her co-author wrote the book for instructors in higher education, the lessons also apply to corporate trainers who are facilitating asynchronous online courses.

Do not be vague about the names of assignments. If you want your students to turn in assignments via electronic means, be very specific about what should go in the subject line of a message (for example, Assignment 1: Theoretical Principles, Student's Full Name). To make sure these assignment names are always accessible, include this information in the course calendar on the Web.

Do not be available to your students all the time. We are constantly reminded that technology allows us to be available anytime, anywhere. But just because it's possible to be available 24 hours a day, seven days a week, does not mean we have to be—or that we should be. Set up a framework for responding to email (24 hours is reasonable). Make it clear that there will be times when the response time will be longer, such as when you're on vacation or attending conferences. You can also set times during which your response time will be shorter, particularly before deadlines. Some instructors even set email office hours.

Don't assume that email is received. We've all heard of letters that get mislaid and are delivered 20 years after they were mailed. Email can be similarly delayed, so don't assume that your message has been received and read by the addressee. Asking students to send a confirmation email on critical messages is wise. Setting up an automatic confirmation when an email is received is another option.

Don't forget to provide feedback. Students want timely and personal feedback on their work. Some faculty are experimenting with the use of audio files for feedback on papers, finding that spoken comments can be completed more quickly than written ones.

Excerpted with permission from *Faculty Guide for Moving Teaching and Learning to the Web* by Judith V. Boettcher and Rita-Marie Conrad, 1999, League for Innovation in the Community College (www.league.org).

teachers. "What's happening is that there are people who are excited and interested in technology, and they're coming forward and volunteering to teach the classes, but that doesn't mean they know how," says Gordon.

She suggests that organizations moving into online learning look at the public school system as a model. Student teachers work with more experienced teachers in highly structured programs designed to give them on-the-job experience that's backed up by expert guidance. Once they're hired, teachers have regular evaluations during which the principal provides feedback and suggestions. Why not apply the same concept to online facilitation at the corporate or academic level?

Until that happens, people who want to learn more about online facilitation may need to take matters into their own hands. Gordon suggests observing someone who's teaching an online course, or taking an online course yourself. "That will help you start thinking visually, in sound bites and small pieces of information," she says.

To learn first-hand how it feels to take part in a heated online debate, Full Circle's White suggests participating in discussion boards such as TableTalk at www.salon.com. "Go someplace and get in the middle of a flamefest. There are plenty of online communities where you can practice, mostly in anonymity, and learn not to take things personally," she says. "Practice is precious."

Amy Sitze is editor of Inside Technology Training *(now* Online Learning Magazine*). She can be reached at asitze@lakewoodpub.com.*

Who Wants to Be a Distance Trainer?

Karen Mantyla

Everyone wants to be a millionaire, but ask a group of trainers whether they want to become distance learning instructors, and you'll see them peer around at colleagues, wondering which brave souls will raise their hands. In this article by co-editor Karen Mantyla, you learn what to look for in potential e-trainers and how to help them succeed in the transition from face-to-face to virtual space.

The 2000-2001 timeframe will produce not only more DL instructors than ever before, but at a faster rate. Many organizations and consultants offer train-the-trainer programs in delivery methods ranging from Web to satellite to videoconferencing, and others. Supporting instructors as they make the switch from classroom trainers to facilitators of learning is a fast-growing service field, and instructors who are considering the change will find help readily available.

I make this point because addressing the real or perceived problems that instructors deal with in distance learning is the first step in the selection process. It's important to check the mindset of instructors that you're considering for these positions. If you provide a forum—such as a workshop—where negative perceptions can be addressed and dealt with effectively, you can enlarge your pool of candidates. Basically, instructors are reluctant to volunteer for these jobs for the following reasons:

- Skepticism that training via distance learning isn't as good as the tried-and-true classroom experience. *Tip:* Offer researched documentation and a list of successful distance learning organizations for benchmarking best practices and successful outcomes.

- Fear of using the technology and appearing less than proficient. *Tip:* Identify the learning technologies being used and allow ample time for trainers' questions and time to practice, practice, practice.
- Training where peers can see them. *Tip:* Have instructors do team teaching with a distance learning instructor or shadow one to get comfortable with these classrooms without walls. Having a mentor is also helpful when making this transition.
- Lack of control. *Tip:* It's important to convey to instructors that distance learning is a team effort, with all members pitching in to support learners' success. The instructor, instructional designer, site facilitator, and technology and administrative contacts form a strong nucleus for supporting the success of distance learning initiatives. When people learn, the team—including the instructor—is given credit for that success.
- Fear of losing their jobs. *Tip:* Provide instructors with resources detailing the new types of jobs that have been created by this new learner-centered environment. Roles, in addition to training, include facilitating, moderating, site coordinating, and learner support. An excellent resource on such new positions is *ASTD Models for Learning Technologies: Roles, Competencies, and Outputs,* by George M. Piskurich and Ethan S. Sanders.

Trainers' perceptions should be addressed openly. The goal is to ensure that their decisions are based on facts, not perceptions. In your e-learning strategic plan, you should build in ways to identify and address people's concerns and resistance to distance learning.

Here are some pointers for the next step, selection. (For additional information, refer to ASTD's *Distance Learning: A Step-by-Step Guide for Trainers,* by Karen Mantyla and J. Richard Gividen.)

Selecting Distance Learning Instructors

Training delivery, especially that first one, will have lots of eyes watching. New mind-set shifts about distance learning are often formed by an organization's initial course or event, so the first one must be successful. A great outcome will help dispel skepticism and, conversely, a poorly delivered course will fuel the fire for "I told you so" while increasing the zeal to minimize change. Ready to select potential DL instructors, here's what to look for:

Enthusiasm about distance learning. It's important to start with these people; you can convert others as you go along. If someone has had prior successful DL experience and is enthusiastic about doing more, put him or her at the top of the list. These instructors can also act as mentors.

Excellent onsite instructors. A track record of excellence in delivering onsite training is a basic requirement for DL instructors.

Learner-centered mindset or willingness to develop one. Those who have a strong instructor-centered mindset will not be your best candidates.

Flexibility. With new skills and technologies to learn, flexibility is an important attribute. Plus, it's a valuable trait for those times when the technology fails and contingency plans are launched.

Adaptability. A DL trainer works with a team and doesn't control what each person on the team does. The trainer is a vital part of the success of the distance learning event and needs to think of delivering training as a collaborative way of supporting the needs of learners. All team members are important, especially the technical people who now become a life-support system that must be included in all planning. The instructor must learn to adapt to recommendations and new ideas by other team members. Rigidity is out.

Sense of humor. Effective use of humor helps remote site learners enjoy the learning experience and want to come back for more (and tell others to come back with them). Good press is invaluable.

Willingness to learn about new technologies. Effective distance learning instructors find out how the equipment works, how the software can be used, and how the hardware and software support the learning experience.

Willingness to create interaction. A talking head or long pages of text on a screen prompt the yawn reflex. Interaction is important and not only helps people learn, but it also can be used to apply the learning to the real world.

Willingness to practice using the equipment and to rehearse delivery. Most DL instructors say the number-one way they learn is to practice, practice, and then do it again. Though instructors may know their content well, it's vital to become confident and comfortable delivering the content with learning technologies.

Training Distance Learning Instructors

Once you've selected trainers, your next job is to help them succeed. There will be differences in training, depending on which technologies they'll use. Such differences include course conversion—including learner support materials—and training delivery methods. Insist that trainers experience the technology before using it for instruction; ask them to take an online course or two and attend a satellite or videoconference event to see what it's like being a learner.

Instructors need practice and a good overview of the job, including how to

- understand different learning technologies and the advantages and disadvantages of each
- select courses for conversion
- convert courses or learning content with a media selection guide (this helps

instructors choose the best technologies for Web-based, CD-ROM, satellite, videoconferencing, and other training).

- design for short segments of 10 to 15 minutes
- build in interactivity for 30 to 50 percent of the program and vary the activities to ensure an active learning event rather than a passive learning experience
- create effective visual aids
- dress properly when using video
- create effective remote site materials
- prepare evaluation tools
- train remote site facilitators
- ensure easy registration and identify precourse administration requirements
- deliver the learning experience based on the selected technologies
- set up contingency plans for when the technology doesn't work
- establish learner support systems before, during, and after learning delivery (help line and email access, for example)
- use all equipment and applications.

Effective onsite instructors learn how to be successful. The same holds true for distance learning instructors. Having a step-by-step process for selecting and training instructors will help ensure that learning is the focus and the technology is seamless.

Karen Mantyla is the president of Quiet Power, located in Washington, D.C. She is the co-author of Distance Learning: A Step-by-Step Guide for Trainers *and the author of* Interactive Distance Learning Exercises That Really Work! *Contact her at QuietPower @aol.com.*

The Life and Times of an E-Trainer

Lesley Darling

This article tells how two online trainers go about their jobs training hundreds of learners who they will never meet face-to-face. How do they succeed? What should you avoid? Read on, and look for the sidebar with tips for new online instructors.

We all know e-learning is hot, that it will have a major impact on how people learn, that it will change how companies train their employees. But, we haven't heard much about the effect online training is having on trainers themselves.

Looking at the typical workday of two e-trainers, it's clear that training in the online world is an entirely different animal. Mickey Dodson and Jeff Bankston each have pursued online learning for years and currently conduct online classes (see the e-trainer profiles, below). Here's a look at their experiences.

The Class Is the Thing

Both Dodson and Bankston teach introductory and higher-level courses. Their online classes, which are conducted using an asynchronous bulletin-board approach, typically run from two to 12 weeks.

Classes begin with a series of postings to a training-site message board. Dodson and Bankston post information about themselves and a general welcome to the class—what learners should expect, how to get the most out of the class, topics, homework, and additional materials. "That's where I set the tone of the class," says Bankston.

The E-Trainers

Mickey Dodson

Home: Granada, Nicaragua

History: Software developer for 20 years; switched to Web development five years ago. Currently owns classroom-training organization Internet Seminar Service.

Online training experience: Has been teaching for SmartPlanet and others since 1998; became full-time online trainer soon after. Teaches topics such as intro to HTML, Webpage design, and Website development.

Student base: Individual consumers and corporate employees.

Jeff Bankston

Home: Atlanta

History: In 1982, began training for Digital Equipment Corporation; has also developed online training for General Electric, the U.S. National Security Agency, and *PC Magazine*. He is vice president of operations and senior network architect for BCI Associates, a small business consultancy.

Online training experience: Began training for Element K (formerly ZD Education) in 1990. Teaches networking topics, such as intro to SQL, network design and implementation, NT server administration, networking essentials, and certification courses.

Student base: Primarily employees of corporate subscribers to Element K.

Dodson has found that she needs to tell learners up front that she's a woman. "With a first name like Mickey, it's only fair," she says. "I've had students in class for 12 weeks, and at the end they'll write a note saying, 'Mr. Dodson, you're the best teacher!'"

Many times, students send introductory emails back. Bankston notes that he's had as many as 100 messages per day during the opening weeks of a class. More typically, he sees around 40 questions and comments each day. At the end of class, student postings "usually taper down to 10 to 20 questions per day." Students review their assigned course materials each week, then post questions and comments to the training-site message board.

Interestingly, interactions in online courses can sometimes be more in-depth than the face-to-face variety. For one thing, the instructor has more time to reflect on the question and respond. Also, says Dodson, "I give a broader answer so the whole class can benefit."

Bankston also conducts live chats in hosted-site chat rooms, usually twice per course. "Students really like the chats," he says. "It's the next best thing to having an instructor actually work on your network."

Class Dynamics

Think controlling a roomful of 30 learners is a handful? Try 500. That's the average number of students in one of Dodson's HTML classes, which are geared for free agent learners.

Typically, she says, only 50 to 60 students of that larger number participate actively with comments and questions, and she has teaching assistants to help with the workload.

Making the online classroom "real" is a conscious process, says Dodson. Feedback and interactivity are the keys. In most online classes, communication peaks during the first weeks and decreases as the weeks progress. She fights to counter that phenomenon.

"In my classes, activity increases as the class goes on," she says. "That's because I give feedback, my teaching assistants give feedback, and I encourage students to visit one another's pages and comment on them. As the students get involved, they build a classroom community. I've seen them respond to the interactivity, and I see it in their course evaluations."

Dodson also strives for a personal touch and sense of humor to increase the comfort level. "I make a point of remembering active students, and I say hello when they come back for another course. And I try to lighten things up if they get frustrated."

The topics that Bankston teaches "can be dry," he admits. "But when you get a spunky, interactive class, it's a ball. Online, I see more sharing of information among students because there's less competition. Instead of taking notes and keeping it to themselves, some students post them online."

Reading personalities into emails becomes an art form for online instructors.

"You get a sense of students' personalities," says Bankston. "You encounter attitudes ranging from 'I've been in this business for three years and designed more networks than God' to 'This is my first class and first network—please help me.' This is typical of people from mixed backgrounds who have used simple networks. A person who's accustomed to one type of network is naturally biased against anything new, but other students often chime in with their unique network experience that helps broaden everyone's knowledge."

What may surprise people is that some of the same class control issues that crop up in live teaching come up in an online course—personality clashes, for example.

"We've occasionally had real flash points," Bankston relates. "Someone on the class message board will say one kind of network server is better, and someone disagrees. Suddenly people start going ballistic!" Fortunately, such interactions are the exception, not the rule. "You have to put on your personnel management hat," he says. "I'll tell them that we can all learn together."

"I don't allow any hotdogging by people who take a class just to show off what they know," says Dodson. "For instance, in my intro to HTML class, I point out that

---

Tips for New Online Trainers

Because online training is still relatively new, instructors may not know all the ins and outs of the delivery medium. Here are some tips:

Be aware of how much time you'll need to spend offline. You still need to prepare for class, and you may need to create extra materials personalized for learners. In addition, you must take time to respond to students in writing, and they often expect in-depth answers to their questions.

Promote interaction among learners. Ask open-ended questions, just as you would in a live classroom setting. Send emails to students who aren't posting questions but who are visiting the message boards. Encourage participants to answer one another's questions and respond to comments. This creates an environment where it's okay to make mistakes.

Pay attention. Your answers are posted permanently, for all to see! Unlike a one-time live classroom workshop, if you feel your answer was lacking, you can go back and add a more informed response to the message thread.

It's about the teaching. Remember, even though online training takes place in a high-tech setting and—at this point, at least—tends to be about technical topics, your stellar teaching skills are the most vital part of your online course.

---

it's an introductory course and that I and the TAs won't comment on any page that doesn't address the assignment."

Both instructors use any conflicts as a catalyst for interaction and learning, while at the same time managing them carefully and coaching students on how to disagree online.

Who's Online?

Bankston and Dodson see differences in the kinds of students they teach in their online courses.

"I see a lot more inexperienced people because online courses are an easy and cost-effective way for them to break into the field," says Bankston. "I have students asking all levels of questions because they're at different experience levels. That can make it tough on the instructor because you sometimes assume a level of knowledge or access to technology that's not always there."

Dodson's experience with her students focuses on another interesting aspect of online learning: "My classes are filled with people from China, New Zealand, and Australia." The classes, she says, "bring the world closer. These people become very close; they begin to help one another and call one another by their first names."

Cultural nuances in such situations are important. "I had a learner from Malaysia," says Dodson, "and he didn't post anything until three weeks into the course when he offered a suggestion to another student's problem. He said he hadn't posted before because he was nervous about his English. I encouraged him—his answer was right on, and his English was perfect. He was posting for the remainder of the class."

Investing the Time

Dodson teaches seven classes, not all at the same time. For each class, she spends two to three hours per day. "If I have five classes going, I work about 12 hours a day," she adds. "Thankfully, that's not often."

Both Dodson and Bankston follow a regular routine. Dodson's day begins around 5 a.m. "I get coffee and go online. I pick up my mail from the sites and from my teaching assistants. The TAs provide student questions that I need to address immediately, or they alert me to sites that I need to look at. Then I sift through the questions and comments and respond to them." Sometimes the learners are still in the classroom, and they're surprised when Dodson's answer pops up.

If any questions require her to do research, she posts a message that she's working on it. "I want my students to know that their questions will be answered within five hours." Dodson goes offline, does any research she needs to, then repeats her visit to the classroom after lunch. In the afternoon, she often designs Web pages that show the solution to student questions; she posts the pages to her own site so everyone can visit and learn from one another's questions. Finally, later in the evening, Dodson visits her classroom again—three times a day is her habit.

Bankston checks messages from his students in the early morning and evening in a procedure much like Dodson's. On average, he spends about two or three hours a day online for new classes, which later tapers down to about an hour per class. He says that he spends about the same amount of time offline preparing for his classes—about three to six hours per Sunday afternoon—as he would prepping for a live class.

Bankston also works offline to make his courses more informative. "If I run across information during a normal business day that would help out in the course, I take notes in a journal. At home, I create material that goes up on my Website for the next class session."

Though they'd never recognize one of their students in a face-to-face encounter, Dodson and Bankston still find the life of an online instructor rewarding.

"I love to teach," says Dodson, "and I've always taught during my career. With online courses, I get to work from home. I don't have to go to an office and sit in a cubicle." Dodson also travels a good bit for her "other" life as a seminar leader, and she still keeps up with her classes: "I can teach anywhere—whether I'm traveling or at the beach."

She also finds rewards in the work itself. "I'll have a student in a FrontPage class, for example, who doesn't even know how to turn on a computer! Twelve weeks later, I visit the Webpage that's his final assignment, and I'm awestruck by how good it is. I love that, because it's something I gave that person—the chance to put his vision on the Internet."

"The best part of online teaching is when you solve a special problem for a student," Bankston says. "When you generate discussion that helps students understand and not fear technology, that leads them to professional growth—the sweet spot."

He, too, travels a good deal as a learning consultant. "Online courses give me the flexibility to connect while I'm traveling and still teach. It's the same for my students; they can take a class any time and place they want to."

Lesley Darling is chief learning officer with Element K, formerly Ziff-Davis Education, and is responsible for the overall online experience at the online education Web site. Darling has more than 10 years' experience in the training industry and has delivered talks and presented at various vendor-specific conferences and events.

Ten Facts of Life for Distance Learning Courses

Annette C. Lamb and William L. Smith

If you're thinking about setting up a distance learning course, you need to understand just what's involved in interacting effectively with students using this methodology. This article summarizes ten important things to remember.

I have been integrating technology into my classroom for twenty years—a Web-based class cannot be that much different, right? Wrong! Each learning environment has unique problems and frustrations. Although your classroom experience will be extremely valuable, you will need to adjust how you think about student-teacher communication, class preparation, and many other things you may take for granted in your traditional classroom.

Whether you are planning a technology course for teachers or a business management course for MBA students, your mission is the same. You want to develop a course where all students can be successful regardless of their prior experiences with distance learning technologies.

The following ten tips review things you already know about teaching but may not have considered as you plan for your distance learning course.

1. Students Are Individuals

Each student and each class is unique. Never is this more apparent than in a distance learning environment. Each student brings a different level of preparedness for the class, and you must be prepared for each individual.

There will be variations in technology experience, content entry skills, and preparedness for the unique characteristics of the distance learning environment. Some students will enter your course with few technology skills, while others will be Webmasters ready to expand their knowledge. In such an environment students who might excel in a traditional classroom may find themselves disoriented among Web-page readings and frustrated with online discussions. It is important to help these students learn to deal with this new class environment. For example, during an initial face-to-face meeting, you might guide students through the online syllabus (see Figure 1), calendar, requirements, and assignments. Demonstrate how they can use the calendar (see Figure 2) to gain access to readings and requirements. Discuss strategies for exploring, skimming, and reading in a Web environment. Talk about the differences between

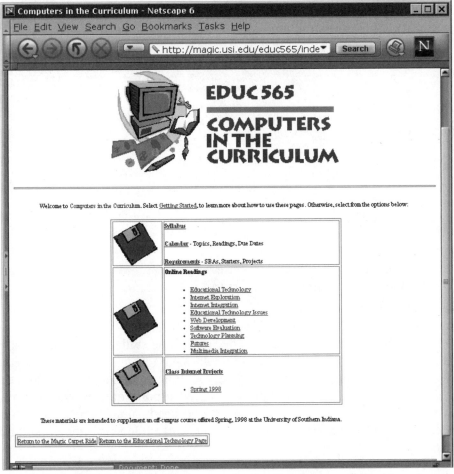

Figure 1. Course overview from Computers in the Curriculum (http://magic.usi.edu/ educ565/index.html)

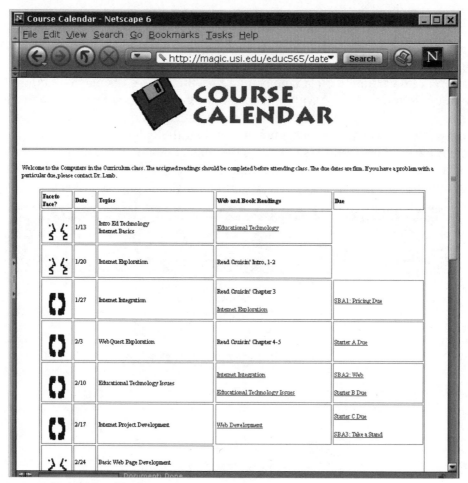

Figure 2. Course calendar from Computers in the Curriculum (http://magic.usi.edu/educ565/dates.html)

live discussions and listserv interactions. A reassuring face-to-face meeting the first week of the semester can go a long way toward making students feel comfortable.

Although most students have little difficulty getting used to this new method of learning, the adjustment period may be long for some students. As an instructor you must be ready to identify potential problems and respond quickly with appropriate, effective help. You may encounter a student who needs almost daily e-mail support and encouragement, while other students may work independently throughout the entire course.

Be prepared to do some remedial work with students who lag behind from the outset. Like all classrooms, there will be variations in the preparedness of the students to deal with the content of the course. These variations are magnified in the distance learning environment because one-on-one, face-to-face help sessions are not available. Consider a help listserv or Web page where students can post questions and help each other.

2. Technologies Change and Evolve

Be prepared to deal with a variety of technologies that are constantly changing. During any particular semester, new Web browsers will appear, alternative versions of systems will be available, and advanced presentation formats may evolve. Although you may be tempted to take advantage of each new technology as it comes along, consider your students, their skills, and their access to technology. Make sure you and your students are confident in a new product before making a commitment halfway through a course.

Distance learning can take place using many different technologies. While a course may start out as a video-based course, it is likely that one or more additional technologies will be available by the next time you teach it. You might add a Web element and later a threaded discussion page or a live chat. There will often be pressure to use new technology, whatever it might be. You should make an informed decision about whether the new technology really contributes to the course and is worth the learning time, development time, and expense to you and your students. The best way to "Be Prepared" is to continuously monitor your learning environment to be aware of which new technology would be of most benefit.

3. Technology Fails

Be prepared for failure. Whether it is your Internet connection, printer cartridge, or a video projector, you can be sure it will be down, out, or just plain dead at the most unexpected and inconvenient time.

Distance learning requires contingency planning. Think through what you will do when technological disaster strikes your class. This planning may be as simple as having a spare bulb handy, carrying a zip drive with a backup disk, or being prepared to postpone a due date if the server goes down. Another approach is to have an alternative plan—perhaps backup technology. Transparencies of a PowerPoint presentation, a print copy of your outline, or a fax machine are possibilities.

This kind of planning is especially important for courses that are dependent on a particular technology. What will you do if the server is down for an extended time? You might, for instance, keep a backup copy of your Web class pages on another server or a hard drive.

4. Planning Shows

Careful instructional design and development is critical for an effective distance learning course. The better the planning, the more successful the implementation.

How often have you been just one week ahead of your students? Do you remember developing course materials the night before class? Have you ever run to the copy center five minutes before class to pick up handouts? This type of procrastination does not work in a distance learning environment. All details of the course should be fully planned and prepared before the course starts.

The distance learning environment tends to exaggerate both the positive and the negative aspects of all the elements of instruction. Anything left to chance will become a major pitfall. Any lack of planning will be exposed. Adhering to the basics of instructional design is essential to success in distance learning.

In an Internet-based course it is essential to have the completed Web pages—including activities, projects, readings, and links—in a final form from the beginning. Although in some courses the pages and projects may evolve and build as students make contributions, the skeleton must be in place from the beginning. An active announcement, discussion, or chat arrangement is essential in communicating changes, updates, and evolution of the site. If your site will be evolving, build in a mechanism to be sure that students are constantly working with the materials. You may find that some students will print pages and not check the electronic bulletin board or announcements as often as you would like.

Good students will appreciate your planning. They like to be able to see the "big picture" before the course begins—including all the assignments, projects, and requirements. With careful planning, the course will run smoothly and students will complete assignments on time with little difficulty.

5. Students Procrastinate

Establish deadlines for each project and activity ahead of time. You can always waive or alter deadlines, but it is difficult to add requirements after the fact.

It is probably not surprising that a disturbingly large number of students will not do assignments until they are under pressure from a firm due date. This situation, too, is exaggerated in the distance learning environment. Because you are not able to see students regularly, look them in the eye, and remind them to get the work done on time, even good students may wait until the last minute. E-mail messages of reminder do not have the same impact, even if you take the time to send them on a timely basis. Also, students will not always read your messages when you expect them to. Use a course calendar as the core page of your course, and include reading and requirement links as well as specific due dates. Encourage students to turn in projects early rather than on the due dates. Use guilt and competition to your advantage by praising good work on your discussion list. When students do good work, include a quote or sample of their work in an online discussion. Encourage students to conduct peer reviews and share their experiences. This type of interaction encourages students to get their work in on time.

Although a Web-based course is a great opportunity for a truly self-paced individualized learning environment, we have found that very few undergraduate or graduate students have the self-discipline to set their own deadlines and complete a course in a reasonable amount of time. This is particularly true when they are taking other courses that contain firm due dates and requirements. It is easy for them to put the "flexible" course on the back burner, and it never seems to get promoted to the front burner.

6. Track Them or Lose Them

Monitor each student's progress regularly. Because you do not see each student in person, it is essential that a planned process be established to monitor students at some specified interval.

If you do not receive an assignment on time, you will have an additional reason to check on a student to be sure he or she is still there and doing okay. Students will "disappear" for a variety of reasons. Illness, personal difficulties, and conflicting work schedules are common problems. A student might even move away and not notify you of the change. The more regular your contacts, the more likely you are to hear from the student in these unusual situations. In addition, it is helpful to have multiple ways to contact each student. At the beginning of the class, be sure to get all students' phone numbers and mailing addresses.

Consider using electronic post cards as a way to maintain contact with students. Greeting cards companies like Blue Mountain (http://www.bluemountain.com), authors such as Jan Brett (http://www.janbrett.com), and companies such as Troll (http://www.troll.com/cardworks/index.html) provide free "postcard" services that can brighten a student's day and encourage him to stay on track.

7. Students Appreciate Feedback

It is a student's responsibility to get assignments in on time. In return, it is your responsibility as the instructor to provide prompt, useful feedback.

A process for quick response and appropriate feedback should be planned into the course. This feedback lets students know that you are concerned about their progress and pleased to get their assignments on time. This communication may be through email, fax, snail mail, phone, or Web page posting.

If students are posting their projects on Web pages, you could open a student's Web page and provide feedback right on her page. You could even highlight ideas in red or green text. Some instructors like to post general feedback for the class to see. For example, you might indicate that Susan has cool clip art on her page that everyone should check out or that David's article review contains some important points that everyone should read.

There are at least three common options for communicating with students through e-mail about their progress. One approach is to respond to student input and inquiry as soon as possible and practical. This option applies the time-management strategy of dealing with paper immediately rather than letting it stack up. In other words, when an e-mail assignment arrives, grade it on the fly, reply immediately, record the grade, and delete the message. You only have to deal with the message once and it is gone.

Some instructors find this task difficult, because they need to get into a particular frame of mind to "grade." Others find it difficult to mix tasks. In other words, personal, professional, work, play, and class e-mail is all mixed together, and it may be hard to move from reading a forwarded joke to grading a student project.

Another approach is to set a particular time each week to respond to all accumulated student input and inquiries. For example, you might find that Sunday night is a good time to quietly go through and respond to all student assignments. The problem with this approach is that it lacks timeliness. A student may have to wait for six days for a response to a simple question. Instead of one day, you may choose three days such as Monday, Wednesday, and Friday mornings at 9AM. If students are aware of your "virtual" office hours, they can plan for feedback during those times.

A third option is to use a separate e-mail account or folder for student assignments. In this way, you can grade projects as they come in, but they are not mixed in with other mail.

You should decide which approach best meets the needs of your students and yourself during each term. The important thing is to set a standard for each class, communicate it to the students early, and follow through during the course. This way, the students will have realistic expectations regarding feedback.

8. Technology Takes Time

Whether you are developing the course, reading a Web-based article, doing an assignment, or grading a project, it will take you twice as long as you think. Although there are many times when technology can be a time saver, at least in the beginning technology can be a time drainer.

Students can get bogged down with reading from the screen. They may complain about "all the reading," when the articles they are reading are no longer than traditional articles on paper. Prepare students by discussing the differences between Web and paper reading.

Distance learning students seem to lose a lot of time trying to solve problems that could be answered immediately in a regular classroom situation. Provide students with time-saving strategies. For example, some students do not realize that they can have the Web and a word processor open at the same time for taking notes. If they are having trouble, it may not occur to them to e-mail another student for help. Encourage students to develop a cohort group and coordinate weekly online study groups.

9. Active Learning Is Critical

Active involvement, student interaction, and varied activities are important for all types of learning, but they are essential in working with students at a distance.

Active involvement is critical in learning. Rather than just assigning a reading, get students to do something with the information they are asked to read. One option is to provide Web pages that contain study guides, Web quests, and other activities that use class materials. Rather than requiring that each assignment be graded by the teacher, use self-evaluation, peer evaluation, or selective grading. For example, students might complete ten "idea exploration" activities but only be required to submit their favorite five activities for a grade.

Keep students interacting through the use of a class listserv, threaded discussion, or other communication tool. Try to get students to choose to participate rather than requiring participation. In other words, if the discussions are helpful to their assignments, projects, or learning, they will participate without an assignment that requires them to "send at least three message to the listserv." Start with nonthreatening discussions that help students get to know each other. Consider developing a Web page, or pages, containing the names and pictures of students so that visual learners can "see" their classmates. Another way to encourage interaction is through the use of peer evaluation, help sessions, and collaborative projects.

Vary your class activities. E-mail messages, a listserv discussion, a threaded Web discussion, Web page development, and a PowerPoint presentation may all be assignments within a business management course. Each assignment would focus on a different aspect of the course The listserv and threaded discussions might be used to synthesize the course reading materials, and the Web page and PowerPoint projects would be used to focus on a particular topic of interest.

10. Students Have Great Ideas

Listen to students. They have great ideas for your course. Encourage them to constantly evaluate the course and provide suggestions. For example, an activity might take twice the time that you planned. Why? Ask your students. Be prepared to trim one assignment, expand another, or cut an activity entirely to meet their needs.

Let students take a leadership role in the class. When things are going well, encourage them to go in expanded directions. If the course is getting off-track, ask students to help refocus activities or assignments. You will be surprised at how motivated they will be when they see that you care enough to involve them in decision making.

Annette C. Lamb has been a full professor, library/media specialist, and computer teacher. She has written more than a dozen books on educational technology integration and has conducted more than 500 presentations at state and national conferences. E-mail her at alamb@eduscapes.com.

William L. Smith is an assistant professor in the School of Business at Emporia State University. Although business is his primary area, Dr. Smith is known for his innovative approaches to integrating technology into college-level business courses. E-mail him at smithwil@esumail.emporia.edu.

Have It Your Way: Adaptive Learning

Bob Oas

Adaptive learning: yet another concept to consider when planning a distance learning course. This article explains more.

As if the e-learning industry weren't complex enough already, there's a new buzzword floating around. It's adaptive learning, and it means many things to many people. For most training types, it refers to computer programming and application interfaces that adjust to the way people learn. The idea is that if people learn in a way that's adapted perfectly to their needs, they retain more knowledge and become more productive in the long run.

Adapting to diverse learners is fairly easy in the classroom. "The teacher has always been the one who paid attention to learning orientations," says Margaret Martinez, co-founder and chief learning officer at The Training Place, an e-learning company in Arlington, Va. "They looked at people who were obviously confused or bored, and they responded on the fly. But now we've taken the instructor away, so we have to build these things into our technology."

The concept of doing that isn't new, says Saul Carliner, assistant professor of information design at Bentley College in Waltham, Mass. "We've had the capability to do some of this for years, just not in such a sophisticated way."

About 15 years ago, for example, researchers came up with the idea of tailored interfaces, which would adjust to a user's level of experience. The most simple example of this approach is a video game that starts out easy for a beginning player, and gets more challenging as that person gains expertise.

Later, academics and researchers refined this model so it would accommodate semantic subtleties. "Let's say you lived in the South and were ordering drinks," Carliner says. "Instead of asking, 'Do you want pop?' the system would say, 'Do you want to order a Coke?'" (In the South, "Coke" is sometimes used as a generic term for soft drinks.)

The architecture has come a long way since then. Much of the adaptive learning currently under development customizes course content to learning styles or attitudes.

Getting Inside Your Head

When you sit down in front of an adaptive learning course developed by IDL Systems Inc., an e-learning company in Washington, D.C., you're instantly in the driver's seat. After taking a brief tutorial that teaches you about learning styles (for example, some people are step-by-step learners while others prefer to look at the big picture), you choose your personal learning style and tell the system whether you prefer audio, video, text or simulation. If you want the system to choose your learning style, you can take a brief quiz that will help the system evaluate your style.

Let's say you tell the system you're a sequential learner who likes video. It instantly creates screens that give you step-by-step video lessons. But what if you don't understand your learning preferences as well as you think you do? Most people make a beeline for video as their preferred media type, says IDL co-founder Brian Roherty, but research shows that very few people learn best that way. So the system jumps in and tells you that audio would probably be a better choice for you.

How does it know? As you're taking the course, the system's artificial intelligence engine tracks every click you make and uses statistical models to give you individualized feedback. For example, if you're taking a math course and bombing all the questions on fractions, the system can actually analyze what you're doing wrong. "Instead of telling you that you don't understand fractions, which isn't helpful, the system tells you that you're getting your subtraction wrong on the denominator. Now that's helpful," Roherty says.

The concept is a good one, but Roherty's challenge was making it happen. Along with Nishikant Sonwalker, IDL co-founder and director of the Hypermedia Teaching Facility at the Massachusetts Institute of Technology (MIT), Roherty realized it was impossible to build thousands of Web pages that would pop up to meet the needs of users with different learning styles and media preferences. Instead, they based the system on information objects—individual elements that reconfigure themselves on a page depending on which choices the user makes.

What this means is that instead of downloading memory-hogging graphic and video files, all you need is a Web browser with a "thin stream" of HTML, Roherty says. "Sometimes it's hard for people to understand that you can't download one of our courses to your hard drive, because there is no course," he says. "There's only a template that pulls up information objects to provide learners with what they're asking for."

Where Are You Coming From?

Similar research is being conducted at the University of Arizona in Tucson, the home of the Virtual Adaptive Learning Architecture (VALA) project. While IDL's efforts are proprietary, the findings of the VALA project—which is primarily funded by the U.S. government and technology giants such as Oracle and Sun Microsystems—will benefit industry, government and academia. "The goal is to create a shell in which anyone can provide content and then anyone can access that content," says VALA project director James Austin.

The project's origins lie in a long-standing interest in doing training on the Navajo Reservation, Austin explains. "People think there is only one path to a goal," he says. "It has always been my contention that there are lots of ways to get there, which in part is what VALA is about. The way I think, as a white male, is not the way a female Hispanic or a Navajo elder or an Asian youngster is necessarily going to think and process information."

The infrastructure of the VALA project, like IDL's, relies on artificial intelligence to serve up customized content. VALA also takes a learner's personality and propensity to learn into consideration. "We're allowing a user to interact with the material in a suggested, not subscribed, manner," Austin says.

Playing on Your Emotions

Catering to a trainee's learning preferences—whether it be learning style, cognitive properties, ability to learn or personality—is a complicated endeavor. But what happens when you add emotion to the mix?

"If we want to personalize, we have to focus first and foremost on emotions and intentions," says The Training Place's Martinez. "We have to look at whether someone's passionate about learning—someone who loves to learn vs. someone who hates to learn, someone who loves to explore vs. someone who is afraid of taking risks."

Martinez's adaptive learning architecture is centered on what she calls "learning orientations": transforming, performing, conforming and resistant. Transforming learners, she says, are assertive and highly motivated. Performing learners are motivated when the subject matter appeals to them, and they enjoy achieving short-term, task-oriented goals. Conforming learners typically do what they're expected to do, but need constant guidance and positive reinforcement. Resistant learners are just that: resistant to learning. They're often more interested in their personal goals than those set by an organization, and they avoid learning altogether when possible.

Martinez's technology gives transforming learners the big-picture view they need without bothering them with unnecessary details. For conforming learners, on the other hand, the technology adjusts to feed them content in a much slower, more simplified way. "You can achieve the same instructional objectives for everyone—it's just that you do it in a different way for people with different learning orientations," she says.

Adaptive learning may be a good idea for the learner, but how does it affect bottom-line business goals? "What's the best way to get up to speed? That's the question that perhaps should be asked," says VALA's Austin. "It may be that the best way is just to throw someone in and let them sink or swim. But if you do that in their preferred environment and in their preferred style, aren't you going to be more effective?"

Bob Oas is a technology writer in Minneapolis. You can reach him at editor@soulgrit.com.

Part Eight

Evaluating Program Success

Y ou've planned and delivered a distance learning course. Now how do you figure out how successful it was and whether your students and the organization got their money's worth? That's the logical topic taken up here in Part Eight. We've included four articles that provide different perspectives and methodologies for evaluating distance learning success.

Jack Phillips and his colleagues have been writing about training evaluation and return on investment for some time, and we're pleased to include "Evaluating the Effectiveness and the Return on Investment of E-Learning" by Phillips along with Patricia Pulliam Phillips and Lizette Zuniga. The article gives you 10 questions to consider as you think about what the success of an e-learning undertaking would involve.

The next piece by Jonathan Goodwin asks the question, "Web-Based Distance Learning: How Effective Is It?" He then proceeds to answer that question, providing a variety of reasons why and how distance learning is an effective way to deliver instruction.

If you'd find a checklist helpful in preparing an evaluation, then see the next piece, "Web-Based Training Evaluation Checklist." This article provides five categories in which to judge the effectiveness of your Web-based training.

We conclude Part Eight with Matthew Champagne and Robert Wisher's "Online Evaluation of Distance Learning: Benefits, Practices, and Solutions." This is an original article written for this yearbook. It explains several strengths of carrying out such evaluations online and provides various case studies to back up their assertions. If you're looking for new evaluation techniques, check out this article.

Evaluating the Effectiveness and the Return on Investment of E-Learning

Jack Phillips, Patricia Pulliam Phillips, and Lizette Zuniga

This article lays out 10 questions to consider in understanding why it's important to focus on the ROI of e-learning programs. It highlights a variety of things to take into consideration as you undertake such training programs.

E-learning is rapidly growing as an acceptable way of training. Whether it's through an intranet, the Internet, multimedia, interactive TV, or computer-based training, e-learning has increased significantly. But what do we know about these innovative approaches to training? Is e-learning effective? Considering the costs of implementing computer-based training, is there a positive return on investment?

While the literature is limited in answering all of our questions about e-learning, there are a few significant findings. First, most of the current evaluation at the business impact or return on investment (ROI) level has been driven by clients of e-learning (those who are funding the project). The designers, developers, and implementers are not driving this level of evaluation. Second, available evidence thus far suggests that traditional classroom instruction yields more favorable responses than e-learning solutions (Level 1). This issue represents a perplexing problem for proponents of e-learning. Third, e-learning is as effective as traditional face-to-face learning. While recipients of face-to-face instruction have expressed more satisfaction (Level 1) with traditional learning solutions, the learning outcomes are not different (Level 2) for participants of e-learning programs. Fourth, the same evaluation strategies (Levels 1-5) and processes utilized in other types of evaluations can be applied to e-learning programs. Fifth, the ROI studies indicate a positive return for companies implementing e-learning programs. Although most studies show a positive return based on cost reduction alone, ROI studies also need to include analysis of benefits. It is important to identify not only improvements in costs, but also the changes in benefits. Sixth, building evaluation into the computerized training process can save time as well as money.

Although recent attention has increased e-learning evaluation, the current research base for evaluating e-learning is inadequate. Due to the initial cost of implementing e-learning programs, it is important to continue to conduct evaluation studies. The following sections will attempt to answer the 10 questions just below on evaluating e-learning and present the most recent research available.

Question 1. Why should I evaluate e-learning?

Question 2. Is there a difference in evaluating e-learning and evaluating classroom training?

Question 3. When evaluating e-learning, what should I evaluate?

Question 4. How do I build support for evaluating e-learning?

Question 5. What processes are necessary to fully implement and integrate ROI into measurement and evaluation?

Question 6. What criteria should be used to decide which e-learning programs to evaluate?

Question 7. How does ROI fit into the evaluation of e-learning?

Question 8. What resources (time and money) are required to evaluate e-learning?

Question 9. Is it really possible to isolate the influence of e-learning solutions from other factors?

Question 10. Can ROI be forecast on proposed e-learning solutions?

Question 1: Why Should I Evaluate E-Learning?

Sound familiar?
- "I don't have time to evaluate e-learning."
- "I am having a hard enough time getting my organization to invest in training, let alone evaluation."
- "I find it difficult to convince people in my organization of the importance of evaluation."

Why is it important to actually evaluate e-learning?
There are many reasons for evaluating any type of learning solution, and several of them apply specifically to e-learning. Many individuals are interested in information about e-learning programs. The developers, coordinators, and even the participants are often interested in receiving data on these programs. Managers of participants and top management often want specific types of information. Finally, those who support and advocate the use of technology need certain types of data about e-learning.

What do we know?

The reasons for evaluating e-learning coincide with the classical reasons for evaluating any type of learning experience. These reasons are:

- to determine whether an e-learning solution is accomplishing its objectives
- to identify the strengths and weaknesses in the e-learning process
- to determine the benefit/cost ratio of an e-learning solution
- to decide who should participate in future e-learning solutions
- to identify who benefited the most or the least from the e-learning solution
- to reinforce major points made to the target group
- to collect data to assist in marketing future initiatives.

In addition, the technology aspect of e-learning brings in other demands for evaluation:

- The tremendous cost of technology often demands accountability, including measuring the actual return on investment.
- The newness of e-learning to many groups brings pressure to develop information about its effectiveness and efficiency as a learning solution.
- Because e-learning is not a proven process in many organizations, there is a need to show value now rather than later when it becomes a routine process.

Question 2: Is There a Difference in Evaluating E-Learning and Evaluating Traditional Training?

Sound familiar?

- "Is there something unique about e-learning that makes it easier to evaluate?"
- "Are there issues specific to e-learning that I should evaluate?"
- "Shouldn't we accept e-learning as a necessary progression in the use of technology and not evaluate it?"
- "There are intranet courses, Internet courses, multimedia, CD-ROM, and computer-based training. With so many different types of e-learning solutions, evaluation seems so confusing."

Why is it important to distinguish the evaluation of e-learning from other learning solutions?

By realizing that some of the same processes used to evaluate other types of learning solutions work with e-learning, the task of evaluation becomes easier. It becomes a matter of expanding the current evaluation techniques and processes to include e-learning as a method of delivery. Consequently, this issue is very important, not only for applying techniques, but for building a database of studies for internal use.

What do we know?

- We know that the techniques to evaluate e-learning are the same as evaluating other solutions:

- The types of data are the same, both quantitative and qualitative.
- The levels of evaluation are the same (five levels of evaluation).
- The data collection methods are the same for each of the levels of evaluation.
- The methods to isolate the effects of e-learning are the same.
- The methods of converting data to monetary values are the same.
- The methods of analyzing and reporting data are the same.

- Several issues are different with e-learning:
  - The methods for collecting data for Level 1 (reaction) and Level 2 (learning) can be built into the process much more easily than traditional methods.
  - Because e-learners can be remotely located, some of the methods of data collection are more difficult to use, such as focus groups and direct observation.

Question 3: When Evaluating E-Learning, What Should I Evaluate?

Sound familiar?

- "We already have ways to measure the effectiveness of training. Can't we just use the same forms to evaluate e-learning?"
- "If I am implementing a new e-learning program, what kinds of things should I be evaluating?"
- "Should I measure results in the same way I always have?"

Why is it important to measure different types of data?

Evaluation of e-learning is a complex issue, and several types of data should be collected. The type of data needed often depends on the purposes of evaluation and the individuals who want the data. Although e-learning does not necessarily add to the complexities of the data mix, it will usually influence the way the data are collected.

What do we know?

- Different types of collected data can be classified into five levels (the first four were developed by Kirkpatrick in the 1950s):
  - Measure participant reaction with the program and capture planned actions during the actual learning activity.
  - Measure change in knowledge skills or attitude.
  - Measure change in on-the-job behavior and specific application actions.
  - Measure changes in business impact for either individuals or work units.
  - Compare the monetary benefits of the program to the actual cost of the program.
- Sometimes it is also helpful to capture intangible data that purposely is not converted to monetary values, but represents important data. This category could overlap with application and impact measures listed above. When this category is combined with the five levels above, a balanced set of six different types of data are collected, representing a comprehensive measurement and evaluation process.

- In addition, certain indicators should be measured or monitored. These include:
  - actual enrollment statistics
  - percent of no-shows
  - retention rates throughout the program
  - cost of the program
  - other volume statistics indicating the level of activity.

Question 4: How Do I Build Support for Evaluating E-Learning?

Sound familiar?

- "I haven't been able to get the decision makers in my organization to think about evaluating e-learning."
- "We don't have the systems and processes in place to measure the effectiveness of e-learning."
- "We do not have the time to measure e-learning in my organization."

Why is it important to build support for evaluating e-learning?

As in any major initiative, evaluation requires commitment and support to be effective. Evaluation is an add-on activity in most situations and represents additional cost. Various stakeholders need to understand the rationale for evaluation and their role in making evaluation work. They must know what type of data is needed, when it is needed, and who needs it.

What do we know?

- We know that support for evaluation rests on six key elements:
  - There must be a commitment from the top of the organization to support the evaluation initiative. Key managers must set the stage by requiring and insisting that evaluation data be collected and utilized throughout the process.
  - The managers in the organization need to provide the necessary support for evaluation. This includes allocating time, allowing others to participate, becoming involved in the activities, and insisting that evaluation data be developed.
  - Policies, procedures, and guidelines must be developed for consistency so that the evaluation data can be compared across programs and so that the most efficient techniques and processes are utilized.
  - Skills and knowledge must be improved with various stakeholders, not only for the purpose of evaluation, but in terms of the technology used with e-learning. All stakeholders must be capable of understanding the need for evaluation and providing the appropriate data.
  - Appropriate technology support must be available to evaluate e-learning. This requires a close coordination and working relationship with the IT function.
  - There must be an action orientation to use evaluation data for process improvement.

- Building support requires several steps:
  - Determine the specific programs to be evaluated and at what level.
  - Determine the specific resources needed for evaluation.
  - Present management the type of data collected and suggest how it can be used in the process.
  - Explain to management the importance of the evaluation and their role.
  - Respond to particular questions or evaluation data quickly.
  - Show management the overall results from the evaluation plan.

Question 5: What Processes Are Necessary to Fully Implement and Integrate ROI into Measurement and Evaluation?

Sound familiar?

- "ROI seems so complicated. How do I know if my organization is ready for this process?"
- "What do I need to calculate an ROI?"
- "How can I satisfy our management group by integrating measurement and evaluation into our system?"

Why is it important to have a process approach to implement and integrate ROI into measurement and evaluation?

Given the interest in ROI, it is imperative to have a comprehensive measurement and evaluation system that improves the actual calculation of ROI. However, for the process to work effectively, several elements must be present to build a comprehensive system. Connections of frameworks and process models, along with implementation and communication issues, will be needed to develop a defensible system that can meet the needs of various target audiences.

What do we know?

The implementation of a comprehensive measurement and evaluation system will require five key elements:

- There must be a framework to collect and categorize data into different types and dictate particular timeframes to predict data. This could be in the form of a balanced scorecard (Kaplan and Norton), the Kirkpatrick four-level framework (Kirkpatrick, 1975), or the five levels of evaluation described earlier.
- A process model is needed to show how data are actually collected and how the effects of e-learning are isolated from other factors. The process also must have a mechanism to convert data to monetary value and to capture the full cost of the program. These key steps are a part of the ROI process model and are designed to ensure that various options are considered and data are properly collected, integrated, processed, and reported.
- Operating standards and guidelines are necessary to ensure that each step of the

ROI process model is consistent from one application to another for the same type of situation. Applying these operating standards ensures that a study can be replicated. Also, the standards reflect a conservative approach to analysis that is often necessary to build credibility to the process.

- A deliberate and methodical approach to implementation must be present to ensure that proper support and resources are in place to fully implement the ROI process. This type of measurement and evaluation process will often require a paradigm shift in terms of design, development, and delivery of e-learning and, consequently, must be properly planned and executed. Additional information for implementation is covered in Questions 4 and 8.
- A track record of successful application of a comprehensive measurement and evaluation process is needed, including ROI. Case studies must be developed within your own organization. Initially, it may be helpful to use many of the published studies around ROI, but eventually case studies will have to be developed internally.

Question 6: What Criteria Should Be Used to Decide Which E-Learning Programs to Evaluate?

Sound familiar?
- "I have budget restraints. How do I decide which training programs need evaluation?"
- "Some of our training programs are mandatory, so why should I evaluate those?"
- "Which programs are most appropriate for evaluation? How do I go about making that decision?"
- "Are some of my e-learning programs inappropriate for ROI?"

Why is it important to establish this criteria for selecting e-learning evaluation?
A comprehensive evaluation system yielding six types of data (reaction, learning, application, business impact, ROI, and intangibles) would be impractical to use for every e-learning project in larger organizations where there are many e-learning programs. Also, certain types of e-learning programs may not be appropriate for evaluating at the ROI level. For example, in compliance programs it may be appropriate to make sure employees understand certain compliance information. It may not be appropriate to measure their business impact or the actual ROI. Thus, a sensible approach must be taken to sort out which programs are appropriate for comprehensive evaluation, including ROI.

What do we know?
- Targets need to be set for evaluating at each level for e-learning programs using the following allocation guidelines as a possible framework:

Evaluation Targets

Level of Evaluation	Target (percent of e-learning programs evaluated at that level)
Level 1. Reaction	100%
Level 2. Learning	80%
Level 3. Job Application	30%
Level 4. Business Impact	20%
Level 5. ROI	10%

- The above targets allocate resources for evaluation, recognizing that it is not economically feasible to conduct 100 percent evaluation on all e-learning programs unless the number of programs is very small.
- When determining which programs to evaluate at Levels 4 and 5, specific criteria need to be developed. These criteria indicate the issues to be considered to make the decision to evaluate at those levels. The following criteria are often used to decide which programs should be used:
  - the life cycle of the e-learning program—a long-term implementation and duration would demand an ROI evaluation at some point during the program.
  - the linkage of the e-learning program to operational goals and measures—a direct linkage should be subjected to ROI evaluation.
  - the importance of the program to strategic objectives—e-learning programs focused directly on strategy should be subjected to business impact and ROI calculations.
  - the cost of the e-learning program—the more expensive the program, the more likely it is a candidate for an ROI calculation.
  - the visibility of the e-learning program—highly visible programs should be subjected to impact and ROI evaluation.
  - the size of the target audience—larger audiences demand higher levels of evaluation, at least for a sample of participants.
  - the investment of time—high commitments of time demand high levels of evaluation.
  - top executives' interest in the evaluation—if executives are interested in business impact and ROI evaluation, then it must be developed.

Question 7: How Does ROI Fit into the Evaluation of E-Learning?

Sound familiar?

- "Some people say ROI is all about money. What does ROI really mean?"
- "I believe in the importance of evaluation, but does that mean I have to conduct an ROI every time I evaluate a training program?"
- "Does ROI always have to be a number?"
- "There is so much talk about accountability these days. How does ROI fit into the picture?"

Why is it important to define ROI and use it consistently?

The term "return on investment" has been one of the most misused and misunderstood terms in our industry. The classical definition of return on investment, from finance and accounting, is earnings divided by investment. In the context of an e-learning evaluation, ROI becomes net monetary benefits from a program divided by the cost of the program. Although different measures are available, other definitions of ROI do not accurately and consistently reflect the investment and the cost involved in e-learning programs.

ROI needs to be utilized consistently so that comparisons can be made from one program evaluation to another. Return on assets (ROA), return on equity (ROE), and return on capital employed (ROCE) are inappropriate for this evaluation because they focus on issues unrelated to the actual investment in e-learning. Other uses of the word "return" should be avoided unless it actually is a monetary value. For example, the return on expectations (ROE) is often used to reflect success related to what the customer expected and may or may not require an actual monetary calculation. This could confuse the audience since many managers would suspect ROE to mean return on equity.

What do we know?

- The actual accounting-related definition for ROI for e-learning is net monetary benefits from the program divided by the actual cost of the e-learning program.
- To build credibility with the target audience for this type of calculation, a conservative approach is needed in the analysis. This approach requires that costs are fully loaded and that monetary benefits are included only if they are directly linked to the program.
- The development of the ROI requires three steps in a process model.

There must be a mechanism to isolate the effects of the e-learning program. There must be some method for converting data to monetary values to use directly in the numerator of the ROI formula. The fully loaded cost of the e-learning program should be tabulated.

- Other related ROI formulas should be avoided, such as return on assets (ROA), return on capital employed (ROCE), return on equity (ROE), or return on stockholders' equity, as they do not necessarily reflect the type of investment that constitutes e-learning investment and expenses.

Question 8: What Resources (Time and Money) Are Required to Evaluate E-Learning?

Sound familiar?

- "I have finally convinced my organization to invest more in training and development. Now you are telling me that I need to invest in evaluation?"
- "My organization is not willing to pay for an expensive impact evaluation."
- "Is ROI economically feasible?"

- "Aren't these elaborate evaluation plans for an organization with a highly equipped staff to follow through on the evaluation?"

Why is it important to determine the resources needed for evaluation?

While many training programs have not been required to undergo evaluation, the time to exercise a complete evaluation plan to measure the effectiveness of learning solutions is prior to the implementation of the program. Practitioners voice concern that the evaluation process requires an exorbitant amount of organization resources, including dollars, time, and people. Due to these concerns, evaluation plans are pushed aside and budgetary resources for training and evaluation continue to be shifted.

Because evaluation will require additional steps in the process and cost additional money, it is very important to indicate how many resources are required and to plan and allocate for those resources. Given the cost for the process, it is then possible to profile the appropriate evaluation mix. In this arrangement, evaluations can be conducted for some programs, leaving more expensive evaluations to those e-learning programs meeting the criteria outlined in Question 6.

Most major organizations pursuing significant change in their evaluation processes are spending 2-3 percent of the total training and development budget on measurement and evaluation. It is estimated that the total expenditures for measurement and evaluation for all training and development organizations are slightly less than 1 percent of the total budget. Although comprehensive measurement plans may require 4-5 percent of total learning solutions budget, an organization can migrate towards this target expenditure level over a period of 2 to 3 years as evaluation data provide economic benefits. Thus, it is possible to use the savings generated from the use of the evaluation information to actually drive the additional required budget expenditures.

What do we know?

- It is important to establish evaluation purposes. Developing evaluation purposes prior to implementation of a learning solution will determine the scope of the evaluation, the type of data collected, and the analysis.
- Evaluation is not an afterthought to be tacked onto the end of a training program. Integrating evaluation into the training process saves time, money, and staff.
- In order to maximize the evaluation process, it is important to share responsibilities for evaluation, including data collection, data analysis, interpreting results, consolidating information into report format, and technical support. Available staff to carry out the evaluation plan is a must.
- Working closely with IT staff in the evaluation process will support aspects of data collection, analysis, and report production.
- To establish a comprehensive evaluation plan, it is important to conduct a needs assessment and link overall purposes with those identified needs.
- Several cost-saving approaches can keep the commitments of time and cost to a minimum:

- Plan for evaluation early in the process.
- Build evaluation into the e-learning process.
- Share the responsibilities for evaluation.
- Require participants to conduct major steps.
- Use short-cut methods for major steps.
- Use sampling to select the most appropriate e-learning programs for ROI analysis.
- Use estimates in the collection and analysis of data.
- Develop internal capability to implement the ROI process.
- Use Web-based software to reduce time.
- Streamline the reporting process.

Question 9: Is It Really Possible to Isolate the Influence of E-Learning Solutions from Other Factors?

Sound familiar?

- "We cannot develop a control group arrangement or other research designs in our business. This is not a laboratory."
- "How do I know that the improvement in business impact is actually related to our e-learning program?"
- "There are too many factors influencing output measures for us to isolate e-learning as a contribution."

Why is it important to isolate the effects of e-learning?

Workplaces are becoming more complex. The implementation of an e-learning program with subsequent skill improvement and knowledge enhancement is only one of many influences which can drive behavior change and business impact. One of the toughest challenges for evaluation of e-learning is to isolate the effects of the e-learning from other influences. Fortunately, many approaches are available and this issue can be addressed in most, if not all, settings. The important point is to deliberately attack the issue, plan for the method of isolation, and follow through so that only the portion of the output data directly linked to e-learning is actually credited to the e-learning program.

What do we know?

- We know that without some method to isolate the effects of the e-learning from other influences, there is a high probability that the study is inaccurate; therefore, some method of isolation must be planned into the process.
- Several methods are accurate for isolating the effects of the process. These include the use of control group arrangements, trend line analysis, and sophisticated forecasting models. Unfortunately, in many settings it is not possible or practical to use these methods.

- Other less sophisticated methods can be used to allocate the actual improvement connected to an e-learning program, including:
  - participant's estimate of the e-learning program impact (percent)
  - supervisor's estimate of program impact (percent)
  - management's estimate of program impact (percent)
  - use of previous studies or expert input
  - calculating/estimating the impact of other factors
  - use of customer input.
- Research data is beginning to validate the accuracy of participant estimates of factors that influence their own performance. Many e-learning participants are able to indicate the extent to which the various influences have had a direct connection to their own performance measures, including business impact.

Question 10: Can ROI Be Forecast on Proposed E-Learning Solutions?

Sound familiar?

- "Senior management is asking for the ROI on our e-learning project before we get started. Is this really possible?"
- "Can I accurately forecast ROI if my company has no history of using e-learning programs?"
- "Why should I waste the time and energy to forecast an ROI on e-learning solutions when I could provide an ROI evaluation after implementing the program?"

Why is it important to forecast ROI?

In many e-learning projects, the client wants to know the projected payback from the project. E-learning projects often require significant investment; to venture into the expensive development process without having some sense of the payback is undesired by many clients. Consequently, there is tremendous pressure to forecast ROI even if it is not very accurate.

What do we know?

- The process for capturing the actual ROI calculation described in Question 7 can be utilized on a forecasting basis. The same elements in the process apply.
- Some e-learning project justifications are based on cost savings alone, where the fully loaded cost of the traditional learning is compared to the cost of e-learning. Cost savings result in a positive ROI. This assumes, of course, that the output of the learning process remains the same and the earnings or net monetary benefits from both approaches are consistent. This may not always be the case.
- The evaluation of an e-learning project should include a mechanism for forecasting the actual expected benefits, converted to monetary values, and then comparing the benefits to the projected cost. The difficulty in the process is to

estimate the actual change in business measures linked directly to the e-learning program.

■ The actual change in business measures can be predicted with input from a variety of groups. It is helpful to obtain input from one or more of the following:
  • program designers and developers
  • vendors, contractor, or suppliers, based on previous types of programs
  • results from other programs in other applications or implementations
  • managers and teams involved in the planned implementation
  • actual participants in the e-learning program
  • other subject matter experts who may understand the process and the dynamics of the e-learning program.

■ With reliable estimates of the actual impact, a sensitivity analysis can be developed showing the anticipated ROI obtained from different assumptions about changes in business measures. This analysis provides an array of possibilities, including the potential break-even point. This allows the client to make a better informed decision than an actual value.

■ Although the actual forecast can be developed using the steps outlined above, it is still an unreliable and inaccurate process. It is much better to try a small-scale implementation in one group, perhaps without all the bells and whistles, conduct an ROI analysis on the pilot program, and then use that data to make a decision regarding the implementation. This way, the six types of data (reaction, learning, application, impact, ROI, and intangible measures) are generated on the pilot program.

References

Kaplan, Robert S., and David P. Norton, "The Balanced Scorecard—Measures That Drive Performance," *Harvard Business Review*, 70, no. 1 (January-February 1992): 71-79.

Kirkpatrick, Donald L., *Evaluating Training Programs*. Alexandria, VA: American Society for Training & Development, 1975.

Jack Phillips, Ph.D. is the founder of Performance Resources Organization, the world's leading consulting firm specializing in accountability issues. He has authored or edited 20 books and 100 articles in the field of human resource development.

Patricia Pulliam Phillips, the vice president of business development for Performance Resources Organization, is responsible for the development of international and national alliances, client relations, and marketing initiatives.

Lizette Zuniga, Ph.D. has over five years of experience in the field of training and development. She currently serves as research associate for Performance Resources Organization.

Web-Based Distance Learning: How Effective Is It?

Jonathan Goodwin

As a follow-up to the lead article in this part of the yearbook, this article asks additional questions and looks at various issues in implementing Web-based distance learning.

Why Should We Look at Effectiveness in Web-Based Distance Learning?

It seems as if most of the attention regarding distance learning has been focused on expensive, synchronous technologies that allow video transmissions between subjects. In spite of these technological advances, web-based distance learning has become more and more popular in academia and in corporate training environments. Traditional courses have migrated to the web, and some "virtual universities" are promising entire academic programs online. Will the unique characteristics of the web limit the effectiveness of distance learning programs, or will the strengths the web has to offer overcome them? This paper discusses this topic in order to get a better grip on the effectiveness of web-based distance learning.

Characteristics of Web-Based Distance Learning

Early on, the web offered static content as the main vehicle for interaction. The first and still most popular format for interaction in web-based distance learning is asynchronous conferencing. With this technology, learners were able to constantly collaborate with others. This idea grew into document sharing, and learners were enabled to work together, regardless of the time and location.

Recently, web content has become more dynamic. Streaming video and audio is becoming more available and more distance learning sites are taking advantage of it. New collaboration tools are also emerging to allow merging of the static content, discussion forums, and multimedia. In the future, with broadband access, video will become an integral component of web-based distance learning.

Problems with Web-Based Distance Learning

Despite the advantages of distance learning, there are a few problems that need to be addressed about web-based distance learning. The main argument against its use is that the tools necessary for web-based distance learning are not ready for the average user. Kreitzberg (1998) points out that "many elements required for effective teaching are missing from today's Internet" (2). These elements are video, consistent look and feel, and the ability to include audio without plug-ins (Kreitzberg 2).

Kreitzberg's claims do hold some merit. At this time, due to telephone line restrictions, it is difficult to guarantee an Internet connection greater than 28.8kbps in the home. With that kind of connection speed, streaming video can be cumbersome. However, many educational and business facilities do have broadband Internet access (T1 lines, DSL, Cable Modems, and ISDN lines). If an instructor knows that their audience will have quick internet access, video becomes a viable medium for web-based instruction.

Extremely high dropout rates also plague early web-based distance learning programs. Wright and Yates (1999) place the dropout rate at 32%, which is much higher than tradition instruction. Despite the use of this statistic by many journals, there are no widely accepted explanations offered that explain why the dropout rate is so much higher on the web.

Benefits of Web-Based Distance Learning

The benefits of web-based distance learning share most of the advantages of other distance learning systems.

Cost-effectiveness. Distance learning cuts the expensive costs of transporting participants and instructors to a centralized location. Duplication costs of materials are also dramatically reduced.

Transcend regional barriers. Corporate and academic learning can take place anywhere. During an employee's lunch break, she could collaborate with classmates in another country. This flexibility allows distance education to reach a much broader audience than traditional instruction.

Increased emphasis on collaboration. With the new distance learning systems, it is less likely that the student will be a passive learner than in the traditional broadcast lecture format. The tools involved (teleconferencing, two-way video, asynchronous forums) encourage active participation and collaboration (Chute, Thompson, and Hancock, 1999).

The web format of web-based distance learning also has its own advantages.

Transcend time barriers. Streaming two-way video has not yet become an integral part of web-based distance learning. As a result, most of the exchanges of information have become asynchronous. Although this may seem to be a limitation, it gives the learners the flexibility to learn at their own convenience. This aspect of web-based distance learning also gives participants time to reflect on ideas and concepts before participating in a class discussion via an asynchronous conference.

Direct access to the experts. The web gives each learner direct access to the instructor of an online class. Discussion forums and email empower the participants to reach the instructor when questions arise without taking up classroom time or taking the risk of speaking to the entire classroom.

Low equipment costs. The web can be a low cost solution to distance learning, especially on the client end. The client requires an internet connection, a web browser, and a computer capable of running it.

Is Web-Based Distance Learning as Effective as Traditional Instruction?

The debate on the effectiveness has heating up lately, as different educators and authors have discussed the significance of moving instruction to the web. Most of this discussion has centered on the technology behind the instruction. Does the Internet lend itself to effective instruction, or does the technical infrastructure hinder the quality of learning? Unfortunately, there was little conclusive evidence to support either position, since most of the debate was framed around opinion (Phipps, 1999).

Recently the NEA has released a report issued to unearth the effectiveness of web-based distance learning. The NEA reported that the quality of instruction is the most important factor that determines the success and effectiveness of web based instruction. A good instructor and curriculum will make or break a classroom, whether it is hosted in a traditional classroom, a two-way videoconferencing system, or a web-based environment.

We can take this position a step further to conclude that the technology involved with web-based distance learning does not hinder the quality of instruction. In order to better understand and evaluate the effectiveness of distance learning, we must put the teaching together with the technology and look at the entire concept as a socio-technical system (Kling, 1999).

If your organization could benefit from a more cost-effective, collaborative, flexible learning environment, and you think the benefits of web-based instruction outweigh the obstacles that come with using the internet as an educational environment, then web-based distance learning might be a solution that can address some of the challenges your organization faces today. Web-based distance learning is already addressing the needs of hundreds of organizations and it is growing in number and sophistication every day.

References

Ashworth, Kenneth H. (1996). "Virtual Universities Could Produce Only Virtual Learning." *The Chronicle of Higher Education,* 6 September 1996.

Bruce, Bertram C. (1999). "Education Online: Learning Anywhere, Any Time." *Journal of Adolescent and Adult Literacy* 42(8): 662-666.

Chung, Curtis. (1999). Interview with Curtis Chung, Slashdot.org. 1999.

Chute, Alan G., Melody Thompson, and Burton Hancock. (1999). *The McGraw-Hill Handbook of Distance Learning: A "How to Get Started Guide" for Trainers and Human Resources Professionals.* New York: McGraw-Hill.

Graham, Steven, and Michael Dorf. (1999). "Distance Learning, Anywhere, Anytime." *Media and Methods* 36(1): 18-20.

Greengard, Samuel. (1999). "Web-Based Training Yields Maximum Returns." *Workforce* 78(2) (February): 95-97.

Gubernick, Lisa, and Ashlea Ebeling. (1997). "I Got My Degree Through E-mail." *Forbes,* 16 June 1997.

Inman, Elliot, Michael Kerwin, and Larry Mayes. (1999). "Instructor and Student Attitudes Toward Distance Learning." *Community College Journal of Research and Practice* 23(6) (September): 11-13.

Kling, Rob.(1999). "What Is Social Informatics and Why Does It Matter?" *D-Lib Magazine* 5(1) (January).

Kreitzberg, Charles B. (1998). "Distance Learning Isn't Going the Distance." *Internetweek* 719 (15 June): 45-50.

Laird, Ellen. (1999). "Distance Learning Instructors: Watch Out for the Cutting Edge." *The Chronicle of Higher Education* 45(38) (28 May): B6-7.

Marcus, J. (1999). "Distance Learning Fails to Close Gap." *Times Higher Education Supplement* (1385): 16.

Meister, Jeanne C. (1994). *Corporate Quality Universities: Lessons in Building a World-Class Work Force.* New York: American Society for Training & Development and Irwin.

Merisotis, James P., and Ronald A. Phipps. (1999). "What's the Difference?" *Change* 31(3) (May-June): 12-18.

Morris, Kathleen. (1999). "Wiring the Ivory Tower." *Business Week,* 9 August 1999: 90-93.

Phipps, Ronald A., and James P. Merisotis. (1999). *What's the Difference? A Review of Contemporary Research on the Effectiveness of Distance Learning in Higher Education.* The Institute for Higher Education Policy, 42.

Wright, Scott W., and Eleanor Lee Yates. (1999). "Distance Learning." *Community College Week* 11(22): 6-9.

Zhang, Ping. (1998). "A Case Study on Technology Use in Distance Learning." *Journal of Research on Computing in Education* 30(4): 398-420.

Jonathan Goodwin is currently with UNext.com, a company that provides online learning for adult students throughout the world. He received his master's degree in instructional systems technology from Indiana University, Bloomington, where he worked in the Center for Research on Learning and Technology in the School of Education. You can contact him at jongoodwin@unext.com.

Web-Based Training Evaluation Checklist

Janeen Rossi and Michael Levick

This is a short but useful checklist you can use to evaluate training Web sites and their utility. You can also use it as a design tool in preparing such a site.

Site Name:

Address:

A. User Friendliness

Layout: Screens and pages are designed well and scrolling is appropriate.

Navigation: Controls are intuitive, and easy to operate and find at all times.

❏ Contents
❏ Index

System Response: Learner knows what the system is doing at all times.

Wait Periods: Response times and file download times are good.

B. Attractiveness and Fun Factor

Interaction: Game, extended metaphor, or other special format engages the learner. Attractive Design: layout, colors, text styles, and graphics are inviting.

Media: "Eye candy" (media and animation used to retain attention) is used wisely.

❏ Graphics
❏ Animation

❏ Audio
❏ Video

Practice Activities: Dynamic, challenging, and engaging.

❏ Games
❏ Prizes and surprises

C. Learner Support Features

Help: Clear help screens/prompts are provided where needed.

Support: Expert/instructor, peer support via email or chat.

Aids: Glossaries, references, job aids and/or links are used effectively.

Status: Tracked and clearly reported to the learner.

❏ Sections completed
❏ Scores

D. Instructional Effectiveness

Goals and Objectives: Clearly communicated and achieved.

Active vs. Passive: Program uses active, student centered learning activities, not passive presentations.

❏ Passive
❏ Passive with quiz
❏ Drill
❏ Game
❏ Prompted practice
❏ Simulation

Chunking: Content is chunked in small, discrete blocks and sequenced in a clear, logical way.

Content: Good information mapping and clear, direct writing make the content easy to absorb.

Media: Support content and objectives, and are not an end in themselves.

E. Practice Activities and Feedback

Practice Frequency: Practice opportunities are frequent and are adequate to ensure mastery and retention.

Practice Quality: Practice activities are dynamic, challenging, and engaging.

❏ Job relevance
❏ Immediacy

Practice Application: Practice and testing require application of content, not just recall of facts and rules.

❑ Scenarios
❑ Simulation
❑ Actual task

Scoring: Practice and testing scores accurately reflect job readiness.

Feedback: Clear and instructive feedback is provided for all answer choices.

❑ Immediate
❑ Delayed
❑ Item-specific

Other Comments:

Janeen Rossi is a partner of eLearning Objects, LLC, an e-learning methods and technologies company in Menlo Park, CA. Janeen applies 10 years of training and development experience to corporate education consulting in Web-based training design and deployment, WBT tracking, learning object systems, and learning management systems (LMS). In 1997, Janeen founded the High Technology Media for Learning Special Interest Group for the Silicon Valley Chapter of ASTD. She holds a master's degree from the Stanford University School of Education. Contact her at janeen@elearningobjects.com.

Michael Levick is managing editor at Breakthebarriers.com, the Web-based training information site of ASTD Silicon Valley Chapter. Write him at editor@breakthebarriers.com.

Online Evaluation of Distance Learning: Benefits, Practices, and Solutions

Matthew V. Champagne and Robert A. Wisher

In this original and thoughtful piece created especially for this book, the authors explore some reasons for using online evaluation techniques of distance learning and explain the methodology, including a variety of examples and case studies.

Distance learning has become an increasingly prevalent form of organizational training in this technology-focused millennium. Frequently, however, proper evaluation of the delivery and design of the distance learning program is not conducted. How well did it work? What did we save? How can it work better next time? Organizations wishing long-term success should examine current training and evaluation products, especially online practices.

Due to the accelerated and enduring growth of the World Wide Web and its widespread influence, Web-based evaluations of training and evaluation products should be of particular concern to organizations (Pettit, 1999). Organizations and practitioners should be vigilant and knowledgeable consumers, wary of distance learning providers who incorporate evaluation products that construct results without accounting for evaluation limitations and base their results on poorly designed evaluations. Evaluations of distance learning programs should constantly attend to psychological and social limitations of the learning environment. Distance learning providers should make every attempt to use evaluation tools as a means of improving technical reliability, enhancing instructor performance, and increasing student learning.

Purpose and Goals

This article begins by articulating why evaluation is important and pondering why it is often underutilized. A popular model of evaluation is used as a reference point to describe how using the Internet removes the barriers of utilizing each level of this model. Four strengths of online evaluation (cost savings, providing feedback, closing the loop, and sharing information with stakeholders) are illustrated with application exercises and case studies from the authors' varied experiences with distance learning programs in corporate, military, and academic settings. Finally, we identify practices to avoid and practices to use that are derived from a psychological framework that considers both the technology and the human learning experience.

Throughout this article, we will discuss the value of using the Internet for evaluation. In particular, we will emphasize that the Internet is a superior method for distributing evaluative measures, collecting responses, and eliminating labor-intensive evaluation procedures. The Internet also makes available real-time evaluation information at nearly zero cost while gaining access to widespread respondents. For readers interested in designing and constructing a successful distance learning evaluation we refer you to our chapter, Champagne and Wisher (2000), in *The 2000/2001 ASTD Distance Learning Yearbook* (Mantyla, 2000).

The Benefits of Evaluation

Evaluation procedures are necessary to ensure the quality of any distance learning program. A sound evaluation will provide feedback to aid the decision-making of stakeholders, provide an objective measure of whether specific goals established by the stakeholders were met, and suggest areas for improvement. Evaluations can also help judge the success and value of a distance learning program, quantify its return on investment, and help prioritize resources for future training. Evaluations can be the impetus for change.

A popular framework for evaluating the effectiveness of a training program is that of Kirkpatrick (1994). The four levels of his model are briefly summarized in the box on the next page and are referred to elsewhere in the chapter.[1] It is generally accepted that conducting evaluation at all levels (reaction, learning, behavior, and results in the Kirkpatrick model) significantly strengthens the evaluation findings. However, this comprehensive approach is rare among organizations, mostly due to the high cost inherent in this practice (Tucker, Glover, Long, Haas, and Alemany, 1999). Even a less comprehensive approach to evaluation is often neglected. Preskill (2000) identified ten unjustified reasons that evaluation is not used, including (1) previous evaluation experiences have been disappointing or disastrous; (2) stakeholders do not believe the results will

---

[1]It should be noted that there are competing models used by practitioners (most notably the ROI model of Phillips, 1998) and our description of the benefits of online evaluation are meant to apply to evaluation in general and not to any specific model.

Kirkpatrick's Four Levels of Evaluation

Level I. Reaction: A measure of how students react to aspects of a training program.
Examples: Ratings of instructor effectiveness
Adequacy of training facilities
Quality of audio and video signals

Level II. Learning: A measure of how much a student increased knowledge, improved a skill, or changed an attitude.
Examples: Measures of performance on a written test or a hands-on assessment of skill, each compared to a before-training baseline

Level III. Behavior: A measure of the extent to which there has been a change in behavior due to participation in a program.
Examples: Surveys of supervisory or subordinate personnel or on-the-job observations. Interpretation can be difficult due to confounding factors from the job climate

Level IV. Results: A measure of the final results that occurred due to participation. in a program.
Examples: Increased sales
Decreased costs
A reduction in turnover

---

be used to make improvements; (3) evaluation costs are perceived to outweigh evaluation benefits; and (4) evaluation is considered an optional activity. It is one goal of this chapter to illustrate that an online evaluation system can not only provide a low-cost, highly efficient method for obtaining information and distributing results to stakeholders, but can also provide the quality and quantity of information necessary to successfully address the often-neglected comprehensive approach to evaluation.

Strength Number 1: Cost Savings

Online surveys, either homegrown or constructed by evaluation organizations, have become a popular tool for collecting responses for many purposes. Online surveys increase the extent and ease of distribution while simplifying or eliminating unwieldy administrative processes. This results in decreased costs and increased productivity due to the time savings typically required to distribute measures, collect responses, and follow through on "missing" returns. This productivity advances the time to analyze data, report findings, and act upon the findings.

Claims that online surveys are cost-effective are generally accepted, yet few systematic comparisons of the cost savings from online assessments have been conducted. Independent evaluations of the National Guard conducted by the Army Research Institute (e.g., Kronholm, Wisher, Curnow, and Poker, 1999) provide a striking example of the cost efficiency of the online assessment approach versus the paper-based approach. The following application exercise is based on short-term training events that are frequently provided during the National Guard's weekend training drills at armories across the country.

Application Exercise I: Efficiency of Online Assessments

The evaluation measure: The generic training evaluation for these events was a one-page instrument with 22 items divided into five evaluation categories: course and learning, instructor, technology, motivation, and demographics. The format was developed according to best practices described in the evaluation literature. Containing the evaluation to a single page, for example, has been shown to improve return rates. A complete review of the construction of this instrument, along with a literature review and evaluation findings from eight training events, is described in Wisher and Curnow (1998), available from the Defense Technical Information Center. For each event, a generic evaluation form was customized. Specifically, revisions were needed on two items concerning the specific training content. Training was conducted through satellite-based video teletraining. The average event had more than 300 participants at 18 remote sites.

Paper-based evaluation: Prior to initiating the online methodology in 1999, the paper-based evaluation of the instructional effectiveness of a DL training event was resource intensive. The production, assembly, and distribution of these paper-based evaluation forms required commitments of time and money. The paper-based approach demanded the tracking of evaluation packages, some delivered overnight. Furthermore, assembling and cleaning returned forms for optical scanning and checking the status of sites that had not yet returned their forms demanded additional time. When the final responses were entered, some by hand, the analysis was performed swiftly and spot reports to the stakeholders were transmitted within a day. For the paper approach, the time between the completion of the training event and initial reporting on training effectiveness and student reaction was seven days, most of the time spent waiting for packages or checking why some had not yet arrived.

A larger resource requirement was printing and distributing the form. Optically scannable forms needed to be forwarded to the sites and returned to the evaluators. The special paper designed for scanning required individual forms be printed directly from a laser printer, rather than be reproduced. The sensitivity of the scanner required demanded careful alignment during printing, with periodic checks and adjustments.

The process: Once printed, the forms were assembled for delivery: counts for each site, with an additional 10% as overage, along with a cover letter, instructions, and a pre-addressed, pre-paid return envelope, were inserted into a package. Facilitators were contacted within two days to ensure that they had received the materials.

Immediately after the training event, students were directed to complete the forms, which were then returned by a facilitator. Follow-up telephone calls were made to sites from which envelopes were not received within five days. Once received, each form was cleaned of stray pencil marks, partially filled circles, or inadvertent chads that could affect the scanning accuracy. The data file created was checked for errors (e.g., two answers to the same question) and ported to a statistical software program for analysis. The steps involved in distributing and collecting the evaluation forms for the paper-based and online methods are summarized in Table 1. (The online method is described shortly.) An important point here is that in the paper-based approach, economies of scale were hardly possible. The labor-intensive nature of production and distribution precluded a lowering of average costs through an increase in production quantity.

Online evaluation: An obvious solution to the labor-intensive approach was to offer the evaluation form through the Internet. In this way, customizing the form to a specific training event as described earlier would be straightforward. It would be possible to add additional items (as the goal of a single-page evaluation form no longer constrained the number of items presented), turn around the evaluation results quickly, and take advantage of the low marginal costs for including additional training sites. By 1999, the customer base had transitioned to Internet access, and nearly all participants have access either at the training site, at the workplace, or through connectivity at home. A reasonable sample, then, could now be reached through the Internet. (Details of the process to convert the paper-based form to an online form can be obtained through the authors.)

Task	Paper-Based	Online
Survey production	Tailored to event Printed on special paper	Tailored to event Posted on Internet
Survey distribution	Prepare overnight delivery Follow-up with sites	E-mail notification of URL
Return of evaluations	Pre-paid return envelopes Follow-up on delays	Automatic encoding of e-mail data file
Scanning and conversion to statistical analysis format	Hand corrections Optical scanning File conversion	One-step conversion of data file to SPSS format

Table 1. Steps in evaluation development, distribution, and data entry

Cost savings: The economic advantages of the online approach to evaluations should be apparent. A quick comparison of costs is offered here. The current analysis is based on the average training event conducted by the National Guard between 1996 and 1998 and evaluated by the Army Research Institute. These statistics are a mean of 17.6 remote sites with a mean of 18.6 participants per site, which equates to 327 participants per event, as derived from data in the Wisher and Curnow (1998) report. Labor costs were assumed to be $15.00 per hour in 1998 dollars, which was the cost for graduate students contracted through local universities. The cost data for the paper-based approach are detailed in Figure 1.

The online cost factors are quite simple: *time to modify the form + time to create a unique URL to that form + time to e-mail the enrollment provider with the new URL = one hour.* Upon completion of the form by participants, usually limited to six hours after the training, responses were automatically encoded into a tab-delimited format and emailed to the Army Research Institute. Converting this format to a dataset for statistical analysis added 15 minutes. There was no need to erase stray pencil marks or correct for multiple responses to an item. The cost for production and distribution for the online approach, then, was $18.75 (assuming the $15 per hour labor rate). This was a cost reduction of 97% from the $568.60 for the paper-based approach. Analyzing on the margin, the cost to add an additional site in the paper-based approach was $32.30 ($568.60 divided by 17.6 sites). Impressively, the cost of adding *additional sites in the online approach was effectively zero.* This is a striking example of a strength of the Internet economy, were the marginal cost of information is zero (Shapiro and Varian, 1999).

The time and costs to analyze data gained by either approach did not differ, requiring about four hours for a spot report limited to the essential findings. Obviously, if a more detailed analysis is needed, such as those requiring contingency breakout by demographic factors or trends between training events, the costs would increase comparably for either method. (Interested readers can use the worksheet provided in Figure 2 as a basis for calculating the costs for your existing paper-based distance learning evaluations.)

Strength Number #2: Ongoing Feedback

The evaluations of most distance learning programs are conducted like autopsies: after the training is over the evaluator tries to discover what went wrong. This is unfortunate because the key to successful evaluation is obtaining meaningful feedback from the respondents in order to provide stakeholders with timely information to make high impact decisions. This information includes not only quantitative responses, but also qualitative comments. The Internet provides a superior method for obtaining comments of higher quality and quantity and a means to organize the comments into meaningful results. For example, a recent evaluation of a distance learning management training course found that students typed an average of four times as many comments (62 words/student) when using an online evaluation form as students completing a paper-based version of the same evaluation form (15.4 words/student). Comments were also judged more detailed and relevant to the training in the online format. In addition, the comments delivered through the online system were automatically sorted by categories and searchable by key words, generating individual results and lists of action-oriented recommendations. Hand-written comments on the paper-based form had to be deciphered and re-typed and provided no clear means of ordering the information for the instructor's benefit.

Task	Marginal Cost	Total Cost
Survey Production		
Optical Forms	360 pages x $0.04 per page	$14.40
Printing	360 pages x $0.015 per page	$5.40
Photocopying	0 pages x $0.07 per page	$0.00
Labor	360 pages x $0.10 per page	$36.00
Subtotal		$55.80
Survey Distribution		
Administrative (sorting, collecting, typing, etc.)	12 hrs per event x $15.00 per hour	$180.00
Overnight delivery*	17.6 sites x $10.00 per site	$176.00
Return envelopes*	17.6 sites x $3.50 per package	$61.60
Follow-up/reminders*	17.6 sites x 8 min per site x $15.00 per hour	$35.20
Subtotal		$452.80
Data Conversion and Entry		
Quantitative data: *Data entry via optical reader/scanner:* Clean and scan forms	3 hrs labor x $15.00 per hour	$45.00
Convert to data analysis package	1 hrs labor x $15.00 per hour	$15.00
Data entry by hand: *Hand type to spreadsheet*	0 hrs labor x $15.00 per hour	$0.00
Qualitative data (Comments) *Transpose to spreadsheet (deciphering illegible comment, typing, proofing, classifying)*	0 hrs labor x $15.00 per hour	$0.00
Subtotal		$60.00
Analysis and Reporting		
Statistical analysis of results	8 hrs labor x $15.00 per hour	$120.00
Spot reporting to stakeholders	8 hrs labor x $15.00 per hour	$120.00
Final report writing	0 hrs labor x $15.00 per hour	$0.00
Subtotal		$240.00
Total Cost		**$808.60**

*events are for distance-based training only

Figure 1. An example of costs to prepare and conduct a paper-based training evaluation

Task	Marginal Cost	Total Cost
Survey Production		
Optical Forms	___ pages x $___ per page	$___
Printing	___ pages x $___ per page	$___
Photocopying	___ pages x $___ per page	$___
Labor	___ pages x $___ per page	$___
Subtotal		$___
Survey Distribution		
Administrative (sorting, collecting, typing, etc.)	___ hrs per event x $15.00 per hour	$___
Overnight delivery*	___ sites x $10 per site	$___
Return envelopes*	___ sites x $3.50 per package	$___
Follow-up/reminders*	___ sites x 8 min per site x $15 per hour	$___
Subtotal		$___
Data Conversion and Entry		
Quantitative data: *Data entry via optical reader/scanner:* Clean and scan forms	___ hrs labor x $15.00 per hour	$___
Convert to data analysis package	___ hrs labor x $15.00 per hour	$___
Data entry by hand: *Hand type to spreadsheet*	___ hrs labor x $15.00 per hour	$___
Qualitative data: (Comments) *Transpose to spreadsheet (deciphering illegible comment, typing, proofing, classifying)*	___ hrs labor x $15.00 per hour	$___
Subtotal		$___
Analysis and Reporting		
Statistical analysis of results	___ hrs labor x $15.00 per hour	$___
Spot reporting to stakeholders	___ hrs labor x $15.00 per hour	$___
Final report writing	___ hrs labor x $15.00 per hour	$___
Subtotal		$___
Total Cost		**$808.60**

*events are for distance-based training only

Figure 2. Worksheet to calculate costs to conduct a paper-based training evaluation

An illustration of the use of an online formative evaluation that provides feedback to improve the delivery of distance learning is exemplified in the following application exercise. The training is conducted for the National Guard through video teletraining to 83 soldiers at five remote sites around the country. The participants meet one weekend each month for approximately 12 hours of qualification training on topics related to a military specialty. The course length is eight months culminating in an intensive two-week hands-on training exercise. This application exercise is based on the first three iterations of training conducted between November 2000 and January 2001.

Application Exercise II: Ongoing Feedback
The evaluation measure: The practice is to have each participant complete an Internet-based evaluation form on site immediately upon completion of that weekend's training. Building on the measure discussed in Application Exercise I, each form has a set of core items that are repeated each month, supplemented with items related to the specific content trained that month and special items, such as established scales that measure motivation. Performance measures recorded during the course are handled separately. The administration time is approximately seven minutes. The form also accepts written comments.

The process: Between November 2000 and January 2001, three training sessions were conducted, each ending on Sunday with an online evaluation. The return rates averaged 88%. The responses were encoded in a tab-delimited format accessible from a Website, allowing the evaluators to import the data directly into a statistical analysis package the following morning. The analysis and preparation of a four-page evaluation "spot report" was completed in six hours and emailed to the primary stakeholders. These included a high-level administrator and the course manager, who in turn provided the report with annotation to technicians and instructors for action.

Two recurring measures have been the ratings on the perceptions of the delivery technology and the comments section. The mean ratings for the first three iterations are provided in Table 2 with the standard deviation reported from the third iteration.

The benchmark data in the second column of Table 2 were derived from historical evaluation data using the same rating scales with a similar demographic group reported in Wisher and Curnow (1998). The benchmark serves to provide a guidepost—ratings should equal or exceed this benchmark if proper adjustments are made during the course. As can be observed in Table 2, the quality of audio remained constant, but slightly below the benchmark. The quality of video and location of the video screen were well below the benchmark during the first iteration, but have steadily improved. The instructor effectiveness has remained slightly below the benchmark. The opportunity to ask questions has remained slightly above the benchmark, as has the responsiveness to those questions. Finally, the overall learning environment has shown a steady increase and has nearly converged with the benchmark. After the first and second iterations, the course manager was able to apply these formative data in directing adjustments to the video and classroom setting, contributing to the improvement in the overall learning environment while the course is still ongoing.

Task	Historical Mean	November Mean	December Mean	January	
				Mean	SD
Quality of audio	3.8	3.6	3.5	3.6	1.04
Quality of video	4.2	3.3	3.2	3.8	0.96
Location of video screen	4.4	3.8	3.7	4.1	0.86
Instructor effectiveness	3.9	3.7	3.4	3.7	0.80
Opportunity to ask questions	3.7	3.9	3.9	4.0	0.92
Responsiveness to student questions	3.9	4.0	3.8	4.2	0.70
Overall learning environment (i.e., lighting, noise, room size, etc.)	4.0	3.5	3.6	3.9	0.92

Table 2. Ratings of perceptions of technology (5-point scale where 1 = poor; 5 = excellent)

As stated earlier, the online form is ideal for collecting and organizing comments more quickly than is possible with a paper-based evaluation. This feedback can be quickly directed to the stakeholders in order to improve the learning process. Some example comments are provided below. For example, an early complaint was the lack of handouts at several of the remote sites. The course manager was able to remedy this problem after the second iteration, the effect of which was no complaints during the third iteration.

Sample Comments:

- "My only problem was not having any type of visual aid for the assessment block of instruction. I feel that my performance on the test was poor due to the fact that I need to see something—slides, or handout to help me get the whole picture."
- "Some things don't seem pertinent; most of it seems good, although a bit redundant. Over-explanation is torture, but some instructors may feel it necessary."
- "I understand that it must be difficult to conduct a course covering so much information, with so many students. The instructors really seem to work hard to get the info across. Personally I'm having a hard time picking up the information, because I'm much more of a "hands on" learner than a lecture learner."
- "Need to provide materials that are relevant to the class in a timely fashion, thereby allowing us to study and come prepared for in class instruction."

Although not all of the shortcomings of the training program or individual preferences can be remedied in a short time, such comments form the basis for improving future courses.

Strength Number 3: Closing the Loop

Feedback is critical for improving training programs. However, not just any type of feedback will do. If basic principles are not followed, feedback will be ineffective. Using the "autopsy" approach, for example, is ineffective because the feedback arrives much too late to be useful. Feedback needs to be specific to the stakeholder in terms of its breadth. Too much feedback will not be digested and too little will not be helpful in the decision-making process. It is also important that the feedback be delivered in a manner targeted to each stakeholder. Use of email, fax, written reports, and telephone calls can all be successful. Stakeholders also need to receive the feedback in a just-in-time fashion. Some stakeholders need to know immediately, others at some point later in the training, and others may need only a full report or accounting at the end of the training program. Tulgan (1999) summarized several of these principles by stating that good evaluation should be FAST (frequent, accurate, specific, and timely).

A final important principle is called "closing the loop" or providing feedback to the feedback. Obtaining responses from the trainees is only one half of the feedback loop. The evaluation process should include a procedure for instructors to respond to trainee feedback. It is not enough to tell respondents that we "appreciate your comments" and will "make necessary changes," as many unsolicited email surveys allege. A program that continues to request feedback from individuals without telling them what changes were made based on their feedback will increase apathy toward future measures and reduce the quantity and quality of feedback.

The following case study illustrates the successful use of these feedback principles in a distance learning program.

Case Study #1: Example of Proper Feedback and Closing the Loop

Albany International is the world's largest manufacturer of paper machine clothing and the industry's leader in technological innovations. In June 1999, as part of its ongoing training program for employees, Albany International (AI) conducted a four-day voluntary training program on supervisory skills training. The instructor-led training was delivered from AI headquarters (Albany, NY) via satellite to 235 company managers, administrators, engineers, and technicians at 21 sites in 10 countries. The trainer had never taught in a distance-learning format, but planned to compensate by "closing the loop": providing feedback to the trainees' feedback.

After the first three-hour training session, consisting of discussion, case studies, and lecture, the trainees returned to their offices, logged into LotusNotes® and retrieved an evaluation form tailored to the training session. The evaluation consisted of reaction measures to the audio, video, and delivery of the training, perceptions of the trainer and instructional materials, outcome measures based on the instruction, and open-ended comments. Trainees completed the 23-item measure and submitted their responses. The data was received by IOTA Solutions where it was automatically collated and analyzed, comments synthesized into action-oriented solutions, and the at-a-glance results emailed to the instructor.

As would be expected on the first day of a distance-learning program, the trainees had many concerns and comments. Rather than ignore the feedback of the trainees, the instructor closed the loop by using the action-oriented solutions at the opening of the second day's training session. He acknowledged that trainees from Brazil did not understand his jokes about the New York Yankees, trainees from Korea wanted more examples relevant to their daily concerns at the plants in Asia, and trainees from France were having technical difficulties with the equipment (which technicians had immediately fixed). The instructor used the at-a-glance feedback to address and remove barriers to training that would otherwise have gone uncorrected until the training program was over.

After the second three-hour training session was completed, the same evaluation process was used. The trainees filled out the measure, submitted their responses, and the instructor received an emailed report summarizing the essential areas of concerns for the trainees. Notably, 85% of the trainees reported that their feedback was satisfactorily addressed—a tremendous accomplishment given the large number of trainees spread across five continents.

During the third training session, the instructor again presented the results of the feedback to the trainees, with the action-oriented solutions focused primarily on learning outcomes rather than barriers to learning. Many of the trainees, although situated thousands of miles away, were pleased that the instructor addressed their individual concerns as if they were in a small classroom. By the end of the four-day training session, the instructor had satisfactorily addressed nearly every barrier to learning and most of the individual learning problems that arose during the training.

"Closing the loop" benefited the organization, the instructor, the trainees, and the training program. By providing meaningful and action-oriented solutions based on trainee feedback, the instructor, technicians, and those responsible for administering the training made changes in midstream, resulting in higher retention levels, tremendous cost savings, more favorable instructor ratings, more satisfied trainees, and a higher-quality training program.

Strength Number 4: Sharing Information with Stakeholders

Stakeholders are the intended users of the results and the decision-makers for whom the evaluation provides feedback. They include administrators, technicians, instructors, and even students. Knowing their interests and defining their expectations is a critical first step. The needs of stakeholders are not identical and vary with position. Some will be concerned at the policy level (do the overall effects warrant continuation?), others will be concerned at the programmatic level (what are the obstacles to learning in this program?), and still others will be concerned at a technical level (is the audio and video quality satisfactory?). In order for an evaluation to provide information to aid the decision-making process of the stakeholders in a distance learning program, it is not enough to provide a single overall report of findings. Rather, each stakeholder needs to be provided with meaningful, just-in-time information in a manageable format that can be quickly reviewed and acted upon.

The following case study[2] illustrates the power of the Internet to create an "embedded assessment" that delivers the correct amount of information in the correct format to each stakeholder in order for meaningful change to occur.

Case Study #2: Embedded Assessment to Aid Stakeholders

Pace University (White Plains, NY) and its partners, the Council for Adult and Experiential Learning (CAEL) and the National Advisory Coalition for Telecommunications Education and Learning (NACTEL), have created a highly successful distance learning telecommunications degree program. All training is delivered asynchronously over the Internet to employees of Citizens Communications, Qwest Communications, SBC, and Verizon Communications.

One of the innovative steps taken by Pace University was the design of an online testing and student authentication system that designated proctors to administer and supervise examinations for these telecommunications employees. This was necessary to ensure that students who earn a degree at an accredited university have learned the knowledge implied by the degree. This system has been successful in verifying that students, who have never set foot on Pace University's campus, have followed all necessary examination guidelines and have earned credit for each course.

In order to evaluate this innovative system and to offer continual improvements, the online testing coordinator (OTC) needed to quickly identify individual problems and provide timely responses to questions from students and proctors after each examination. Initially, a paper-based survey was emailed or faxed to proctors and students to collect the necessary information. However, this method suffered from the many inefficiencies of paper-based methods. A second form was constructed by retyping the survey questions into the administration tools available within the online learning platform (Blackboard®). This eliminated the need for paper-based surveys and would save time by automatically calculating the average responses. However, the proctors did not have access to the administration tools and they continued with the paper-based method.

To analyze the results of the surveys, the OTC entered the data and comments by hand, and used Microsoft® Excel to create the statistics, charts and graphs necessary for her reports. Not only was this a very time-consuming process, but she was unable

[2]The work described in this case study was funded by the Learning Anytime Anywhere Partnerships (LAAP) program, which is administered by the Fund for the Improvement of Postsecondary Education (FIPSE), a unit of the U.S. Department of Education. The LAAP program supports academic and corporate partnerships involving asynchronous, innovative, scalable, and nationally significant distance education projects.

to track at the individual level. For example, if a student said that his proctor did not receive the exam password, the identity of the student or proctor could not be determined and the problem would be difficult to resolve.

The OTC needed richer and more timely information than could be provided by either one of these methods. She needed to have a process to allow frequent and ongoing feedback from students and proctors in order to quickly address problems and concerns while the course was still in session. The solution was to incorporate an embedded assessment into the online testing program. This system would allow the OTC to view real-time trends from the respondents as well as pinpoint individual problems. She could then close the loop by immediately calling or emailing the proctors and students with the answers and for follow up.

The embedded assessment consisted of surveys with reliable and valid questions, designed to provide specific solutions and allow for informative comments. The stakeholder interface was designed to provide the OTC with the appropriate feedback necessary to quickly interpret the massive amount of data and pinpoint problems. The result was that the OTC could now monitor and immediately address the concerns of nearly 600 students and proctors across 12 courses.

According to the OTC, this embedded assessment had the following benefits: 1) instant check of the number of students completing the surveys; 2) moment-by-moment view of the raw results; 3) students were more willing to complete the survey honestly because their responses were independent of the course and there was less fear that their responses would affect their grade; 4) surveys could be accessed via the internet by both students and proctors; 5) easy to read printable report, including all comments; 6) tracking of individual responses necessary for updating information and correcting problems; 7) centralized the data and a complete summary report over a given time frame to expedite comparisons between surveys and across time; and 8) automatic drill-down features to determine why students and proctors gave particular responses.

This embedded assessment system was tailored to provide a single stakeholder with a view of all available information. However, other organizations could tailor the assessment to provide various stakeholders with varying amounts of information necessary to make important decisions.

Successful Evaluation Practices

The evaluations of most distance learning programs are conducted in a post-hoc manner: after the training is over the evaluator tries to figure out what happened. Other evaluations are conducted without providing the necessary quality and quantity of feedback to the stakeholders. These and many other unsuccessful practices can lead to ambiguous results, lack of improvements, and frustration by all parties. Evaluators should avoid these practices by implementing some of the successful evaluation prac-

---

Unsuccessful and Successful Evaluation Practices

Unsuccessful evaluation practices

1. Evaluate performance and attitudes only after training has ended
2. Fail to give the right amount of feedback to stakeholders when they need it most
3. Focus on the "average" learner, rather than the individual learner
4. Do not provide learners or instructors with timely feedback
5. Give instructors feedback that is unwieldy and difficult to interpret

Successful evaluation practices

1. Develop process to allow frequent and ongoing feedback from trainees
2. Use the correct amount, type, and delivery style of feedback
3. Provide "just-in-time" solutions to all stakeholders
4. Provide meaningful, action-oriented, at-a-glance feedback to stakeholders
5. Allow procedure for instructors to respond to trainee feedback
6. Emphasize individual difference
7. Focus on learning, behavioral, results, and ROI outcomes
8. Use valid and reliable measures of learning, attitudes, and behaviors
9. Incorporate "Embedded Assessment" tools

---

tices illustrated in this chapter. The box on this page contains a more complete checklist of both successful and unsuccessful evaluation practices.

Conclusions

The current end-of-training, paper-based evaluation systems used by many organizations do not provide the quality, quantity, or timeliness of feedback required to make interim improvements to a distance training program. An online evaluation system could better serve organizations by providing the many benefits outlined in this chapter. The conversion to an online evaluation system is not difficult, particularly since the same technology that is readily available to deliver distance learning can also deliver evaluation measures while the training is still in session. For example, some development packages for online courses include automatic assessment features for tracking student performance, identifying course improvements, and enabling certification.

The complex and time-consuming stages of an evaluation, including measurement construction, production, and distribution, data collection and analysis, and reporting of results, may all be conducted more efficiently via technology-based means. Popular models of evaluation, such as those of Kirkpatrick and Phillips, which are rarely implemented in full form due to the labor-intensive nature of the process, may be fulfilled by using the tools and processes described in this chapter. By incorporating a continuous process of input, feedback, and change into current distance learning program evaluations, organizations can begin data mining the wealth of information collected online. Organizations can then better manage training as an agent of change.

References

Champagne, M. V., and Wisher, R. A. (2000). Design considerations for distance learning evaluations. In K. Mantyla (Ed.), *The 2000/2001 ASTD Distance Learning Yearbook.* New York: McGraw-Hill.

Kirkpatrick, D. L. (1994). *Evaluating training programs: The four levels.* San Francisco: Berrett-Koehler.

Kronholm, E.A., Wisher, R.A., Curnow, C.K., and Poker, F. (1999). *The transformation of a distance learning training enterprise to an Internet base: From advertising to evaluation.* Paper presented at the Northern Arizona University NAU/web99 Conference.

Pettit, F.A. (1999). Exploring the use of the World Wide Web as a psychology data collection tool. *Computers in Human Behavior, 15,* 67-71.

Phillips, J. J. (1998). Level 4 and beyond: An ROI model. In S. Brown and C. Seidner (Eds.), *Evaluation corporate training: Models and issues.* (pp. 113-140). Boston: Kluwer Academic Publishers.

Preskill, H. (2000). *Taking evaluation into the 21st century: Linking evaluation to the organization's learning systems.* Paper presented at the American Society for Training and Development conference.

Shapiro, C., and Varian, H. (1999). *Information Rules: A strategic guide to the network economy.* Boston: Harvard Business School Press.

Tucker, R. L., Glover, R. W., Long, D. W., Haas, C. T., and Alemany, C. (1999). *Return-on-investment (ROI) analysis of education and training in the construction industry.* Retrieved 10 February 2001 from the World Wide Web: http://www.cdc.gov/niosh /elcosh/docs/d0100/d000132/d000132.html.

Tulgan, B. (1999). *FAST feedback* (2nd ed.). Amherst, MA: HRD Press.

Wisher, R. A., and Curnow, C. K. (1998). *An approach to evaluating distance learning events.* Technical Report 1084, Alexandria, VA: U.S. Army Research Institute for the Behavioral and Social Sciences.

Notes

The views expressed here are those of the author and do not necessarily reflect the views of the U.S. Army Research Institute or the Department of Army.

The authors would like to thank Christina Curnow, Kara Orvis, and Jim Hunter for technical assistance in application exercise number two, and to thank Nina Y. Lee for her valuable assistance on earlier drafts of this article.

Dr. Matthew V. Champagne has served as a faculty member, researcher, practitioner, and consultant in the area of evaluation for over 10 years. He has authored numerous articles on research design and evaluation of distance learning and training programs and is President of IOTA Solutions, Inc. Dr. Champagne holds a doctorate degree in industrial and organizational psychology from Purdue University.

IOTA Solutions creates online evaluation instruments that deliver immediate feedback and meaningful solutions to stakeholders while training is in process. IOTA's evaluation methodologies and embedded assessment tools have become the standard for dozens of training organizations and higher education distance learning programs.

Dr. Robert A. Wisher is a Senior Research Psychologist with the Army Research Institute in Alexandria, Virginia. Dr. Wisher conducts research on the effectiveness of distance learning on a broad range of learning categories and training technologies. He was awarded the U.S. Distance Learning Association 1999 Most Outstanding Achievement Award by an Individual for his contributions in research and evaluation. He was a Visiting Scholar to the Center for Research on Learning and Technology, Indiana University, during the 2000-2001 school year. Dr. Wisher holds a doctorate degree in experimental psychology from the University of California, San Diego.

Part Nine

Distance Learning Case Studies

ow have others done it? Answering that question is what Part Nine is about. We've selected three case studies dealing with different aspects and problems incurred with implementing distance learning. The first article, "E-Learning at IBM: A Case Study" by Nancy Lewis, the director of management development for IBM in its Armonk, NY headquarters, explains the details of how IBM approached the implementation of e-learning for its executives across the organization—from planning to execution to evaluation to lessons learned. This is a very useful article for those interested in the successful implementation of blending e-learning with classroom-based training in their organization.

Next we include Ramona R. Materi's "Choosing an Authoring Tool for Web-Based Training: A Case Study." Authoring tools are software that facilitates the effective development of Web-based courses. There are different types of tools available, and this case study looks at how the training staff of a large but unidentified company found the tools they were looking for. While this article focuses on the selection of tools, the concerns involved in making decisions go beyond tools. It gives a good sense of what issues need to be addressed in setting up Web-based training.

The final article here, "Will CBT Produce the Results You Need? A Case Study" by Steven V. Benson, attempts to answer the question in the title, using his firm, Kinetic Concepts, Inc., a therapeutic products company. He explains why the company went to CBT and includes various charts used to determine the efficacy of this decision and then documents the positive results they achieved.

E-Learning at IBM:
A Case Study

Nancy Lewis

This article documents how IBM implemented e-learning into its training strategy. Specifically, you will get an inside look into how "Big Blue" created the "Basic Blue Program" for managers around the globe. What is interesting to note is that they did not eliminate a classroom experience *for the learners; they enhanced it by surrounding it with a strong e-learning foundation. As well, they built in evaluations from Level I to Level V. Here's their story including documentation of the facts.*

Managers' leadership development is critical to our company's long-term success. Ongoing training and skills improvement is very important. In assessing our training programs, we recognized several problems and opportunities for improvement.

Problem #1. Previously we trained 13,000 US managers. In 1997, our training division was reorganized, downsized and given global responsibility. We are now responsible for the leadership development of 30,000 managers in 72-plus countries worldwide—with fewer resources.

Problem #2. Managing in a matrixed organization; collaborating across functional and national boundaries, teaming within electronic spaces, hiring and retaining talent in a competitive industry—these are just a few of the growing leadership challenges not being addressed by our previous five-day in-class programs.

Problem #3. Our managers are pressed for time. Most work 10- to 12-hour days. Taking them off-site for additional class time is prohibitive.

Our Task

To design and deploy a richer, more extensive learning experience for managers worldwide, covering five times as much material for a time-pressed audience, yet positively received by participants.

A Twofold Solution

1. Change one-time week-long classroom "event" into a one-year learning *process*
2. Employ a blended, multi-modality approach to management development, integrating intranet *e-learning* with a *classroom experience*. The approach incorporates:
   - online performance-support modules and interactive simulations
   - virtual collaborative workspaces
   - customized personal assessments
   - online content mastery tests
   - on-the-job training via second-line manager coaches
   - develop and implement an evaluation framework

Results

Level I. a new blended e-learning process enthusiastically received by participants
Level II. knowledge-gain is five times previous new-manager intervention
Level III. positive changes in behaviors of targeted competencies and managerial styles
Level IV. increased productivity and improved business results
Level V. substantial cost savings, template re-use savings, and lawsuit avoidance

Background

In mid-1997, our company reorganized. Our training staff was cut, while our student base was expanded from 13,000 managers in the United States to *all* 30,000 company managers worldwide. Marketplace changes simultaneously were broadening managers' development needs, creating pressure to include more skills development in an already jam-packed five-day classroom program.

Challenge. We were faced with developing a wider range of leadership skills for nearly twice as many students, worldwide—and with fewer resources. As our manager audience is typically time constrained (most work 10-12 hours/day, some longer), the option of increasing our five-day off-site class time was unfeasible. We needed a new approach.

Proposed Solution and Goal. Our proposal: (1) to reconceptualize management development as an extended process, rather than a week-long classroom "event," and (2) to employ technologies to augment and enhance the classroom intervention. Our initial goals were: (1) that the new model must be enthusiastically received by its time-pressed students despite their having to learn five times as much material than previously delivered, and (2) that our new delivery must be equally as effective in knowledge-gain and behavior change as our in-class intervention.

Design. Since January 1999, our new process has been delivered to 6600 new first-line managers worldwide. These new "first-lines" are 17% of the total management population (30,000) in a company numbering over 300,000 employees. Students are from every company profession (programming, research, marketing, services, distribution, etc.) and every geography (North America, Latin America, Europe, Africa, and Asia Pacific). The design of the process encompasses three distinct phases, together lasting 52 weeks:

The Three Phases

Phase I: 26 weeks of self-paced, online learning

Upon appointment, new first-line managers engage in 48 hours of self-paced instructional activities within a Lotus LearningSpace, available 24 hours/day on the company intranet via each manager's desktop or laptop computer. Each LearningSpace cohort numbers 24 new managers, who engage with each other in a virtual, asynchronous workroom. However, each manager progresses individually at his or her own pace, at an average of two hours/per week, working through five online units of modular content: in all, a total of 18 mandatory and elective managerial topics, custom-developed for our company's particular culture and business environment, with additional content from the online *Harvard ManageMentor* (Harvard Business School Publishing).

- Each mandatory topic requires the manager to display knowledge mastery by achieving a minimum score on an online test, which can be repeated until mastery is attained.
- Fourteen interactive online simulation modules immerse the user into typical, real-life business scenarios—situations in Human Resource Policies and Programs issues. The manager makes decisions by consulting the company intranet's HR policy database, and learns from his or her mistakes how to search effectively within this huge and critical online information resource.
- A LearningSpace tutor (an experienced company manager/trainer skilled in facilitating in a collaborative online workspace) guides managers via online and telephone support.
- Each new manager's second-line manager works closely with him or her to support four "in-field" activities (meeting management, goal setting, retention, etc.) with direct reports.

Phase II: The in-class five-day "Learning Lab"

This is held at company learning centers worldwide. Because information transfer has occurred in Phase I, the Learning Lab focuses on experiential, higher-order learning. For example, the Coaching Model based upon Sir John Whitmore's *Coaching for Performance* was introduced in the Phase I online activities. Managers practiced applying this new knowledge in the eight interactive scenarios within the 5000-screen Coaching Simulator accessed online. In the Phase II Learning Lab, students move directly into action learning, as all managers bring a real-life situation from their jobs and are coached by a student colleague to define and address the issue. Participants are thus able to jump into higher-order application because both the basic information transfer and skills practice first occurred though *e-learning*. Other leadership/management topics are addressed similarly.

The focus of the Learning Lab is for the manager to gain self-knowledge as an individual, understand the role as a team or group leader and as a member of the organization. Validated 360-degree instruments, case studies, and experiential exercises are used to address each perspective. These include the Leadership Competencies Survey, Hermann Brain Dominance Instrument, the Hay/McBer Climate and Managerial Style Assessment, and a validated feedback tool created by our company's research division. Case studies include cases customized from *Harvard Business Review* and several developed by in-house subject matter experts. Experiential exercises were created from work done at the US Military Academy at West Point and the Fuqua School of Business at Duke University. Teaming is important in our business, and students are assigned to learning teams. This creates small learning communities as teams remain together though all three phases. This recursive approach creates an environment where students learn from each other as much as they learn from experts. Within the entire five-day Learning Lab, less than one hour is used for lecture.

Phase III: 25 weeks of online learning
This is similar to Phase I. However, Phase III content is more complex and focused on application of skills and knowledge. Upon conclusion of the Learning Lab, each manager creates an Individual Development Plan and an Organizational Action Plan. During Phase III, these plans are reviewed with the first-line's manager. When satisfied that the student has demonstrated competency in the workplace, the second-line manager signs off. This final step in the learning process ensures that learnings are applied in the workplace. In addition to such application activities, students also complete more *e-learning* modules. Unlike Phase I, where most modules are mandatory, the student chooses topics of personal relevance in Phase III. This design encourages managers to take an active role in the planning and execution of their own development. Phase III completes the new manager process.

Development Resources

Eight full-time employees are involved in our program development, engaged with selected vendors in overall needs assessment, design, delivery, and evaluation, and redesign. Technologies included Lotus LearningSpace, online simulators, Harvard ManageMentor, web-based QuickCase modules, online personal assessment instruments, and performance-support QuickViews. The per-day student cost of 5000 managers worldwide participating in a traditional classroom 128-hour program would have been $350.00 for module development, instruction, participant time, travel, and room and board. This new e-learning approach costs $136 per student day, resulting in delivering five times more content at one-third the cost.

Documentation

Needs Identification. Given our company's large size (307,000 employees), our needs analysis is generated from a variety of sources:

- Managers—ongoing qualitative interviews with managers provide day-to-day perspective of what actual line-managers need.
- Global Learning Integrators—seven senior executives, representing all geographies and all industries within our company, raise specific business-related and geography-related issues to be solved via a global approach.
- HR Solutions Focus Team surveys all employees, legal divisions, and employee-relation officers for management problems and concerns.
- Our business unit enjoys founding-membership status in the Harvard Business School Publishing New Media Partners Council. This consortium comprises 20 non-competing *Fortune* 500 companies identifying overall trends in industry that impact management development.
- Company CEO and Vice Presidents introduce large organizational issues to be solved and future direction of our company to follow.
- Internal development specialists communicate insights, thoughts, and trends from academic conferences and colloquia (e.g., the Conference Board, ASTD's and *Training* magazine's annual conferences and expositions, etc.).
- Mayflower Survey. Our organization is provided a comparative analysis of our management standing vis-à-vis 20 other companies within our industry in regard to retention statistics, employee attitude, hiring, emerging employee relations, trends and issues, bench marking practices and policies.
- Global Employee Survey. Each year our company surveys one-third of our entire employee population. The questionnaire typically includes 24 questions on perception of the manager and company management to identify specific management education needs.
- Interviewed 47 line executives from units to identify issues and impact on management.
- The results from 51,400 360-degree management assessment surveys were reviewed.

These sources identified a significant increase in the number of core, common, and critical managerial and leadership skills required to drive our future business success, including 11 specific leadership competencies validated by the Hay/McBer study (e.g., breakthrough thinking, coaching, building organizational capability, straight talk, etc.). Managing in a remote-and-mobile environment, collaborating across geographic boundaries and in virtual spaces, understanding and accommodating cultural differences in communication and negotiation were among other important behaviors warranting inclusion within extremely limited class time.

Design Values

Organizational Interests. Design efforts were guided by two organizational objectives: to develop superior leadership skills in our new managers and to harness the potential of e-learning. Superior leadership has been found to foster a high-performance working environment to increase business results, and *e-learning* allows us not only to reach students globally but also, just as important, to put into our own practice our company's new external-client "e-business" approach, i.e., to "walk the talk" of using distance, networked technologies to reach our "customers" who are distributed around the world.

Research conducted for IBM by a leadership consulting firm (Hay/McBer) found that 11 specific Leadership Competencies differentiate outstanding from typical leaders in our company. Linkage of these competencies to managerial styles and ultimately to organizational climate formed the basis for the corporate leadership framework. This model, with supporting research, ties leadership quality to business results. This provides the content road map for driving desired learning, is endorsed and supported at senior levels of the company, and is the model for all leadership training in our organization.

Employee Needs. Our managers are pressed for time. Most work 10-12 hours per day, some more. Being able to enhance leadership and management skills in the most time-efficient way is of critical importance to managers. Moreover, being able to fulfill managers' individual performance-support needs in a "just-in-time" manner is equally compelling. The task was to create an instructional model that employs our network infrastructure to allow managers to make best use of resources to fulfill both the organizational learning needs and the performance-support and skill-building needs of our managers worldwide.

The New "Blended" Design. Our new design blends four "tiers" of delivery in the tradition of a learning hierarchy. Each tier builds upon learnings developed at the previous tier, beginning with information exchange and progressing on to skills development to collaborative person-to-person interaction. The four tiers together comprise a system of tools and applications that constitute a continuing *process* of learning, instead of mere "events" such as one-time classes or workshops.

The Four Tiers

Tier 1. Information and just-in-time online performance support. These online resources are available to the manager via the company intranet anytime, anywhere. Their purpose is primarily to address an ongoing, immediate management concern. The manager with an existing problem accesses the relevant topic either via an index

---

or the keyword search engine and brings the material directly to desk top for online reading, printing to hard copy, or mailing to an e-mail account. Best thinking on over 50 leadership and people-management topics of concern to our managers is available, including materials provided by Harvard Business School Publishing. Tools—printable worksheets and checklists—are also available for specific action issues. Links to important external web sites are also highlighted. Because we team globally, managers need to have access to policies and practices in different countries. Tier 1 offerings allow managers quick and easy access to all global HR material.

Tier 2. Interactive online learning. Managers further enhance their knowledge and personal development beyond the awareness level by engaging in immersive simulations of the issues presented in Tier 1. The online Coaching Simulator alone comprises eight different scenarios, with over 5000 screens of actions, decisions points, and branching results. Eighteen other simulations cover other Human Resources topics such as Business Conduct Guidelines, Multicultural Issues, Work-Life Issues, Retention, and Personal Business Commitments.

Tier 3. Online collaboration. Lotus Learning Space allows learners to team with other managers in virtual groupware spaces. Here they learn collaboration skills, and create and build real-life learning networks to enhance our company's own intellectual capital. Collaborative spaces using same-place, different-time communication enable a truly global learning environment, eliminating the problems of time zones and travel.

Tier 4. Classroom "Learning Labs." For developing people skills, face-to-face human interaction is arguably the most powerful of learning interventions. Classroom activities provide immediate responses, are flexible to human needs, and can adapt as needed to different learners' styles. For leadership development, nothing quite duplicates face-to-face learning. In addition, a classroom of peer learners can provide added motivation, inspiration, and a community environment further stimulating interest and involvement. Management Development continues to offer interactive classroom experiences. Our five-day in-class experience requires the learner to master the material contained in Tiers 1, 2, and 3 so that the precious time spent in classroom Learning Labs can target deeper and richer skills development.

Alignment

The new blended learning process:

- Allows new managers to access material when and where they need it and to learn five times more than previously delivered in our classroom-only approach.
- Enables new managers to work at their own pace and at their own convenience to build a foundation of knowledge.

- Maximizes the precious limited time spent face-to-face in the classroom experience.
- Provides more opportunity for additional critical skills areas to be addressed across all geographies and business units.
- Provides a set of permanent, updatable resource tools for the new manager to access instantly to solve workday problems.

Blending a variety of learning modalities (online just-in-time performance support, interactive simulations, virtual collaborative spaces, and in-class activities) is essentially an integration of different learning opportunities combining to reinforce critical leadership and people management skills. Basic knowledge gain in, for example, leadership competencies are accessed by the new manager in our online Manager QuickViews and Harvard ManageMentor. Managers can then build and practice skills in these areas by using online simulators, learn from peers in these issues via LearningSpace's collaborative groupware, and finally deepen their skill building in face-to-face Learning Lab role plays and in-field learning with their second-line manager. All of these focus on managers strengthening their leadership competencies and styles/climate approaches, which constitute the model for all leadership development across our company. These modules are being integrated into our global technical and professional certification programs for critical skill paths.

A critical organizational goal is for managers to become adept at using our internal technologies for communication (Lotus Notes) and collaboration (Lotus TeamRoom, Lotus WorkRoom, Lotus CustomerRoom). Managers are immersed in a Lotus LearningSpace for nearly a year, an interface which closely replicates all of the aforementioned Lotus products. In addition, *all* of our online materials—QuickViews,

---

Partnerships Within and Outside the Organization

All the instructional materials comprising the four tiers of the process have been designed and developed in concert with other organizations, within and outside the company. For example, the online Coaching Simulator was co-designed with our Executive Development Group; the simulator contains four manager scenarios and four executive scenarios. Both groups together benchmarked the coaching field and, for the purpose of alignment up and down the company, agreed to adopt the same coaching model.

The Manager QuickViews were co-developed by our Management Development and Harvard Business School Publishing (HBSP). As HBSP was building its Harvard ManageMentor and we were building our Manager QuickViews, we mutually shared our best design ideas, feedback from our users, and interface suggestions. Consequently, not only do the two tools work in nearly similar fashion, but the

HBSP content fits perfectly within our interface, allowing us the advantage of easily adding any HBSP content appropriate to our needs. We were also the first company to be permitted to customize *Harvard Business Review* case studies, which are used in the five-day Learning Lab.

Our company's Solutions Focus Team, charged with identifying critical line issues, was accorded the role of a decision maker on what QuickView topics would be written and incorporated, in order to align these performance-support tools with real business issues and concerns of managers.

One of our Learning Services divisions customized Lotus LearningSpace to meet the special needs of our new practice and the 5000 new managers served this year by this tool.

Our Multicultural QuickView and web site was co-designed with the Intercultural Business Institute of the University of North Carolina, Charlotte. The cross-cultural model and all of the 300 interactive cross-cultural scenarios were co-developed with the director of the Institute. Other QuickViews are designed and maintained by internal subject-matter experts from across the HR and Policy functions.

We participate in professional endeavors to share knowledge with thought leaders in the field: In 2000, we cosponsored benchmarking studies on e-learning with Dr. Brandon Hall and an ASTD/Elliott Masie study on e-learning preferences and sponsored and participated with ASTD in the Learner Preference study.

In evaluation, we used our company's Research division, two studies by Harvard Business School, and two studies assisted by research consultant support from University of Texas Professor Rajiv Rimal.

Simulators, remote learning modules—have been designed using the Lotus interface to further solidify alignment with these other important communication tools.

Evaluation Strategy

Using the Kirkpatrick model on training impact evaluation, we evaluated the overall effectiveness along two dimensions, *leadership* and *e-learning*, that correspond to our primary objectives. Outcomes were also evaluated along a continuum that comprised a "chain of impact" leading from direct training effects to higher-order business outcomes. When investigating business outcomes, we distinguished between cost avoidance and business result enhancements. Because this program represents a full year of investment in development in each manager, we considered it important to measure success throughout the different phases of the program, not just at the end, and also eight months after the intervention. Furthermore, because our ultimate interest is in documenting long-term organizational changes, results from the previous year were also used as comparisons. We strive for two goals with our new evaluation framework—1) to spread training effectiveness information throughout the internal staff in order to drive continuous improvement, and 2) to measure with sufficient research rigor to illuminate true training effects.

Level I. (1) Two separate and independent studies of representative cohorts of students (N = 520 managers) were done in 8/99 and 8/00 via confidential questionnaires and in-depth telephone interviews by a Harvard Business School professor assess student satisfaction with content and delivery modality. (2) At the end of every Learning Lab, a company-administered student perception survey assesses content and delivery of every participant (N = 6600 +). Results are analyzed formally each quarter, and modules are changed and/or supplemented to respond to student needs. (3) In Phase III, student feedback is posted in LearningSpace, and Learning Lab facilitators receive individual feedback.

Level II. (1) In Phase I, 15 mastery tests (220 items on basic leadership and people-management principles and theory, legal and policy understanding, etc.) are taken, and all students must achieve 90% passing grades in order to move on to Phase II (Learning Lab). (2) Mastery is also demonstrated in Phase II through collaborative role-playing, feedback, and case studies. (3) In Phase III, mastery tests measure advanced content areas that are dependent on knowledge mastered in Phases I and II. (4) Individual assessment is done via 360-degree feedback from managers, peers and direct reports of students on competencies, managerial styles, and climate.

Level III. An alumni assessment is conducted eight to nine months after completion (the time lag between course completion and measurement is intended to capture ingrained behavior change versus immediate, post-training effect) to measure two behavior change dimensions: (1) actual observed behavior changes and (2) changes in factors that social science research has indicated are strong predictors of behavior. These behavioral precursors include gains in self-efficacy and reduction of perceived barriers. For new managers, perceptions of barriers to effective leadership can be powerful in influencing behavior. Hence, a large part of the training is spent on building skill in overcoming leadership barriers, as well as building intention to increase positive change activity. The assessment is one of two online, anonymous surveys administered to *all* graduates (we believe this follow-up intervention further reinforces the importance of desired behavior transfer). The 40% response rate from the first wave of alumni (637 students who completed course work in 1999) was pleasing, and the data was examined for response pattern match to other assessments to confirm representativeness of the respondent group.

Level IV. (1) Business impact attributable to training was measured in the same survey used for Level III measurement. These include extent to which students have become better leaders, extent to which their teams have been positively affected, and types of impact on business results (e.g., impacts on people/teamwork/morale, productivity/effectiveness and customer and financial indicators). (2) Large-scale leadership effectiveness was measured as well. (3) The Employee Research group conducts a global opinion survey each year in which many items critical to the corporation are measured. Recently, a detailed analysis investigated the connection between leadership and the key corporate measurement of customer satisfaction. This piece of research was examined for high-level leadership trends and linkage to important business outcomes. These results are widely distributed and strategically used across the corporation, so our quest to isolate training effects is confounded. For evaluation purposes, the research is important nonetheless because we believe that using multiple measures representing a variety of depth and specificity of impact can help to triangulate on global training effects.

Level V. Most easily measured was the cost efficiency achieved using e-learning approach over classroom-only delivery. Cost of development returns and learner efficiencies have been quantified and tracked since the inception of the program. More difficult is the measurement of the ultimate success of training—the extent to which it has a noticeable impact on business success. The bottom-line impact of leadership training on business operations is notoriously hard to measure, but we endeavored using a "chains of impact" approach, following the trail of training effects down two paths: (1) cost avoidance/savings and (2) results enhancement. For example, tangible cost savings from cost of discrimination and harassment lawsuit avoidance are estimated by comparing internal legal action rates with other top-tier corporation rates. In addition to savings, we measured ROI by results enhancements, such as manager estimation of business impact due to leadership improvements.

Our Results

Level I. All three satisfaction instruments yielded high participant satisfaction with both content and modes of delivery. HBS' findings (N = 520) indicated that "the company made significant strides in selecting learning modalities that are most appropriate to the learning situation, and implementing those modalities in an effective fashion.... The student interview results revealed *unequivocal enthusiasm for [the company's] implementation of both the online and classroom components of the program ...* [and that the company] has appeared to recognize that when implemented appropriately, learning modalities can be synergistic, rather than competing."

The internally conducted student survey showed that certain modules, such as coaching and climate, consistently receive the most positive scores. Summary ratings (5-point scale, 1 is highest score): overall satisfaction mean = 1.16, lessons learned were useful mean = 1.06, overall experience valuable = 100% yes, recommend program to others = 100% yes.

Level II. The program's second goal was that attainment of Level II (knowledge gain) would be greater than the previous classroom-only new-manager intervention. On the 15 knowledge mastery tests, slightly over 96% of the 6600 participants to date have achieved mastery in all 15 subject areas, and these students attained an average of 92% mastery on the 220 online-delivered knowledge items. Moreover, *five* times as much content is covered in the new year-long process than in the previous five-day New Managers' classroom program.

Usage of the e-learning architecture is regularly monitored. Based on a student population of 3,000 students per year, nearly 500,000 intranet Web page requests per year signifies an average of approximately 150 page requests per year per student. Since the program's inception, there has been a cumulative total of 2.3 million page requests.

Level III. Based upon the alumni survey, significant behavior change occurred as a direct result of training, and the largest behavior changes occurred in the content areas most heavily emphasized in training: coaching, competencies, styles, and climate. Samples of the most powerful findings include (5-point scale of degree of change, 1 representing greatest degree of change): straight talk (mean = 1.82), coaching as a competency (1.9), teamwork (1.92), active listening (1.94), using the intranet to increase leadership knowledge (1.96), team leadership (1.97), and coaching as a managerial style (1.97). These results match facilitator observations of degree of behavior change throughout the course. Further, they demonstrate that the overall goals for themes of behavior change are being met.

Self-efficacy items also showed great results—the graduates believe they can make a difference and they are still enthusiastic about it after eight to nine months since completion of the course—the impact has staying power. Most powerful results: confidence in ability to be an effective leader (1.75, representing biggest change found in the survey), belief that positive changes in team are within my control (1.87), increased knowledge of leadership capabilities and needs (1.93), belief that I can make a positive impact on climate (1.95). The greatest barrier reduction was found for lack of understanding of how to resolve "people" issues (2.31) and difficulty in leading remote employees (2.62).

Level IV. Self-reports on observable changes in leadership behavior and impact on the business were also uniformly positive. Regarding "overall effect of the training on their leadership": 8% of managers reported "extraordinary improvement," 50% reported "large amount of improvement," and 41% reported "some improvement." Most frequently selected types of impact on subordinate teams that resulted directly from leadership improvement: development of the group as a team (71%), increased focus on strategy and goals (68%), morale improvement and empowerment of staff (both 65%), stronger relationships among teams (53%), and increased productivity (50%). To further establish the relationship between behavior change and business impact, 11 indices were created from the key behavior topics, and then correlated with the measures of business impact. The strongest correlation (or "prediction" of impact) was found between behaviors regarding changing organizational climate and impact (correlation = .41, indicating a high degree of relationship, statistically significant at the p < .0001 level) and leadership competency behavior and impact (correlation = .35, p < .0001). A factor analysis on 11 index variables yielded a three-factor solution, consisting of Impact on Business Measures, Impact on Strategic Outcomes, and Impact on Relationships. Impact on Business Measures correlates with many of the behavior-change indices, most notably self-efficacy (correlation = .35, p = 0.0001) and managerial styles (correlation = .33, p = 0.0003). We conclude that alumni perceive leadership improvements that relate to improvements in their business as a result of training. This finding is supported by results from the internal Research study, which showed proof of linkage between leadership and customer satisfaction that were particularly compelling. A company-specific linkage model was created via the use of structural equation modeling to demonstrate that leadership quality influences teamwork, and ultimately, customer satisfaction.

Level V. Total financial cost including room and board, travel and infrastructure cost, not typically included in standard education industry accounting templates, is calculated by estimating per student cost for 128 hours of learning:

Per Student Cost:	$8,708
Per Student Cost, previous	
classroom program (@128 hrs. instr.)	$14,586
Per Student Savings	$5,878
Total Savings (first 5000 students, US)	$29,390,000

Given the $8708 cost per student for program completion, our estimated delivery ROI is 17 to 1. (The ROI is based on the total cost of creating and deploying a module and the tangible cost benefits based on the usage over the past 18 months.)

Reuse of the e-learning methodology, via content object templates and/or simulation templates, is another source of savings. Use of templates by other internal organizations has resulted in development savings totals of $780-$905K, as follows: 1) Managerial QuickViews, given to five organizations at $50-$75K each, 2) NetObject Fusion Template, given to three organizations at $10K saving each, 3) Learning Simulator, given to two organizations at $100K savings each, 4) LearningSpace Customization, given to three organizations at savings of $100K each. In addition, our Training Services external provider is now using our design as a standard for many of their internally developed programs.

Tangible cost savings from cost of discrimination/harassment lawsuit avoidance have been estimated by comparing internal legal action rates with other top-tier corporation rates. Lawsuit avoidance by our target student population is lower due to emphasis in the training on early issue identification and prevention content, resulting in an estimated savings of $4.5M annually for US managers attending the program.

Within the survey venue, we asked graduates to assess the first year annual impact, in dollars, that the leadership change due to training has had on their departments. The average direct impact value managers placed on department improvement

Attribute Emphasized in Training	Correlation with Financial Indicators
Increase in leadership competencies	.34***
Improvement in managerial style behaviors	.31***
Increase emphasis on aspects surrounding organizational climate	.27**
Increase in coaching behaviors	.32***
Improvement in managing telling behaviors	.29**
Better diagnosing and managing resistance to change	.24*
Gains from case-study approach adopted in program	.35***
Increase in knowledge about leadership	.22*
Improved efficacy (confidence in managerial ability)	.26**
Reduction in perceived barriers to behavior change	.19^

^p < .1, *p < .05, **p < .01, ***p < .001

Improved behavior effect on the business

was $415K. This leads to an ROI of 47 to 1.

Correlates of impact on revenues: based on responses from graduates (N = 121), impact on financial indicators was predicted by key behavior change indices. Improvement in the following areas predicted impact on financial indicators:

Together these analysis lead us to the conclusion that students perceive real and lasting leadership improvements directly linked to the training, which drive observable and financial value for their business.

In making the content available to all managers worldwide via our company Internet, we have contributed to establishing a greater consistency of language, knowledge, and company culture across the globe than previously when different geographies developed and deployed their own separate new-manager programs.

The early success of this practice has sparked interest and enthusiasm across others parts of our company to use a similar blended approach for other company professions. Not only have other divisions begun planning their development based on our blended four-tiered approach, but as our templates are reusable, they are being adapted for content beyond management development. Five other company divisions now use our templates to deliver their own QuickViews and Simulations. Our customization of Lotus LearningSpace to our students' needs—e.g., to provide a progress view for each student and an aggregate progress tracking map for administrators—and our successful deployment for such a huge number of students has helped inform and improve subsequent LearningSpace endeavors within the company.

We have also begun to sell components of the practice externally. Besides providing revenue for the business, it has also helped to create a greater acceptance of the materials internally across company divisions.

Other selected impacts of the new process include:

- **Adaptation of common nomenclature and conceptual models.** Prior to the practice, different organizational functions and geographies used different terms and concepts to describe the work of managers. For example, seven dissimilar change models were used within the company. That has now been replaced with one commonly agreed-upon model. Common approaches and ideas have subsequently fostered more cross-functional understanding and teamwork.
- **Online workplace behavior evaluations.** Online 360-degree survey instruments with input from direct reports and peers on Managerial Styles, Leadership Competencies and Organizational Climate are now used via our intranet to measure the behaviors exhibited by participants.
- **Participants also now develop an Organizational Action Plan** (OAP) aimed at measurable improvements in the business. Completion of the program is dependent on the new manager's manager sign-off that real workplace behaviors have changed, as evidenced by completion of OAP objectives. This new approach has been well received.
- ***Rip and Read* requests.** Participants can use the print version of online learning modules to retain the content in hard copy for later use. Nearly 50% of 896,000 annual site hits are print requests. This suggests that managers are using the material for purposes beyond the immediate learning objectives within the course.

All impacts above are believed to be long-term, as the e-learning approach appears to be increasingly accepted throughout our company.

Lessons Learned

1. Learning preferences are poor predictors of e-learning acceptance. Moon's studies reveal it is difficult for our pre-intervention students to express accurately their preference for a particular learning modality (e-learning) because their range of classroom experiences far exceeds that of online learning. E-learning should thus be viewed as an *innovation* with attributes unclear to its users. Using this approach, we used the findings of nearly 50 years of "Diffusion of Innovations" research (especially Everett Rogers, 1995, *Diffusion of Innovations*) to inform our design and deployment.

2. "Relative advantage" of e-learning must be salient and promoted. The degree to which the innovation is perceived as better than existing alternatives is the primary driver of its use. With online learning and our students, it is anytime/any-place access and the advantage of being able to focus on a specific skill or information module desired instead of having to sit through an entire class program covering a broader set of skills or wade through a larger body of information.

3. The "compatibility" of e-learning with already existing tools, navigation, and usability is important to students. Any learning design features inducing students to regard the innovation as "familiar" increases satisfaction and speeds its adoption. For instance, if online applications are consistent with already familiar interfaces and navigation, such as their e-mail, learners feel more comfortable adopting the new learning technology. (Moon, "Evaluation of Innovation in Online Learning," 8/00).

4. The simplicity of an e-learning application, as perceived by its potential adopters, will speed its rate of adoption. Conversely, perceived complexity of installing "plug ins," which are commonly required for various online learning programs, is one example of how complexity slows adoption of online learning. Thus we designed and built everything with simple "point and click" in mind.

5. "Trialability"—the degree to which e-learning can be experimented with on a limited basis—helps dispel uncertainty and drives its adoption. Deploying e-learning features with "no risk to try" helped speed adoption. All simulators, online cases, and web pages are neither tracked nor password-required, so users could try them—and make mistakes—without feeling they were being watched. Trialability appears to be especially critical for earlier adopters who have no precedent to follow when they adopt, unlike later adopters who may be surrounded by peers whom they can observe and experience via "vicarious trialability."

6. "Observability"—the degree to which the results are visible to others. Some effects of e-learning are more immediate and easier to see, and these help drive future usage. For example, we learned that building in observable and practical management skills content that can be used immediately by the student helps whet appetites for more e-learning. So we made these available first. Such immediate skill gains are more quickly observed than other leadership skills which typically have long-term accrued effects, and these immediately perceived benefits help promote continued adoption of our new e-learning approach.

Nancy Lewis is Director of Management Development for IBM in Armonk, New York. To find out more about the program, call 800 IBM TEACH.

Choosing an Authoring Tool for Web-Based Training: A Case Study

Ramona R. Materi

Authoring tools are software that facilitate the creation of effective Web-based courses to train employees. When companies have little background in the development of such courses, how can they select the authoring tool that will work best for them? This article is a case study of how one large company did this.

Web-based or Internet training is a fast-growing educational option. A 1998 survey by the American Society for Training and Development (ASTD) estimated that by 2000, the market for training delivered via new technologies would be to be 35% of the corporate training market, with web based training accounting for a sizeable chunk (Bassi 1999).

With this technological bandwagon rolling through the corridors of large companies (or at least in the training press), strong pressures may exist for managers to leap aboard. Pushing the wheels along, a growing number of authoring software programs are available to design Web-based training, each with their own enthusiastic advocates. If managers do decide to go ahead, however, they have almost no role models to follow. Few companies actually use Web-based programs. Despite the fanfare, the same ASTD study cited above showed that in 1998, only 10% of American employee training was computer-based, with only 3% of companies surveyed using the Internet. Hence, managers who attempt to develop Web-based training programs must largely learn by trial and error.

Faced with these forces, what can managers do, particularly if they have a minimal background in technology? If they decide to use a Web-based system, how can they make appropriate choices about the type of authoring software to use? What criteria should they use to make this decision?

This paper explores some of these questions through a case study of a department in a large company. Although space requirements limit the scope and depth of the analysis, it attempts to provide some guidelines, or at least options to consider. The paper concludes with a recommendation about the type of authoring system that would best meets the needs of the department.

Background

The customer affairs department of a large company (hereafter referred to as "The Department") faces training challenges. A portion of its 20 professional staff rotate in and out regularly, while another group consists of older workers who have been in their positions for over 15 years. The work demands a thorough understanding of the company's business, as well as complex government regulations. The officers must also deal with often irate customers, usually on the telephone and, less often, in person.

Currently, new officer training is fairly rudimentary. Officers arrive, receive a brief overview of the department from a more senior staff member, then spend the next three to four days reading through old reports and letters. After this introduction, they are "on the phones," dealing with customer inquiries. The thought behind this practice is that new staff will learn best by doing, by making mistakes and learning from them. Officers receive no follow-up training. Everyone is under tremendous pressure: time is constrained, there are too few people to address the complaints received and volume is rising steadily.

This training, or lack thereof, has led to problems. New officers often make mistakes, so more experienced staff must sometimes deal with problems that have become more complex due to further errors on the company's part. Managers try to compensate by maintaining stricter control over customer response letters, but this increased scrutiny leads to even slower turnaround times. It is difficult to control who responds to telephone calls, a problem worsened by the frequent absence of staff nearing retirement. New officers often are quite stressed, as they try to calm angry customers by defending company policy or government legislation over which the company has limited control.

To address the problems, the department's managers have developed an outline for a proposed training plan for new staff. Its major goals and objectives include:

- An orientation program for new members to the department;
- An ongoing, in-house program to upgrade and update current members;
- A provision for retaining information and training materials for future reference and self-help on an intranet site;
- the eventual development of self-training components through the intranet.

These items are the division's written objectives. Our interviews with managers and observation of actual practices reveal additional goals that provide a more nuanced perspective. For the Department, the training priorities appear to be the following:

1. Minimize the time required by old staff to train new staff, since "production" remains the overall priority.
2. Develop standard material so that officers can provide consistent information to clients and reduce the number of easily avoided errors.
3. Train officers to deal more effectively with irate and stressed clients.
4. Acquire information from older officers about solutions to unusual problems and the history of policy development before they retire.
5. Train officers to be more efficient and deal with files more quickly.

At this stage, managers are willing to explore a Web-based training pilot. Some of the equipment to implement the training innovation is already in place; as part of the company's Y2K preparations, all staff received updated computers, with a connection to the company intranet and browser software. Cost is a consideration, but managers are willing to examine slightly more expensive options, if they deliver better training.

What Software? The Managers' Decision

Having decided to use a Web-based system, the managers must now select the tools to build it. They have two options:

1. Using a simple HTML editor, HomeSite 4.5, to produce a simple, largely text and graphics program. The Department has a licence for the program and the company provides some technical support for it.

Product Description: Allaire's HomeSite is a Web site editor. Users must be familiar with Hypertext Markup Language (HTML), since HomeSite is code-based. The product is a favourite of developers, since it allows for extensive customization. In 1998, HomeSite 4.0 won the CNET Builder award as the Best Code-based HMTL editor. (Gatlin 2000)

2. Purchasing a more elaborate authoring tool, like WebCT or another commercial product, to design a more elaborate (video, audio) course. With such software, the division would have to rely on outside technical support.

Product Description: WebCT is an example of an on-line education system. Like Blackboard, TopClass, Lotus Learning Space and similar packages, WebCT offers "one-stop-shopping" for neophyte Web-based designers. It provides for asynchronous communication between faculty and students, supports on-line quizzes and tests and can be integrated with video and audio elements from other programs. WebCT allows for easy design of a basic course and is one of the less expensive programs in its class. (For further details and a comparison of WebCT to other products, see *Online Educational Delivery Applications: A Web Tool for Comparative Analysis* by Dr. Bruce Landon [www.ctt.bc.ca/landonline] or the University of California at Berkeley *Reviews of Web-Based Instructional Tools* [ist-socrates.berkeley.edu:7521/wbi-tools].)

Selecting the Tool: An Analysis

Phillips (1998) and Hall (1997) offer models for selecting appropriate on-line course authorware. Using a blend of their models as a starting point, this section analyzes the circumstances in the Department.

Step One: Assess In-House Capabilities

Phillips and Hall suggest a company begin by assessing its internal resources. These include:

- Course Development Skills—Does the company already have trainers experienced in computer-based delivery or computer programming?
- Current Software Available—Has the company already invested significant time and money in an authoring system?
- Development and Deployment Infrastructure—Do all sites use the same platforms? Does the software require a special server, or technological "bells and whistles" like sound cards, additional programs or plug-ins on the computers of the end users? Are users capable of installing these additions, or will a technical specialist need to configure work stations?

The Department: The Department has no staff member with computer delivery or programming skills. It has one contractor experienced with database material. The larger company has developed some CD-ROM based programs, but Department officers do not use them. All officers have the same computers, configured similarly. Their stations, however, have no audio or video capabilities. Skills with computers vary immensely, so a technical specialist would need to make any changes to work stations.

Step Two: Assess Learning Content Needs

The second step is to determine the objectives of the educational content, then try to match the authoring system to its demands. As Phillips wryly notes, "Design and delivery should follow the demands of your content, rather than the desires of your design team to use a new system because it boasts a "cooler" animated spin feature for the company logo" (p. 4).

The Department: In its plan, the division identified three broad areas for officer training:

- Knowledge of Policies and Procedures: Background on divisional and corporate policies and procedures, overview of legislation, the company's key relationships.

- Dealing with Customers and Issues: Case management of complaints, dealing with customers, other departments, outside agencies.
- Computer Software Training: Case management software, word processing, spreadsheet, Internet search skills.

Darrah (1999) believes that computer-based training is inadequate for training in interpersonal skills and high-level analytic requirements. Thus, the customer and stakeholder management module would likely be more effectively delivered through face-to-face training. The Department could conceivably use the Web-based training system to educate officers about policies and procedures. A more sophisticated application could also train officers to use the computerized case management system the Department has recently implemented.

Step Three: Assess Audience/Client Needs

As Wolfe (1990, cited in Fahy 2000) and Levison (1990) note, successful technology adaptation depends on the response of the implementers to the needs and desires of the users. Hall and Phillips suggest that companies review such variables as:

- Reception Capabilities: How big is the "pipe" or connection that will deliver the program to users? Will users rely on the company intranet, or will some access the program using the generally slower and less reliable Internet?
- Audience: Who are the users? What is their technical background and familiarity with computer or Web-based training? What is their readiness for it? Will adding technology-based training increase their stress levels? Where will they take the training (e.g., in a special lab or at their desktop)?
- Time Frames: When does the training need to occur? When does the solution need to be implemented and the results realized?
- Course Management and Administration: What kinds of reports do managers need at the end of each training activity?

The Department: The Web-based training would use initially use the corporate intranet. If the program expanded to other divisions, officers outside of headquarters would have to rely on the Internet. As for the audience, the innovation is somewhat compatible with existing practices. All officers use their computers to track files and read company e-mail and some do their own word processing. Some officers are quite versed in Net tools, but others have never even opened their browser software. Most staff would probably use a Web-based course individually, at their desktops.

Given that formal training in the department is almost non-existent, most newer officers would welcome any innovation that provided more information in a readily available fashion. For them, the innovation would likely relieve some of their stress. For older officers, though, the system might increase stress. These people generally have weak computer skills and see no reason to learn word processing or Net browsing shortly before retirement. They would have the least need for the system's knowledge components and, in fact would likely be net contributors to their development. They could likely make use of any computer skills training made available.

Departmental management has set no time frame for the training project. Reporting requirements would likely be minimal, since managers must deal with daily crises and lack the time to monitor individual progress or performance on training tests and tools.

Step Four: Assess Potential Costs

Training costs can vary considerably, depending on the amount and sophistication of the media used. (See Bates 1995 for a fuller discussion of these issues.) Barkdale and Lund (cited in Hall 1997) suggest developers consider a variety of administrative, development, personnel and travel related costs. Matkin (cited in Fahy 2000) and Phillips (1998) have also developed Return on Investment (ROI) models. Most developers believe that an ROI study is unnecessary for a small pilot project, although they offer no specific figures as to what might be regarded as a "small project" (Webb 1999).

The Department: The Department's Web-based training will initially be for about 20 people. Such a small number would not seem to warrant an extensive ROI study. In addition, since the division has spent little on training in the past, it would be difficult to develop measures to use as a basis for comparison.

Recommendation

With this analysis in hand, which way should the Department proceed?

We recommend that the managers proceed using the simpler HomeSite tool. Indeed, while space prohibits a fuller discussion, a more traditional CD-ROM-based course or even a knowledge management system might better meet the Department's needs. Two of the great strengths of Web-based training are its potential for interactivity and the ability for designers to make up-to-the-minute changes. With time and training personnel in short supply, these attributes may be largely wasted in Web courses designed for Department staff.

Perhaps the best reason for choosing a simple, existing tool is that the entire training project has a high risk for failure or, more accurately, non-implementation. The Department lacks a training culture and managers have had no time to implement the plan they drew up. Further, as outlined above, only certain modules are suited to Web-based training. Even if the designers were able to get the project under way, it is unclear if many officers will use a computer-based tool, particularly the older ones. (Their reluctance may be quite typical. Weiss (2000) reports that some companies have retention rates of less than 10% for internal Web-based courses.) As seems to be the case in many companies, designing an elaborate Web-based training program might be like giving expensive chocolate to a group of toddlers—they may or may not bite and, if they do, they might have no appreciation for the quality they are receiving.

Can it be argued that, however many the users, a more powerful program would enable the creation of more attractive training? In the case of the Department, the designers face limitations. The officers' work stations have no audio or video capabilities. It is unlikely managers would invest in upgrades until they had evidence that officers liked the Web-based model. So, the designers would have to rely primarily on text and graphics to deliver the training content. A tool like Web CT might enable them to deliver this material more easily, but they would have little need of its more powerful design or record-keeping functions. Further, if a managerial goal is to reduce staff time spent on training, it is unlikely designers would gain ongoing access to a "training guru" to provide tutoring and respond to on-line questions and concerns. Students could pose questions, but would probably receive a delayed response or never hear from anyone.

In fact, one of the few reasons *for* buying Web CT or a similar tool relates, in this case, to the needs of the designers. Web CT is meant to be easy to learn and use. Rather than thrashing about with often awkward and confusing HTML coding, the designers could point, click and drag their way to an attractive course in short order. This option would no doubt be of interest to the design staff with minimal technical background in Web design and programming.

In conclusion, we believe the right choice for the Department is to keep it simple— and cheap. As Wolfe 1990 (cited in Fahy 2000) notes, readily available, technologically less sophisticated tools may accomplish an organization's goals as well as complex ones. HomeSite may be a bit clunky for the job and contribute to a longer development period, but it will accomplish what the Department needs, for now.

Bibliography

Bassi, L.(1999). Are employers' recruitment strategies changing: Competence over credentials? In Stacey, N.G. (Ed.), *Competence Without Credentials*. Retrieved April 20, 2000 from the World Wide Web: http://www.ed.gov/pubs/Competence/section3.html.

Bates, A.W. (1995). *Technology, Open Learning and Distance Education*. New York: Routledge.

Bechky, B. (1999). Summary of the workshop. In Stacey, N.G. (Ed.), *Competence Without Credentials*. Retrieved April 20, 2000 from the World Wide Web: http://www.ed.gov/pubs/Competence/section7.html.

Darrah, C. (1999). Learning tools within a context: History and scope. In Stacey, N.G. (Ed.), *Competence Without Credentials*. Retrieved April 20, 2000 from the World Wide Web: http://www.ed.gov/pubs/Competence/section5.html.

Fahy, P. (2000). MDE 620: *Advanced Technology for Distance Education and Training Course Notes*, Winter. (Available from Athabasca University, 1 Athabasca Boulevard, Athatbasca, Alberta, T9S 3A3, Canada.)

Gatlin, P. (2000). Allaire HomeSite 4.5: CNET Review. Retrieved April 20, 2000 from the World Wide Web: http://www.builder.com/Reviews/HomeSite45/ss01.html.

Hall, B. (1997). *Web-Based Training Cookbook*. Toronto: Wiley Computer Publishing.

Levison, E. (1990). Will technology transform education or will the schools co-opt technology? *Phi Delta Kappan*, October, 121-126.

Nath, R. (1994). Difficulties in matching emerging information technologies with business needs: A management perspective. *Information Processing and Management, (30)3*, 437-444.

Phillips, V. (1998). Selecting an online course authoring system: Corporate markets. *Training Magazine*, April 1998. Retrieved April 18, 2000 from the World Wide Web: http://www.geteducated.com/articles/corpauth.htm.

Webb, W. (1999) Show me the return. *Inside Technology Training*, November 1999. Retrieved April 20, 2000 from the World Wide Web: http://www.trainingsupersite.com/ittrain/pastissues/November99/nov99coverstory.htm.

Weiss, M. (2000). Distance Education. Retrieved April 25, 2000 from the NETTRAIN mailing list. Archives available at http://listserv.acsu.buffalo.edu.

Ramona R. Materi is president of Ingenia Training, in North Vancouver, British Columbia. A trainer and instructional designer with degrees in economics, public affairs, and environmental science, she has a half-dozen years' experience designing and delivering Internet training and more than 10 years' experience as a project manager. She has worked and studied in India, Australia, and Switzerland as well as Canada and the U.S. She is currently pursuing a master's degree in distance education, with a focus on Web-based training.

Will CBT Produce the Results You Need? A Case Study

Steven V. Benson

This article includes useful tables to help you in making decisions with regard to setting up CBT courses and figuring out whether such courses are for you. It also documents the experience of one company in setting up CBT.

Kinetic Concepts, Inc. (KCI) is a leading innovator of specialized therapeutic products and services for patients in hospitals, nursing homes, and home health agencies. The company began 23 years ago and has grown into a multimillion-dollar company doing business worldwide. Our growth didn't come without growing pains; our success caused us to grow out of our traditional method for training newly hired employees and led to our use of computer-based training (CBT).

New hire training is for sales and service employees who work out of our network of service centers. Traditionally, sales employees were trained during a three-week stay at our corporate office. Service employees were trained at our service centers. But company growth made both approaches inadequate. Training was not offered frequently enough to keep up with demand. Record keeping was time-consuming and difficult to maintain. Furthermore, maintaining content continuity in our service courses was difficult because of the many different instructors and training locations. We worried that these problems may have had an adverse impact on our competitiveness.

If someone asked you to put together a short list of reasons why you are better than your competitors, what would you include on your list? I expect you would include your workforce's knowledge. Most performance experts would agree with you. The combined knowledge of the workforce is a key competitive advantage for a company. Like the saying goes—knowledge is power!

Today's challenge is finding a way to provide enough training fast enough to stay competitive. This is especially true when it comes to training newly hired employees. Here you face the challenge of offering both an orientation and a training program.

At KCI we needed an orientation program to tell new employees about the company and explain specific issues in their working conditions (such as Occupational Safety and Health Administration (OSHA)-related safeguards) and benefits and compensation. We also needed a training program that included roughly a week's worth of highly technical work performance issues. Both programs had to be tailored to each position, because different positions had to be informed about different subjects. And the program information had to be available 24 hours a day, seven days a week for approximately 1,200 people who worked at about 140 locations.

In looking for a better way to deliver our training programs, we also looked at our training challenges. Budget cutbacks, limited personnel, and distant locations all contributed, especially the need for training that is offered when a person needs it, is quantifiable, provides sufficient documentation, and is cost efficient and effective! All these needs were present; finding a solution was important.

Selling the Boss on CBT
Is CBT Right for Your Organization?

Before asking for CBT, you need to see if it is the right solution for the problems you face. Included with this paper you will find a survey that helps determine if CBT is an appropriate solution for your training needs (Figure 1). It comes from Brandon Hall's *Web-Based Training Cookbook* (Hall, 1997) and helps answer the question of whether CBT is right for your organization.[1]

How does it work? The survey lists a wide range of topics for consideration. Your answer to each consideration is weighted according to how much it supports doing CBT. You get your overall score by adding up the individual scores. There is more to the survey than just a score. Reading the topics lets you see the wide variety of issues to consider when selecting CBT. Using this aid, you can see that making a CBT decision requires a thorough review of many different topics.

Should you find that CBT appears to be an appropriate solution, the next thing you need to do is sell your boss on using it. The boss may be your immediate supervisor, but more likely it includes a number of upper-level executives. Preparing for this step helped us develop a rationale for explaining the benefits of a CBT training approach.

---

[1]This chart will be helpful in determining how practical CBT is for your training needs. Brandon Hall says, "A score of less than 135 indicates [CBT] should probably not be considered as a training solution for the project in question; a score of 136 to 200 indicates [CBT] may be worth considering, and a score over 200 indicates [CBT] is most likely an appropriate solution."

Consideration	Instructions	Points	Score
Number of learners	If < 50 learners > 50 & < 100 learners > 100 learners	0 5 10	
Number of training sites	If learners are at 1 site 2 to 5 sites > 5 sites	0 5 10	
Distance of learners from existing training site	If the average distance learners are from an existing training site Does not require overnight stay Requires overnight stay Requires many overnight stays	0 5 10	
Number of times program will be offered	If program will be offered 1 time 2 to 5 times 6 to 19 times > 20 times	0 3 5 10	
Frequency of integrated updates	Integrated updates are needed < Every 3 months Between 3 & 6 months > 6 months	0 5 10	
Development time available	If training must be available in < 3 months 3 to 6 months > 6 months	0 5 10	
Preferred learning style	If learners prefer Group learning Independent learning	0 10	
Preferred training schedule	If it is more appropriate to Set training schedules Allow learner to set schedule	3 10	
Current computer proficiency	If learners Don't know how to use a computer and don't need a computer for their job Don't know how to use a computer and do need a computer for their job Know how to use a computer	0 5 10	
Current learner skill level	If learners All have the same skill level Have widely varying skill levels	5 10	

Figure 1. Is CBT right for your organization? (continued on next page)

Consideration	Instructions	Points	Score
Need for individualized remediation	If learners probably Won't need remediation Will need remediation	 5 10	
Importance of subject consistency	If consistency is Not important Somewhat important Very important	 0 5 10	
Need for performance tracking	If performance tracking across multiple courses or modules is Not needed Desirable Required	 0 5 10	
Content	If skills are Soft Hard	 5 10	
Content already available on CBT	If CBT program Must be developed to meet requirements Can be purchased and modified to meet requirements Can be purchased for use without modification	 0 5 10	
Management's past experience with CBT	If past experience with CBT was Not favorable Neutral Very favorable	 0 5 10	
General view of technology	If management views technology as Awful A necessary evil Great	 0 5 10	
Budgeting scheme	For cost comparisons, if development costs Are separate from costs of delivery Are included with delivery costs	 0 10	
Availability of hardware at learner's site	If hardware at learner's site is Not available at all Available but has to be upgraded Available	 0 5 10	

Figure 1. Continued

Consideration	Instructions	Points	Score

Cash flow (Can the company spare the cash now for development in order to save later?)	If cash flow is
	   Slow
	   Okay
	   Good
		
		0
		5
		10	

Management's perception of person making recommendation	If person making recommendation
	   Has poor track record
	   Has a great track record
		
		0
		10	

Availability and skills of project management staff	If staff
	   Cannot manage a CBT project
	   Can manage a CBT project
		
		0
		10	

Availability of production hardware	If production hardware is
	   Not available at all
	   Available but has to be upgraded
	   Not needed
	   Available
		
		0
		5
		10
		10	

Availability and knowledge of CBT design and authoring language	If staff
	   Knows nothing about authoring
	   Will buy off-the-shelf CBT
	   Can design and author CBT
		
		0
		5
		10	

Availability of hardware troubleshooters	If troubleshooters
	   Cannot be made available
	   Can be made available
		
		0
		10	

Availability of content experts	If content questions must be answered and experts
	   Cannot be made available
	   Can be made available
		
		0
		10	

Use of existing trainers	If exisiting trainers
	   Will no longer be needed
	   Can be transferred to new positions
	   Can be used on CBT projects
		
		0
		5
		10	

TOTAL			

Figure 1. Concluded

Preparing Our Rationale

In preparing to ask for money, we took a close look at what we were doing in the current training system. In our case, we were doing training, but it wasn't working. We had the opportunity to show how CBT could bring efficiency and savings to our company.

We developed our rationale around those things that would show the biggest benefit; these points became our tangible benefits. We defined tangible benefits as those things that were measurable and shown to be correlated with a proposed action.

Our biggest problem had to do with adequate documentation of training. The solution we chose included a course management system. Our plan called for recording an employee's training each time he or she logged onto the system. This guaranteed documentation of the completed CBT lessons and quizzes.

CBT also solved the problem of training someone when he or she was hired. We were able to keep our current training policies in place, and we now had a system that supported them. Using CBT, a new employee would log into the system on their first day. The new employee would go through approximately six hours of CBT orientation. This met our policy for providing health and safety training during the employee's initial few days of employment and before he or she was allowed to do any meaningful work. Next, approximately 40 hours of CBT training would be included on job-specific topics. This training was supposed to be done during an employee's initial 120 days of employment. Our new system made it possible to meet this goal, too. However, our system was not going to end there.

We also wanted to document each employee's on-the-job performance. We were confident the CBT program would teach an employee what each needed to know, but that was not everything we needed to do. We also needed a system for documenting that employees could demonstrate proficiency of a task while on the job. We did this by setting up a special course-management screen for supervisors. Using this screen a supervisor produces an "On-the-Job Training (OJT) Certificate" when an employee proficiently performs a job task. This expanded the system's capability by providing documentation for non-CBT training, too.

Our greatest tangible benefit was in the improvement in training documentation. In the current system, training documentation was often missing or hard to find. Different departments kept their own paper records. It was a full-time job for many people to follow up requests for records and to file. Our proposed system would track both CBT and non-CBT training—at a cost saving. Using CBT we could consolidate the work done across many departments and put everything in one database without any increase in staff. In fact, all this could be done with fewer people than our current system used.

To have a tangible benefit, training must increase or decrease something. Usually, it is an increase in revenue, productivity, morale, or some other favorable outcome. Or, it brings about a decrease in turnover, accidents, theft, lost customers, or some other unfavorable outcome. For example, you might say training has reduced turnover. The tangible benefit is lower turnover; the cost savings is spending less for recruiting than for training. Unfortunately, tangible benefits are not easy to prove, so intangible benefits must often be substituted for them.

Intangible benefits are those for which you cannot prove a direct correlation, but "common sense" suggests they should exist, such as employee morale. Many things can affect how satisfied employees feel about their jobs. Elton Mayo's classic study at Western Electric's Hawthorne Works demonstrates this point (Mayo, 1977). You would like to say that employee morale would improve when training is done, but can you actually prove it? Let's say you measured morale before and after you conduct a program. Your data show morale has gone up, but did this happen because of your program? Or were other factors influencing morale?

Most of the time, you cannot say with absolute certainty that your program was the reason, so improving employee morale is offered as an intangible benefit. Common sense seems to say that if you do a better job training your employees, more employees will be satisfied.

Picking Your CBT Vendor

After selling our boss on using CBT, we were ready to begin developing the program. We did not have the in-house talent to do this, so we searched for an outside vendor to help. Picking a CBT vendor was a critical step in this process. Making a mistake could result in a product that is developed late, costs more than its estimate, or—in the worst case—does not do the job!

To pick the best vendor for the job, we developed a questionnaire. Getting bids from vendors immediately is risky because you do not know if all the vendors have the necessary qualifications to perform the work that you need. Our questionnaire (Figure 2) allowed us to make an objective comparison of vendor strengths and weaknesses. By using the questionnaire we were able to eliminate unqualified vendors before asking about cost. This approach added another step to our vendor selection process.

The questionnaire contained 10 criteria for weeding out unqualified vendors. The criteria were weighted for importance, with the more important items having a higher number of potential points. They are also listed from most important to least.

Outcomes from CBT

The heart of the matter is, what's in it for you and your organization when using CBT? I will try to answer this question three ways: First, by explaining some benefits we saw from using CBT, next by demonstrating that CBT was an economical alternative to other kinds of training, and finally by reporting on the impact of CBT inside KCI.

Benefits from Using CBT

Our program included both CBT and a course management system. About 15% of our program's cost was for development of the course-management system, which allowed us to track employees' training activities and provided us with automated documentation. It also offered online reports and a report-writing feature. The reports benefited employees and managers alike. Employees saw immediate results. Every time they finished a lesson they could see progress in the accumulated online report; we called this online screen the Course Book.

Managers had access to the training records according to their responsibilities. Immediate supervisors saw their staff's training records. Middle and upper management saw records for everyone. These records are seen online or through a special

Criteria	Rationale	Points	Score
Hardware and software capabilities	Everything the vendor produces must integrate into existing or planned hardware and software. Pay special attention to specifications, capacities, communication connections, and potential conflicts.	20	
Vendor experience	The more experienced the vendors, the more efficient and proficient they should be. Staff skills and capabilities should include: ▪ Computer graphic art ▪ Narration ▪ Database programming ▪ Multimedia development ▪ Instructional systems design ▪ Digital photography and videography ▪ Senior-level authoring programming ▪ Local area network administration ▪ Website design ▪ Project management	20	
Delivery schedule commitments	Projects can take a long time. You want someone who knows how to work efficiently and understands the importance of project deadlines and milestones.	14	
Goodwill support	Consider what "freebies" the vendor provides as goodwill, such as free software and technical support both during and after production.	13	
Similarity of previous projects	You want someone with the vision and experience to do what you need. If you are doing training, find someone who's done training programs. Also, look for someone who's done multimedia content similar to what you want.	11	
Scope of contracts	Choose a vendor with experience producing projects similar in scope and effort to your project.	10	
Geographic region of vendor	The closer the vendor, the easier the working relationship.	5	
References	It is nice to know someone else likes them.	3	
CD duplication capability	This is a small issue, but it adds to the final product's image and cost.	2	
Familiarity with your company's products and terminology	Things should be easier and faster if the vendor knows your business and users.	2	
TOTALS		**100**	

Figure 2. CBT vendor selection criteria

report writer that works off our database. The report writer has the capability to show individual training, work group summaries, and special categories of training.

Another benefit gained with CBT is a standardized format. Our experience with instructor-led programs showed us that program content varied each time a class was taught. In our technically oriented work environment this presented problems. Our learning content is complex and it is easy to overlook something important. A CBT program teaches the content the same way, every time.

We discovered another problem; all training material did not conform to a standard look. This problem shows up when different trainers create their own handouts and do not follow an overall template. This was a common problem because many different people taught both our week-long sales classes and our field-based courses. Our CBT program gives all the content a similar look.

We also discovered a problem with some tasks being done different ways. For example, one task could be done five different ways; each way would lead to the correct result. When a new employee was learning this task and was shown more than one way to do it by various instructors, it took the employee longer to learn the task. To make learning faster, it is important that every task be taught the same way every time.

CBT can also take into account that people learn things different ways and at different paces. Again, our classroom instruction experience showed that we focused our teaching on one type of learner and excluded others. When an instructor focused on slower learners, the faster learners got bored. And our instructional material often lacked adequate visual aids, making learning harder for learners who prefer pictures and diagrams to lists. Thus, we made sure our CBT included a rich multimedia environment. Our programs included pictures, diagrams to show detailed information, video segments, and computer simulations of our products' operations.

Timing is also critical. With CBT you have 24-hour, seven-day availability. Employees do not have to wait until it is convenient for someone else to orient or teach them. Furthermore, CBT can be watched again and again. This is especially useful when a job task is done infrequently.

We also shared a little bit about the company with all our employees. The opening screen of our program shows a picture of our headquarters' lobby. Many service center-based employees do not get a chance to see the corporate office, so CBT allowed us to add a little something extra.

Comparing CBT Cost with Other Forms of Training

The question of cost and cost comparisons is important. We were not concerned with the salary costs associated with training, since these costs occur no matter how training is done. What we wanted to do was compare the cost of CBT to our current training programs. To do this we chose to calculate the cost for delivering an hour of training for our current training programs and compare that to the cost of delivering CBT.

Our plan for comparing costs was hardest to do with service training. Service center training was done in our service centers, where an instructor either taught a small group of employees or met with an employee one on one. We had been doing service training without a budget line item for it; therefore, we had to estimate our expenses. Our biggest expense was the time an instructor spent with new employees. We determined the average cost per hour for service training by using the instructor's salary. Our review of past training showed that about three-fourths of new employees were taught one on one or one on two. Therefore, we decided to calculate the hourly cost of service training by dividing the instructor's salary by 2080 (the average hours worked per year).

Unlike service training, sales training was done in the classroom. The cost per hour was easy to calculate. The biggest expense of classroom training is travel. So we took the average travel cost per student and divided it by the number of hours of training to arrive at the cost of an hour of classroom training.

It was a little harder estimating CBT into cost per training hour. We had to estimate the average number of training hours included in the new program. Next, we had to estimate the "life span" of the product. We then estimated how many employees would be using the program over its life span. The cost per hour of CBT represents the number of training hours estimated over a three-year time span. Figure 3 shows the cost per hour of training we found at KCI.

Method	Cost per Hour
CBT	$7
Service (one-on-one)	$10-$30
Sales (classroom)	$32-$38

Figure 3. Cost of training per hour

Our estimates showed that CBT was a cost-efficient alternative. Classroom training was the most expensive form of training—up to as much as five times more expensive than CBT. Another cost consideration was the purchase of new equipment. We were already using computers in our service centers, and we did not want to start a program that could not use the existing equipment. Fortunately, our program was developed to work over our existing WAN, which primarily used 28.8 modems. We were also able to design a system that effectively ran using the current PCs. Being able to minimize our capital costs made CBT very attractive.

CBT's Positive Impact on KCI

At KCI there were many positive outcomes from the CBT. Figure 4 shows the benefits we found with using our CBT program.

Lower	Higher
Litigation vulnerability	Productivity
Turnover	Positive morale
Product down time	Job satisfaction
Recruiting costs	Safety
Accidents	Positive company image
Idle time due to new employees waiting on training	Rapid response to change in program content

Figure 4. Benefits of CBT for KCI

CBT replaced a program where all documentation was done on paper. In prior years, only a small percentage of new hire training was sufficiently documented. With CBT, 100% of our new hires have their training documented. Adequate documentation is important for showing compliance to OSHA and the US Food and Drug Administration regulations. This added documentation reduces our litigation vulnerability.

Other Outcomes

We received anecdotal reports that the CBT increased productivity. In one case, it was reported that newly hired employees who complete their training have more product knowledge than do three- to five-year employees.

The course management system brings a whole new level of accountability to training. Before CBT, training had gotten lip service about being important, but we did not have good documentation to support these comments. Since the implementation of CBT, it is easier to report on training progress. The course management system has raised training's visibility to the same level as other important business factors. As a result, management has started paying more attention to training.

The fact that we have a systemwide training program has not gone unnoticed by our customers either. They see us in a more positive way because of our training system. They tell us that our CBT gives us a more positive image and helps "sell" us to them.

We have gotten numerous reports back from employees who are using our system, saying that they appreciate working for a company that takes an interest in training new employees. In a recent survey, it was reported that eight out of ten employees said the availability of training was important to them (Schaaf, 1998). Our CBT program has demonstrated our concern for employees and fostered a positive company image with new employees.

The most notable unintended outcome from our CBT program has been on employee retention. During a periodic review of our turnover, we discovered that the new hires we retained were those who used the new training system. In fact, those employees who stayed were three times more likely to have used our CBT system.

Making it easier to train new employees has brought about a change in our recruiting program. First, the success of the CBT proves we can train new employees faster, better, and cheaper. Second, the use of CBT led to a favorable increase in new employee retention. Third, we feel it is possible to relax a previous work-experience requirement because we are doing a better job training. This work-experience requirement has in the past limited our recruiting ability, so by eliminating it we expect to have a larger candidate pool for entry-level employees. Our action mirrors the actions of other companies that are able to modify their entry-level requirements because of improvements in training and other systems. In today's tightening job market, this action is critical. We are confident we can expand our candidate pool, and by using CBT we can get our new hires to become productive employees faster.

Conclusion

CBT solved critical training challenges and provided other benefits for KCI. To determine if CBT can furnish you with similar benefits, I would recommend you first complete the survey in Figure 1. It provides an excellent beginning in selecting CBT.

Next, you should come up with a business plan for using CBT that you can use to sell your boss on the idea. If you are doing training now, then find a way to show—dollar for dollar—that CBT is the best alternative. Point out the potential tangible and intangible benefits of using CBT.

If CBT is right for you, you must decide if the work can be in house or if you should outsource it. If you cannot do it yourself, then you must find a qualified vendor. Use the questionnaire in Figure 2 to help. It screens out unqualified companies by objectively comparing 10 potential vendor strengths.

What can you expect to gain from using CBT? We experienced immediate results in many areas. Most impressive was the increase in documented training. We also showed our training had a positive relationship to new hire retention.

We gained unexpected benefits, too. By doing a better job of training we were able to improve our recruiting. Our improved training makes recruiting easier because we can now consider less experienced candidates.

What makes this news even better is knowing that our CBT is doing a better job training new hires. We expect the people hired will use CBT to know more and know it faster than employees who had learned using the old training system.

References

Hall, B. (1997). *Web-Based Training Cookbook*. New York: John Wiley and Sons Inc.

Mayo, E. (1977). *The Human Problems of an Industrial Civilization*. New York: Arno Press.

Schaaf, D. (1998, September). "What Workers Really Think about Training." *Training Magazine*.

Steven V. Benson is an organizational development, human resource development, and human resource professional. He is now Director of Organizational Development for Kinetic Concepts, Inc. He can be reached at stevebenson@worldnet.att.net.

Part Ten

Benchmarks for Successful Distance Learning Programs

───────────────────────────

P art Ten is designed to help you benchmark by looking at successful practices in different companies. In this part we are providing articles from two
publications based on a survey carried out by Brandon Hall. The first of
these, "The Benchmarking Study of Best Practices: E-Learning Across the
Enterprise," looks at e-learning in 11 exemplary organizations, including Cisco
Systems and the U.S. Navy, and documents the benefits these organizations
achieved through using this training approach.

The second article is also derived from this study and appeared first in a special
section in *Forbes* devoted to e-learning. In it we learn some important conclusions
regarding actions necessary to ensure that e-learning programs will succeed.

Part Ten concludes the anthology section of this yearbook.

The Benchmarking Study of Best Practices: E-Learning Across the Enterprise

Brandon Hall and Jacques LeCavalier

How is e-learning being implemented and used in different companies? What are the best companies doing? This article summarizes the result of a benchmarking study undertaken by Brandon Hall and provides information on the current state of e-learning in American companies. This article is followed by a second take on this same study written for a different publication. Together, they will give you a good sense of where things are with regard to the use of distance and e-learning.

Purpose of the Study

This is an intensive research study which spans 11 domestic and foreign companies across the board with significant e-learning success stories, including online employee training, orientation and education. The study lets us identify the best practices in large-scale implementations and state-of-the-art execution of enterprise-wide e-learning. "E-learning across the enterprise" describes the best practices of these companies and how they have overcome challenges to rise to the top.

The organizations we highlight are a reflection of business today—they cover a wide range of varying industries, with different e-learning needs, sizes, structures, markets and sectors. This report serves to set criteria for rating e-learning in terms of quality, quantity and business impact, which will benefit the e-learning community.

Searching for organizations that are potential world-class examples of the implementation of e-learning requires conducting extensive research and following a rigorous protocol. E-learning is a global industry; representing that fact was an important factor in the selection process. By researching and choosing a wide variety of companies from different countries and industries, we were able to avoid limiting the scope of success of our e-learning study.

The research activities included:

- Sending e-mail surveys to 5,000 industry professionals;
- Placing notices in major industry publications;
- Placing notices in industry listserves; and
- Interviewing industry writers and speakers.

We chose organizations based upon excellence in one or more particular research areas, which included: e-learning scope, management support, purchase of e-learning content and services, development of custom e-learning content, staffing, budgeting and taking it across the enterprise.

The businesses profiled for this report were Cisco Systems, IBM, Dell Computer Corp., GTE, Air Canada, the Internal Revenue Service, Rockwell Collins, Shell International Exploration & Production, Ernst & Young, Unipart, and the U.S. Navy.

Leadership, Vision and Culture

The general rationale for e-learning across the reporting corporations is "access above all." Best practice organizations are moving from a perception of learning as a cost to one of learning in order to maximize value. This leads to increasing demand for skills and knowledge delivered in a shorter cycle time.

E-learning as a driver for e-culture. E-learning driving business strategy is somewhat of a surprise concept. E-learning is seen by some as a key driver of e-culture, because it has the greatest power to engage employees and to be part of an overall e-business strategy and transformation.

We asked organizations to tell us when (if at all) they implemented various e-learning practices in the enterprise. Out of those responses, we extracted eight practices which are indicative of the progressive level of sophistication of e-learning implementations. These are: online courses, online catalogs, blending classrooms/online, Web-based learning management systems, live e-learning, e-competencies, online mentors and streaming video.

Cisco focused on their biggest training challenge: training the sales force—about 20 percent of their employees. Now, 80 percent of the sales staff use the Field E-learning Connection (100 percent is the goal for 2001, with 80 percent of sales and technical training Web-enabled). Some form of e-learning also is offered by Cisco's 30 training organizations, making Cisco the most pervasive e-learning implementation studied.

IBM focused many of their efforts on leveraging e-learning for management development, addressing core, critical and common skills in this top-priority area. Now 70 percent of management training is conducted via e-learning.

Mentors. As far as online mentors are concerned, two distinct concepts are in use: tutors (individuals providing administrative and content support during e-learning courses) and true mentors (individuals providing coaching and support in a broader job context). The U.S. Navy also uses this approach in a just-in-time context, bringing experts and sailors together via the Internet when complex and rare tasks need to be carried out flawlessly.

With regard to our participants and the depth of their e-learning systems, none of the implementations studied is truly enterprise-wide. In order to ensure success, companies have generally opted for a more focused, high-leverage approach to implementation. Nevertheless, the numbers are impressive.

As the proportion of training time delivered via e-learning rises, total training time could be seen to drop off in some organizations, given the higher efficiency of e-learning. For some companies, the imperative was to start where the need was greatest.

Upon finding they were unable to keep up with the pace of the products and technology, Cisco decentralized their training. Air Canada suggests recognizing your project limitations, especially in terms of expert people resources available. And Unipart confirms the critical importance of sustainability.

An e-learning implementation is as difficult to plan for, if not as costly, as an ERP implementation. Accordingly, best-practice organizations invest significantly in planning and strategy development.

Some strategic planning guidelines used by several of our participating corporations included: ensuring the plan was aligned to the company vision, specified key objectives, projects, measures, owners and impact. The plans also need to address resources and capabilities. Shell shared two versions of their Open University approach. The Alpha version provided for the development of a first-choice, one-stop-shop learning portal, a self-assessment and competence gap analysis, provision of links to their Learning Partner programs and the implementation of LMS capabilities. The beta version of this approach called for a fully operational Web site, with more than 50 registered users, the development of new course templates, the implementation of self-registration and GEC compliance, evaluation of mentoring, one-to-one tutoring and updated course EPT-HL category.

Executive Sponsorship Is Critical and Attainable

When Cisco's CEO, John Chambers, stated that e-learning was the next big killer application, his pronouncement made everyone in the company and the industry react. Chambers believes that e-learning will determine an organization's success and competitive advantage.

Bosses like e-learning. Chambers fully believes that e-learning will determine an organization's success and competitive advantage. Likewise, Kodak understands that regional managers are rarely all on board for corporate-wide initiatives, but that e-learning is a shining exception.

E-learning likes bosses. Regardless of how participants evaluated the degree of exec-utive-level support, they all considered that a high level of support was critical to the success of their implementation.

Organizations such as IBM use terms like "commitment" to describe their execu-tives' degrees of involvement. Dell's CEO, vice chairman and the executive committee will have an opportunity to teach in the executive education program, where the fac-ulty consists exclusively of top leaders.

The core of Dell's online program is a unique direct-to-customer approach called the Dell Business Model. The content for this course was developed through an inten-sive series of interviews with Michael Dell. After extensive reviews, improvements and additions were made and approved by the CEO.

When the company decided to move into e-business, Dell asked that an online training module be created to teach the company's Internet strategy. Know the Net teaches and tests individuals on how to use the Internet. Dell personally sends e-mails, communicates attendance at staff meetings and insists on receiving a status report on the percentage of people completing the training successfully.

For IBM, the e-learning model is where distributed learning and knowledge man-agement intersect. There is a feeling that IBM is more nimble because of e-learning, and linking it to their knowledge management efforts lets them better refine their strat-egy and future plans.

While Shell's dovetailing efforts have not been easy, it has largely succeeded in integrating human resources, recruitment, retention, knowledge management and learning strategies. Shell's Exploration and Production knowledge management system includes a Web-based expertise directory, as well as numerous knowledge-sharing forums and eight centers of excellence.

Most companies have strategies to track and maximize completion rates. Course schedules at Cisco are adhered to as closely as possible, while NCR employees are encouraged to display "e-learning in progress" signs to reduce interruptions. Along the same lines, IBM confronted procrastination on the part of Basic Blue participants, and limited commitment from second-level managers by implementing additional strategies.

Most participating organizations report that with the advent of e-learning, training is at last seen as having an integral role to play in overall organizational strategy.

- Communications strategies and vehicles are offered as counsel for other execu-tives and managers: From Air Canada—build a compelling case and craft a strategic vision designed to add demonstrated value to the enterprise; from Ernst & Young—presentations, one-on-one and meetings in a box.
- For employees and other users: From IBM—opinion leaders are key (diffusion of innovations); from the U.S. Navy—they have had success with approaching

---

E-learning makes training an integral role in overall organizational strategy:
- E-learning offers numerous opportunities to learn new skills and exercise new roles.
- E-learning does not eliminate face-to-face education—it enhances it.
- Classrooms will change, but not go away.
- E-learning increases work-life balance due to reduced need to travel.

---

receptive instructors suggesting they develop an e-learning offering.
- "What's in it for them" messages for executives and managers: From Cisco—e-learning accelerates the metabolism of any corporation that embraces it and any individual that exploits it; from Ernst & Young—e-learning provides scalability, a key enabler in driving globalization efforts.
- For concerned instructors, classrooms will change, but will not go away; e-learning offers numerous opportunities to learn new skills and exercise new roles. For learners: from IBM—e-learning does not eliminate face-to-face education, it enhances it; from Ernst & Young—e-learning provides increased work-life balance due to a reduced need to travel.

Successful e-learning implementations for multinational corporations are seen as confirming the need to combine the impact of standardized, enterprise-wide activities with flexible and quick innovations and efforts, both locally and internationally. On a global level, translation and adaptation of e-learning content to local languages sometimes requires a tricky balance between corporate instructional and information standards and local preferences.

Content, Technology and Human Resources

Many topics benefit from e-learning. There is little favoritism as far as topic areas are concerned. With the popularity of blended learning solutions, any topic can be addressed by an e-learning system. For example, IBM built a Web-based e-learning environment specifically for their employees and their partner salespeople, which they called Sales Compass.

Building e-learning content from scratch is prohibitive, even for large companies. Most buy and/or adapt some content from other uses. Organizations serious about achieving real results from e-learning also are serious about instructional design, and choose not to cut corners in the development of their mission-critical programs.

IBM found that it was not possible to take the content from prior programs and port them into an e-learning model. E-learning requires a totally different thought process in terms of delivery methods. Air Canada has had considerable difficulty in attempts to reuse legacy aircraft and other documentation in their e-learning and performance support system. Near-obsolete document formats and unclear responsibilities for conversion have been obstacles.

For its part, Cisco appears to have had success with a systematic repurposing process of identifying existing content available from all sources (among them, about 10 million Web pages!), then editing, tagging and organizing it into meaningful groupings for each audience. Finally, this "information" content is converted into learning by adding assessments, exercises and labs.

The U.S. Navy specifically targets courses with high throughput, attrition or setback rates for repurposing.

In some cases and contexts, people need and prefer to have information in a rough state. Cisco claims its learners require data instantaneously. Hence, the training approaches include on-demand, just-in-time and at-your-desk training.

Controlling costs and speeding up dissemination of critical knowledge are the key goals of several participating organizations' learning object strategy.

Blended Instruction Has Come of Age and Is Here to Stay

Most participating organizations report that with the advent of e-learning, training has an integral role to play in overall organizational strategy.

The advantages of this strategy are self-evident:

- The closer the learning vehicle is aligned with a particular learning style, the more effective the educational experience.
- When combined, media technologies have greater impact on delivering messages.

Selecting optimal e-learning blends adds a certain level of complexity to the old "instructor vs. computer-based training" decision.

Powerful Self-Instructional Techniques

In an effort to engage learners and accelerate learning, best-practice organizations are using technology and instructional design expertly to create highly potent self-instructional materials.

Dell America Operations knows that not everyone in manufacturing has access to a computer. They developed a visual work instruction system with large icons based on usability survey information, with 20- to 30-second bites, that conveys the new procedures.

Staffing for E-Learning

E-learning sometimes results in major skill shifts:

- From instructional designers/course developers to program/project managers;
- From instructors to facilitators, in a classroom and an e-learning context;
- From instructor to on-the-job coach, and from e-mentor to individuals and groups;
- From instructors and subject matter experts to instructional/information designers and developers;

- Some instructional designers with the aptitude become new media developers;
- Coaches need to develop higher-level coaching skills; and
- IBM finds that e-learning also requires increased teaming to provide global facilitation learner support.

While in the pilot and ramping-up stages of e-learning, organizations commonly struggle with insufficient staff to achieve all of their objectives. However, once e-learning is truly operational, staff requirements decrease. Organizations tend to use their internal development group as a primary resource for specific development.

IT as Partner and Service Provider

For some organizations experiencing difficulties getting quick response from Information Technology (IT) departments, it has become necessary to hire their own external IT resources. While not the ideal solution, this can expedite the resolution of certain technical challenges.

Whether the IT function is internal or outsourced, its key role in an e-learning implementation cannot be overstated. One cannot deny the value of what IT brings to the table: experience with implementing enterprise-wide software.

In achieving a partnership with a sometimes hesitant IT department, there is no substitute for support and direction from above. This is a sure way to avoid or correct responses from IT which suggest that e-learning is not a legitimate business application.

Hosted Solutions

External e-learning service providers may be an appropriate alternative to developing and integrating a complex e-learning infrastructure.

Effective IT partnership strategies may involve:
- Knowing and exploiting IT's key initiatives and dates that could impact e-learning;
- Getting IT staff on your selection committees, or at least in the room when vendors come; and
- Leveraging e-commerce expertise in the IT function to help with distribution of e-learning.

LMS Selection and Implementation: Lessons Learned

Almost half of the participating organizations developed their own in-house learning management systems. Commercial systems with all the required functionality were generally not available when needed. The adage for these companies was "Take your time to do it right; there is no hurry!"

Standards Help Everyone

IBM's e-learning team retained the standard corporate Lotus Notes interface to ensure consistency and to make life easier for employees. Cisco found that you can solve organizational problems but create a corporate problem by not using corporate- or IT-supported tools.

The issue of how to develop a global learning network with a common open architecture is a key strategy question. It goes well beyond the software you are using. While some of the participants have the resources and expertise to put it all together, expenses often have been greater than anticipated.

Putting Vendors to the Test

NCR took an aggressive and efficient approach to dealing with "spouted-not-tested" vendor claims. It asked them to make their pitches to an audience made up of key NCR staff and competing vendors. Besides the obvious impact of such an exercise, there also were fruitful discussions among some vendors about how to combine their wares to offer a more complete solution.

Cisco developed tools such as the content upload tool (CUT/CAB), a tool to synchronize various media types to create an Internet presentation, and Cisco interactive mentor (CIM), executable programs with a built-in simulator that accepts student input, parses it and returns a response. When a custom e-learning tool can be used for purposes other than training, its uptake in the organization will be quicker.

In devising such tools, Cisco recommends that a company use emerging/evolving tools on a limited basis, that tools should be flexible and easy to use, and that a company needs different authoring tool templates for different author types and outputs.

Dell uses consolidated tools and applications across businesses, such as the DLS-negotiated master service level agreements for technology, which let them get a competitive pricing structure for the Dell Enterprise.

Measurement, Accountability, Spending and Results

Real spending on e-learning is tough to isolate. While the summary data on spending suggests considerable variability among participating organizations, about half of them had a difficult or impossible time obtaining this information. The median value of 30 percent suggests that e-learning is well-entrenched in some organizations.

Companies that want to move fast with their e-learning implementation tend to work harder at pulling together budgets from several sources into a sizable "pot." In order to reduce the financial load on the training department and make the e-learning implementation less vulnerable to budget cutting, some organizations spread the costs over several departments.

Air Canada spent about $500,000 on the pilot phase, using seed money. The Navy budgeted and spent $3 million on the pilot phase over a one-year period. Shell spent $5 million over three years in the pilot phase.

Added to these costs were implementation and infrastructure expenditures. Rockwell spent $1.2 million over a year; Cisco budgeted about $8 million in application development and support over 18 months; Shell planned for and spent $1.5 million over a year; IBM claims that e-learning didn't cost them real money; and Kodak states that increased IT costs almost canceled out their savings in training costs.

A final area of spending includes operating costs. Cisco said that e-learning operating costs are unclear, and that the current client-funded charge-back models are becoming obsolete and need changing. IBM notes they instituted a "library card" as a method, which lets employees access online learning with a single charge per user.

Competency Management

The majority of participating organizations have implemented competency management as a fundamental element and a key driver of their e-learning system. By placing an important part of the responsibility in employees' hands, competency management accelerates the penetration of e-learning.

While at least one organization had difficulty mapping out competencies for less well-defined jobs, most have invested heavily in the effort. Air Canada made significant investments before much courseware was developed. Cisco invested heavily from September 1999 to March 2000.

Assessment Methods

Formal assessment of e-learning is proving difficult, and concern for measurement is not unanimous. For instance, Shell has little evaluation data to support its e-learning business case, but senior management is already sold on the idea. As e-learning efficiencies drastically cut training time and organizations move increasingly to merge knowledge, measures of learning quantity become less relevant and likely more confusing for managers.

Air Canada completed a formative evaluation of the pilot version of the Ramp Performance Safety & Support System (RPSS) between July and December 1998. IBM noted that instructional design without rigorous evaluation of its effectiveness is meaningless; they believe that knowing whether learning objectives are met is an essential part of any intervention.

Some managers may have unrealistically high return on investment expectations for e-learning—an 18-month payback period is unacceptably long for some. Several organizations point to training penetration as a key metric to communicate to management.

However, companies clearly perceive the value of e-learning once they have used it. At Cisco, 13,000 employees have logged onto the GTMS registration training system since October 1999. At IBM, their Basic Blue program was deployed to over 3,000 managers in 1999.

Air Canada noted that 7 to 10 percent of end users are in the high-use category (at least once a day) and that 25 to 40 percent are casual users (at least once per cycle, or six days).

At Dell, their One-Stop URL and On-line Product Training segment increased usage of online materials substantially and broadened their employees' access to best practices and industry trends.

Performance improvement

Cisco reports increased productivity and reduction in support of tools, improved efficiencies while using business tools and increased workloads, while requiring fewer people. The time to get someone up to speed in a manufacturing facility has gone from three months to about four weeks.

Since implementation of its system in May 1999, Air Canada reports that while more training is occurring on-line, there is not yet any appreciable corresponding drop in classroom time/costs.

The concept of at-home learning is not new, but e-learning further encourages employees to get training on their own time and dime. Most companies prefer to explicitly allocate training time, and when necessary, compensate employees for learning done outside business hours.

Summary

"E-learning across the enterprise" focuses on 11 major corporations. These companies' e-learning success stories include online employee training, orientation and education. The study let brandon-hall.com identify the best practices in large-scale implementations of enterprise-wide e-learning, describing the methodologies used and the obstacles encountered by these well-known companies, and how their success in the implementation of their e-learning practices came only after they had overcome numerous challenges.

See Brandon Hall's biography on page 439.

Jacques LeCavalier is a senior consultant and partner in LeGroupe Mentor, a firm based in Montreal. E-mail him at jacques@grmentor.com.

E-Learning: Benchmark Study of Best Practices

Brandon Hall

This article provides more information from Brandon Hall's benchmark study. This appeared in a special section of Forbes *devoted to e-learning.*

In July 2000 brandon-hall.com completed a benchmark study of best practices titled *E-Learning Across the Enterprise*. This intensive research study spans 11 domestic and foreign organizations with the most significant e-learning success stories, including online employee training, orientation and education. They include Cisco Systems, IBM, Dell Computers, GTE, Shell, Unipart, Rockwell Collins and the U.S. Navy.

These organizations completed an extensive questionnaire consisting of numerous in-depth questions pertaining to the entire scope of e-learning, as well as basic background information. The best practices survey was designed to measure the efficiency and progress of e-learning throughout different types of organizations, as well as to pinpoint the weaknesses and potential drawbacks in an attempt to help further define the e-learning industry.

The benchmark study identifies the best practices in large-scale implementations and documents state-of-the-art execution of enterprise-wide e-learning. *E-Learning Across the Enterprise* describes the best practices of the companies surveyed and how they overcame challenges to rise to the top. Participating organizations are a reflection of business today. They cover a wide range of varying industries, e-learning needs, sizes and structures, markets and sectors. This report serves to set criteria for rating e-learning in terms of quality, quantity and business impact, which will benefit the entire e-learning community. The information that follows was excerpted from that study.

E-Learning: The Business Imperative

Best-practice organizations are moving from a perception of learning as a cost to one of maximizing value. This leads to increasing demand for skills and knowledge delivered in a much shorter cycle time—in summary, a greater demand for access and speed.

Overall, meat-and-potatoes business reasons (access, costs, speed) were the driving factors in incorporating e-learning. The effort had to be justified in terms of the bottom line (performance, flexibility, accountability).

Why are best-practice organizations implementing e-learning on a large scale? One participant states it most succinctly: it's about "getting more training to more [employees], anytime, anywhere, at less cost."

Big-Time Cost Savings

All of the benchmarked organizations that were far enough along to measure cost savings/avoidance and return on investment reported positive results. This includes IBM's $200 million savings from e-learning in one year. The company provides five times as much training at one-third the cost in its management development program.

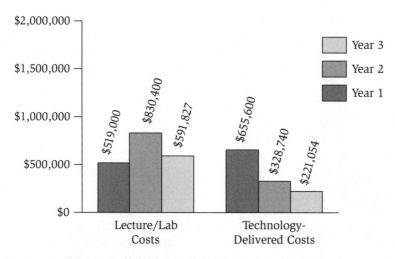

Figure 1. Comparison of costs for lecture/lab vs. multimedia courses over three years
Note: The costs for the technology-based course include the cost of development for the lecture/lab course on which it is designed. The pattern of costs over several years for this course is similar to that found in other organizations: development costs for technology-delivered courses are higher, but delivery costs are lower when compared to instructor-led courses. Source: brandon-hall.com, *Return on Investment and Multimedia Training* (1995)

Planning for E-Learning

An e-learning implementation can be difficult. Accordingly, best-practice organizations invest significantly in planning and strategy development. Participants caution that each organization's e-learning plan will be very specific to its own context.

Executive Sponsorship Is Critical

Given the very substantial business imperative and impact of e-learning, it is not surprising that the extent of executive-level support and involvement is high among most best-practice organizations. As one participant says simply, senior management "supports e-learning because it delivers what is needed when it is needed."

All best-practice companies considered that a high level of support was critical to the success of their implementation. One organization claims that "without it, our project would have been lost in the shuffle of changing priorities and other commitments for capital."

Beyond mere management "support," organizations use terms like "commitment" to describe executives' degree of involvement. In one organization where the faculty consists of top leaders, the chief executive officer, the vice chairman and the executive committee all have an opportunity to teach in the executive education program. The core of this company's online program is a unique direct-to-customer approach. The content for this course was developed through an intensive series of interviews. When the company decided to move into e-business, the chief executive officer asked that an online training module be created to teach the company's Internet strategy. In this way, e-learning is part of the company's change effort.

In another participating organization, the chief executive officer declared early on that e-learning would play a big part in determining the organization's success and competitive advantage. Senior management quickly got on board, integrating into their objectives that 50% of all education would be conducted through e-learning.

In some organizations, a single champion or evangelist is responsible for jump-starting the e-learning implementation. Most participants suggest, however, that the impact of e-learning on the organization is significant, forcing change in areas including accounting processes, IT and training staff assignments and skills. It is therefore logical that most organizations continuously improve their implementation and ensure that learning meets business needs, using a learning council or steering committee that consists mostly of business managers.

Learning and Training: Finally a Seat at the Big Table

Most participating organizations reported that with the advent of e-learning, training is at last seen as having an integral role to play in overall organizational strategy. Those who see e-learning as an enabler of e-culture also see the synergy among e-learning, knowledge management, performance support and high commitment management practices. To implement e-learning effectively, best-practice organizations first develop

or adapt a clear, purposeful vision of optimizing learning, knowledge and performance—a "North Star"—and how current technology can activate this vision. They
ensure that the vision is compelling enough to increase all stakeholders' openness to
change. Change is, after all, both the reason and the fuel for e-learning.

Persistent and Targeted Communications

While e-learning is a relatively easy sell to senior managers, it is not always easily
embraced by employees. Best-practice organizations are persistent in the use of a variety of communication vehicles, along with targeted and compelling messages, to
inform, educate and motivate line managers, instructors, employees and other stakeholders affected by e-learning.

Acting Locally and Globally

Successful e-learning implementations confirm the need to combine the impact of
standard enterprise-wide activities with flexible and quick local innovations and
efforts. Programs need to integrate sophisticated courseware with rapidly deployed,
time-sensitive information and knowledge.

Global organizations implementing e-learning are also addressing regional and cultural issues and are adapting content and practices to deal with them effectively.
Collectively, best-practice organizations are using e-learning in all topic areas—new
product training, management development, leadership, sales, service, manufacturing,
safety—you name it, they've got it.

Content from Here, There and Everywhere

The leading organizations get their e-learning content from three sources equally:
packaged courseware providers, custom developers or their own internal development.
Most organizations use a clear set of guidelines based on content, audience, resource
availability and strategic factors to decide what elements of content development to
outsource and what to handle internally or via partnerships. Well-entrenched strategies for managing the high cost of content include syndication of content, participation in content-sharing consortia and working with development houses that are willing to share or resell their knowledge assets.

Basic, Quick Instructional Design

Organizations that are serious about achieving real results from e-learning are also
serious about instructional design, choosing to avoid cutting corners in their mission-
critical programs.

Smart organizations also know that speed and immediacy sometimes take prece-
dence over rigorous design. Therefore, their instructional processes are lean, which
leads to some impressive savings in development effort. They also don't shy away
from quickly deploying information (as opposed to interaction-rich training) when

employees require more immediate access, such as the specs on the latest product. Indeed, a clear understanding of information-sharing and training allows best-practice organizations to deliver time-sensitive content quickly without compromising their instructional design standards.

Using Templates

Controlling costs and speeding up the rollout of critical knowledge are key goals for many of the organizations in this benchmark study. These goals are being achieved through the use of templates and "learning objects," which allow for reuse of content in various courses.

Blending the Best of Online and Classroom

As one participating organization notes, e-learning is not about using the latest technology to replace the classroom. Nor is it about posting content on the Web to be downloaded or read. E-learning provides a new set of tools that can add value to all of the traditional learning modes—from classroom experiences to learning from books.

As learning moves closer to the job, blended instruction addresses the need for more just-in-time and project-based learning, performance support, open and distance learning, expert assistance and a generally greater variety of events and experiences.

The emerging e-learning model blends online learning for information transfer and procedural skill training, classroom learning for role plays and face-to-face discussions, and on-the-job learning, integrated with knowledge management and competency evaluation.

These best-practices companies say that classroom-based training will continue to play an important role for a few reasons: it is the best delivery approach for certain types of high-level learning, it is the way some people prefer to learn and it is still the way many trainers prefer to teach.

Competency Management: Turning "Push" into "Pull"

The majority of participating organizations have implemented competency management or learning profiles based on the job as a key driver of their e-learning systems.

By placing the responsibility for learning in employees' hands, competency management accelerates the use of e-learning. One participant claims, "With e-learning, you can empower the learner—the student becomes a knowledge broker, and therefore, a power broker. The learner, as well as the mentoring system, is held accountable." One company implements this principle via an open resourcing system for job assignments—individuals must market themselves internally and understand that they'll get the job if they have the competencies. Accreditation opportunities provide further motivation to engage in e-learning.

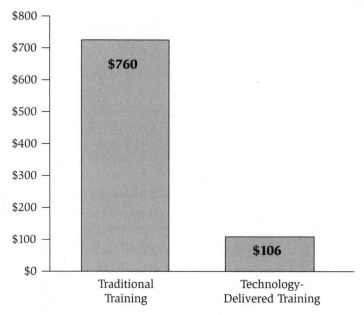

Figure 2. Cost per learner over five years
Note: Comparison by Price Waterhouse of cost-per-learner over five years for traditional instructor-led training ($760) vs. technology training ($106)
Source: brandon-hall.com, *Return on Investment and Multimedia Training* (1995)

Learning Management Systems

The learning management system (LMS) is the "operating system" for e-learning in the enterprise. When organizations select from the 100-plus commercial learning management systems, these key success factors stand out:

- Identify business and technical requirements. Save yourself time by bringing in only those vendors that can meet at least 80% of your requirements.
- Articulate your business needs and your vision of the future.
- Involve stakeholders who will be using the new LMS.
- Ensure that the product is compatible with your existing IT systems.
- Ensure that the product has been demonstrated to be robust and scalable, and to have multiplatform capability. Preferably, pick a vendor whose product is being used by companies with a similar need.
- Choose a partner that will provide exceptional customer service. Implementation is key.

To examine one of the best learning management systems, check out Saba Software. The company is considered by many to be on its way to becoming the Siebel Systems of learning management. Siebel Systems, across Highway 101 from Saba in California, has emerged as the number one vendor in the Customer Relations

Management (CRM) category.

Saba has depth at the executive level, excellent funding, more engineers than many of its competitors combined and a product that is reliable and full of features.

Authoring and Other Tools

Participating organizations have not overwhelmingly adopted any authoring or design tool, nor have they settled the issue of authoring versus programming. Authorware, Toolbook, Dreamweaver, HTML and JavaScript are the most frequently cited tools or programming languages, but, as in the case of learning management systems, many custom tools are used for a variety of development, delivery and conversion purposes. Cisco's arsenal of sophisticated tools is particularly impressive.

Development

Organizations tend to use their internal development groups as a primary resource for specific content development. When they use external resources, they do so to obtain a unique skill set, speed up the development process, access generic content and reduce costs (at least one organization outsources simulation coding to a development company in India).

IT as Partner and Service Provider

Whether the IT function is internal or outsourced, its key role in an e-learning implementation cannot be overstated. One cannot deny the value that IT brings to the table: experience with implementing enterprise-wide software.

In achieving a partnership with the IT department, there is no substitute for support and direction from senior management. This is a sure way to avoid or correct reactions that suggest e-learning is not a legitimate business application.

One company's e-learning team retained the standard corporate Lotus Notes interface to ensure consistency and make life easier for employees. Another company found that it could solve organizational problems, but created a corporate problem by not using corporate- or IT-supported tools. That said, balancing standards while allowing for innovation is very important to this company, whose many divisions have quite diverse requirements.

Effective IT partnership strategies:

- Understand the challenges of e-learning for your IT department—there are many.
- Know and exploit IT's key initiatives and dates for software and network upgrades, annual equipment purchases, enterprise resource planning implementation and other investments that impact e-learning.
- Include IT staff on your selection committees and in meetings with vendors.
- Leverage e-commerce expertise in the IT function to help with distribution of e-learning.

Getting a Handle On E-Learning Costs

As you plan your global e-learning strategy, a necessary step is to compare costs from different vendors. You need to know the questions to ask, but like buying a home, you also need to go in with some expectations.

Evidence indicates that computer-based training reduces the total cost of training when compared with instructor-led training. The total cost of training includes the cost of development and the cost of delivery. Interactive training has a higher cost of development and a lower cost of delivery, while traditional training has a lower cost of development and a higher cost of delivery. The lower delivery cost for interactive training results primarily from a reduction in training time and the elimination of travel. A positive return on investment requires a training population large enough for the savings in delivery to offset the development cost.

Computer-based training also requires less time for training compared with instructor-led training. The amount of reduction ranges from 20% to 80%, with 40% to 60% as the most common. Time reduction for computer-based training is usually attributed to a tighter instructional design, the option for participants to bypass unnecessary content and the opportunity for participants to focus on those sections of the course not yet mastered.

There is very strong evidence that computer-based training results in an equal or higher quality of learning over traditional instruction. A number of scientific studies have investigated this issue. The settings for the studies have included business and industry, the military, higher education institutions and elementary schools.

Following is an overview that is designed to help you ask the right questions as you develop your training budget. One aspect of understanding the various costs involves defining from whom you can purchase products. Some of the emerging distribution channels include:

- *Resellers*: You may not always be able to tell whose course you are buying. Resellers include Internet service providers, and content aggregators such as TrainingNet. Some resellers identify the content developer, while others use private labels.
- *E-Learning Partnerships*: Company names may change because the e-learning marketplace is constantly transforming. As rapidly as companies release new titles and new vendors enter the market, there are consolidations in other areas and partnerships on products. E-commerce training sites offer volume discounts to organizations. They act as content aggregators and often provide non-online courses through books, CD-ROMs and videos.
- *Learning Portals*: One of the most significant emerging trends, learning portals are Web sites that create a learning community and provide access to content and learning resources. Some learning portals are new companies that are building on Internet-based business models. Others are traditional training

organizations that have moved into the Internet environment. As a result, there are a few commonalities among the sites.

Content acquisition is a top priority. Independent content providers are being inundated with proposals to make their content available on these learning portals, so you will see much of the same content on numerous sites.

To get people to your Web site, you might consider offering free content and entertaining activities. Most sites have a mix of both professional and consumer-oriented content. Look for learning portals that allow customization. Some learning portals specialize in a niche area, such as sales or accounting and finance, creating the opportunity for a strong community.

Tutoring and Mentoring Services

More and more companies are including mentoring or tutoring services as part of their e-learning packaged courses. These services may be in real-time or have time delays, with e-mail questions and even virtual tutoring in development. Mentoring services are a key differentiator in e-learning, and a variety of options will become available. Companies either are formalizing their own services or will partner with independent content providers.

Course Delivery Models, Pricing Schemes

One thing is clear: there is not an easily discernible average price for an e-learning packaged course because there is no definitive paradigm. This is due to emerging technologies and the rapid creation and evolution of learning features, which make it difficult to pin down a definition and set boundaries for e-learning. However, a research study entitled *The Cost of E-Learning Packaged Courses* that was conducted by brandon-hall.com this year offers a per-student price as well as a per-student, per-course price, when applicable, to create some constant price point examples across all pricing schemes.

For instance, in purchasing a subscription library of e-learning courses, vendors will use a per-student, per-course price. This is the actual price if every student in the target population takes every course. For example, say 500 users intend to take a self-paced course over the Internet, ranging in length from 15 minutes to 12 hours. This would cost $12 to $25 per course, and $1.20 to $33 per student. If you take that up to 5,000 users, the cost becomes $20 to $26 per course and $2.60 to $20.65 per user.

Even though the cost of a product depends on many factors, you will find price ranges within specific course-delivery models. In addition, understanding the actual price points of specific products will make you a better informed consumer when working with e-learning vendors.

Achieving the lowest prices usually requires a large student population, a great number of courses and a long contract. In general, an average price point along the pricing spectrum corresponds to the respective point along the product complexity and components range. Usually, the self-directed and shorter courses are on the lower-price end and the complex, expert-facilitated courses are on the higher end.

An understanding of the cost of e-learning includes awareness of pricing models for packaged courses. Prices range from a low of 11 cents to a high of nearly $1,000 per student, per course. You will want to consider factors such as the instructional quality of the courses, technical support, access to collaborative tools, breadth and depth of titles, course duration and the tracking and reporting system.

Pricing Models

Here is a summary of available pricing models:

- Subscription-based library
- Subscription-based mini-library
- Per-server
- Per-course (purchaser-selected)
- Per-unit usage-based, by course
- Usage-based, by time.

When comparing and contrasting vendor offerings, one should also factor in other alternatives—from the internally developed courses, to third-party training-management systems, to outsourcing components such as mentoring or technical support. Some of the participating vendors include DDI, InfoSource, Vital Learning, NETg, DBM Knowledge Communication, McGraw-Hill, SkillSoft, DigitalThink and GEOLearning. A list of other distribution or development sources of e-learning packaged content, such as learning portals and e-commerce sites, is available at www.brandon-hall.com. Overviews of Web sites are included.

Think First

E-learning is taking new forms and incorporates new terms, trends and technologies at a fiery rate. A study by *Training Magazine* states that corporations save 50% to 70% of their overall training cost by replacing traditional training with online delivery. A WR Hambrecht & Co. study, *Corporate E-Learning: Exploring a New Frontier* (March 2000), shows that while $500 million was spent on Internet training in 1999, spending is projected to skyrocket to $7 billion in 2002. So it doesn't take such a leap of faith to begin integrating e-learning into employee training programs. The training demands will grow dramatically as companies partner, acquire, change names, improve processes and upgrade technology. While there is much pressure to move quickly, place quality high on your list of priorities and carefully construct an enterprise-wide e-learning plan that meets all of your corporate training needs.

The rewards will be an empowered workforce, an efficient, adaptable training infrastructure and incredible savings in time and money. Those are competitive advantages that will help your company get ahead and stay ahead.

Brandon Hall, Ph.D. industry analyst and lead researcher of brandon-hall.com, has 23 years of experience in research, writing, advising, and presenting in corporate training. He has been a contributing editor to the American Society for Training & Development's Training & Development *magazine and an editor for* Technology for Learning *newsletter. He regularly presents at conferences such as ASTD and Online Learning. He received his Ph.D. in educational psychology and has served on the faculty of San Francisco State University's multimedia studies program.*

brandon-hall.com provides independent, objective reports, information, and advice, helping organizations make the right decisions about technology for learning. Publications from brandon-hall.com include Building the Business Case for E-Learning, Learning Management Systems 2001: How to Choose the Right Systems for Your Organization, E-Learning Across the Enterprise: The Benchmarking Study of Best Practices *(from which this article was taken),* Collaboration Tools for E-Learning, Live E-Learning, *and* The Web-Based Training Cookbook. *The organization also works to recognize and advance the industry with the annual Hall of Fame Awards, now in its fifth year and the first recognition program dedicated entirely to the e-learning industry.*

For more information or to contact Brandon Hall, call 408 736-2335 or write him at brandon@brandon-hall.com. Or visit www.brandon-hall.com.

Part Eleven

A Distance Learning Resource Guide

P arts One to Ten make up the anthology section of this yearbook. We now come to the reference section of the book. Here we have developed a variety of directories and other materials to help you learn even more about the field and to assist you in finding organizations, publications, events and other resources. Here's what we've put together:

- **Distance Learning Magazines, Journals and Newsletters**. This is a comprehensive listing of publications that directly or indirectly deal with distance learning and technology-based training.
- **Best Current Books on Distance Learning**. This is an annotated list of 15 of the most useful publications on DL that have appeared over the past two years.
- **Distance Learning Resources on the Web**. It would be impossible to be anywhere near inclusive of all the Web sites devoted to distance learning. So this is just a brief listing of sites we think are important, many of which include links to other sites. Think of this as a starting point for learning more on the Web.
- **Directory of Distance Learning Organizations and Associations**. This directory includes nearly every organization involved in DL in the United States plus a good selection of international associations.
- **Glossary of Distance Learning Terms**. Prepared by Christine Olgren of the University of Wisconsin, this is a complete list of terms and definitions to help you master the language of technology.
- **Major Distance Learning Meetings and Conferences in 2001-2002**. To assist you in planning and figuring out which meetings might be useful to attend, we include this calendar of events that provides dates, locations, and Web addresses for learning more.

Distance Learning Magazines, Journals, and Newsletters

T raditionally, the greatest difficulty in compiling a list of periodicals in a given area was in being comprehensive, in defining the area and deciding what publications to include. Now, the greatest difficulty might be in deciding what constitutes a "periodical" and what "publication" means. As more and more print periodicals make some or all of their contents available online, as electronic publications proliferate, and as Web sites renew their contents regularly, it's increasingly difficult to define the terms "periodical" and "publication."

Active Learning in Higher Education

biannual (July and December), ISSN: 1469-7874, published by Sage Publications, Inc., 2455 Teller Road, Thousand Oaks, CA 91320, Phone: (805) 499-0721, (800) 818-SAGE 7243) (customer service), Fax: (805) 499-0871, E-mail: info@sagepub.com, Web: www.sagepub.com, www.ilt.ac.uk/resources/publications/alhe.htm

Subscriptions: Individual: $36/£23. Institutional: $146/£93.

Active Learning in Higher Education is a refereed, international journal published by the ILT in conjunction with Sage Publications to foster and disseminate research and good practice in learning, teaching, and assessment in higher education.

Adult Learning

six issues, ISSN: 1045-1595, published by the American Association for Adult and Continuing Education, 1200 19th Street, NW, Suite 300, Washington, DC 20036-2422, Phone: (202) 429-5131, Fax: (202) 223-4579, E-mail: thomas.kinney@albany.edu, Web: www.cdlr.tamu.edu/tcall/aaace

Subscriptions: Free to AAACE members. Nonmembers: U.S., $29; Canada, $34; elsewhere, $39.

This publication covers cross-cutting issues with an emphasis on practical solutions to problems faced by all adult educators from secondary and post-secondary education, business and labor, military and government, and community-based organizations.

ALN Magazine

semiannual, online, ISSN: 1092-7131, published by the Asynchronous Learning Network, John Bourne, Editor-in-Chief, P.O. Box 1570, Station B, Nashville, TN 37235, Phone: (615) 322-2118, Fax: (615) 343-6449, E-mail: john.nourne@vanderbilt.edu, Web: www.aln.org/index.htm

Subscriptions: Free.

This magazine is devoted to topics in Asynchronous Learning Networks that do not fall in the traditional journal format. These topics include reports of uses of technology, experiences with ALN courses, reports of activities on various campuses or in industry, and summaries of ALN activities. The aim is to make it more news- and method-oriented than a formal journal.

ALT-Journal

three issues, ISSN: 0968-7769, published by the Association for Learning Technology, ALT-J Subscriptions, University of Wales Press, 6 Gwennyth Street, Cathays, Cardiff CF2 4YD, Wales, Phone: 0222 (+ 44 222 rom abroad) 231919, Fax: 0222 (+ 44 222 from abroad) 230908, E-mail: press@press. wales.ac.uk, Web: www.warwick.ac.uk/alt-E/Publications/ALT-Journal

Subscriptions: Individuals, £40; institutions, £60. Concessionary rates are available to members of ALT.

This is an international journal devoted to research and good practice in the use of learning technologies within higher education, covering innovative teaching, independent and collaborative learning, computer-assisted learning, learner support, interactive media, knowledge representation and acquisition, networking, and on-line information.

The American Journal of Distance Education

three issues, ISSN: 0892-3647, published by the College of Education, The Pennsylvania State University, 110 Rackley Building, University Park, PA 16802-3202, Phone: (814) 863-3764, Fax: (814) 865-5878, E-mail: ACSDE@psu.edu, Web: www.ed.psu.edu/acsde/ajde/jour.asp

Subscriptions: Institutional, $75.00; Individual, $45.00. Outside the U.S., add $15.00 for shipping and handling.

This peer-reviewed journal promotes the study of distance education scholarship, research, and practice worldwide. Subscribers to the *AJDE* also receive a free one-year subscription to DEOSNEWS, the Distance Education Online Symposium, the monthly electronic journal.

The Australian Journal of Educational Technology
three issues, published by the Australian Society for Educational Technology and the Australasian Society for Computers in Learning in Tertiary Education, Roger Atkinson, Production Editor, Teaching and Learning Centre, Murdoch University, Murdoch WA 6150, Australia, Phone: +61 8 9360 6840, Fax: +61 8 9310 4929, E-mail: atkinson@ cleo.murdoch.edu.au, Web: cleo.murdoch.edu.au/ajet/ajet.html

Subscriptions: AU$30 in Australia, New Zealand, Singapore, Malaysia, Indonesia, Papua New Guinea, and other countries in Australia Post's Asia-Pacific charging zone; AU$40 in all other countries (Australia Post's Rest of World charging zone).

This is a refereed journal publishing research and review articles in educational technology, instructional design, educational applications of computer technologies, educational telecommunications, and related areas.

Canadian Journal of Educational Communication
semiannual, ISSN: 0710-4340, published by the Association for Media and Technology in Education in Canada, 3-1750 The Queensway, Suite 1318, Etobicoke, ON M9C 5H5, Canada, Phone: NA, Fax: NA, E-mail: NA, Web: www.amtec.ca

Subscriptions: Free.

This journal covers the latest in research, application, and periodical literature. It also publishes reviews on significant books and films, and critiques on computer programs.

CIT Infobits
monthly, online, published by Information Resources Consultant, Center for Instructional Technology, Academic & Technology Networks, 08 Smith Building, CB# 3420, University of North Carolina at Chapel Hill, Chapel Hill, NC 27599, Phone: (919) 962-6042, Fax: (919) 962-0784, E-mail: cit@unc.edu, Web: www.unc.edu/cit/infobits/ infobits.html

Subscriptions: Free.

CIT Infobits (formerly titled *IAT Infobits*) reports on news in information technology and instructional technology.

Communiqué
three issues, online (pdf), published by the Western Cooperative for Educational Telecommunications, P.O. Box 9752, Boulder, CO 80301, 1540 30th Street, Boulder, CO 80303,

Phone: (303) 541-0231, Fax: (303) 541-0291, E-mail: infowcet@wiche.edu, Web: www.wiche.edu/telecom

Subscriptions: Free.

This is the official newsletter of the Western Cooperative for Educational Telecommunications, an initiative of the Western Interstate Commission for Higher Education.

Communiqué

six issues, published by the Canadian Association for Distance Education, Suite 204, 260 Dalhousie Street, Ottawa, ON K1N 7E4, Canada, Phone: (613) 241-0018, Fax: (613) 241-0019, E-mail: cade@csse.ca, Web: www.cade-aced.ca

Subscriptions: Free to CADE members. Nonmembers: in Canada, CDN$32.10; outside Canada, US$30.00.

This is the association newsletter, providing members with news and information from within Canada and outside.

Compute-Ed

online, ISSN: 1328-0635, Geralyn E. Stephens, Chief Editor, Assistant Professor, College of Education, Wayne State University, 5425 Gullen Mall, Detroit, MI 48202, Phone: NA Fax: NA, E-mail: editor@coe.wayne.edu, Web: computed.coe.wayne.edu/index.html

Subscriptions: Free.

This refereed journal is concerned with issues and applications in teaching with and about technology in primary, secondary, and higher education. It publishes articles, letters, and reviews about a broad range of issues in information technology in education, with an emphasis on classroom practice.

Computers and Education

eight issues, ISSN: 0360-1315, Elsevier Science, Regional Sales Office, Customer Support Department, P.O. Box 945, New York, NY 10159-0945, Phone: (212) 633-3730, (888) 4ES-INFO (437-4636), Fax: (212) 633-3680, E-mail: usinfo-f@elsevier.com, Web: www.elsevier.nl/inca/publications/store/3/4/7

Subscriptions: Individual: all countries except Europe and Japan, $150; Europe, NLG 297 (euro 134.77); Japan, JPY 18,600. Institutional: all countries except Europe and Japan, $1,151; Europe, NLG 2,267 (euro 1028.72); Japan, JPY 142,400.

This journal publishes papers in the language of the academic computer user on educational and training system development using techniques from and applications in any knowledge domain.

Converge

monthly, Victor Rivero, Editor, published by e.Republic Inc., 100 Blue Ravine Road, Folsom, CA 95630, Phone: (916) 363-5000, Fax: (916) 363-5197, E-mail: vrivero@convergemag.com, Web: www.convergemag.com

Subscriptions: Free to qualified applicants in U.S. Other countries, $269.

This magazine's mission is "to interest, inform, and inspire educators in the K-12, college/university, corporate, and lifelong learning domains." It highlights "the use of technology to improve the content and quality of learning, educational instruction, and organization management."

Corporate Universities International Newsletter

bimonthly, published by the Corporate University Xchange, Inc., 381 Park Avenue South, Suite 713, New York, NY 10016, Phone: (800) 946-1210, (212) 213-2828, Fax: (212) 213-8621, E-mail: info@corpu.com, Web: www.corpu.com

Subscriptions: Free to members ($199).

This is "the only newsletter dedicated to in-depth research and analysis of corporate university trends, and the only newsletter targeted to senior corporate university practitioners and to representatives of institutions of higher education." It provides advice on all aspects of managing a corporate university.

Corporate University Review

bimonthly, published by IQPC, 150 Clove Road, Little Falls, NJ 07424-0401, Phone: (800) 882-8684, (973) 256-0211, Fax: (973) 256-0211, E-mail: info@traininguniversity.com, Web: http://www.traininguniversity.com.

Subscriptions: Free to members of the Corporate University Collaborative: U.S., $295, elsewhere, $395.

This publication focuses on how companies train their employees.

DEOSNEWS

monthly, online journal, published by the Distance Education Online Symposium, The American Center for the Study of Distance Education, College of Education, The Pennsylvania State University, 110 Rackley Building, University Park, PA 16802-3202, Phone: (814) 863-3764, Fax: (814) 865-5878, E-mail: ACSDE@psu.edu, Web: www.ed.psu.edu/acsde/deos/deos.asp

Subscriptions: $12 or free with subscription to *The American Journal of Distance Education.*

DEOSNEWS complements *The American Journal of Distance Education* by promoting distance education scholarship, research, and practice.

Distance Education: An International Journal

biannual (May and October), ISSN: 1326-0065, published by DEC Publications, Distance Education Centre, University of Southern Queensland, PO Darling Heights, Toowoomba, Queensland 4350, Australia, Phone: +61 7 46 31 2290, Fax: +61 7 46 31 1502, E-mail: grundonm@usq.edu.au, Web: www.usq.edu.au/dec/decjourn/demain.htm

Subscriptions: AU$55 surface mail, AU$72 overseas airmail.

Distance Education is the official journal of the Open and Distance Learning Association of Australia Inc. The aim of the journal is to engender and disseminate research and scholarship in distance education, open learning, and flexible learning systems.

Distance Education Report
bimonthly, published by Magna Publications, Inc., 2718 Dryden Drive, Madison, WI 53704, Phone: (608) 246-3580, (608) 246-3590, Fax: (608) 246-3597, E-mail: cust-serv@magnapubs.com, Web: www.magnapubs.com/Newsletters/Der/main.html

Subscriptions: $399.

This newsletter provides distance educators, administrators, and staff with information to design, implement, and manage distance education programs courses. The focus is on practical applications and new developments, with concise reports on changing technologies, institutional case studies, governance, and international initiatives.

Education and Information Technologies
quarterly, ISSN: 1360-2357, published by Kluwer Academic/Plenum Publishers, 233 Spring Street, New York, NY 10013-1578, Phone: (212) 620-8000, (800) 221-9369, (212) 20-8468 (customer service), Fax: (212) 807-1047, E-mail: services@wkap.nl, Web: www.wkap.nl/journalhome.htm/1360-2357

Subscriptions: Individual, $65/EUR 65. Institutional, $363/EUR 363.

This is the official journal of the IFIP Technical Committee on Education. It publishes papers from all sectors of education on all aspects of information technology and information systems.

ED—Education at a Distance
monthly, electronic, published by the U.S. Distance Learning Association, 140 Gould Street, Suite 200B, Needham, MA 02494-2397, Phone: (800) 275-5162, (781) 453-2388, Fax: (781) 453-2389, E-mail: kclemens@usdla.org, Web: www.usdla.org

Subscriptions: Free.

This magazine is an official publication of the United States Distance Learning Association. It covers developments in the field of distance learning.

Education Technology Research and Development
quarterly, published by the Association for Education Communications and Technology, Inc., 1800 North Stonelake Drive, Suite 2, Bloomington, IN 47404, Phone: (812) 335 7675, Fax: (812) 335-7678, E-mail: aect@aect.org, Web: www.aect.org/Pubs/etrd-web/etr_d.html.

Subscriptions: AECT members, $35; nonmembers in U.S., $55; elsewhere, $63 (surface mail) or $83 (airmail).

This is a refereed, scholarly journal dealing with research and development in educational technology and instructional design at the school, higher, and adult education levels. Articles tend to be a blend of theory and application. Includes a book review section.

Educational Media International

quarterly, ISSN: 0952-3987, published by Taylor & Francis Group (Routledge), Customer Services, 325 Chestnut Street, Suite 800, Philadelphia, PA 19106, Phone: (800) 354-1420, Fax: (215) 625-8914, E-mail: info@taylorandfrancis.com, Web: www.tandf.co.uk/journals

Subscriptions: Institutional, US$270/£163; Individual: US$70/£41.

This journal provides an international forum for the exchange of information and views on new developments in educational and mass media. Contributions come from academics and professionals whose ideas and experiences come from a number of countries and contexts.

Educational Technology

bimonthly, published by Educational Technology Publications, Inc., 700 Palisade Avenue, Englewood Cliffs, NJ 07632-0564, Phone: (800) 952-2665 or (201) 871-4007, Fax: (201) 871-4009, E-mail: edtecpubs@aol.com, Web: bookstoread.com/etp

Subscriptions: U.S., $119; other countries, $139.

Subtitled "The Magazine for Managers of Change in Education," this publication is aimed at both education and training, with a blend of theoretical and practice-oriented articles dealing with the use of electronic technology, including computers, video, and multimedia.

Educational Technology Abstracts

bimonthly, published by Taylor & Francis Group (Carfax), Customer Services, 325 Chestnut Street, Suite 800, Philadelphia, PA 19106, Phone: (800) 354-1420, Fax: (215) 625-8914, E-mail: info@taylorandfrancis.com, Web: www.tandf.co.uk/journals

Subscriptions: Institutional, US$862/£523; Individual, US$318/£193.
ISSN: 0266-3368

This is an international abstracting service to help teachers, lecturers, educational technologists, and instructional designers identify important recently published material in the field of the technology of education and training.

Educational Technology & Society

quarterly, online, ISSN: 1436-4522, published by Kinshuk, Massey University, Private Bag 11222, Palmerston North, New Zealand, Phone: (64) 06 350-5799 x 2090, Fax: (64) 06 350-5725, E-mail: kinshuk@massey.ac.nz, Web: ifets.ieee.org/periodical/

Subscriptions: Free.

The journal of the International Forum of Educational Technology & Society and the IEEE Learning Technology Task Force, this peer-reviewed journal covers issues affecting the developers of educational systems and educators who implement and manage such systems.

Educational Technology Research and Development
quarterly, ISSN: 1042-1629, published by Association for Educational Communications & Technology, 1800 N. Stonelake Drive, Suite 2, Bloomington, IN 47404, Phone: (812) 335-7675 or (877) 677-AECT, Fax: (812) 335-7678, E-mail: aect@aect.org, Web: www.aect.org

Subscriptions: Institutional Print: $150, Print and Electronic: $250, Personal Print: $65, Print and Electronic: $105, AECT Members Print: $40, Print and Electronic: $65, (outside US add $20 for surface and $40 for airmail).

This refereed, scholarly journal focuses entirely on research and instructional development in the field of educational technology. In addition to separate Research and Development sections, regular departments feature book reviews, including international works.

Educational Technology Review
biannual, ISSN: 1065-6901, published by the Association for the Advancement of Computing in Education, P.O. Box 3728, Norfolk, VA 23514, Phone: (757) 623-7588, Fax: (703) 997-8760, E-mail: info@aace.org, Web: www.aace.org

Subscriptions: Free to AACE members. Nonmembers: U.S., $40; other countries, $50. Outside the U.S., add $15 for postage.

Subtitled "International Forum on Educational Technology Issues and Applications," this journal enables AACE members to exchange information, ideas, and practical solutions to contribute toward improving education through information technology.

Educause Review
bimonthly, 1150 18th Street, NW, Suite 1010, Washington, DC 20036, Phone: (202) 872-4200, Fax: (202) 872-4318, E-mail: info@educause.edu, Web: www.educause.edu

Subscriptions: U.S., Canada, Mexico: $24. Other countries: $48.

This magazine is devoted to "exploring the impact of information technologies on higher education."

e-Journal of Instructional Science and Technology
bimonthly, online, published by Distance Education Centre, University of Southern Queensland, Toowoomba, Australia 4350, E-mail: jegede@ouhk.edu.hk (Olugbemiro Jegede), s.naidu@meu.unimelb.edu.au (Som Naidu), Web: www.usq.edu.au/elect-pub/e-jist

Subscriptions: Free.

This is an international peer-reviewed electronic journal that publishes manuscripts based on original work of practitioners and researchers with specific focus or implications for the design of instructional materials. The materials are intended for practitioners, policy makers, and academics within education and training.

e-Learning Magazine

monthly, published by Advanstar Communications, Publishing Office, 201 Sandpointe Avenue, Suite 600, Santa Ana, CA 92707, Phone: (714) 513-8400, (800) 598-6008 or (218) 723-9180 (circulation), Fax: (714) 513-8632, E-mail: ccoates@advanstar.com, Web: www.elearningmag.com

Subscriptions: Free to qualified subscribers in the U.S. and Canada. Others: U.S., $35; Canada and Mexico $45; other countries, $55.

"The Magazine of Distributed Learning" aims to educate executive decision-makers in the public and private sectors on the benefits of learning tools, programs, and applications.

EMedia Magazine

monthly, P.O. Box 2036, Skokie, IL 60076, Phone: (800) 806-7795, (847) 588-0340, Fax: (203) 761-1444, E-mail: emediasub@onlineinc.com, Web: www.emediapro.net

Subscriptions: Individual, $55; corporate, $98. Canada, add $9 postage. Other countries, add $50 postage.

This magazine covers the tools and technologies that professionals use to publish, archive, distribute, and network digital content. The magazine is for producers and the business users of CD-ROM, CD-Recordable, DVD, CD-ROM/online hybrid, and Internet-based electronic media applications and products.

European Journal of Open and Distance Learning

irregular, online, Martin Valcke and Anne Bruce, Editors, E-mail: martin.valcke@rug.ac.be, Web: www1.nks.no/eurodl/index.html

Subscriptions: Free.

The goal of this online journal is to "publish scholarly work and solid information about open and distance learning, education through telematics, multimedia, on-line learning and co-operation, ... or whatever you prefer to call this field."

First Monday

monthly, online, ISSN: 1396-0466, Edward Valauskas, Chief Editor, P.O. Box 87636, Chicago, IL 60680-0636, Phone: NA, Fax: NA, E-mail: ejv@uic.edu, Web: www.first-monday.org

Subscriptions: Free.

First Monday is a peer-reviewed journal on the Internet that publishes original articles about the Internet and the Global Information Infrastructure.

Indian Journal of Open Learning

three issues (January, May, and September), ISSN: 0971-2690, published by Staff Training and Research Institute of Distance Education, Indira Gandhi National Open University, Maidan Garhi, New Delhi, 110 068, India, Phone: 91 11 6515399, Fax: 91 11 6857073, E-mail: stride@del2.vsnl.net.in, Web: www.ignou.org/stride/journal.htm

Subscriptions: NA.

This international journal was started in 1992 to disseminate information about theory, practice, and research in the field of open and distance education.

Information Technology & People

quarterly, ISSN: 0959-3845, published by MCB University Press Ltd., 60/62 Toller Lane Bradford BD8 9BY, England, Phone: +44 (0)1274 777700, Fax: +44 (0)1274 785200, E-mail: customerservices@mcb.co.uk, editorial@mcb.co.uk, Web: www.mcb.co.uk/itp.htm

Subscriptions: North America, $1499. Other areas, check Web site for rates.

This journal provides a communication medium for academics and practitioners concerned with social and organizational issues in the design and use of information technology.

Innovations in Education and Teaching International

quarterly, ISSN: 1470-3297 (Print), 1470-3300 (Online), published by Taylor & Francis Group (Routledge), Customer Services, 325 Chestnut Street, Suite 800, Philadelphia, PA 19106, Phone: (800) 354-1420, Fax: (215) 625-8914, E-mail: info@taylorandfrancis.com, Web: www.tandf.co.uk/journals

Subscriptions: Institutional: US$244/£148, Individual: US$68/£39.

This journal, formerly *Innovations in Education & Training International*, is the official journal of the Staff and Educational Development Association, newly merged with the Association of Education and Training Technology. It covers developments in education and training for teaching staff, staff developers and managers in higher and further education, continuing education, and training organizations.

Interactive Educational Multimedia

biannual, online, ISSN: 1576-4990, published by Interactive Educational Multimedia (José Luis Rodríguez Illera), ICE - Universitat de Barcelona, Passeig de la Vall d'Hebron, 171, 08035 Barcelona, Spain, E-mail: mme@d5.ub.es, Web: www.ub.es/multimedia/iem/index.htm

Subscriptions: Free.

This journal, launched in 2000 by The Multimedia Teaching and Learning Group of the University of Barcelona, is intended to provide "a space for dialogue and reflection about the application of the multimedia technologies in education." It publishes articles related to research into the educational aspects of multimedia technologies in all its facets: implementation and design of materials, teaching and learning, experiences, etc.

Interactive Learning Environments

three issues, ISSN: 1049-4820, published by Swets & Zeitlinger Publishers, P.O. Box 825, 2160 SZ Lisse, Netherlands, Phone: (+31) 252 435 111, Fax: (+31) 252 415 888, E-mail: pub@swets.nl, Web: www.swets.nl

Subscriptions: Individuals: $79; institutions, $213.

This journal covers technologies such as Internet, groupware, and multimedia and "their impact on the fields of education and training, lifelong learning, and sharing knowledge in the global village."

InterMedia

bimonthly, ISSN: 0309-118X, published by International Institute of Communications, 3rd Floor, Westcott House, 35 Portland Place, London W1B 1AE, England, Phone: +44 (0)20 7323 9622, Fax: +44 (0)20 7323 9623, E-mail: enquiries@iicom.org

Subscriptions: Free to IIC members. Nonmembers, £70.

The journal of the International Institute of Communications—a global, independent and interdisciplinary network of senior decision makers and thinkers—takes a multi-disciplinary approach to emerging communications issues that relate to broadcasting, telecommunications, and new media. Its readers are policy makers, regulators, academics, content providers, technologists, and industrialists in over 70 countries.

International Journal of Artificial Intelligence in Education

quarterly (print), ongoing (online), ISSN: 1560-4292 (print), 1560-4306 (online), published by The International AIED Society, Computer Based Learning Unit, University of Leeds, Leeds LS2 9JT, England, Phone: +44 113 2334626, Fax: +44 113 233 4635, E-mail: ijaied@cbl.leeds.ac.uk, Web: cbl.leeds.ac.uk/ijaied

Subscriptions: Free to members of the International AIED Society. Nonmembers, £40. Institutions, £60.

This is the official journal of the International Artificial Intelligence in Education Society. It publishes "papers and other items concerned with the application of artificial intelligence techniques and concepts to the design of systems to support learning."

International Journal of Educational Technology

semiannual, Michelle Hinn, Department of Educational Psychology, 1310 South Sixth Street, College of Education, Champaign, IL 61820, E-mail: IJET@lists.ed.uiuc.edu, Web: www.outreach.uiuc.edu/ijet

Subscriptions: Free.

This is an international refereed journal in the field of educational technology, created in 1999 and sponsored by faculty, staff, and students at The Graduate School of Education at the University of Western Australia and the College of Education at the University of Illinois at Urbana-Champaign.

International Journal of Educational Telecommunications

quarterly, ISSN: 1077-9124, published by the Association for the Advancement of Comput-ing in Education, P.O. Box 3728, Norfolk, VA 23514, Phone: (757) 623-7588, Fax: (703) 997-8760, E-mail: info@aace.org, Web: www.aace.org/pubs/ijet/index.html

Subscriptions: Free to AACE members ($80). Institutions, $115. Outside the U.S., add $15 for postage.

This journal as created to serve as a forum to facilitate the international exchange of information on the current theory, research, development, and practice of telecommunications in education and training.

International Journal of Human-Computer Studies

monthly, ISSN: 1071-5819, published by Academic Press, Inc., 525 B Street, Suite 1900, San Diego, CA 92101-4495, Phone: (619) 231-0926, (619) 231-6616, (800) 543-9534 (customer service), Fax: (619) 699-6715, E-mail: IJHCS@harcourt.com, Web: www.apnet.com/ijhcs

Subscriptions: £1064.

This journal publishes original research on the theory and practice of human-computer interaction and the human-machine interface. The journal covers the boundaries between computing and artificial intelligence, psychology, linguistics, mathematics, engineering, and social organization.

International Review of Research in Open and Distance Learning

Janice Thiessen, Managing Editor, Institute for Research in Distance and Open Learning, Athabasca University, 1 University Drive, Athabasca, AB T9S 3A3, Canada, Phone: (780) 675-6727, Fax: (780) 675-6722, E-mail: irrodl@athabascau.ca, Web: www.irrodl.org

Subscriptions: Free with registration through Web site.

This refereed electronic journal seeks to advance theory, research, and practice in open and distance learning worldwide.

Interpersonal Computing and Technology Journal

online/e-mail, two/four times a year, Susan Barnes, Editor, Association of Educational Communication and Technology, 1800 N. Stonelake Drive, Suite 2, Bloomington, IN 47404, Phone: (812) 335-7675, (877) 677-AECT, Fax: (812) 335-7678, E-mail: sbbarnes @pipeline.com, aect@aect.org, Web: jan.ucc.nau.edu/ ~ ipct-j

Subscriptions: Free.

This is a scholarly, peer-reviewed journal that focuses on computer-mediated communication and the pedagogical issues surrounding the use of computers and technology in educational settings.

Journal of Asynchronous Learning Networks

irregular, online, ISSN: 1092-8235, John Bourne, Editor-in-Chief, P.O. Box 1570, Station B, Nashville, TN 37235, Phone: (615) 322-2118, Fax: (615) 343-6449, E-mail: john. bourne@Vanderbilt.edu, Web: www.aln.org/alnweb/journal/jaln.htm

Subscriptions: Free.

The journal publishes research articles that describe original work in ALN, including experimental results, as well as reviews and articles that outline current thinking. The articles deal primarily with educational settings and issues, but some are also relevant to business training.

Journal of Computer-Mediated Communication

quarterly, online, ISSN: 1083-6101, Margaret L. McLaughlin, Co-Editor, Annenberg School for Communication, University of Southern California, Los Angeles, CA 90089, Phone: (213) 740-3938, Fax: (213) 740-0014, E-mail: jcmc@usc.edu, Web: www. ascusc.org/jcmc

Subscriptions: Free.

This journal covers all areas of computer-mediated communication. It was launched in 1994 to publish original essays and research reports.

The Journal of Computing in Higher Education

Carol B. MacKnight, Executive Editor, P.O. Box 2593, Amherst, MA 01004-2593, Phone: (413) 545-4232, Fax: (413) 545-3203, E-mail: cmacknight@oit.umass.edu, Web: www-unix.oit.umass.edu/ ~ carolm/jche

Subscriptions: Individuals / Personal Check: U.S., $35, Canada, $45; other countries, $65 surface mail, $75 airmail. Institutions: U.S., $65; Canada, $75; other countries, $80 surface mail, $90 airmail.

This journal publishes "peer-reviewed essays, reviews, reports, and research articles that contribute to our understanding of the issues, problems, and research associated with instructional technology and educational management information systems."

Journal of Distance Education/Revue de l'Education à Distance

biannual (Spring and Fall), ISSN: 0830-0445, Canadian Association for Distance Education, Suite 204, 260 Dalhousie Street, Ottawa, ON K1N 7E4, Canada, Phone: (613) 241-0018, Fax: (613) 241-0019, E-mail: cade@csse.ca, Web: www.cade-aced.ca

Subscriptions: Free to CADE members. (Regular individual membership: CDN$75.00. Student or retired individual membership: CDN$37.50. Organizational membership:

CDN$280.00 for up to four people, CDN$65.00 for each additional person. Outside Canada, pay in US$.) Nonmembers: in Canada, CDN$40 + CDN$2.80 (GST) = CDN$42.80; outside of Canada, US$40.

An international publication of the Canadian Association of Distance Education, the journal promotes empirical and theoretical scholarly work relating to distance education in Canada and throughout the world.

The Journal of Distance Learning

annual, Administration Secretary, Distance Education Association of New Zealand, 4 Ronald Woolf Place, Churton Park, Wellington, New Zealand, Phone: (64 4) 478-5839, Fax: (64 4) 478-5832, E-mail: wilcol@xtra.co.nz, Web: http://www.deanz.org.nz/jour.htm

Subscriptions: New Zealand, NZ$25 (including GST); Australia and South Pacific NZ$30; rest of the world, NZ$35. Price includes including airmail delivery outside New Zealand.

A refereed journal from the Distance Education Association of New Zealand, this publication is devoted to exploring both the theory and practice of distance education and open and flexible learning. The focus is on the "distinctive and interesting ways" in which distance learning is developing in New Zealand, the Pacific, and Australia.

Journal of Educational Computing Research

eight issues, ISSN: 0735-6331, published by Baywood Publishing Co., Inc., 26 Austin Avenue, P.O. Box 337, Amityville, NY 11701, Phone: (631) 691-1270, (800) 638-7819 (orders), Fax: (631) 691-1770, E-mail: baywood@baywood.com, Web: baywood.com

Subscriptions: Individual, $114. Institutional, $275.

This interdisciplinary journal addresses four primary areas of concern: the effects of educational computing applications, the design and development of innovative computer hardware and software for use in educational environments, the interpretation and implications of research in educational computing fields, and the theoretical and historical foundations of computer-based education.

Journal of Educational Multimedia and Hypermedia

quarterly, ISSN: 1055-8896, published by the Association for the Advancement of Computing in Education, P.O. Box 3728, Norfolk, VA 23514, Phone: (757) 623-7588, Fax: (703) 997-8760, E-mail: info@aace.org, Web: www.aace.org/pubs/jemh/Default.htm

Subscriptions: Free to AACE members. Nonmembers: U.S., $40; elsewhere, $50. Institutions, $115. Outside the U.S., add $15 for postage.

This journal is designed to provide a multi-disciplinary forum to present and discuss research, development, and applications of multimedia and hypermedia in education. The main goal is to contribute to the advancement of the theory and practice of learning and teaching using these technological tools that allow the integration of images, sound, text, and data.

Journal of Educational Technology Systems
quarterly, ISSN: 0047-2395, published by the Learning Technology Institute, 50 Culpeper Street, Warrenton, VA 20186, Phone: (540) 347-0055 or (800) 457-6812, Fax: (540) 349-3169, E-mail: info@lti.org, Web: www.lti.org

Subscriptions: Available only to SALT members: $60 (individual). Institutions: $146. Add $6.50 in U.S. and Canada or $11.75 elsewhere for postage.
This journal deals with systems in which technology and education interface and is designed to inform educators who are interested in making optimum use of technology.

Journal of Instruction Delivery Systems
quarterly, ISSN: 0892-4872, published by the Society for Applied Learning Technology and the Learning Technology Institute, 50 Culpeper Street, Warrenton, VA 20186, Phone: (540) 347-0055 or (800) 457-6812, Fax: (540) 349-3169, E-mail: info@lti.org, Web: www.lti.org

Subscriptions: SALT members, $40; others, $60. Outside North America, add $18 for postage.
The journal is devoted to enhancing productivity through appropriate applications of technology systems in education, training, and job performance and to heighten awareness of technology-based learning.

Journal of Instructional Science and Technology
See e-Journal of Instructional Science and Technology

Journal of Interactive Instruction Development
quarterly, ISSN: 1040-0370, published by the Society for Applied Learning Technology and the Learning Technology Institute, 50 Culpeper Street, Warrenton, VA 20186, Phone: (540) 347-0055 or (800) 457-6812, Fax: (540) 349-3169, E-mail: info@lti.org, Web: www.lti.org

Subscriptions: SALT members, $40; nonmembers, $60. Outside North America, add $18 for postage.
This journal provides instructional systems developers and designers with important perspectives on emerging technologies and design methodologies.

Journal of Interactive Learning Research
quarterly, ISSN: 1093-023X, published by the Association for the Advancement of Computing in Education, P.O. Box 3728, Norfolk, VA 23514, Phone: (757) 623-7588, Fax: (703) 997-8760, E-mail: info@aace.org, Web: www.aace.org/pubs/jilr

Subscriptions: Free to AACE members. Individuals, $80. Institutions, $115. Outside U.S., add $15 shipping/handling.

This journal publishes papers "related to the underlying theory, design, implementation, effectiveness, and impact on education and training of the following interactive learning environments: authoring systems, cognitive tools for learning computer-assisted language learning, computer-based assessment systems, computer-based training, computer-mediated communications, computer-supported collaborative learning, distributed learning environments, electronic performance support systems, interactive learning environments, interactive multimedia systems, interactive simulations and games, intelligent agents on the Internet, intelligent tutoring systems, microworlds, virtual reality based learning systems."

Journal of Interactive Media in Education
irregular, online, ISSN:1365-893X, Simon Buckingham Shum, Knowledge Media Institute, The Open University, Milton Keynes, MK7 6AA, United Kingdom, Phone: NA Fax: NA, E-mail: jime@open.ac.uk, Web: www-jime.open.ac.uk

Subscriptions: Free.

This online journal is intended to foster a multidisciplinary and intellectually rigorous debate on the theoretical and practical aspects of interactive media in education.

Journal of Online Learning
quarterly, published by the International Society for Technology in Education, 480 Charnelton Street, Eugene, OR 97401-2626, Phone: (800) 336-5191, (541) 302-3777, Fax: (541) 302-3778, E-mail: iste@iste.org, Web: www.iste.org/publishing/jol/index.html

Subscriptions: Free to SIG/Tel members: U.S., $29; other countries, $39.

This journal is published by the ISTE Special Interest Group for Telecommunications, a network of educators involved with computer-based communications. It features articles on aspects of K–12 and college instructional use of telecommunication, with emphasis on computer-mediated communication.

Journal of Research on Computing in Education
quarterly, published by the International Society for Technology in Education, 480 Charnelton Street, Eugene, OR 97401-2626, Phone: (800) 336-5191, (541) 302-3777, Fax: (541) 302-3778, E-mail: iste@iste.org, Web: www.iste.org/publishing/jrce

Subscriptions: $38. Outside U.S., add $10 shipping/handling.

This journal publishes articles that report on original research, system or project descriptions and evaluations, syntheses of the literature, assessments of the state of the art, and theoretical positions that relate to educational computing. International in scope and thorough in its coverage, the theoretical and conceptual articles in the *JRCE* define the state of the art and future horizons of educational computing.

Journal of Technology Education
semiannual (fall and spring), ISSN 1045-1064, James E. LaPorte, JTE Editor, 144 Smyth Hall, Virginia Tech, Blacksburg, VA 24061-0432 , Phone: (540) 231-6480, (540) 231-8169, Fax: (540) 231-9075, E-mail: laporte@vt.edu, Web: scholar.lib.vt.edu/ejournals/JTE

Subscriptions: U.S.: individual, $12; library, $20. Other countries: individual, $20; library, $25.

This journal, sponsored by the Council on Technology Teacher Education and the International Technology Education Association, provides a forum for scholarly discussion on topics relating to technology education—research, philosophy, and theory. It also publishes book reviews, editorials, guest articles, comprehensive literature reviews, and reactions to published articles.

The Lakewood Report on Technology for Learning
See Technology for Learning

Learning Circuits
monthly, online, published by American Society for Training & Development, 1640 King Street, Box 1443, Alexandria, VA 22313-2043, Phone: (703) 683-8100, (800) 628-2783, Fax: (703) 683-1523, E-mail: info@astd.org, Web: www.learningcircuits.org

Subscriptions: Free.

This online magazine focuses on workplace e-learning, with feature articles, departments, columns, and peer interaction. Very useful resource.

MultiMedia
quarterly, ISSN: 1070-986X, published by the Institute of Electrical and Electronics Engineers (IEEE Computer Society), IEEE Customer Service Center, 445 Hoes Lane, P.O. Box 1331, Piscataway, NJ 08855-1331, Phone: (800) 678-4333, (732) 981-0060, Fax: (732) 981-9667, E-mail: storehelp@ieee.org

Subscriptions: $440. Outside U.S., Canada, and Mexico, ass $25 shipping/handling. (Discount for IEEE members.)

This magazine focuses on multimedia computing and communications systems. It covers such topics as hardware and software for media compression, media storage and transport, workstation support, data modeling, and abstractions to embed multimedia in applications programs.

Multimedia & Internet Training Newsletter
See Technology for Learning

Networking
biweekly, online, ISSN: 1206-9450, published by The Node Learning Technologies Network, 410 Dufferin Avenue, London, ON N6B 1Z6, Canada, Phone: (519) 457-465, Fax: (519) 457-4659, E-mail: info@node.on.ca, Web: thenode.org/networking

Subscriptions: Free.

This newsletter covers developments in distance education and learning technologies at Canadian colleges, universities, and organizations and provides news, reviews, and analysis.

On the Horizon
bimonthly, ISSN: 1085-4959, published by Camford Publishing Limited, Sidney House Sussex Street, Cambridge, CB1 1PA, United Kingdom, Phone: +44 (0) 1223 509161, Fax: +44 (0) 1223 509162, E-mail: oth@camford.demon.co.uk, Web: www.camford-publishing.com

Subscriptions: Individual, $59 or £39. Institutional, $95 or £55.

This international publication provides analysis and comment on the future of postsecondary education. It informs key decision makers concerned with postsecondary education in its many and emerging forms, from traditional institutions to corporate universities, from private/for-profits to non-profits around the world.

Online Journal of Distance Learning Administration
quarterly, online, Melanie Clay, Editor-in-Chief, The State University of West Georgia, Center for Distance Education, 1600 Maple Street, Carrollton, GA 30118, Phone: (770) 836-4647, Fax: NA, E-mail: mhill@westga.edu, Web: www.westga.edu/~distance/jmain11.html

Subscriptions: Free.

This journal covers all areas of distance education management, practical and theoretical.

Online Learning Magazine
monthly, Circulation Dept. 50 S. Ninth Street, Minneapolis, MN 55402, Phone: (612) 340-4809 (editorial), (800) 328-4329, Fax: (612) 340-4819 (circulation), (612) 333-6526, E-mail: editor@onlinelearning.mag, circwork@billcomm.com, Web: www.onlinelearningmag.com

Subscriptions: Free to qualified applicants in U.S. and Canada; otherwise, $89; elsewhere, $129.

Formerly *Inside Technology Training*, this magazine focuses on e-learning, including concepts like knowledge management, performance support and virtual collaboration.

Open Learning: The Journal of Open and Distance Learning
three issues ISSN: 0268-0513, published by Taylor & Francis, Editorial: Greville Rumble,

Editor, Open University, Walton Hall, Milton Keynes, MK7 6AA, United Kingdom, E-mail: g.rumble@open.ac.uk, Subscriptions: Taylor & Francis Group Journals, 325 Chestnut Street, Suite 800, Philadelphia, PA 19106, Phone: (800) 354-1420, Fax: (215) 625-8914, E-mail: info@taylorandfrancis.com, Web: www.tandf.co.uk/journals/car-fax/02680513.html

Subscriptions: Individual: US$57/£35. Institutional: US$174/£105.

Published on behalf of the Open University, this journal publishes theoretical and practice-based articles reflecting global developments in distance, flexible, and open education and training, as well as book reviews.

Open Learning Today

quarterly, published by the British Association for Open Learning, Pixmore Centre, Pixmore Avenue, Letchworth, Hertfordshire, SG6 1JG, United Kingdom, Phone: 01462 485588, Fax: 01462 485633, E-mail: info@baol.co.uk, Web: www.baol.co.uk/olt.htm

Subscriptions: United Kingdom, £55. Other countries, £65.

The goal of the journal of the British Association for Open Learning is to promote best practice in open and flexible learning, extend awareness of open and flexible learning, and act as an information bridge across the different sectors, and between the individual organization and the general pool of knowledge. It addresses issues and topics as they impact on the wide world of lifelong learning.

Performance Improvement

10 issues (monthly, with combined May/June and November/December issues), ISSN: 1090-8811-AE, published by the International Society for Performance Improvement, ISPI Publications, 1300 L Street NW, Suite 1250, Washington, DC 20005, Phone: (202) 408-7969, Fax: (202) 408-7972, E-mail: info@ispi.org, Web: www.ispi.org

Subscriptions: Complimentary to ISPI members; for nonmembers, $69.

This journal covers a range of topics related to training and performance improvement in the workplace, with articles written by practitioners.

Performance Improvement Quarterly

quarterly, ISSN: 0898-5952, published by the International Society for Performance Improve-ment, ISPI Publications, 1300 L Street NW, Suite 1250, Washington, DC 20005, Phone: (202) 408-7969, Fax: (202) 408-7972, E-mail: info@ispi.org, Web: www.ispi.org

Subscriptions: $40 for members, $50 for nonmembers.

This journal serves as a vehicle for "the scholarly publication of studies reflecting cutting-edge research in the field of human performance technology" and a forum for discussion among professionals in the field of issues related to human performance, instructional design and development, and learning.

Quarterly Review of Distance Education
quarterly, published by the Association for Education Communications and Technology, Inc., 1800 North Stonelake Drive, Suite 2, Bloomington, IN 47404, Phone: (812) 335-7675, Fax: (812) 335-7678, E-mail: aect@aect.org, Web: www.aect.org/Publications/qrde.htm

Subscriptions: AECT members: $40. Nonmembers: $65. Institutions: $150. Outside U.S., add $20 for surface mail and $40 for airmail.

The official journal of AECT, this refereed journal publishes articles, research briefs, reviews, and editorials dealing with the theories, research, and practices of distance education in the public and private sectors.

Syllabus Magazine
monthly, published by Syllabus Press, 345 Northlake Drive, San Jose, CA 95117, Phone: (800) 773-0670, Fax: (408) 261-7280, E-mail: info@syllabus.com, Web: www.syllabus.com

Subscriptions: Free in U.S. to qualified applicants. Canada and Mexico, $24. Other countries, $75.

This publication is intended to be "the definitive technology magazine for high schools, colleges, and universities." It focuses on the use of technology in education and related learning environments, to inform educators on how technology can be used to support their teaching, learning, and administrative activities.

Tech Trends: For Leaders in Education and Training
bimonthly, published by the Association for Educational Communications and Technology, 1800 North Stonelake Drive, Suite 2, Bloomington, IN 47404, Phone: (812) 335-7675, Fax: (812) 335-7678, E-mail: aect@aect.org, Web: www.aect.org

Subscriptions: AECT members, free; nonmembers: check Web site.

This is a peer-reviewed periodical for practitioners that features practical articles about technology and its integration into the learning environment. Regular departments include news items, new products, copyright, ethics, new books, and software.

TechKnowLogia: International Journal of Technologies for the Advancement of Knowledge and Learning
bimonthly, published by Knowledge Enterprise, Inc., P.O. Box 3027, Oakton, VA 22124, 9926 Courthouse Woods Court, Vienna, VA 22181-6019, Phone: NA, Fax: (703) 242-2279, E-mail: information@KnowledgeEnterprise.org, Web: www.techknowlogia.org

Subscriptions: Free (registration).

This international online journal is described as "a one-stop magazine that deals with the whole domain of issues related to technologies for knowledge and learning" and "a forum for dialogue and sharing of knowledge and experiences, and an instrument to encourage thinking 'outside the box.'"

Technological Horizons in Education
See T.H.E. Journal

Technology for Learning: Multimedia & Internet Training Newsletter (Lakewood Report on Technology for Learning)
monthly, published monthly by Bill Communications, Inc., Human Performance Group, 50 S. Ninth Street, Minneapolis, MN 55402, Phone: (800) 328-4329 or (612) 333-0471, Fax: (612) 333-6526, E-mail: nswanson@lakewoodpub.com, Web: www.trainingsupersite.com/publications

Subscriptions: $189. Canada, add $10 plus 7% GST or 15% HST (#123705485). All other countries, add $20.

This newsletter provides practical ideas, how-to case studies, and product reviews that can help trainers accelerate learning in their organizations. It covers emerging technologies, including computer-based training and electronic performance support systems, and effective uses for them in the workplace.

The Technology Source
bimonthly, online, ISSN: 1532-0030, James L. Morrison, Editor-in-Chief, CB #3500, Peabody Hall, University of North Carolina, Chapel Hill, NC 27599-3500, Phone: NA, Fax: (919) 962-1693, E-mail: morrison@unc.edu, Web: horizon.unc.edu/TS

Subscriptions: Free.

The purpose of this peer-reviewed bimonthly periodical is "to provide thoughtful, illuminating articles that will assist educators as they face the challenge of integrating information technology tools into teaching and into managing educational organizations."

Technos: Quarterly for Education and Technology
quarterly, ISSN: 1060-5649, published by the Agency for Instructional Technology, Box A, Bloomington, IN 47402-0120, Phone (812) 339-2203, Fax: (812) 333-4218, E-mail: info@technos.net, Web: www.technos.net

Subscriptions: U.S., $28. Other countries, $32.

The journal of the Agency for Instructional Technology, this is a forum for the discussion of ideas about the use of technology in education, with a focus on reform.

Teleconference Magazine—The Business Communications Magazine
bimonthly, ISSN: 0739-7208, published by Advanstar Communications, Inc., 7500 Old Oak Boulevard, Cleveland, OH 44130-3369, Phone: (440) 243-8100, Fax: (440) 826-2833, E-mail: information@advanstar.com, Web: www.advanstar.com

Subscriptions: Free to qualified applicants in U.S. and Canada. Mexico: $80. All other countries: $110.

This magazine covers applications, case studies, technology, news, and information on audio conferencing, video conferencing, telemedicine, and distance learning. It's aimed at presidents, CEOs, CTOs, CFOs, network managers, telecom managers, sales and marketing VPs, and VARs.

T.H.E. Journal

11 issues (monthly except July), 17501 East 17th Street, Suite 230, Tustin, CA 92780, Phone: (714) 730-4011, Fax: (714) 730-3739, E-mail: editorial@thejournal.com, Web: www.thejournal.com

Subscriptions: Free to qualified applicants. In Canada, add $29 for mailing. In other countries, add $95 for mailing.

This journal, formerly *Technological Horizons in Education,* covers applications of technology in learning.

Training

monthly, published by Bill Communications, Inc., Human Performance Group, 50 S. Ninth Street, Minneapolis, MN 55402, Phone: (800) 328-4329 or (612) 333-0471 (editorial) or (800) 328-4328 (subscriptions), Fax: (612) 333-6526 (editorial) or (612) 340-4819 (subscriptions), E-mail: edit@trainingmag.com (editorial) or nswanson@lakewoodpub.com (subscriptions), Web: www.trainingsupersite.com/publications

Subscriptions: U.S., $78. Canada, $88 plus 7% GST or 15% HST (#123705485). All other countries, $99.

This magazine covers issues of interest to corporate trainers and managers in general, on all aspects of training, management and organizational development, motivation, and performance improvement. One of the leading magazines for trainers.

Training & Development

monthly, published by the American Society for Training and Development, 1640 King Street, Box 1443, Alexandria, VA 22313-2043, Phone: (800) NAT-ASTD (628-2783) or (703) 683-8100, Fax: (703) 683-8103, E-mail: info@astd.org, Web: www.astd.org

Subscriptions: ASTD members, $60. Nonmembers: U.S., $85; other countries, $165.

This journal covers a wide variety of topics relating to training, human resources, performance, and management issues. Articles are aimed at keeping readers current with the field, with lots of practical features, including book reviews and new learning tools sections.

Training Media Review

bimonthly, TMR Publications, P.O. Box 381822, Cambridge, MA 02238-1822, 21 Watson Road, Belmont, MA 02478, Phone: (877) 532-1838 or (617) 489-9120, Fax: (617) 489-3437, E-mail: tmr1@tmreview.com, Web: www.tmreview.com

Subscriptions: Print edition, $229. Online edition, $189.

This magazine was founded in 1993 "to facilitate decision making by providing the training community with authoritative, objective evaluations of media-based business training."

Training Strategies for Tomorrow

six issues (six dispatches), ISSN: 1369-7234, published by MCB University Press Ltd., 60/62 Toller Lane, Bradford, West Yorkshire, England BD8 9BY, Phone: +44 (0) 1274 777700, Fax: +44 (0) 1274 785200, E-mail: help@mcb-usa.com, Web: www.mcb.co. uk/tst.htm

Subscriptions: North America, $899. Other areas, check Web site for rates.

This journal covers management development, customer service training, outdoor training, evaluation of training programs and strategies, lifelong learning, participation and empowerment, training for quality, teambuilding, career development, performance appraisal, self-development, leadership skills training, selection and use of multimedia programs, and the impact of training and development on organizational performance.

The Training Technology Monitor

eight issues, published by Carswell, Thomson Professional Publishing, 2075 Kennedy Road, Scarborough, ON M1T 3V4, Canada, Phone: (800) 387-5164 or (416) 609-3800, Fax: (416) 298-5082, E-mail: customercare@carswell.com, Web: www.carswell.com

Subscriptions: Canada, $150 CDN + GST. Other countries, US$103.45.

This newsletter covers practices, trends, and issues related to the use of technology in delivering training for the workplace. It features profiles of innovative projects and individuals, features on new software and hardware, summaries of research focusing on technology-assisted learning, and a calendar of conferences, seminars, and workshops.

Upside

monthly, ISSN: 1052-0341 published by Upside Media, Inc., 731 Market Street, 2nd Floor, San Francisco, CA 94103-2005, Phone: (415) 489-5600, Fax: (415) 377-1961, E-mail: feedback@upside.com, Web: www.upside.com

Subscriptions: Free to qualified applicants in U.S. Otherwise: U.S., $19.95; elsewhere, $50.

This business technology magazine "analyzes technology business developments and the strategies behind them in entertainment, media, and telecommunication; profiles the industry's current and future leaders; and examines how changes in technology are affecting the way people live, work, and communicate."

Virtual University Business Digest

monthly, published by geteducated.com, LLC, 4 Carmichael Street, #2160, Essex

Junction, VT 05452, Phone: (802) 879-1379, Fax: (802) 288-1083, E-mail: info@geteducated.com, Web: www.geteducated.com/vubd/vubd.htm

Subscriptions: U.S., $265; other countries, $295.

Launched in March 1999, this newsletter focuses on "the Internet-enabled, for-profit, e-education industry." It is aimed at "executives, deans, analysts, and suppliers who are building or servicing for-profit, Internet-enabled, adult education enterprises." It covers new products and platforms, mergers, partnerships, funding sources, acquisitions, and emerging market leaders.

The Virtual University Gazette
monthly, online, ISSN: 1099-4262, published by geteducated.com, LLC, 4 Carmichael Street, #2160, Essex Junction, VT 05452, Phone: (802) 879-1379, Fax: (802) 288-1083, E-mail: gazette@geteducated.com, Web: www.geteducated.com/vugaz.htm

Subscriptions: Free.

This newsletter covers "the Internet university movement" for "distance learning professionals and students at the adult, postsecondary levels."

Virtual University Journal
monthly, online, ISSN: 1460-745X, published by VUP International, Anne Christie, Publisher, Association of International Management Centres, Castle Street, Buckingham, England MK18 1BP, Phone: +44 (0)01280 817222, Fax: +44 (0)1280 22205, E-mail: achristie@imc.org.uk, Web: www.openhouse.org.uk/virtual-university-press/vuj/welcome.htm

Subscriptions: Individual, £50 Sterling (+ VAT in EU Member States) or $85. Group rates available.

This international journal covers "the field of academic facilitation of learning through the use of communications technologies," publishing "papers relating to research, innovative thinking, and practice in this field."

WebNet Journal
quarterly, ISSN: 1522-192X, published by the Association for the Advancement of Computing in Education, P.O. Box 3728, Norfolk, VA 23514, Phone: (757) 623-7588, Fax: (703) 997-8760, E-mail: pubs@aace.org, Web: www.webnetjrl.com

Subscriptions: Individual, $45; institutional, $115. Outside the U.S., add $12 postage/handling.

Subtitled "Internet Technologies, Applications & Issues," this magazine is written for "an international readership of researchers, developers, and Internet users in educational, business, and professional environments."

Best Current Books on Distance Learning

I n collaboration with the ASTD and with the help of Karen White, manager of the ASTD Information Center, we present the following annotated list of 15 recently published books distance learning professionals will find particularly useful.

1. *Technology-Based Training: The Art and Science of Design, Development, and Delivery* by Kevin Kruse and Jason Keil, Jossey-Bass Publishers, 2000, 395 pp, ISBN: 0-7879-4626-5
Provides a comprehensive overview of technology-based training (TBT). Reviews and compares learning technologies, particularly CD-ROMs vs. the Web. Applies instructional system design theories to designing technology-based learning. Discusses managing TBT, working with a vendor, and selling projects internally. Contains four case studies that illustrate the design and use of TBT. Appendices include a glossary, a list of Internet resources, a list of useful associations, examples of a vendor proposal, and a cost-benefit worksheet.

2. *On-Demand Learning: Training in the New Millennium* by Darin E. Hartley, HRD Press, 2000, 171 pp, ISBN: 0-87425-539-2
Describes the future of on-demand learning, where the learner decides when, where, and how, to facilitate learning. Discusses the knowledge worker vs. the blue collar worker, multitasking, and competencies of the on-demand learner. Provides guidelines on how to enable on-demand learning, and identifies technological considerations. Concludes with examples of best practices particularly in the high-tech field.

3. *Managing Web-Based Training: How to Keep Your Program on Track and Make It Successful* by Alan L. Ellis, Ellen D. Wagner, and Warren R. Longmire, ASTD, 1999, 158 pp, ISBN: 1-56286-115-8
Written for managers tasked with designing, developing, and managing Web-based training initiatives even though they may have a limited understanding of what's involved in these activities. Provides direction in managing a Web-based program by including topics such as assessing the benefits and drawbacks of Web-based training, unique considerations, desiging and developing learning interventions, constructing the instructional Web site and staffing it, and evaluation and maintenance issues. Contains a glossary of terms and extensive list of resources.

4. *How to Design Self-Directed and Distance Learning Programs* by Nigel Harrison, McGraw-Hill, 1999, 360 pp. ISBN: 0-07-027100-3
Contrasts the differences between education and training. Emphasizes the importance of a systematic approach to developing learning programs. Provides guidelines specific to distance or self directed learning through the analysis, design, development, implementation, and evaluation steps. Includes specific advice for page and screen design.

5. *Open and Distance Learning: Case Studies from Industry and Education* by Stephen Brown, Kogan Page Ltd., 1999, 210 pp, ISBN: 0-7494-2934-8
Contains a collection of case studies on the effectiveness of distance learning in business and education. Profiles Lloyds Bank, Barclays Bank, Reuters, and several university programs in the UK and Australia. Covers such issues as open learning, corporate cultural change, integrated courseware, flexible learning, and computer-based learning.

6. *In Action: Implementing HRD Technology* by James Hite Jr., ed., ASTD, 1999, 301 pp, ISBN: 1-56286-127-1
Part of the "In Action" series. Contains 18 case studies that describe ways in which electronic technologies are being integrated into people and organizational development activities. The case studies include infrastructure and operational applications as well as direct learning support examples. Provides cases from the public and private sectors.

7. *Interactive Distance Learning Exercises that Really Work!* by Karen Mantyla, ASTD, 1999, 192 pp, ISBN: 1-56286-128-X
Outlines the steps involved in converting exercises, games, and other learning activities for use in a distance learning environment with special emphasis on interactivity. Demonstrates the steps involved in converting materials by using case studies from several companies. Includes a glossary of distance learning terms.

8. *Technology-Based Learning: Maximizing Human Performance and Corporate Success* by Michael J. Marquardt and Greg Kearsley, St. Lucie Press, 1999, 320 pp, ISBN: 1-57444-214-7
Discusses the impact technology has had on organizations, work, and workers. Identifies 14 ways that technology has transformed the workplace. Explains the connection between technology and the learning organization. Describes the learning capabilities of electronic publishing, television/video, teleconferencing, and interactive multimedia. Summarizes how technology is used for managing knowledge through the use of electronic performance support systems, networks, and knowledge engineering. Discusses the future of technology in the workplace. Includes a glossary.

9. *A Trainer's Guide to Web-Based Instruction: Getting Started on Intranet-and-Internet-Based Training* by Jay Alden, ASTD, 1998, 81 pp, ISBN: 1-56286-084-4
Presents an overview of preparing and presenting Web-based multimedia training over an intranet or the Internet. Discusses the advantages and disadvantages, visual design, structure, and interactive capability of Web-based training. Includes a glossary.

10. *ASTD Models for Learning Technologies: Roles, Competencies, and Outputs* by George M. Piskurich and Ethan S. Sanders, ASTD, 1998, 136 pp, ISBN: 1-56286-083-6
Presents a matrix of roles, competencies, and outputs for HRD professionals. Defines learning technologies and organizes them into instruction, presentation, and distribution methods. Discusses the ethics of using technology for learning purposes. Includes a self-assessment worksheet and a glossary.

11. *Open and Flexible Learning in Vocational Education and Training* by Judith Calder and Ann McCollum, Kogan Page Ltd., 1998, 146 pp, ISBN: 0-7494-2172-X
Identifies the environment in which training strategy is determined, the major stakeholders, and the types of training made available. Discusses the features and options in open and flexible learning. Reviews case studies of many different companies in the UK that are using open learning techniques. Part of the Open and Distance Learning series.

12. *Teaching and Learning Materials and the Internet, 2nd Edition* by Ian Forsyth, Kogan Page Ltd., 1998, 197 pp, ISBN: 0-7494-2606-3
Discusses using the Internet to deliver training. Presents a model for developing courses and materials to be used via the Internet. Reviews the costs/benefits of using the Internet as a training/learning delivery system. Discusses intranets along with home offices, small offices, and teleworking.

13. *Quality Standards for Evaluating Multimedia and Online Training* by Lynette Gillis, McGraw-Hill Canada, 2000, 240 pp, ISBN: 0-07-086385-7

Helps organizations select the most effective training programs from off-the-shelf courseware. Offers a rating scheme for comparing design features in different programs. The standards can also be used in preparing requests for proposals for e-learning or for formative evaluation. Includes six evaluation booklets, usability tests for learners, and tracking sheets.

14. *Multimedia-Based Instructional Design* by William W. Lee and Diana L. Owens, Jossey-Bass Pfeiffer, 2000, 359 pp, ISBN: 0-7879-5159-5
Explains how to design and develop computer-based, Web-based, or distance broadcast training. Covers needs assessment and analysis, instructional design, development and implementation, and evaluation. Includes a CD-ROM with multiple tools, checklists, and templates.

15. *Web-Based Training* by Margaret Driscoll, Jossey-Bass Pfeiffer, 1998, 278 pp, ISBN: 0-7879-4203-0
Guides training managers and designers through the process of determining whether Web-based training (WBT) is the appropriate method to use; defining the type of WBT to use in different situations; applying adult education principles to designing the program; managing the expectations of senior management, clients, and users; and designing effective WBT programs. Includes a CD-ROM with document templates, job aids, worksheets, resource lists, and presentations to senior management about WBT.

Distance Learning Resources on the Web

There are thousands of Web sites devoted to distance learning. It would not be possible to begin to catalog these here. However, to get you started at some of the most useful sites, we include this brief directory. These sites include basic information on DL and many links to other sites.

The American Center for the Study of Distance Education
http://www.ed.psu.edu/ACSDE/
This is the home of The American Center for the Study of Distance Education (ACSDE) and *The American Journal of Distance Education* (AJDE) at The Pennsylvania State University. Dr. Michael G. Moore is the Director of ACSDE and Editor of *AJDE*.

American Society for Training and Development
http://www.astd.org
ASTD's site provides articles from the last two years of the defunct *Technical Training* magazine, links to other sites, and areas of resources and discussion groups.

The Army Distance Learning Program
http://www.tadlp.monroe.army.mil
If you'd like to know something about the Army's approach to DL, check this site. The military is ahead of many other organizations in the implementation of distance learning.

ASTD Learning Circuits
http://www.learningcircuits.org
Run by ASTD, this is an online publication devoted to distance and e-learning.

Blackboard.com

http://www.blackboard.com

Convert a course to the Web for free! This site provides templates for easy conversion and access.

The Chronicle of Higher Education, Distance Learning

http://chronicle.com/distance

This is the distance education page from *The Chronicle of Higher Education*. A good place to stay updated on DL in post-secondary education.

Distance Education at a Glance

http://www.uidaho.edu/evo/distglan.html

Bookmark this site as soon as possible! This is the home of "Distance Education at a Glance," written by Barry Willis and the University of Idaho Engineering Outreach staff. The guide highlights information detailed in Dr. Willis' books, *Distance Education—Strategies and Tools* and *Distance Education—A Practical Guide*. This site contains 13 valuable guides to key areas in distance education.

Distance Learning Exchange

http://dle.state.pa.us

This site of the Distance Learning Exchange provides information about a variety of distance learning activities such as Web quests, satellite teleconferences, electronic field trips, videoconferencing courses and e-mail exchanges.

Distance Learning on the Net by Glenn Hoyle

http://www.hoyle.com/distance.htm

As described at the site: "Distance learning on the Net celebrates 5 years of bringing descriptions of distance education Web sites, along with links to lead you to further Distance Learning and education resources."

Distance Learning Organizations

http://ccism.pc.athabascau.ca/html/ccism/deresrce/institut.htm

This includes a wide variety of links to virtual campuses, open and distance learning institutions, distance education departments within conventional institutions, and distance learning networks.

Distance Learning Resource Network

http://www.dlrn.org

This Web site is the home of the U.S. Department of Education's distance learning dissemination project. It includes a variety of resources for K-12, adult learners, educators, and more.

Distance Learning Resources

http://www.unc.edu/cit/guides/irg-06.html

This site is a resource for information on distance learning and for contacting others in the field for assistance. It includes World Wide Web sites, addresses for journals and newsletters, and information on electronic discussion lists.

Distance Learning Web Resources

http://www.kimsoft.com/dista.htm

This site includes a large number of links to other sites dealing with every aspect of distance learning.

Distance Learning Week

http://www.pbs.org/als/dlweek/whatis.htm

Run by PBS, this is an online magazine devoted to distance learning, especially in schools.

geteducated.com

http://www.geteducated.com

A variety of topics can be found at this site prepared by distance learning consultants. It is also the home of the Virtual University Gazette.

"Learning, Teaching, and Interacting in Hyperspace: The Potential of the Web"

http://www2.ncsu.edu/ncsu/cc/pub/teachtools/ConfReport.htm

This site features a report by several members of the North Carolina State University faculty and staff who attended a three-day workshop held in May 1997, "Learning, Teaching, and Interacting in Hyperspace: The Potential of the Web."

The MASIE Center

http://www.masie.com

Your link to Elliott Masie, President of The MASIE Center and the Technology and Learning ThinkTank. The site also provides you with the opportunity to subscribe to the free online newsletter, "TechLearn Trends," and offers a wealth of information resources and articles.

MindEdge

http://www.mindedge.com/home/index.phtml

An Internet company described as follows: "MindEdge, Inc. serves this emerging market by providing the Web's premier resource for personal development, distance learning, continuing education, on-campus and corporate training courses."

National Technological University

http://www.ntu.edu/

This is the home of PBS The Business & Technology Network, offering satellite-delivered programs. (PBS The Business Channel was acquired by National Technological University Corporation in June 1999.)

Quisic, The Essence of Learning
http://www.quisic.com/
A new and very useful site dealing with management e-learning topics. Includes articles from many different sources as well as useful links.

A Teacher's Guide to Distance Learning
http://fcit.coedu.usf.edu/distance
This is an online manual for teachers planning distance learning courses, especially at the K-12 level. Well done.

TrainingSuperSite
http://www.trainingsupersite.com
This site is hosted by Lakewood Publications, publisher of *Training* magazine. Many articles relating to distance learning are included in the magazine and selected articles are published at this site. In addition, there are links that will take you to over 200 training and education Web sites.

UNext.com
http://www.unext.com
The site describes UNext this way: "UNext.com was created to deliver world-class education. We are building a scalable education business that delivers the power of knowledge around the world. To bring people the finest curricula, we collaborate and co-brand with some of the world's leading universities. We plan to form partnerships with leading establishments throughout the world."

United States Distance Learning Association
http://www.usdla.org
This is the site of the USDLA and includes a wide variety of information about the association and its state affiliates.

The University of Wisconsin Distance Education Clearinghouse
http://www.uwex.edu/disted/home.html
Bookmark this site! This is one of the finest sources of distance education information. The University of Wisconsin-Extension provides a listing of courses delivered via distance education and a valuable index of other distance education resources and links, including:

Certificate Programs
http://www.uwex.edu/disted/certificates.html
This section will point you to a dozen of the leading universities providing certificate programs for distance learning.

Future Conferences
http://www.uwex.edu/disted/conf/

Here you will find the constantly updated list of conferences specifically designed for all aspects of distance learning.

Online Articles

http://www.uwex.edu/disted/lobart.htm

Leading articles spanning all aspects of distance education. This site contains practical guides, tools, and additional resources for anyone interested in learning what to do, how to do it, lessons learned, and future trends.

Online Journals

http://www.uwex.edu/disted/lobline.htm

This section provides direct links to over 35 electronically delivered journals, newsletters, and magazines.

Vendors, Products, and Services

http://www.uwex.edu/disted/vendors.htm

Over 100 providers of distance learning products and services can be found at this site and all are hyperlinked for easy access to each site. What a time-saver!

Web Development Resources

http://www.uwex.edu/disted/webdevel.htm

This section provides links to Web development articles, "how to's," best practices, tools, teaching guides, instructional design and delivery, and more!

World Bank Global Distance EducationNet

http://www1.worldbank.org/disted/

The Global Distance EducationNet (Global DistEdNet) is a knowledge guide to distance education designed to help clients of the World Bank and others interested in using distance education for human development.

Directory of Distance Learning Organizations and Associations

Agency for Instructional Technology
Michael F. Sullivan, Executive Director
Box A
1800 North Stonelake Drive
Bloomington, IN 47402-0120
Phone: (812) 339-2203, (800) 457-4509
Fax: (812) 333-4218
E-mail: info@ait.net
Web: www.ait.net
AIT is a nonprofit education organization established in 1962 to develop, acquire, and distribute quality technology-based resources and to provide leadership to the educational technology policy community.

Alliance for Public Technology
P.O. Box 27146
Washington, DC 20038-7146
919 18th Street, NW, Suite 900
Washington, DC 20006
Phone (voice/TTY): (202) 263-2970
Fax: (202) 263-2960
E-mail: apt@apt.org
Web: www.apt.org
APT is a nonprofit, tax-exempt coalition of public interest groups and individuals whose goal is to foster broad access to affordable, usable information and communi-

cation services and technology. APT provides an effective grassroots voice for equitable and affordable access to the benefits of telecommunications technology. It publishes the *Alliance Quarterly Newsletter.*

American Association for Higher Education
1 DuPont Circle, Suite 360
Washington, DC 20036
Phone: (202) 293-644
Fax: (202) 293-0073
E-mail: info@aahe.org
Web: www.aahe.org
The American Association for Higher Education envisions a higher education enterprise that helps all Americans achieve the deep, lifelong learning they need to grow as individuals, participate in the democratic process, and succeed in a global economy.

American Center for the Study of Distance Education
The Pennsylvania State University
110 Rackley Building
University Park, PA 16802-3202
Phone: (814) 863-3764
Fax: (814) 865-5878
E-mail: acsde@psu.edu
Web: www.cde.psu.edu/ACSDE
ACSDE, established in 1988 in the College of Education, seeks to promote distance education research, study, scholarship, and teaching and to serve as a clearinghouse for the dissemination of knowledge about distance education.

American Distance Education Consortium
Janet Poley, President
C218 Animal Science Building
Box 830952
Lincoln, NE 68583-0952
Phone: (402) 472-7000
Fax: (402) 472-9060
E-mail: jpoley@unl.edu
Web: www.adec.edu
ADEC is "an international consortium of state universities and land grant institutions providing high-quality and economic distance education programs and services via the latest and most appropriate information technologies."

American Society for Training and Development (ASTD)
1640 King Street
Box 1443
Alexandria, VA 22313-2043
Phone: (703) 683-8100, (800) 628-2783
Fax: (703) 683-1523
E-mail: info@astd.org
Web: www.astd.org
ASTD represents more than 65,000 individuals from more than 100 countries. ASTD is the leading resource on workplace learning and performance issues, providing information, research, analysis and practical information to its members.

Association for Applied Interactive Multimedia
Jared A. Seay, President
P.O. Box 892
Charleston, SC 29402-0892
Phone: (843) 953-1428
E-mail: seayj@cofc.edu
Web: www.aaim.org
AAIM was created to support professionals who use and develop interactive multimedia for education and training. Its mission is to bring together through communication, workshops, conferences, and its Web site practicing multimedia professionals, educators, trainers, and those considering using multimedia and related applications.

Association for Educational Communications and Technology, Inc.
1800 N. Stonelake Drive, Suite 2
Bloomington, IN 47404
Phone: (812) 335-7675, (877) 677-AECT
Fax: (812) 335-7678
E-mail: aect@aect.org
Web: www.aect.org
The mission of AECT is "to provide leadership in educational communications and technology by linking professionals holding a common interest in the use of educational technology and its application to the learning process."

Association for Learning Technology
Oxford Brookes University
Gipsy Lane Campus
Oxford OX3 0BP
United Kingdom

Phone: 01865 484125
Fax: 01865 484165
E-mail: alt@brookes.ac.uk
Web: www.warwick.ac.uk/alt-E
ALT is an educational organization formed in April 1993 at the CAL'93 conference in York to bring together all those with an interest in the use of learning technology in higher and further education. It publishes an international peer-reviewed journal, *ALT-Journal*, three times a year.

Association for Telecommunications Professionals in Higher Education
Kellie Bowman, Membership Manager
152 W. Zandale, Suite 200
Lexington, KY 40503
Phone: (859) 278-3338
Fax: (859) 278-3268
E-mail: kbowman@acuta.org
Web: www.acuta.org
ACUTA is an international non-profit educational association serving nearly 800 colleges and universities. ACUTA is dedicated to the enhancement of teaching, learning, research, and public (community) service by providing leadership in the application of telecommunications technology for higher education.

Association for the Advancement of Computing in Education
P.O. Box 3728
Norfolk, VA 23514
Phone: (757) 623-7588
Fax: (703) 997-8760
E-mail: info@aace.org
Web: www.aace.org
Founded in 1981, AACE is an international, educational, and professional organization dedicated to advancing the knowledge, theory, and quality of learning and teaching at all levels with information technology. It encourages scholarly inquiry related to information technology in education and the dissemination of research results and their applications through publications, conferences, divisions, societies, chapters and inter-organizational projects. AACE produces several print publications, including *Educational Technology Review*.

British Association for Open Learning
Pixmore Centre, Pixmore Avenue
Letchworth, Hertfordshire, SG6 1JG
United Kingdom

Phone: 01462 485588
Fax: 01462 485633
E-mail: info@baol.co.uk
Web: www.baol.co.uk
BAOL exists to promote quality and best practice in open, flexible, and distance forms of learning throughout the education and training sectors of the United Kingdom, Europe, and internationally.

British Interactive Multimedia Association
6 Washingley Road
Folksworth, Peterborough PE7 3SY UK
Phone: 01733 245700
Fax: 01733 240020
www. bima.co.uk
BIMA is the trade association representing the interactive media industries in the UK. Established in 1985, the British Interactive Multimedia Association brings new media into focus.

Center for Distance Learning Research
Texas A&M University
College Station, TX 77843-1588
Phone: (409) 845-3016
Web: www.cdlr.tamu.edu
The mission of the Center for Distance Learning Research at Texas A&M University is to provide timely and appropriate information on the development, application and maintenance of information technology systems. This information is provided through demonstration, training, publications and technical assistance. The Center's services are available to all public agencies and private businesses that are interested in the welfare and education of people through the use of appropriate information technology and distance education.

The Digital Learning Organization
901 Burlington Avenue, Suite #2
P.O. Box 445
Western Springs, IL 60558
Phone: (877) 533-4914
Fax: (877) 533-6451
E-mail: info@digitallearning.org
Web: www.digitallearning.org
The Digital Learning Organization is a worldwide trade organization composed of the industry's leading vendors of work-related learning. Its mission is to foster growth in the global digital learning industry and help its member organizations succeed.

Distance Education and Training Council

1601 18th Street, NW
Washington, DC 20009-2529
Phone: (202) 234-5100
Fax: (202) 332-1386
E-mail: detc@detc.org
Web: www.detc.org
DETC (formerly the National Home Study Council) is a non-profit educational association that serves as a clearinghouse of information about the distance study/correspondence field and sponsors a nationally recognized accrediting agency, the Accrediting Commission of the Distance Education and Training Council. The Council's goal is to promote sound educational standards and ethical business practices within the distance study field.

Distance Learning Resource Network

2020 N. Central Avenue, Suite 660
Phoenix, AZ 85004-4507
Phone: (602) 322-7003
Fax: (602) 322-7007
E-mail: dlrn@dlrn.org
Web: www.dlrn.org
The Distance Learning Resource Network (DLRN) is the dissemination project for the Star Schools Program, a federally funded distance education program which offers instructional modules, enrichment activities and courses in science, mathematics, foreign languages, workplace skills, high school completion and adult literacy programs.

EDUCAUSE

1150 18th Street, NW, Suite 1010
Washington, DC 20036
Phone: (202) 872-4200
Fax: (202) 872-4318
E-mail: info@educause.edu
Web: www.educause.edu
The mission of EDUCAUSE is to help shape and enable transformational change in higher education through the introduction, use, and management of information resources and technologies in teaching, learning, scholarship, research, and institutional management.

European Association for Distance Learning

Henricus Verweijen, Executive Director
Bastiengasse 41/1

A-1180 Vienna
Austria
Phone/Fax: +431 470 9192
E-mail: HenricusV@compuserve.com
Web: www.eadl.org
EADL is the European association of schools, institutions, and individuals working in correspondence and distance education. With members from more than 15 European countries, the Association is a representative forum for the exchange of information and ideas on current practice and developments in this expanding field of education and training.

European Association of Distance Teaching Universities
EADTU Secretariat
Post Office Box 2960
6401 DL Heerlen
Valkenburgerweg 177
6419 AT Heerlen
The Netherlands
Tel: +31 45 576 2214
Fax: + 31 45 574 1473
E-mail: secretariat@eadtu.nl
Web: www.eadtu.nl
This is "a strategic level organisation whose European activities and projects support and advance goals towards achieving its mission: to promote and support the creation of a European network for higher level distance education." The association was established in January 1987 by the principals of Europe's major distance teaching institutions to foster cooperation between European organizations dedicated to higher education through distance teaching methodology.

European Distance Education Network
EDEN Secretariat
Dr. András Szûcs, Secretary General
Mrs. Anna Wagner, Office Manager
Budapest University of Technology and Economics
H-1111. Budapest, Egry J. u. 1.
Hungary
Phone: + 36 1 463 1628, + 36 1 463 2259
Fax: + 36 1 463 1858
E-mail: eden@khmk.bme.hu
Web: www.eden.bme.hu
EDEN is a non-governmental educational association formally established in May 1991

following the first pan-European conference on distance education in Budapest in 1990. Its aim is to foster developments in distance education through the provision of a platform for co-operation and collaboration between a wide range of institutions, networks, and individuals concerned with distance education in Europe.

Institute for Electronic Education

1155 State Street, Suite 608
Bellingham, WA 98225
Phone: (360) 647-5823
Fax: NA
E-mail: info@institute.org
Web: www.institute.org
The Institute is a non-profit organization formed to help people using technology in learning. This includes research, public seminars, curriculum development and "train-the-trainer" support to introduce new methods and techniques to practitioners of technology training.

Institute for Learning Technologies

Columbia University
525 West 120th Street
Box 144
New York, NY 10027
Phone: (212) 678-4000
Fax: (212) 678-4048,
E-mail: info@ilt.columbia.edu
Web: www.ilt.columbia.edu
ILT was founded in 1986 to advance the role of computers and other information technologies in education and society. Through its program of practice, the Institute seeks to empower the creative reform of education.

Institute for the Transfer of Technology to Education

c/o National School Boards Association
1680 Duke Street
Alexandria, VA 22314
Phone: (703) 838-6722
Fax: (703) 838-7590
E-mail: info@nsba.org
Web: www.nsba.org/itte
ITTE is a program developed "to help advance the wise use of technology in public education." It hosts the Technology + Learning Conference.

Instructional Telecommunications Council
Christine Dalziel, Executive Director
1 Dupont Circle NW, Suite 410
Washington, DC 20036-1176
Phone: (202) 293-3110
Fax: (202) 833-2467
E-mail: cdalziel@aacc.nche.edu
Web: www.itcnetwork.org
An affiliated council of the American Association of Community Colleges established in 1977, ITC represents nearly 600 institutions in the United States and Canada, and is leader in advancing distance education. ITC provides leadership, information, and resources to expand and enhance distance learning through the effective use of technology.

International Centre for Distance Learning
Institute of Educational Technology
Walton Hall
Milton Keynes MK7 6AA
United Kingdom
Phone: +44 1908 653216, +44 1908 274066
Fax: +44 1908 654173
E-mail: IET-Queries@open.ac.uk
Web: www-icdl.open.ac.uk
ICDL is a center for research, teaching, consultancy, information, and publishing activities based in the Institute of Educational Technology. ICDL promotes international research and collaboration by providing information from its library and databases and through its publications.

International Council for Open and Distance Education
International Head Office
International Chief Executive Officer
Reidar Roll, Secretary General
Gjerdrums vei 12
N-0484 Oslo
Norway
Phone: +47 22 02 81 70
Fax: +47 22 02 81 61
E-mail: icde@icde.no
Web: www.icde.org
ICDE is a global membership organization of educational institutions, national and regional associations, corporations, educational authorities, and agencies in the fields

of open learning, distance education, and flexible, lifelong learning. ICDE facilitates international cooperation in distance education and open learning throughout the world. Through the ICDE membership and partnership structure, more than 130 countries are represented.

International Technology Education Association
1914 Association Drive, Suite 201
Reston, VA 20191-1539
Phone: (703) 860-2100
Fax: (703) 860-0353
E-mail: itea@iris.org
Web: www.iteawww.org
ITEA is the professional organization of technology teachers. Its mission is to promote technological literacy for all by supporting the teaching of technology and promoting the professionalism of those engaged in this pursuit. ITEA strengthens the profession through leadership, professional development, membership services, publications, and classroom activities.

Internet Society
11150 Sunset Hills Road, Suite 100
Reston, VA 20190-5321
Phone: (703) 326-9880
Fax: (703) 326-9881
E-mail: isoc@isoc.org
Web: www.isoc.org
The Internet Society is a non-profit, non-governmental, international, professional membership organization. The Society helps train key information technology leaders around the world through programs. Its membership consists of more than 175 organizations and 8,600 individuals in over 170 nations.

Learning Technology Institute
50 Culpeper Street
Warrenton, VA 20186
Phone: (540) 347-0055
Fax: (540) 439-3169
E-mail: info@lti.org
Web: www.lti.org
The Learning Technology Institute was founded in 1975 as a non-profit public interest corporation devoted to research, development, organization management, and education activities in connection with the use of technology and computers in knowledge engineering, systems design, and technology-based information delivery systems.

Masie Center, Inc., The Technology and Learning Thinktank
P.O. Box 397
Saratoga Springs, NY 12866
Phone: (518) 587-3522
Fax: (518) 587-3276
E-mail emasie@masie.com
Web: www.masie.com
The MASIE Center is an international thinktank located in Saratoga Springs, NY. The Center is dedicated to exploring the intersection of learning and technology.

National Educational Computing Association
Web: www.neccsite.org
NECA is a non-profit federation of 14 national scientific and professional societies that exists solely to sponsor the National Educational Computing Conference.

National Educational Telecommunications Association
P.O. Box 50008
Columbia, SC 29250
939 S. Stadium Road
Columbia, SC 29201
Phone: (803) 799-5517
Fax: (803) 771-4831
Web: www.netaonline.org
NETA was organized in July 1997. It is composed of members of the former Pacific Mountain Network and the Southern Educational Communications Association. The NETA staff serves public television and education in all 50 states, the U. S. Virgin Islands, and Puerto Rico.

Open and Distance Learning Association of Australia
Distance Education Centre
University of Southern Queensland
PO Darling Heights
Toowoomba, Queensland 4350
Australia
Phone: +61 7 46 31 2290
Fax: +61 7 46 31 1502
E-mail: grundonm@usq.edu.au
Web: www.usq.edu.au/dec/decjourn/odlaa.htm
ODLAA is a professional association of members interested in the practice and administration of distance education and open learning.

Open and Distance Learning Quality Council
16 Park Crescent
London W1B 1AH
United Kingdom
Phone: 020 7612 7090
Fax: 020 7612 7092
E-mail: odlqc@dial.pipex.com
Web: dspace.dial.pipex.com/odlqc
ODLQC was founded in 1969 as the Council for the Accreditation of Correspondence Colleges. It is an independent body, though set up at the request of government, and has continued to benefit from governmental support and cooperation. ODLQC helps to enhance quality in education and training and to protect the interests of learners through the accreditation of open and distance learning providers.

Society for Applied Learning Technology (SALT)
50 Culpepper Street
Warrenton, VA 20186
Phone: (540) 347-0055
Fax: (540) 349-3169
E-mail: info@lti.org
Web: www.salt.org
SALT is oriented to professionals whose work requires knowledge and communication in the field of instructional technology.

Society for Information Technology and Teacher Education
Association for the Advancement of Computing in Education
P.O. Box 3728
Norfolk, VA 23514
Phone: (757) 623-7588
Fax: (703) 997-8760
E-mail: info@aace.org
Web: www.aace.org/site
SITE is an international association of individual teacher educators and affiliated organizations of teacher educators in all disciplines, who are interested in the creation and dissemination of knowledge about the use of information technology in teacher education. The Society seeks to promote research, scholarship, collaboration, exchange, and support among its members and to foster the development of new regional and national organizations.

The Education Coalition
31 Segovia

San Clemente, CA 92672
Phone: (949) 369-3867
Fax: (949) 369-3865
E-mail: TECemail@aol.com
Web: www.tecweb.org
TEC is a not-for-profit educational organization, created in 1993 to serve the needs of the business and education communities. We are comprised of diverse agencies from across the nation working together to promote systemic educational reform through the use of multiple technologies. TEC includes elementary, secondary, and post-secondary schools, educational agencies, broadcast agencies, and high-tech industry corporations.

The TLT Group
1 Dupont Circle, NW, Suite 360
Washington, DC 20036-1110
Phone: (202) 293-6440
Fax: (202) 467-6593
E-mail: info@tltgroup.org
Web: www.tltgroup.org
This is the teaching, learning, and technology affiliate of the American Association for Higher Education. Its goal is "to help educational institutions improve teaching and learning by making more sensible use of technology."

United States Distance Learning Association
John G. Flores, Executive Director
140 Gould Street, Suite 200B
Needham, MA 02494-2397
Phone: (800) 275-5162, (781) 453-2388
Fax: (781) 453-2389
E-mail: jflores@usdla.org
Web: www.usdla.org
This is a nonprofit organization formed in 1987 to promote the development and application of distance learning for education and training. It serves constituents in Pre-K through grade 12, higher education, home school education, continuing education, corporate training, military and government training, and telemedicine.

University Continuing Education Association
1 Dupont Circle, NW, Suite 615
Washington, DC 20036-1168
Phone: (202) 659-3130
Fax: (202) 785-0374
E-mail: postmaster@nucea.edu

Web: www.nucea.edu

Founded in 1915, the University Continuing Education Association (formerly the National University Continuing Education Association) is the principal U.S. organization for continuing higher education. UCEA helps institutions of higher learning and affiliated nonprofit organizations increase access to higher education through educational programs and services. UCEA also provides national leadership in support of policies that advance workforce and professional development.

Western Cooperative for Educational Telecommunications

P.O. Box 9752
Boulder, CO 80301
1540 30th Street
Boulder, CO 80303
Phone: (303) 541-0231
Fax: (303) 541-0291
E-mail: Infowcet@wiche.edu
Web: www.wiche.edu/telecom

This program, established by the Western Interstate Commission for Higher Education, helps states and institutions to use new technologies more effectively for improved education.

World Association for Online Education

E-mail: waoe@waoe.org
Web: www.waoe.org

WAOE is an international professional organization concerned with online pedagogy. WAOE offers membership services relevant to educators concerned with teaching online, public services for international society, and collaboration with other educational organizations functioning in cyberspace. It maintains a discussion list, WAOE-VIEWS.

Glossary of Distance Learning Terms

Christine Olgren

D istance learning is a technical field. It is possible because of the wide availability of electronic and information technology. While this technology is familiar to us, it involves a rather large vocabulary of technical terms, most of which people in the field have heard or used but may not know the exact definition of. Thus, this glossary, developed by Christine Olgren of the University of Wisconsin-Madison, one of the leading institutions in the field of distance learning.

Analog Information that is transmitted by means of modulations of a continuous signal, such is a radio wave. *See Digital.*

Applets Mini-programs that can be downloaded quickly and used by any computer equipped with a Java-capable browser.

Asynchronous Anytime, anyplace access to education or training materials, or anytime communications.

Asynchronous Transfer Mode (ATM) A high-speed, cell-switching technology with speeds ranging from 128 Mbps (megabytes per second) to more than 6 Gbps (gigabytes per second).

Audio Teleconferencing Two-way voice communication between two or more groups, or three or more individuals, who are in separate locations linked by a telecommunications medium.

Reprinted with permission from Distance Education Technology, Core Module, Distance Education Professional Development Program, University of Wisconsin-Madison. www.wisc.edu/depd.

Audiographics The transmission of images and graphics over ordinary telephone lines or the Internet to enhance audio interaction. The audiographics family includes computer-generated graphics, electronic whiteboards, electronic tablets, document sharing, and computer-based multimedia systems or combinations thereof.

Audiotext An automated computer-based telephone messaging technology, it operates similar to an answering machine. It allows for calling a computer and tapping into information on a 24-hour basis.

Authoring Tools or Systems Software for creating graphics, multimedia presentations, Web documents, text files, and other resources to produce learning materials, modules, or courses.

Backbone A high-speed line or series of connections that forms a major pathway within a network.

Bandwidth The range of frequencies that can be carried by a telecommunications medium without undue distortion, such as a broadcast television signal of 3 million Hertz or a telephone voice signal of 3,000 Hertz.

Bit Binary digit, the smallest unit of information in a computer.

BRI (Basis Rate Interface) Used in ISDN to refer to three digital signals carried over a single telephone line; one BRI (one line) can carry compressed video and voice at 112 kbps.

Bridge A device that is designed to interconnect three or more telephone lines; used to link multiple locations for audio or audiographic teleconferencing.

Broadband A telecommunications medium that carries high-frequency signals; includes television frequencies of 3-6 million Hertz.

Broadcast The one-way transmission of information.

Browser A software application that permits browsing, retrieval, and viewing of content from the World Wide Web and Intranets. Examples are Netscape and Internet Explorer.

Bulletin Board or **Bulletin Board Service (BBS)** A forum for users to read and post electronic messages via a personal computer and modem.

Byte The unit of computer memory typically consisting of 8 bits; 64K = 64,000 bytes or 64 kilobytes.

C-Band The range of frequencies from 4-6 gigaHertz on which most satellites and terrestrial microwave systems receive and transmit signals.

Cable TV Transmits programs to subscribers through coaxial cable rather than over the air. Most cable systems have the potential for two-way communication in addition to broadcast television.

CCTV (Closed-Circuit Television) The system for sending cable signals to subscribers or designated locations.

CD-I Computer Disc Interactive.

CD-ROM Computer Disc, Read Only Memory. A computer storage medium similar to an audio CD.

CD-V Computer Disc Video.

Chat The exchange of electronic messages among people who are using their computers at the same time; real-time computer communications.

Client A software application that is loaded on an end-user's computer to communicate with and perform tasks associated with similar software located on a server.

Codec Hardware and/or software components that provide digital compression and decompression of video signals so they can be sent more efficiently.

Compact Disk (CD) A plastic device that can contain video, audio, text, and graphics information for storage and access.

Compressed Video Video images that have been compressed to remove redundant information, thereby reducing the amount of bandwidth required to send them over a telecommunications channel.

Computer-Based Training (CBT) Training or instruction where a computer program is used to provide content and feedback to the learner. CBT can be delivered via CD-ROM, local area network (LAN), Intranet, or Internet.

Computer Conferencing Software of computer capabilities that enables individuals at different locations to communicate with each other through computers.

Computer Mediated Communications (CMC) *See Computer Conferencing.*

Cookie Information stored on a user's computer after visiting a Web site; tracks data about the user.

DBS (Direct Broadcast Satellite) A satellite designed with sufficient power that smaller earth stations can be used for direct on-site reception of signals.

Desktop Videoconferencing Videoconferencing on a personal computer.

Digital Electronic information based on the binary code, sent as a series of "on"/"off" pulses and is less subject to interference.

Discussion Board *See Bulletin Board.*

Distance Education, Distance Learning Learning where the instructor and the students are in physically separate locations and some form of media is used to provide content and/or communications (print, audio, video, computer, multimedia).

Distributed Learning Learning that makes use of computer technology or communications networks for content delivery, feedback, and communications. Sometimes called *networked learning*. Similar to *e-learning*.

Document Sharing or **Document Conferencing** Participants at different locations can view and edit the same computer document.

Domain Name The unique name that identifies an Internet site. Domain names always have two or more parts, separated by dots. For example, wisc.edu

Downlink A verb—the process of beaming signals from a satellite to earth stations; (noun) an antenna shaped like a dish that receives signals from a satellite.

Download/Upload To download is to transfer (retrieve) a file from another computer to the user's computer. To upload is to send a file to another computer.

Downstream An audio or video signal traveling from the cable TV headend to a subscriber point in the community.

DVD Digital video (or versatile) disk; an optical disk for storing information.

Echo Cancellation The elimination of acoustic echo in a conferencing room or on an audio bridge. *See Bridge.*

E-Learning Short for electronic learning; any learning that uses a network for delivery, interaction, or facilitation. Often refers to Internet or computer delivery, but can include any distance learning mode other than pure print-based packages or correspondence study. *See Distributed Learning.*

Electronic Bulletin Board Holds information that can be accessed by computers via a modem. *See Bulletin Board Service.*

Electronic Whiteboard or Blackboard A device that looks like an ordinary whiteboard or blackboard but has a special conductive surface for creating freehand information that can be send over a telecommunications channel, usually a telephone line.

E-Mail (Electronic-Mail) Messages sent to and from a computer linked by telephone lines.

F2F Face to face; a classroom environment.

FAQ Frequently asked questions about information technology.

Fax or **Facsimile** Copies of documents and graphics that are sent via phone lines to another copier.

Fiber Optics A technology that transmits voice, video, and data by sending digital pulses of light through hair-thin strands of flexible glass.

Firewall A system through which all traffic must pass between an internal network and external network. A firewall allows only authorized traffic into the internal network, where "authorized" is defined by the firewall owner's security policy.

Footprint The geographic area on the globe in which a given satellite signal can be received.

Ftp (File Transfer Protocol) A networking protocol for moving computer files between machines.

Gateway Hardware or software that connects two computers or systems.

Geosynchronous Orbit The altitude 22,300 miles above the equator at which the satellite's orbit is synchronous with the earth's rotation, making the satellite appear stationary.

GigaHertz One billion Hertz (cycles per second).

Groupware Software that supports online group collaboration for e-mail communications, shared files, online chats, and similar activities.

Hardware A term used for electronic equipment.

HDTV (High Definition Television) Doubles the number of lines in a broadcast or cablecast signal, creating a very high resolution signal.

Headend A cable system's central location, where it receives, amplifies, and converts incoming signals before redistributing them to subscribers.

Hertz Cycles per second, unit of broadcast frequency.

Home Page The first Web page a user sees when visiting a World Wide Web site. Similar to a table of contents or main menu to a Web site.

Host A computer that serves as a central site or node on a network.

HTML (HyperText Markup Language) A software code for defining page layout and hypertext links between documents; the standard language of the World Wide Web.

HTTP (HyperText Transfer Protocol) A networking protocol for retrieving HTML documents.

Hyperlink A highlighted word or graphic in a Web document that, when clicked upon, takes the user to a related piece of information.

Interactive Technology Technology that permits two-way participation.

Interactive Television (ITV) Two-way transmission of both voice and video, enabling participants to talk to and see each other.

Interface The place at which two systems or pieces of equipment meet and interact with each other.

Internet The global network that connects computers for electronic mail, telnet, ftp, and World Wide Web applications.

Internet Service Provider (ISP) Any organization that provides access to the Internet.

Intranet A private network inside a company or organization that uses similar kinds of software that you would find on the public Internet, but it is only for internal use.

ISDN (Integrated Services Digital Network) A digital telecommunications channel that allows for the integrated transmission of voice, video, and data.

ITFS (Instructional Television Fixed Service) A group of channels in the ultra-high frequency range that has been set aside since the 1960s for educational use. It transmits via microwave equipment not more than 20-30 miles (line of sight) from the transmitter.

Java A programming language used to create computer software or small applications (applets) that can run on a Web page.

Ka-Band A satellite transmission in the 20 and 30 gigaHertz frequency spectrum; still an experimental technology.

KiloHertz One thousand Hertz (cycles per second).

Ku-Band A satellite transmission in the 11 to 14 GigaHertz frequency spectrum; a newer technology than C-Band.

Laser Light amplification by stimulated emission of radiation. This highly focused beam of light (or its device) is used in fiber optics and optical video disc.

Learning Object A piece of content material; a modular building block that can be used as a portion of the subject matter content.

Learning Management Systems Software that tracks student progress in a course, records test scores, and indicates completions. Typically used in conjunction with other capabilities for online learning, such as bulletin boards, chats, and Web materials.

Listserv (listserver) Software that permits a group of people to share information via electronic mail sent to a central address.

Local Area Network (LAN) A network in which all hosts are in close proximity (e.g., within the same building or set of adjacent buildings).

MegaHertz One million Hertz (cycles per second).

Microprocessor The heart of the computer. A silicon chip that processes data and controls the computer's components.

Microwave High-frequency radio waves, above 500 megaHertz, that can transmit television signals. They are easily disturbed by trees, buildings, etc., and require direct line-of-site to operate.

Modem (Modulation-Demodulation) The hardware that facilitates communication between two or more computers; a device that links the computer to a phone line.

MPEG (Motion Picture Experts Group) A standard for compressing digital video images.

Multiplexor Equipment used to combine signals from different sources for transmission over a single channel.

Narrowband A telecommunications medium that carries low-frequency signals, such as telephone voice signals.

Narrowcast Sending out television or audio signals to a small, narrow, specific audience.

Netiquette Internet etiquette or accepted ways of behaving and communicating when using the Internet.

Online In direct communication with a computer.

Online Learning Learning via the Internet or an intranet.

Optical Video Disc (Laser Disc) A video playback laser beam is reflected against microscopic pits on a disc to retrieve frames of prerecorded information. The disc can contain more than 54,000 frames that can be located instantly.

Origination Site The place from which a teleconference originates.

Packet A sequence of bits or bytes that make up all or part of a message communicated on a network.

Plug-in A (usually small) piece of software that adds features to a larger piece of software. For example, several kinds of plug-ins are available for Netscape to add multi-media or communication features.

Point-to-Point Protocol (PPP) A protocol for making computer connections over a telephone line.

Portal Usually used as a marketing term to describe a Web site that is intended to be the first place people see when using the Web. Typically a "portal site" has a catalog of Web sites, a search engine, or both. A portal site may also offer e-mail and other services to entice people to use that site as their main "point of entry" (hence "portal") to the Web.

Posting A single message sent to a bulletin board, listserv, or newsgroup.

Protocol An agreed-upon sequence of bits, bytes, or characters exchanged between programs for purposes of transmitting and receiving information.

Random Access Locating information at any point on a disc or in an information file.

Receive Site A location that receives transmissions from another site, such as a satellite receive site.

Room Integration Design or construction of a total teleconferencing room, including the equipment, associated electronics, and environment.

Satellite An orbiting antenna, also called a "bird," that relays signals (voice, data and video) from and back to earth.

Search Engine Software that enables users to find information or specific files on the Internet/Web. Three common search engines are Yahoo, Google, and Lycos.

Software Programs created for computer use.

Streaming Technology (Audio or **Video)** Allows audio or video files to be played as they are downloaded from the Internet.

Synchronous Same-time or real-time communications.

T-1 High-speed digital transmission system with a bit rate of 1.544 Mbps; can be subdivided into 24 channels, with a bit rate of 64 Kbps (kilobytes per second).

TCP/IP (Transmission Control Protocol/Internet Protocol) The drive software that connects computers and networks to the Internet.

Telecommunications The use of wire, radio, optical, or other electromagnetic channel to transmit or receive signals for voice, video, and data communications; communications over distance using electrical means.

Teleconferencing Two-way electronic communication between two or more groups, or three or more individuals, who are in separate locations; includes group communication via audio, audiographics, video, and computer systems.

Teleport A facility, usually in large urban areas, that offers various telecommunications services.

Teletext One-way textual graphic information sent on unused scanning lines (Vertical Blanking Intervals, VBI) of television pictures.

Telnet Allows users to access a remote computer via a telephone call or network connection from their computer.

Transponder The device on a satellite that receives, amplifies, and retransmits audio, video and data signals from the earth.

TVRO (Television Receive Only) Consists of an antenna (dish), low-noise block down converter and a satellite receiver. The antenna size varies with location.

UHF (Ultra High Frequency) Channels 14-69.

Uplink The transmitting station or site for communicating with a satellite. An antenna shaped like a dish that sends signals to a satellite.

Upstream An audio or video signal traveling from a subscriber point in the cabled community to the cable TV headend.

URL (Universal Resource Locator) The address used to locate a special resource or site on the World Wide Web.

Usenet A world-wide system of discussion groups, called newsgroups, on the Internet.

VBI (Vertical Blanking Interval) The 21 unused lines on television that appear as a heavy black line when the horizontal hold stops. These lines are useful for messages for the blind, E-Mail and other data.

VHF (Very High Frequency) Channels 1-13.

VHS (Video Home System) The most common type of video home recorder. The less common system is called Beta. They are not compatible.

Video Bridge Computerized switching system that allows multipoint videoconferencing. *See also Bridge.*

Video Teleconferencing Two-way voice and video between two or more groups, or three or more individuals, who are in separate locations linked by a telecommunications medium.

Videotex An interactive technology that uses phone line or two-way cable to connect the television set to a central computer. The user retrieves information or transacts business using a keypad or keyboard.

Virtual Space A type of video conference in which each participant is assigned to a separate camera and is seen on a separate monitor, large screen or assigned spatial area.

Web *See World Wide Web.*

Web-Based Training (WBT) Training which is delivered in Web page formats over a network (LAN, WAN, Intranet, or Internet). Can be either instructor-led or computer-based.

Web Page A single document containing information that can be accessed over the World Wide Web.

Web Site An organization's or individual's location on the Web that contains their file of information accessible to others.

Whiteboard An electronic space or window for creating and editing graphics information that can be shared with others via computer networks.

Wide Area Network (WAN) Any internet or network that covers an area larger than a single building or campus. Contrast to LAN (local area network).

World Wide Web (Web or **WWW)** A part of the Internet network that provides access to multimedia resources—text, graphics, sound, video—located on computer servers connected to the network.

XML (Extensible Markup Language) The next generation HTML that will enable Web site developers to program their own markup language.

Major Distance Learning Meetings and Conferences in 2001-2002

T he following is a calendar of major meetings and conferences of interest to professionals working in distance and e-learning. We've done our best to give you the dates and locations of events occurring between June 2001 and May 2002. In some cases, the dates for the 2002 meetings have not been set, but we have still included information on the month and where you can find additional information.

June 2001

ICIMADE International Program Committee
International Conference on Intelligent Multimedia and Distance Education (ICI-MADE 2001)
June 1-3, 2001
Fargo, ND
venus.ece.ndsu.nodak.edu/ece/research/conferences/icimade01

Association for Media and Technology in Education in Canada
28th AMTEC Conference (AMTEC 2001): "Making It Work: Effective Educational Technology in the New Millennium"
June 3-6, 2001
Halifax, NS, Canada
amtec2001.ednet.ns.ca

American Society for Training & Development
ASTD 2001
June 3-7, 2001
Orlando, FL
www.astd.org

Purdue University Calumet
Annual Conference: Topics on Distance Learning
June 5-6, 2001
Hammond, IN
www.calumet.purdue.edu/todl/index.html

Internet Society
INET 2001: The Internet Global Summit: A Net Odyssey—Mobility and the Internet
The 11th Annual Internet Society Conference
June 5-8, 2001
Stockholm, Sweden
www.isoc.org/inet2001

Online Journal of Distance Learning Administration
The State University of West Georgia
Distance Learning Administration 2001
June 6-8, 2001
Pine Mountain, GA
www.westga.edu/ ~ distance/conf.html

European Distance Education Network
10th Anniversary Conference: Learning Without Limits: Developing the Next
    Generation of Education
June 10-13, 2001
Stockholm, Sweden
www.eden.bme.hu/contents/conferences/Stockholm/stockholm0.html

VNU Business Media
17th Annual Training Director's Forum
June 10-13, 2001
Las Vegas, NV
www.trainingdirectorsforum.com

National University Telecommunications Network
19th Annual National Distance Learning Conference: "2001: A Digital Odyssey"
June 16-19, 2001
Denver, CO
www.odu.edu/nutn

EDINEB (Mastricht University, Netherlands)
EDHEC School of Management (Lille and Nice, France)
Formations Hommes et Conseils (Paris, France)
8th Annual EDINEB International Conference: Technology, Pedagogy, and
   Innovation
June 20-22, 2001
Nice, France
www.edineb.net or www.edineb.com

WebCT
3rd Annual Users Conference: "Transforming the Educational Experience"
June 23-27, 2001
Vancouver, BC, Canada
www.webct.com/2001

National Educational Computing Association
NECC 2001: National Educational Computing Conference
June 24-27, 2001
Chicago, IL
www.neccsite.org

Learning Resources Network
Learning Online 2001
June 25-26, 2001
Minneapolis, MN
www.lern.org/learning_online

Malaysian Institute of Corporate Governance
LEO Training & Consultancy Sdn Bhd
Education for the 21st Century: New Trends and Perspectives for Learning in the
   Future
June 25-27, 2001
Kuala Lumpur, Malaysia
www.hkleo.com/corp-training/training-micg.htm

Association for the Advancement of Computing in Education
ED-MEDIA 2001—World Conference on Educational Multimedia, Hypermedia &
    Telecommunications
June 25-30, 2001
Tampere, Finland
www.aace.org/conf/edmedia

The Inter-American Distance Education Consortium
Virtual Educa 2001: International Conference on Education, Training, and New
    Technologies
June 27-29, 2001
Madrid, Spain
www.virtual-educa.net

**International Association of Science and Technology for Development,
Technical Committee on Education**
International Conference on Computers and Advanced Technology in Education
    (CATE 2001)
June 27-29, 2001
Banff, Canada
www.iasted.com

National-Louis University
2nd International Conference on Technology in Teaching and Learning in Higher
    Education
June 27-29, 2001
Samos Island, Greece
nlu-ln01.nl.edu/conferences

Intermedia Exhibitions & Conferences
E-Learning Expo Amsterdam
June 28-29, 2001
Amsterdam, Netherlands
www.elearnexpo.com

July 2001

Learning and Teaching Development, Loughborough University
Fifth International Computer Assisted Assessment Conference
July 2-3, 2001
Leicestershire, UK
www.lboro.ac.uk/service/fli/flicaa/conf2001

Faculty of Engineering, Kumamoto University, Japan
International Conference on Information Technology-Based Higher Education and
    Training
July 4-6, 2001
Kumamoto, Japan
www.eecs.kumamoto-u.ac.jp/ITHET01

International Quality & Productivity Center
Training World 2001
July 8-12, 2001
San Diego, CA
www.iqpc.com

101communications
Syllabus Summer 2001 Conference
July 20-24, 2001
Santa Clara, CA
www.syllabus.com

Society for Applied Learning Technology Information
Education Technology Conference 2001
July 24-26, 2001
Arlington, VA
www.salt.org

Asociación Iberoamericana de Educación Superior a Distancia
IX Encontro biannual
July 25-27, 2001
Cartagena de Indias, Colombia
www.uned.es/aiesad

Association for Educational Communications and Technology
Summer Leadership Institute 2001
July 26-29, 2001
Baltimore, MD
www.aect.org/Events/Baltimore/default.htm

Association for Telecommunications Professionals in Higher Education
30th Annual Conference and Exposition
July 29-August 2, 2001
Orlando, FL
www.acuta.org/events/calendar.cfm

International Federation for Information Processing
WCCE 2001: 7th World Conference on Computers in Education: Networking the
  Learner
July 29-August 3, 2001
Copenhagen, Denmark
www.wcce2001.dk

August 2001

University of Wisconsin-Madison, Department of Industrial Engineering
Chinese Academy of Sciences
Human Factors and Ergonomics Society
Japan Ergonomics Society
International Ergonomics Association
Japan Management Association
Institute of Industrial Engineers
HCI International 2001: 9th International Conference on Human-Computer
  Interaction
August 5-10, 2001
New Orleans, LA
hcii2001.engr.wisc.edu/index.html

IEEE Computer Society
International Conference on Advanced Learning Technologies (ICALT 2001)
August 6-8, 2001
Madison, WI
lttf.ieee.org/icalt2001

University of Wisconsin, Graduate Program in Continuing and Vocational
Education
17th Annual Conference on Distance Teaching & Learning
August 8-10, 2001
Madison, WI
www.uwex.edu/disted/conference

National Educational Telecommunications Association
Firstview 2001
August 10-14, 2001
Dallas, TX
www.netaonline.org/firstview.htm

Cultural Society POLYGON
ERASMUS
5th Romanian Internet Learning Workshop: Internet as a Vehicle for Teaching and
   Learning
August 11-18, 2001
Sumuleu Ciuc, Romania
rilw.emp.paed.uni-muenchen.de/2001/index.html

Association for Computing Machinery
Twelfth ACM Conference on Hypertext and Hypermedia: Hypertext '01
August 14-18, 2001
Århus, Denmark
www.ht01.org

September 2001

CMP Media Internet & Mobile Group
Web2001 International Conference and Exposition
September 4-8, 2001
San Francisco, CA
www.web2001show.com/index2.html

Universiti Malaysia Sarawak
MIMOS Berhad
Ministry of Education, Malaysia
2nd Annual International Symposium on Online Learning: SOLE2001
September 5-8, 2001
Kuala Lumpur, Malaysia
www.calm.unimas.my/sole2001

Heller Reports
EdNET 2001, Educational Technology and Telecommunications Markets Conference
September 8-12, 2001
Washington, DC
hellerreports.com/ednet01

Oxford Brookes University, Oxford Centre for Staff and Learning Development
9th Improving Student Learning Symposium: Improving Student Learning Using
   Learning Technologies
September 9-11, 2001
Edinburgh, Scotland
www.brookes.ac.uk/services/ocsd/1_ocsld/isl2001.html

Government Technology
13th Annual Government Technology Conference East 2001
September 10-14, 2001
Albany, NY
www.govtech.net/conferences/gtc/gtceast2001/index.phtml

Association for Learning Technology
ALT-C 2001: Changing Learning Environments
September 11-13, 2001
University of Edinburgh
www.ed.ac.uk/altc2001

CMP Media Events
Internet Telecom Expo 2001: "Where Telecommunications and the Internet Meet—
    the New World of Open Communications"
September 19-21, 2001
New York, NY
www.i-telecomexpo.com/itx

Georgia Distance Learning Association
2nd Annual Conference
September 23-25, 2001
Athens, GA
www.ga-distance-learning.org/index_flash.asp

Open and Distance Learning Association of Australia
The University of Sydney
The Open Training and Education Network
15th Biennial ODLAA Forum: Educational Odyssey: Issues in Open, Flexible and
    Distance Learning
September 24-27, 2001
Sydney, Australia
www.oten.edu.au/odlaa

October 2001

VNU Business Media
OnLine Learning 2001 and Performance Support Conference and Exposition
October 1-3, 2001
Los Angeles, CA
www.onlinelearningconference.com

Instructional Telecommunications Council
The TeleLearning People
Telelearning 2001
October 6-9, 2001
Costa Mesa, CA
www.itcnetwork.org/telelearning.htm

Benjamin Franklin Institute of Global Education
Global Learn Day V
October 7, 2001
virtual
www.bfranklin.edu/gld5

Open University
9th Cambridge International Conference on Open and Distance Learning:
   Supporting the Student in Open and Distance Learning
October 7-10, 2001
Cambridge, England
ebony.open.ac.uk/cic

Global Alliance for Transnational Education
6th Annual GATE Conference: Quality Transnational Education: A Vehicle for
   Sustainable Development
October 8-10, 2001
San Jose, Costa Rica
www.edugate.org/conferences.html

American Society for Training and Development
ASTD TechKnowledge 2001
October 9-12, 2001
Charlotte, NC
www.astd.org/virtual_community/conferences

University of New Brunswick, Instructional Technology Unit
NAWeb 2001: North American Web-Based Learning Conference
October 13-16, 2001
Fredericton, NB, Canada
www.unb.ca/naweb

The Pennsylvania State University
The Ohio State University
University of Wisconsin Extension
Outreach Scholarship 2001: Learning, Discovery, and Engagement
October 14-16, 2001
State College, PA
www.outreach.psu.edu/C&I/OutreachScholarship2001

Government Technology
2nd Annual Government Technology Conference Southeast 2001
October 15-19, 2001
Raleigh, NC
www.govtech.net/conferences/gtc/gtcsoutheast2000/contact.phtml

Advanstar Communications
TeleCon 2001 Conference & Expo: Solutions for Enterprise Collaboration & E-Learning
October 22-25, 2001
Anaheim, CA
www.teleconexpos.com

Association for the Advancement of Computing in Education
WebNet 2001: World Conference on the WWW and Internet
October 23-27, 2001
Orlando, FL
www.aace.org/conf/webnet

The Consortium of College and University Media Centers
Annual Conference
October 25-29, 2001
New Orleans, LA
www.indiana.edu/ ~ ccumc/conf.html

EDUCAUSE
EDUCAUSE 2001: An Edu Odyssey
October 28-31, 2001
Indianapolis, IN
www.educause.edu/conference/e2001/csp.html

The Masie Center
TechLearn 2001
October 28-31, 2001
Orlando, FL
www.masie.com

Western Cooperative for Educational Telecommunications (Western Interstate Commission for Higher Education)
13th Annual Conference: eRevolution@edu
October 31-November 3, 2001
Coeur d'Alene, ID
www.wiche.edu/telecom

November 2001

Association for Educational Communications & Technology
AECT 2001 Annual Conference
November 7-10, 2001
Atlanta, GA
www.aect.org

National School Boards Association
15th Annual Technology + Learning Conference
November 7-10, 2001
Atlanta, GA
www.nsba.org/T + L

Asia-Pacific Chapter of the Association for the Advancement of Computing in Education
ICCE/SchoolNet 2001: International Conference on Computers in Education
November 12-15, 2001
Seoul, Korea
www.icce2001.org

League for Innovation in the Community College
Conference on Information Technology
November 14-17, 2001
Minneapolis, MN
www.league.org/cit2001

Asynchronous Learning Networks Center
7th International Conference on Asynchronous Learning Networks (ALN 2001)
November 16-18, 2001
Orlando, FL
www.aln.org

United Entertainment Media
Government Video Technology Expo 2001
November 28-29, 2001
Washington, DC
www.gvexpo.com

Learning Resources Network (LERN)
Annual Convention: Lifelong Learning 2001
November 28-30, 2001
San Francisco, CA
www.lern.org/annual_convention

Online Educa Berlin
7th International Conference on Technology Supported Learning & Training
November 28-30, 2001
Berlin, Germany
www.online-educa.com

101communications
Syllabus Fall 2001 Conference
November 29-December 2, 2001
Danvers, MA
www.syllabus.com

December 2001

Center on Education and Work, University of Wisconsin
6th Annual Workplace Learning Conference
December 2-4, 2001
Chicago, IL
www.cew.wisc.edu/workplace

Australasian Society for Computers in Learning in Tertiary Education
18th Annual Conference: ASCILITE 2001: "Meeting at the Crossroads"
December 9-12, 2001

Melbourne, Australia
www.medfac.unimelb.edu.au/Ascilite2001

January 2002

Center for Distance Learning Research, Texas A&M University
9th Annual International Distance Education Conference
January 2002 (date and location to be determined)
www.cdlr.tamu.edu

The Center for Lifelong Learning & Design
CSCL (Computer Support for Collaborative Learning) 2002: Foundations for a CSCL
   Community
January 7-11, 2002
Broomfield (Denver), CO
www.cscl2002.org

February 2002

Euro Education
Euro Education 2002: 4th International Conference on ICT in Education
February 5-7, 2002
Aalborg, Denmark
E-mail: euro@akkc.dk

March 2002

Center for Internet Technology in Education
3rd Annual CITE Conference
March 2002 (date to be determined)
Denver, CO
www.cite.eCollege.com

Influent Technology Group
Studio 2002: The Conference on Designing the User Experience
March 2002 (date to be determined)
Seattle, WA
www.influent.com

International Conferences, Exhibitions, and Fairs
The Pan-American Distance Learning Exchange, International Marketplace for
   Providers and Buyers of Distance Learning Programs
March 2002 (date to be determined)

Miami, FL
www.icef.com
VNU Business Media
Online Learning 2002 Europe
March 4-7, 2002
London, United Kingdom
www.vnulearning.com

Association for the Advancement of Computing in Education
SITE 2002 (Society for Information Technology & Teacher Education)
March 18-23, 2002
Nashville, TN
www.aace.org/conf/site

April 2002

Advanstar
e-Learning Conference and Expo
April 2002 (date to be determined)
Washington, DC
www.elearningexpos.com

E-Learning Conference & Expo (formerly TeleCon East/IDLCON)
Washington, in DC
April 2002 (date to be determined)
www.elearningexpos.com

Influent Technology Group
WBT Executive Summit
April 2002 (date and place to be announced)
www.influent.com

Influent Technology Group
Web Producer 2002
April 2002 (date and place to be announced)
www.influent.com

International Society for Performance Improvement
Annual International Performance Improvement Conference and Expo
April 2002 (date to be determined)
www.ispi.org/

United States Distance Learning Association
E-Learning Conference & Expo
April 2002 (date to be determined)
Washington, DC
www.usdla.org

University Continuing Education Association
UCEA 87th Annual Conference
April 2002 (date and place to be determined)
www.nucea.edu

May 2002

European Association for Distance Learning
The EADL Conference 2002
May 2002 (date and place to be determined)
www.eadl.org

Government Technology
17th Annual Government Technology Conference West 2001
May 2002 (date and place to be determined)
www.govtech.net

International Conference on Technology and Education
20th Annual International Conference on Technology and Education
May 2002 (date and place to be determined)
www.icte.org

VNU Business Media
OnLine Learning 2002 Asia
May 2002 (date and place to be determined)
www.vnulearning.com

Index

About the Editors

Karen Mantyla is president of Quiet Power, Inc. a Washington, D.C.-based distance learning training and consulting company. She is the co-author of *Distance Learning: A Step-By-Step Guide for Trainers* (ASTD 1997) and *Consultative Sales Power* (Crisp Publications 1995), *Interactive Distance Learning Exercises That Really Work* (ASTD 1999), and *Blending E-Learning: The Power Is in the Mix*, which will be published by ASTD in the fall of 2001.

Ms. Mantyla is the Secretary of the Federal Government Distance Learning Association (FGDLA). She is the Editor of *Distance Learning News*, the Official Publication of the FGDLA, a specialized chapter of the United States Distance Learning Association (USDLA). Ms. Mantyla is an active member of the American Society for Training and Development (ASTD), a Certified Facilitator for The Human Performance Improvement Certification Program offered by ASTD, and a member of the Publishing Committee for ASTD. She consults with both public- and private-sector clients to help design, develop, implement, and maintain distance learning systems. Her focus is on the "human side" of the distance learning equation to ensure that the trainers receive proper support, guidance, and training in selecting and utilizing distance learning methods of delivery. In addition, she helps design learner support systems, tools, and methods to ensure success and continuous process improvement for all remote site facilitators and learners. Ms. Mantyla has over 20 years of specialized experience in the development and implementation of workplace education programs, with specific emphasis on reaching learners in dispersed geographic locations. She has held many senior leadership positions, including Vice President of a *Fortune* 500 corporation. She received her Professional Certification in Distance Learning from the University of Wisconsin-Madison, a renowned leader in distance education. Ms. Mantyla's biography is featured in the 2001 editions of *Who's Who in the World*, *Who's Who in America*, *Who's Who of American Women*, and *Who's Who in Finance and Industry*.

John Woods is president of CWL Publishing Enterprises (www.cwlpub.com), a Madison, Wisconsin-based company that specializes in the development of business books. His company is responsible for the Briefcase Books series (basic management books) published by McGraw-Hill (www.briefcasebooks.com). He is the co-author of *Supervision* (a college textbook, South-Western), *The McGraw-Hill Encyclopedia of Quality Terms and Concepts*, and author of *The Ten-Minute Guide to Teams and Teamwork*. His company has also developed six titles for the Complete Idiot's Guides series (Macmillan) and he is co-editor of *The ASTD Training and Performance Yearbook* (published annually by McGraw-Hill since 1997). He is a graduate of the University of California, Berkeley and served in the Peace Corps.